Istiḥsān

ISTIḤSĀN

The Doctrine of Juristic Preference in Islamic Law

❖

Saim Kayadibi

IBT
Islamic Book Trust
Kuala Lumpur

Published by
Islamic Book Trust
607 Mutiara Majestic
Jalan Othman
46000 Petaling Jaya
Selangor, Malaysia
www.ibtbooks.com

Islamic Book Trust is affiliated with The Other Press.

Perpustakaan Negara Malaysia Cataloguing-in-Publication Data

Kayadibi, Saim
Istihsan : the doctrine of juristic preference in Islamic law / Saim Kayadibi.
Includes index
Bibliography : p. 309
ISBN 978-967-5062-46-9
ISBN 978-967-5062-47-6 (pbk.)
1. Presumptions (Islamic law)--Research. 2. Islamic law-- Research.
I. Title.
340.59072

For my wife Yasemin
and our children
Zeynep Pınar, Mehmet Edip Taha,
Mevlana Musa & İsmail Yahya
who are the joys of our life.

Contents

Glossary ix
Preface xxi
Acknowledgements xxiii
Introduction xxvii

1 The Sources of Islamic law 1
Definition of some juristic terms 3
Unanimous sources of Islamic law 14
The Qur'an 14
The *Sunnah* 16
Ijmāʿ (consensus) 18
Qiyās (analogical deduction) 22
Controversial sources of Islamic law 29
Definition of *istiṣḥāb* 30
Maṣlaḥah Mursalah (public interest) or *al-istiṣlāḥ* 33
'Urf (customary law) 38
Sadd al-Dharāʾiʿ (blocking the means) 40
Qawl ṣaḥābī (the saying of a Companion of the Prophet) 42
Sharʿ man qablanā (revealed laws preceding to the Sharīʿah) 44
Istiqrāʾ (induction) 45
Conclusion 45

2 Development of *Ijtihād* by *Ra'y* 57
Concept of *ijtihād* 63
Validity of *ijtihād* 69
Implementations of *ijtihād* at the time of the Prophet 75
Conclusion 99

3 Definition of *Istiḥsān* and Analysis 114
Istiḥsān—a historical perspective 115
View point of *istiḥsān* amongst the scholars 128
Further evidences of the validity of *istiḥsān* 169
Application of *istiḥsān* in the early Ḥanafi school 185
Conclusion 207

4 Various Types of *Istiḥsān* 237
Istiḥsān in the sense of departing from one ruling 240
Istiḥsān based on *sanad* in terms of the departure 250
Conclusion 281

Conclusion 298
Bibliography 309
Index 339

Glossary

A

'adl: justice.
adillah (pl. *dalīl*): proofs, evidences, indication.
adillah Sharī'ah: proofs of Islamic law.
adhān: call to prayer.
af'āl: acts.
aḥkām (pl. *ḥukm*): rules, laws, and ordinances.
aḥkām 'amaliyyah: practical rulings.
aḥkām 'aqliyyah: rational rules.
aḥkām al-dīn: rulings of religion.
aḥkām ḥissiyyah: law of sense perception.
aḥkām i'tiqādiyyah: creed/ convictional, which is belief in the existence of God, His oneness, His qualities, the truth of the mission of the Prophet (ṣ), belief in the Day of Judgment etc.
aḥkām khuluqīyyah: ethical and moral rules.
aḥkām lughawiyyah: linguistic rules.
aḥkām al-mu'āmalāt: transactions.
aḥkām shar'iyyah: legal rules.
aḥkām waḍ'īyyah: declaratory rules.
ahl al-iṣābah: the residual heirs.
ahl al-bayt: the household of the Prophet (ṣ).
ahl al-bid'ah: people of innovation.

A

ahl al-ḥadīth: the traditionalist group or school.
ahl al-kahf: People of the Cave.
ahl al-ra'y: the rationalist group.
ahl al-farā'iḍ: portions for heirs designated in the Qur'an.
al-aḥsan: the best.
ahwan al-sharr: lesser evil.
'āmm: general.
amārah: indication, signs or allusions, probable evidence.
al-anṣāb: gambling.
arkān: essential requirements.
'aql: intellect, reason.
'aqlī: rational.
'aṣabah: those entitled to the remainders of the shares, agnates.
asās: foundation.
asḥābi furūḍ: Spouses, parents, grandfather, grandmother, daughter, son's daughter, sister, mother's son.
aṣl: root, origin, source, and used original case in the context of analogy.
āyāh (pl. *āyāt*): proof, evidences, lessons, signs.
'azīmah: strict or unmodified law which remains in its original rigour due to the absence of mitigating factors.
azlām: arrows for seeking luck or decision.

B

bāṭil: wrong, null and void.
bayt al-Māl: treasury, exchequer.
bay' al-ṭa'āṭī: give-and-take sale.
bid'ah: innovation.
burhān: proof, evidence.

D

daf' al-fasād: avoid evil.
dalā'il (pl. *dalīl*): indication, proof, evidence.
ḍalāl: error.
ḍalālah: error.
dalīl 'ām: general evidence.

dalīl ijmālī or *kullī*: general evidence.
dalīl qaṭ'ī: definite proof.
dalīl tafṣīlī: specific evidence, detailed proof.
ḍarar: harm.
ḍarūrah: necessity.
ḍarūriyyāt: essentials.
dharī'ah (pl. *dharā'i'*): means.
dirhams: silver coins.

F

fahm: understanding.
fuqahā' (pl. *faqīh*): jurist, one who is learned *fiqh*.
far': lit. a branch or a sub-division, and in the context of *qiyās* a new case.
farḍ: obligatory, obligation.
farḍ 'ayn: individual duty and obligation.
farḍ kifāyah: a collective duty, the fulfilment of which by a sufficient number of individuals excuses the other individuals from fulfilling it.
fasād: evil.
fatwā: formal legal opinion.
fawāḥish: corruptions.
fi'lī: physically.

G

ghanīmah: booty.
ghusl: ritual ablution of the whole body.

H

ḥadīth: tradition.
ḥadīth mashhūr: well known Tradition.
ḥadīth mutawātir: widely spread Tradition.
ḥadīth ṣaḥīḥ: authentic tradition.
ḥajj: pilgrimage, the once-in-a lifetime obligation of pilgrimage to the holy Ka'ba.
Ḥājiyyāt: complementary.
ḥaqīqī: true, genuine, authentic, real and literal as opposed to metaphorical.
ḥaqq: right.

H

ḥaqq al-irtifāq: all of the ancillary rights.
ḥaqq al-masīl: the right of flow.
ḥaqq al-murūr: the right of passage.
ḥaqq al-shurb: the right of water.
ḥarām: prohibited.
ḥasan: good.
hawā': inclination, whim.
ḥimār: donkey.
ḥimāriyyah: donkey case.
ḥissī: sensory.
ḥujjah: *dalīl*, evidence, proof.
ḥukm (pl. *aḥkām*): rule, as in *ḥukm shar'ī*; law, value or ruling of Sharī'ah.
ḥukm taklīfī: the obligation, creating rule, defining law.
ḥukm waḍ'ī: declaratory law.

I

ibṭāl al-istiḥsān: invalidating juristic preference.
iḥram: the ritual garment worn for *ḥajj*.
iḥtiyājāt: needs.
ijārah: leasing.
i'jāz: inimitability.
ijmā': consensus, agreement.
ijmā' ṣarīḥ: explicit agreement.
ijmā' sukūtī: tacit agreement.
ijtihād: is the expenditure of efforts to arrive at righteous judgement; it could be either physical such as walking, working or intellectual such as inference of a ruling, or juristic and linguistic theory: Kamāl Ibn Al-Humām defines *ijtihād* as the expenditure of efforts by the *faqīh* to arrive at a juristic ruling, such ruling being either rational (*'aqlī*) or transmitted (*naqlī*), definitive (*qaṭ'ī*)or speculative (*ẓannī*).
ijtihād taqdīrī: which allows jurists all to give rulings and on which there is no cause for disagreement amongst the scholars.

ikrāh: means forcing someone to do or say something against his will, coercion.

ilhām: inspiration.

'illah: cause and reason.

'ilm: knowledge.

imām: founder.

intifā': usufruct.

'iqāb: punishment.

iṣābah: target.

ishārah: indication, sign, token, and symptom.

ish'ār: marking animals.

iṣmah: infallibility, immunity from making errors.

istaḥsana: approved as the better judgment.

istidlāl: inference.

istiḥsān: Juristic Preference.

istiḥsān istithnā'ī: exceptional *istiḥsān*.

iṣṭilāḥī: technical.

istiqrā': induction.

istiqrā' tāmm: complete induction.

istiqrā' nāqiṣ: incomplete induction.

istiṣḥāb: presumption of continuity.

istiṣlāḥ: consideration of public interest..

istiṣwāb: discretion.

istithnā: This is the giving of an order to a labourer or artisan to make a definite article with agreement to pay a definite price for that article when made.

'itāb: blame.

i'tibār: admonition.

i'tiqād: faith, belief.

J

jahd: which means the forbearance of hardship, that is striving and self-exertion in any activity which entails a measure of hardship.

jalb al-ṣalāḥ: obtaining benefit.

jināyah: criminal offence.

jadhr: root.

J

juhd: which means exertion of effort or energy.
junub: a state requiring a ritual ablution of the whole body.
juz'ī: partial.

K

kaffārah: expiation.
kamāliyyāt: embellishments.
khabar: news or report.
khabar wāḥid: solitary *ḥadīth.*
khamr: wine.
kharāj: land tax.
khāṣṣ: specific, individual.
khayr: good deed.
khalwah: privacy.
kufr: unbelief.
kullī: whole.

L

lughawī: linguistic.

M

maḍarrāt: evils.
madīnah: town.
mafqūd: missing person.
mafsadah: harm, evil.
al-Majallah: Ottoman court manual.
makrūh: discouraged, adversity.
makrūh karāḥat al-taḥrīm: strongly disapproved.
makrūh karāḥat al-tanzīh: disapproval.
mandūb: recommended, optional.
manfa'ah: benefit.
māni': impediment, obstacle, hindrance..
maqāṣid: objectives, aims, purposes, goals.
maqāṣid al-'āmmah: general purposes.
maṣdar: source.
mashaqqah: hardship, difficulty.
Mashhūr: is defined as a ḥadīth which is originally reported by one, two or more Companions from the

Prophet (ṣ) or from another Companion but which has later become well-known and transmitted by an indefinite number of people.

maṣlaḥah: benefit.

maṣlaḥah mursalah: consideration of public interest.

maytatah: unlawful meat.

minārāh: minaret.

miqyās: scales.

muallafah al-qulūb: conciliation of hearts.

mubāḥ: permissible.

muḍārabah: This means a contract of co-partnership, in which one of the parties (the proprietor) is entitled to a profit on account of the capital (*ra's al-māl*) he has invested. He is designated as the owner of the capital (*rabb al- māl*). The other party is entitled to profit on account of his labour and is designated as the *muḍārib* (or the manager) in as much as he derives a benefit from his own labour and endeavours.

muftī: the authority of giving *fatwā*-ruling.

mujtahid: competent jurist.

mukallaf: subjects.

mukhaṣṣaṣ: particularized agent.

mukhaṣṣiṣ: particularising agent.

munkar: evil.

mansūkh: abrogated.

muʿāmalāt: contracts.

muftī: judge.

muqallid: the close and faithful followers of established rules, follower.

muqayyad: dependent, limited.

mursal: discontinued.

murshid: guide, conductor.

musāqah: This is a contract between two parties whereby one party takes charge of the fruit tree of the other partner on condition that the crops shall be divided between them on specific terms; share tenancy.

M

mushtarik: shared.
mustaqil: independent.
mut'ah: maintenance.
mutaraddiyah: dead by headlong fall.
mutawātir: literally means continuously recurrent. In the present context, it means a report by an indefinite number of people related in such a way as to preclude the possibility of their agreement to perpetuate a lie.
muṭlaq: absolute.
muzāra'ah: This is a contract between two persons whereby one party is the landlord and the other the cultivator. They both agree that whatever is produced by cultivation of the land shall be divided between them in specified proportions; an agreement of crop sharing.

N

nabīdh: fermented dates.
nāfilah: supererogatory.
naqlī: Transmitted.
naqṣ: deficiency.
nasab: lineage and stock.
naskh: abrogation.
naṣṣ: text.
naẓarī: theoretical.
nikāḥ: marriage.

Q

qā'idah fiqhiyyah: jurisprudence rule.
qadhf: slander, accusation.
qāḍī: judge.
qal'ah: fort.
qalbī: which takes place in the heart.
qaṭ'ī: definitive.
qatl: murder.
qawā'id pl. *qā'idah*: principles..
qawā'id kullīyyah: general principles.
qawāi'd fiqhiyyah: general principles of jurisprudence.

qawl: saying.
qawlī: relating to speech, verbal.
qawl ṣaḥābī: The sayings of a Companion of the Prophet (ṣ).
qiyās: analogy.
qiṣāṣ: retaliation.
al-qiṣāṣ: the law of equality in punishment.
qiyās adnā: analogy of the inferior.
qiyās awlā: analogy of the superior.
qiyās jalī: obvious analogy.
qiyās khafī: latent, hidden, implicit analogy.
qiyās musāwāh: analogy of equals.
qiyās ẓāhir jaliyy: apparent clear analogy.

R

rājiḥ: preference.
raf' al-ḥaraj: avoidance of hardship.
ra'y: opinion.
ra'y bāṭil: invalid; null, and void.
ra'y mashkūk: doubtful, uncertain.
ra'y saḥīḥ: valid, authentic.
riwāyah: transmitted *ḥadīth*.
rujḥān: preference, preferability.
rukhaṣ: concessions.
rukn: condition, essential requirement.
ru'yah: to perceive an object which is seen.

S

sabab: cause.
sadd: blocking.
sadd al-dharā'i': blocking the means.
ṣaḥābī: pl. *ṣaḥābah*: a Companion.
salam: contract of purchase of goods with pre-payment, forward sale, prepaid sale.
salām: conclusion of prayer.
ṣalāt: prayer.
sanad: basis, proof, authority..
shahādāh al-zur: false testimony.

S

shāhid: witness.
shahwah: passion.
*shār*ʿ: Lawgiver.
sharʿ man qablanā: revealed laws preceding to the Sharīʿah of Islam.
Sharīʿah: Islamic law.
sharṭ (pl. *shurūṭ*): condition.
shufʿah: pre-emption.
shūrah: consultation.
sudan: uncontrolled,without purpose, a state of lawlessness.

T

taʿabbudī: worship.
tadbīr: precaution.
taʿdiyah: referring a ruling to another case.
tafsīr: interpretation.
taḥsīniyyāt: embellishment.
taḥrīf: distortion.
taḥrīm: prohibition.
takhṣīṣ: specifying the general, particularization of the general.
takhṣīṣ ʿillah: specifying the cause.
ṭalab or *iqtiḍā*ʾ: request.
ṭalāq bāʾin: divorce to be absolute.
ṭalāq rajʿī: revocable.
taladhdhudh: deriving pleasure.
tark: departure.
taṣarrufāt: transactions.
tashahhud: To say while sitting: "There is no god but Allah and Muḥammad (ṣ) is Allah's Apostle.".
tawātur: continuous testimony.
tawbah: repentance.
tayammum: to wash with clean sand or earth where water is unavailable.

U

ʿudūl: the departure.
*ʿulamā*ʾ: scholars.

'ulū al-amr: those in authority amongst Muslims.
'umūm al-balwā: general calamity.
ummah: the whole Muslim community.
'urf: custom.
'urf 'āmm: general custom.
'urf khāṣ: special custom.
uṣūl: pl. *aṣl;* root, origin, source.
uṣūlī: juristic scholars.
uṣūl al-fiqh: the principle of Islamic jurisprudence.

W

wahmī: imaginary.
waḥy: divine revelation.
wājīb: obligatory.
waqf: charitable endowment.
wasā'il: means.
waṣf (pl. *awṣāf*): attribute, quality, adjective.
wujūb: necessity, obligation, rendering something obligatory..

Y

yanqadihu: embedded.

Z

zakāh: alms.
ẓann: speculation, doubt, conjecture.
ẓannī: speculative, doubtful..
ẓanni ghālib: mostly probable.
ẓāhir: manifest, apparent..
zinā: illegal sexual intercourse, fornication, adultery.

Preface

The research work embodied in this thesis constitutes a critical analysis of classical and modern aspects of the concept of *istiḥsān* (juristic preference) in Islamic law, an important principle in Islamic legal legislation throughout history. This area of legislation has been investigated by many researchers and scholars; however, the research work conducted to evaluate the true nature and role of *istiḥsān* with regard a combination of classical and modern approaches still requires further investigation.

The thesis consists of four chapters. The introductory chapter is the theoretical basis of the study and comprises a brief understanding of some general principles of Islamic law; the Qur'an, the Sunnah, *ijmā'* (consensus), *qiyās* (analogy), *maṣlaḥah mursalah* (consideration of public interest), *istiṣḥāb* (presumption of continuity), *qawl ṣaḥābī* (the saying of the Companion of the Prophet), *'urf* (custom), *sadd al-dharā'i'* (blocking the means), *shar' man qablanā* (revealed laws preceding to the Sharī'ah of Islam) and *istiqrā'* and so on.

Chapter 2 deals with the development of *ra'y* and *ijtihād* in the context of *istiḥsān*. This chapter introduces the concept of *ra'y* and *ijtihād* as related to historical background and implementation, with their methods of development where *istiḥsān* originated from. *Istiḥsān* was practiced well before the formation of the Islamic legal schools of thought and can be referred back to the time of the Prophet (ṣ), the Companions and the Successors.

Chapter 3 begins with definitions of the term of *istiḥsān*, identifying its true nature with an extensive analysis both linguistically and technically. Historical development is investigated, and then the viewpoints of the scholars and their discourses that form the main cornerstone of this study. Also in this chapter the validity of *istiḥsān* is discussed and explained with special reference to the reason behind the disagreement over *istiḥsān* as the scholars introduce their evidences to justify the claims of those who consider it a valid source of law and those who do not recognize it as such. Consideration of *istiḥsān* and its implementation in the early Ḥanafī school of thought by eminent scholars is also elaborated.

Chapter 4 is devoted to the types of *istiḥsān* and the division among the scholars with practical examples. Other related terms as *iḥtiyāj* (need), *ḍarar* (harm), *raf' al-ḥaraj* (avoiding hardship), *mashaqqah* (hardship), *ḍarūrah* (necessity).

Acknowledgements

Numerous individuals have assisted, directly or indirectly, in the production of this thesis; to mention them all would require an added chapter. In general, I would like to thank everyone who has encountered me throughout my research and hope that those whom I have not listed will forgive me.

Firstly, I would like to thank my supervisor Dr. Colin P. Turner without whose scholarly guidance and support this study could have never been achieved. He has been a constant source of encouragement throughout the difficult period of my research, and his patient and yet compassionate approach, at times when seemingly insuperable obstacles emerged has been of inestimable help.

My sincere thanks also go to the staff of Durham University School of Government & International Affairs/ Institute for Middle Eastern and Islamic Studies and in particular to its head, Professor Anoush Ehteshami who has been of tremendous support on many occasions.

I am also grateful to the library staff of Durham University, the Graduate Society, Ustinov College and the IT centre. My special thanks also go to SGIA postgraduate secretary, Mrs. Barbara Farnworth.

I would also like to thank the staff of the Islamic Studies Libraries at Al-Azhar, 'Ayn Shams, Cairo, Tanta, Alexandria and American Universities in Egypt, Selçuk and Marmara University in Turkey, Jordan, Irbid University and The International Institute of Islamic Thought (IIIT) in Jordan, and the Universities of Edinburgh, Oxford and London (SOAS) for their assistance during my countless research trips to those places.

My sincere gratitude goes to my spiritual teacher, Prof. M. Es'ad Coşan (d. 2001) who persuaded me to conduct research in Islamic law, and without whose scholarly advice and guidance I would not have been able to accomplish this study. Special thanks must also go to Prof. Dr. Orhan Çeker, Prof. Dr. Ahmet Yaman, Selçuk University, Prof. Dr. Ahmet Davutoğlu, Boğaziçi University and currently Foreign Minister of Turkey, Prof. Dr. Muḥammad 'Alī Sawwā', University of Jordan Faculty of Sharī'ah. Dr. Aḥmad al-Raissounī, University of Muḥammad Khāmis, Rabat. Prof. Muḥammad M. 'Abd al-Laṭef Jamāl al-Dīn, University of Al-Azhar, Egypt. Prof. Ṭāha Jābīr al-'Alwāni, the president of the *Fiqh* Council of North America. Thanks also go to Ustādh Shaykh Shu'ayb al-'Arnawūṭī, whose suggestion brought me to this country (England) to complete my PhD study.

Special thanks also go to Mrs. Denise Smith who edited my English writings, and to my dear friends, Filiz Çelik, İsmail Kılın, Alev & Hüsamettin and İlhan Kurt. Their help, advice and endless encouragement have been priceless; at a time when I was faced with many difficulties, they saved the day and enabled me to pursue my study. In conclusion, I cannot thank them enough.

The financial support given by "Muslim Aid" for the first year at my study, and further aid from the Turkish Community Association is also appreciated. I would like to give a special mention to my friend Maḥmoud Rāḍī in Egypt, 'Ādil from Singapore, Wassef Obeid and Prof. Dr. Hakan Aslan. Thanks also to my beloved brother-in-law Prof. Dr. Fatih Gültekin for his encouragement and sympathy whenever I was in despair whilst completing the study.

I would like to express my deepest gratitude to my dear mother Zülfüye, my late father, Mehmet, and my brothers and sister who have always provided their unlimited and unconditional spiritual support. I would also like to thank my father-in-law, İsmā'il, and mother-in-law, Adeviye, for looking after my family while I have been away.

I would like to remember those who would like to study but are denied the opportunity, to encourage them to continue and always carry the passion in their hearts even though they have to endure much hardship.

Finally, I cannot express with words my deepest gratitude to my family for their persistent moral support, love, friendship and encouragement throughout my academic career. They have all lived patiently with this study for longer than any of us cares to remember, and thus it is dedicated to my dearest wife Yasemin, and to our children Zeynep Pınar, Mehmet Edip Taha and twins Mevlana Musa & İsmail Yahya those who are the joys of my both academic and family lives.

Introduction

OBJECTIVE OF THE RESEARCH

Justice is one of the fundamental principles to keep a society alive, and thus law has to be based on justice. It is a fact that abusing the system of justice causes corruption for the society. The subject that I have researched has a vital role that has substantially contributed to the development of law based on justice and equity.

The objective of my research is to investigate the concept of *istiḥsān* from every possible aspect. Islamic law has been developed over the centuries using the methods of *ra'y* and *ijtihād*. However, the development of the principle of *istiḥsān* opened for Islamic law a new horizon for the future phenomenon.

The present work initially began as a study of the nature and reality of the concept of *istiḥsān*. In the very early stage of legislation of Islamic law, the growth of the Islamic world presented people with new challenges. These included rapid urbanization, multi-cultural relationships and new responses that required the Islamic jurists to provide vigorous efforts to resolve the problems and issues of the Muslim community using their personal discretion and *ijtihād* based on *naṣṣ* (text). The process of systematic reasoning, which is analogy (*qiyās*), began as a methodological solution to operate with the appearance of the juristic schools of thought; in fact the process of legal reasoning is technically called model of legal reasoning (*ijtihād*).

However, the application of the process of systematic reasoning (analogy) in certain situation has not always responded to the needs of the people and sometimes was detrimental to the objectives of the Lawgiver. In such cases, the situation has to be studied in the light of justice, wisdom, equity and necessity in order to remove its rigidity and harms by way of departing from the already established rule. One who studied such cases on that manner and developed justifying it as a principle of Islamic law was the Ḥanafī school of thought, on the basis of a number of verses in the Qur'an and in traditions. "And follow the best (i.e. this Qur'an) of that which is sent down to you from your Lord" (39:55). "Those who listen to the Word (good advice) and follow the best" (39:18) "Whatever the Muslim community views as good, it is also considered by God as good".[1] Later on, despite much opposition, *istiḥsān* was embraced and used by many other schools of thought, including the Shāfi'ī school of thought who never accepted the term *istiḥsān*, but implemented the same principle under the name of *maṣlaḥah*, *istiṣḥāb*, *istiṣlāḥ* and so on.

In this context, I have faced many issues, and have had to question whether Islamic law can accommodate the challenges of modern life, providing adequate solutions to it without violating the religion and interfering with God's commands. Are there any possibilities that the jurist in Islam might interpret the revealed laws without being accused of legislating arbitrarily? The reply to this question is the focal point of the investigation carried out in this research, benefiting from the institution of *ijtihād* that created the power of the concept of *istiḥsān* to provide adequate solutions to modern problems. *Istiḥsān* is a form of *ijtihād* in which jurists use their personal discretion within the guidelines of the Sharīʿah to choose the better legal judgment in a case which has more than one possible solution. As explained in the ḥadīth of Muʿādh[2] the better and adequate solution is required by jurists to secure what is deemed to be of benefit, easier and most suitable for a community without contradicting the objectives of the Lawgiver.

Istiḥsān, therefore, is an attempt on the part of the jurist to understand the commands and objectives of God. It goes back to the time of the Prophet (ṣ), and from the outset opened the way for the development of Islamic law.

THE IMPORTANCE OF THE RESEARCH

Few works of note have been done on the sources of Islamic law, which is why I was encouraged to carry out this research on the concept of *istiḥsān*.

Whilst much academic attention is given to Islamic law in the western world, the Muslim world itself is sadly lacking in this area. This reflects the extent to which the Muslim world has fallen behind, not only in terms of science and technology, but also in the social sciences and the study of religion. And one of the reasons for the academic and intellectual stagnation in the Muslim world is the perception which many have that the gate of *ijtihād*—of which *istiḥsān* is an important part—is closed. The present work is a study of an extremely under-researched area—namely *istiḥsān* or juristic preference—which is itself a long-forgotten source of law and principle of *ijtihād*; hence the title of this thesis: "*Istiḥsān* (juristic preference): the forgotten principle of Islamic law."

During the early Islamic period the term *istiḥsān* was neither known nor directly defined, and therefore when it was applied in judgments, it was applied without giving any specific definition or explanation. Supporters of *istiḥsān* considered the fundamental principle of ease and the avoidance of hardships as the sole basis for the concept of *istiḥsān*. It could be said that the opponents of *istiḥsān* misunderstood the procedure of the usage of *istiḥsān*. Applying *istiḥsān* without giving precise definitions to the term led even those who support *istiḥsān* to fall into the trap that sparked intense debates amongst the various schools of thought. The opponents of *istiḥsān* were—and still are—those who consider it to be "Arbitrary law-making within religion", thus possibly missing what its supporters, Ḥanafīs, Mālikīs, Ḥanbalīs meant by *istiḥsān*.

Although acquainted with the distinction between the concept of *ra'y* and the concept of *ijtihād* in Islamic legal philosophy, my general assumption was that they are two complementary facets of a similar approach to the Islamic concept of law. However, what gradually became clear was that these two aspects have been used interchangeably. It is difficult to distinguish between *ra'y*, *ijtihād* and *istiḥsān*, all of which are based on personal judgment. Moreover, it is viewed that *istiḥsān* is a product of *ijtihād*.

In fact, Abū Ḥanīfah used to implement *ijtihād* based on his personal opinions, but conforming to the Qur'an and the Sunnah by saying, "*Qiyās* rules this, but we '*Nastaḥsinū*' (prefer) that; or we proved this by *istiḥsān* contrary to *qiyās*; or, the *qiyās* of this is so and so and the *ijtihād* of this is so and so, and the *ijtihād* we take".[3] For the development of Islamic law *ijtihād* plays one of the most important roles in comprehending the purposes of the Qur'an and the Sunnah.

With this realization, I then began to explore the concept of *istiḥsān* from every possible aspect. Historically the technical term *istiḥsān* began with Abū Ḥanīfah, although its practical implementation goes back to the period of 'Umar. In my extensive research, I realized that this concept was used on various occasions in the very early period of legislation, without its name being mentioned. Eventually my investigation led me to believe that *istiḥsān* as a juristic term was not in use before 'Iyās bin Mu'āwiyah (d. 122/740).

I then began to study the viewpoints of scholars from different schools. Ḥanafī scholars perceive *istiḥsān* as a valid source of Sharī'ah, according to which action could be taken in juristic rulings; it is also recognized by the Mālikī, Ḥanbalī and Zaydī Schools. However, the first scholar who rejected and strongly criticized *istiḥsān* was Imām Shāfi'ī (d. 204)[4] who wrote a book titled "*Ibṭāl al-Istiḥsān*" (Invalidating Juristic Preference) and made his famous statement: "*Man istaḥsana faqad sharra'a*" (whoever approves of juristic preference is making himself the Lawmaker)[5]; his disciples also followed this view:[6] Isnawī (d. 772/1370), Bishr b. Qays (d. 218/833), Shīrāzī (d. 476/1083), and Ghazālī (d. 505/1111). Dāwūd al-Zāhirī (d. 270/884)[7], and Ibn Ḥazm (d. 456/1064)[8] who founded the Ẓāhirī School, not only rejected *qiyās*, but was also strongly opposed to *istiḥsān*,[9] as were the Imami Shī'ah.[10]

The concept of *istiḥsān* in Islamic law has been discussed and commented upon by both its supporters and its detractors. One of the major factors behind the tendency to reject, or the inability to distinguish between arbitrary law-making and personal judgment based on evidence, is the fact that the early Ḥanafī scholars had not provided any direct definitions to identify their claims and the usage of the concept. In that respect, the earlier Ḥanafī scholars' examples of how to apply the concept has been discussed and their ramifications for Islamic law pointed out.

More importantly, the validity of *istiḥsān*, namely whether it is a source of law, was also the subject of debate amongst the various scholars. I have discussed their arguments through the evidence supplied and have covered the reasons behind the disagreements among the *'ulamā'*. In addition the various types of *istiḥsān* have also been explored. There are many types of *istiḥsān*, and the scholars give basic and general classifications which have been identified and simplified in this study. Another interesting aspect related to the concept of *istiḥsān* is the objectives of the lawgiver (*maqāṣid al-Shārī'*). Those objectives, also, have been discussed and explored in this final chapter.

During my research, I have realized the importance of the concept of *istiḥsān* in terms of development and renewal in Islamic law. Over the past four years, I have gained the experience that the concept of *istiḥsān* is a crucial factor in the development of Islamic law. As Kamālī says, "A clear and well-defined role for *istiḥsān* would hopefully mark a new opening in the evolutionary process of Islamic law".[11]

METHOD AND SOURCES

My main concern throughout has been to make an extremely complex subject as approachable as possible, without compromising either detail or depth of analysis. My main approach has been a phenomenological one, based on a comparative analysis of the main historical sources. My base has been the works of the Ḥanafi School, which is the source and origin of *istiḥsān* in its technical sense.

Abū Ḥanīfah and his disciples often used many works on *istiḥsān* which are no longer extant. An example is "*Kitāb al-Istiḥsān*" which is attributed to Shaybānī but which has not reached us, despite the many quotations made by Sarakhsī and Jaṣṣāṣ. The principle was not often expounded in Ḥanafī texts as an independent subject but was usually dealt with in connection with related concepts such as *qiyās* (analogy).

Information on *istiḥsān* could also be found in the books of "*Al-Qawā'id al-fiqhiyyah*", and the Ottoman Courts Manual "*Al-Majallah*", from which I have benefited. Single works dedicated to *istiḥsān* are conspicuous by their absence in juristic circles. However, as I have indicated above the true nature of *istiḥsān* can be gleaned from Ḥanafī books. Some selected Ḥanafī uṣul books are Abū Bakr Al-Jaṣṣāṣ's "*Al-Fuṣūl fī al-Uṣūl*", Abū Zayd al-Dabbūsī's "*Taqwīm al-Adillah*", Fakhr al-Islām al-Bazdawī's "*Uṣūl* al-Bazdawī on the Margin of 'Abd al-'Azīz al-Bukhārī "*Kashf al-Asrār*", and Sarakhsī's "*Al-Uṣūl*" and this "*Kitāb al-Mabsūṭ*".

I have realized that, despite the many contemporary research works that have been made, there is much that is left to be desired, especially in those works that emphasize the classical understanding of *fiqh* and its connection with the principles.

In addition, general *uṣūl al-fiqh* (principles of Islamic law) books, independent works about principles of Islamic law such as *qiyās*, *ijmā'*, *maṣlaḥah*, *'urf*, *ḍarūrah*, *istiṣlāḥ* etc; ḥadīth collections; dictionaries; and general books which are related to my work have been used and benefited from. Also a wide range of contemporary works related to *ijtihād* and Sharī'ah reform have been consulted.

The introductory chapter (chapter 1) looks at a number of important juristic terms relevant to the study, such as *uṣūl*, *fiqh*, *aḥkām*, *adillah*, Sharī'ah and so on. It also defines and critically analyses all of the main sources of law: These are divided into two categories: the unanimously accepted sources; and the controversial sources. The former comprises the Qur'an, the Sunnah, *ijmā' qiyās*; the latter includes 'forgotten principles' such as *maṣlaḥah*, istiṣlaḥ, *'urf* and so on. The main works consulted for this have been the major classical works of jurisprudence such as Ibn al-Qayyim, Laknawī, Ibn Amīr al-Ḥajj, Ibn Taymiyyah, Ṣadr al-Sharī'ah, M. Hāshim Kamālī, Wahbah Zuhaylī, and so on.

The fundamental sources of *istiḥsān*, namely *ra'y* and *ijtihād*, form the subject of chapter 2. This area has been covered extensively in classical and modern works by a wealth of eminent scholars such as Āmidī, Ibn al-Qayyīm, Bazdawī, 'Abd al-'Azīz al-Bukhārī, Ibn Khaldūn, Ibn Ḥazm, Shafi'ī, Ghazālī, Sarakhsī, Shawkānī, Ibn Taymīyyah, Isnawī, Qarafī, Ibn al-Humām, etc. as well as western scholars such as Schacht, Hallaq, Emile Tyan, Noel J. Coulson, George Makdisi, and Yasin Dutton and it is upon their works and other erudite contemporary individuals that I have drawn for inspiration in the development of this chapter.

The heart of the study, namely the main arguments concerning the concept of *istiḥsān*, is chapter 3. In the definition of *istiḥsān*, linguistically and technically, I have referred to many classical dictionaries such as Ibn Manẓūr's "*Lisān al-'Arab*", Jowharī's "*Tāj al-Lughah* and *Ṣiḥāḥ al-'Arabiyyah*", Zabīdī's "*Tāj al-'Arūs* from *Jawāhir al-Qāmūs*", Fīrūzabādī's "*Qāmūs al-Muḥīṭ*". I have also referred to classical and modern *uṣūl al-fiqh* (principles of Islamic law) books whilst introducing scholars' viewpoints and arguments about *istiḥsān*. Several previously neglected works have been used extensively in the research for this chapter, and also throughout the study. On the application of *istiḥsān*, my main sources were Sarakhsī's "*Kitāb al-Mabsūṭ*" and his "*Uṣūl*", Jaṣṣāṣ's "*Al-Fuṣūl fī al-Uṣūl*", Abū Yūsuf's "*Kitāb al-Kharāj*" and "*Kitāb al-Athar*", Ibn Al-Humām's "*Sharḥ Fatḥ al-Qadīr*", Shaybānī's "*Al-Aṣl*" and "*Al-Siyar al-Kabīr*", Sha'bān Muḥammad Ismā'īl's "*Al-Istiḥsān Bayn al-Naẓariyyah wa al-Taṭbīq*", Madīḥah 'Alī 'Abd al-Ḥāfiẓ's "*Al-Istiḥsān wa Atharuh fī Binā' al-Fiqh al-Islāmī*'", Ridwān Aremū Yūsuf's "*The Theory of Istiḥsān in Islamic law*", Muḥarrem Önder's "*Ḥanafī Mezhebinde İstiḥsān Anlayışı ve Uygulaması*" and so on. Besides these sources, other primary source materials have also been used; a complete list of sources is presented in the bibliography.

I have made an effort to access as many sources as possible. To this end I travelled to Egypt twice, spending approximately four months on my second trip, and travelled to Jordan and Saudi Arabia as well as Turkey. I conducted research in the places mentioned at many independent and university libraries, as well as through personal discussions with eminent scholars such as Prof. Muḥammad 'Alī Sawwā', University of Jordan Faculty of Sharī'ah; Dr. Aḥmad al-Raissounī, the University of Muḥammad Khamis, Rabat; Prof. Muḥammad M. 'Abd al-Latef Jamāl al-Dīn, University of Al-Azhar; Prof. Dr. Orhan Çeker and Prof. Dr. Aḥmet Yaman Konya Selçuk University /Turkey; Prof. Ṭāha Jābīr al-'Alwani, the president of the *Fiqh* Council of North America; and Ustādh Shaykh Shu'ayb al-Arnawūṭī in Jordan.

Chapter 4, on the different types of *istiḥsān*, draws almost entirely upon the classical and modern sources that I have introduced previously. Besides the previous sources, I have also benefited from the works of many contemporary scholars to develop my thesis, particularly on issues such as the concept of *maqāṣid al-Sharī'ah*. Some of the selected sources that I have referred to include Shāṭibī's "Muwāfaqāt", Ibn 'Āshūr's "*Maqāṣid al-Sharī'ah al-Islāmīyyah*", and "*Naẓarīyyāh al-Maqāṣid*" by Aḥmad al-Raissounī, which is an academic dissertation on Imām Shāṭibī. It investigates his perception of *maqāṣid* and is now a text book being taught at the University of Jordan by Muḥammad 'Alī Sawwā'. Other sources include 'Allāl Fāsī's, "*Maqāṣid*", Juwayni's "*Al-Burḥān*", Ghazālī's "*Al-Mustaṣfā*", Ṭūfī's "*Risālah fī al-Maṣlaḥah al-Mursalah*" and "*Sharḥ Mukhtaṣar al-Rawḍah*", etc.

Notes

1. Ibn Ḥanbal, "*Al-Musnad*", vol. 1, p. 379; Ibn Mājah "*Sunan*", ḥadīth no. 2340, vol. 2, p. 784.

2. Abū Dāwud, "*Sunan*", trans. Aḥmad Ḥasan, edt. Muḥammad Ashraf, (Lahore: 1984), ḥadīth no: 3585, vol. 3, p. 1019.
3. Shalabī Muḥammad Muṣṭafā, "*Uṣūl al-Fiqh al-Islāmī*", (Beirut: 1986), p. 258.
4. Shāfi'ī "Al-Risālah", p. 503; and, "Al-Umm", vol. 7, p. 309.
5. Anṣārī, "*Ghāyat al-Wuṣūl*", p.139; 'Alwānī, "*The Ethics*", p. 75; Ghazālī, "*Mustaṣfā*", vol. 1, p. 274, ibid, "*Mankhūl*", p. 374; Isnawī (d. 772/1370), "*Nihāyat al-Sūl*", vol. 4, p. 399.
6. Shīrāzī, "*Sharḥ al-Luma'*", vol. 2, p. 969; Juwaynī, "*Talkhīs*", vol. 3, p. 310; Ghazālī, "*Mustaṣfā*", vol. 1, p. 274; Ghazālī, "*Al-Mankhul*", p. 374; Rāzī, "*Maḥsūl*", vol. 2, p. 559; Āmidī, "*Al-Iḥkām*", vol. 4, p. 390.
7. Shīrāzī, "*Tabaqāt al-Fuqahā*", pp. 92-93; Ibn Subkī, "*Tabaqāt*", vol. 2, pp. 284-293.
8. Ibn Ḥazm, "*Al-Iḥkām*", vol. 6, p. 192.
9. Shāfi'ī, "*Al-Umm*", vol. 7, p. 298; Shāfi'ī, "*Risālah*", vol. 3, p. 219; Ibn Ḥazm, "*Al-Iḥkām*" vol. 6, p. 757; Ghazālī, "*Al-Mankhul*", p. 374; Ghazālī, "*Al-Mustaṣfā*", vol. 1, p. 275; Isnawī, "*Sharḥ*" vol. 3, pp. 139.
10. Abū Zahrah, "*Al-Imām al-Ṣādiq Ḥayātuhu ve 'Aṣruhu Ārāuhu wa Fiqhuhu*", (Cairo: Dār al-Fikr al-'Arabī, n.d.), pp. 527-529,
11. M. Hāshim Kamālī, "*Principles*", p. 264.

1

The Sources of Islamic Law

A starting point for understanding the concept of *istiḥsān*, an explanation of some basic components of Islamic law is necessary. Basically, all rulings of Islamic law are based ultimately on the Qur'an and the Sunnah. In other words, the *Aḥkām Sharīʿah* (legal rules) are produced using particular methods and mechanisms which are applied to the general rules given originally by God Himself.

Islamic legal theory is, in general, based on four sources[1]—the Qur'an, the Sunnah, *ijmāʿ* (consensus), and *qiyās* (analogy)—which are unanimously accepted by all the Sunnī schools of law. Shīʿī and Ẓāhirī legal theory is different.[2]

The Qur'an is the first source of law for Muslims who seek guidance. If one finds the answer within the Qur'an there is no need to resort to other sources.

However, if one does not find his answers within the Qur'an, one should seek enlightenment from the Sunnah. If the required knowledge is not obtained from these two sources, one should look to *ijmāʿ* (consensus) for an answer; if the desired information is still not forthcoming, one must finally turn to *qiyās* (analogy).

The ḥadīth below, narrated from Mu'ādh ibn Jabal (d. 18/640), shows the sequence in which rulings are to be sought from the sources. Explaining the methodology of the jurists in discovering and applying the law, scholars usually quote this Tradition. When the Prophet (ṣ) intended to send Mu'ādh ibn Jabal to Yemen, the Prophet (ṣ) asked him:

> "How will you judge when the occasion of deciding a case arises?" He replied: "I shall judge in accordance with God's book." The Prophet (ṣ) asked: "What will you do if you do not find guidance in God's book?" He replied: "I will act in accordance with the Sunnah of the Messenger of God." The Prophet (ṣ) asked: "What will you do if you do not find guidance in the Sunnah of the Messenger of God and in God's Book?" He replied: "I shall do my best to form an opinion and spare no pains in my search for truth". The Messenger of God then patted him on the chest and said: "Praise be to God who helped the messenger of the Messenger of God to find an answer which pleases the Messenger of God."[3]

Also, the same method of discovering and applying the law was used by the Companions of the Prophet (ṣ).[4] Mihrān bin Maymūn reports that Abū Bakr (d. 13 AH) referred to the Qur'an whenever a claimant-defendant asked him for guidance. If he was unable to find the result in the Qur'an, he would then seek a judgment in the Sunnah. Failing to discover the answer within these sources, he would then consult the righteous men of the community who would convene to discuss the matter and arrive at a solution. If they arrived at an opinion which was unanimously accepted, the consensus was that he should judge accordingly. 'Umar and other companions of the Prophet (ṣ) applied these methods of judgment and consequently the Muslim community also accepted this procedure.[5]

This shows that Islamic Law is able to find answers for human problems and develops itself naturally. Based on Mu'ādh's answer, "I shall do my best to form an opinion and spare no pains" can we say that human opinion influences Islamic law? Is this a proof that Islamic Law can deal with any issues relating to human life? And, is Islamic law itself developing further and evolving over time?

DEFINITION OF SOME JURISTIC TERMS

We shall now explain some important terms that are crucial to an understanding of the discipline of *uṣūl al-fiqh* (the principles of Islamic jurisprudence), and thus for our central topic, which is *istiḥsān*.

Uṣūl

In certain cases, this is defined as something upon which another thing is constructed, be it material or spiritual; here it gives the meaning of foundation (*asās*).[6] The term a-*ṣ-l* is used in the sense of the Arabic word "*maṣdar*" (source). The term *uṣūl* is the plural of *aṣl*, and it is "something from which another thing originates or is sourced." Thus, the origin of a thing is its *aṣl* that is the reason for translating the word *aṣl* as "root" (*Jadhr*). It also means *nasab* (lineage and stock), *'illah* (cause and reason). Another meaning is *ḥaqīqī* which means true, genuine, authentic and real.[7] Technical applications of the word (*a-ṣ-l*) in Islamic Law are as follows: One of the uses of *a-ṣ-l* is the meaning of *dalīl*. The word *dalīl* was applied to mean a guide leading a caravan, or scout finding the trail. In this sense, a directory, like a telephone directory, may be called a *dalīl*, because it leads us to a number or an address.

In Islamic law, the word *dalīl* is used in two ways: *dalīl tafṣīlī* is like an individual verse of the Qur'an or an individual *Sunnah* in a *ḥadīth*. We may refer to it as "specific evidence", though it is sometimes translated as "detailed proof". For example, God says "Forbidden to you (for marriage) are your mothers, your daughters, your sisters..." (4:23). It indicates a *ḥukm* (rule), which is obvious, that marriage to mothers, daughters and sisters is forbidden. "And come not near to unlawful sexual intercourse..." (17:32). This verse indicates a *ḥukm* (rule), which is also obvious: do not commit adultery.

As compared to *dalīl tafṣīlī* (specific evidence), the *dalīl ijmālī* or *kullī* is general evidence, because it contains within it a large amount of specific evidence. The *dalīl ijmālī* has nothing to do with direct, absolute order and prohibition. However, it produces general rulings as *wujūb* (necessity) and *taḥrīm* (prohibition). The Qur'an is general evidence: it contains a large number of specific evidences:[8] "And perform *as-ṣalāt*" (2:43), is the *aṣl* which makes prayer obligatory in the Qur'an.

The word (*a-ṣ-l*) is also used to indicate the foundation upon which analogy is constructed. An example in the Qur'an: "O you who believe! Intoxicants (all kinds of alcoholic drinks) ... are an abomination of Satan's handiwork. So avoid (strictly all)" (5:90). This is the general prohibition of drinks which contain intoxicants. As *ḥadīth* confirms it: "Every drink which contains intoxicant is *khamr* (wine) and every *khamr* is forbidden".[9] Therefore, *khamr* is an original case (*a-ṣ-l*) or basis for the prohibition of *nabīdh* (fermented dates); the *'īllah* of intoxication is found in both, but is extrapolated from *khamr*, which is the *aṣl*.[10]

In addition, *aṣl* is sometimes applied in the sense of the original rule. Hence, the maxim says: "*Al-aṣlu fī al-ashyā' al-ibāḥah*", which means the original rule for all things is permissibility. Another use of *aṣl* is that the meaning of general principles of jurisprudence (*qawāi'd fiqhiyyah*) governs the law and its interpretation. An example is "*lā ḍarara walā ḍirār*" which means "Harm is neither inflicted nor reciprocated in Islām"[11] is an *aṣl* in the principle of Islamic Law. It also means *al-rujḥān* (preference, preferability), and as jurists say: "*al-aṣl fī al-kalāmi al-ḥaqīqah*" which means in that literal meaning rather than metaphor is to be understood.[12]

Dalīl (proof) is distinguished from *amārah* (indication), which literally means sign or allusion. A sign indicates the existence of a thing without the need for rational proofs like the *minārāh* of a mosque, and milestone of the road.[13] *Dalīl* could only relate to evidence which leads to a definitive ruling or to positive knowledge (*'ilm*). *Amārah* on the other hand is reserved for evidence or indication that only leads to a *ẓannī* (speculative) ruling.[14] In this way, the term *dalīl* could only be concerned with the definitive proofs, namely the Qur'an, the *Sunnah,* and *ijmā'*, while the remaining proof which contains a measure of speculation, such as *qiyās, istiḥsān, istiṣḥāb, maṣāleḥ mursalah,* etc, could fall under the category of *amārah* (signs or allusions, probable evidence). However, most jurists consider both *dalīl* and *amārah* whether *qaṭ'ī* (definitive) or *ẓannī* (speculative), as a *dalīl* (proof). *Amārah* becomes *dalīl* if *ḥukm shar'ī* is deduced from it.[15]

After all these explanations of the concept of the term *aṣl* we can say that the term *aṣl* is actually *dalīl,* which is a proof or an evidence of Islamic Law.[16] The jurist seeks the *dalīl ijmālī* or *kullī* (general evidence), yet the *adillah al-tafsīliyyah* (specific evidence) is the subject field of the *mufti.* Therefore, the *uṣūl al-fiqh* (the principles of Islamic Jurisprudence) is called *adillah al-fiqh al-kulliyyah* (proofs or evidences of general *fiqh*). The juristic scholars (*uṣūlī*) define the term of *uṣūl al-fiqh* in two separated parts as *uṣūl* and *fiqh.* As I have covered the term of *uṣūl* (plural of *aṣl*) above, the term of *fiqh* now will be elaborated.

Fiqh

In the linguistic sense, the term *fiqh* is synonymous with *al-fahm* (understanding).[17] The Qur'an has used the word *fiqh* in its general sense of "understanding" as: "O Shu'ayb! We do not understand much of what you say," (11:91) and "So what is wrong with these people that they fail to understand a single fact."(4:78), "They have hearts wherewith they understand not."(7:179) It implies an understanding of Islām and consideration of religion. The same meaning is also revealed in the *ḥadīth* of the Prophet (ṣ) as saying: "He for whom God wills His blessings is granted the understanding of dīn."[18] In addition the term, *'ilm* (knowledge) was used for the same meaning of *fiqh* (understanding) in the early time of Islām, as the Prophet (ṣ) blessed Ibn 'Abbās (d. 68) saying: "*Allahumma faqqihhu fī al-dīn*" (O God, give him understanding in religion).[19] The Prophet (ṣ) could not have meant absolute knowledge of the law. However, it is clear that the Prophet (ṣ) meant a deeper understanding of Islām in general.

The term *fiqh* also means *kalām*, which Abū Ḥanīfah (d. 150) defines as "*Ma'rifat al-nafsi mā lahā wamā 'alayhā*" which means "A person's knowledge of his rights and obligations".[20] *Al-Fiqh al-Akbar* which is attributed to Abū Ḥanīfah (d. 150) against the beliefs of *ahl al-qadar* deals with the basic tenets of Islām like faith, unity of God, His attributes, the life hereafter, prophecy, etc. These are problems which are dealt with in *kalām* and not in the discipline of law.[21]

Fiqh is used for the meaning of exercise of intelligence as the Successors of the Companions of the Prophet (ṣ) at most were *fuqahā'* (jurists), who gave legal judgments using their own intelligence and reason in solving legal problems, in that respect the term *fiqh* is also used for the knowledge of the law. Technically, the definition of *fiqh* is confined to Islamic law alone.

Among the scholars, Shāfi'ī's (d. 204/819) definition is widely known: "The knowledge of the legal rules (*aḥkām shar'iyyah*), pertaining to conduct, have been derived from their specific evidences." On the other hand "It is a compilation of the legal rules pertaining to conduct that have been derived from their specific evidences."[22] The definition of *fiqh* can be understood in stages. Then the meaning of *fiqh* will be the knowledge of the *aḥkām shar'iyyah.*

Uṣūl al-fiqh

The meaning of *uṣūl al-fiqh* (the principle of Islamic jurisprudence) is combined by the understanding of the meaning of *uṣūl* and *fiqh* individually. The term of *uṣūl al-fiqh* now can be defined as: "The principles by the use of which the *mujtahid* arrives at legal rules through the specific evidences."[23] It is a discipline of Law, a kind of methodology, which explains the reasoning behind *istiḥsān* (juristic preference), *qiyās* (analogy), *istiṣḥāb* (presumption of continuity). These are taken from general evidences, the rules of interpretation, deduction and the sources of Islamic law. *Uṣūl al-fiqh* also includes the kind of general evidences that are indicative to the *aḥkām* of God and the sources of Islamic law, as well as proofs or evidences on how to arrive at the *aḥkām.*

Aḥkām

Aḥkām (rules) is the plural form of *ḥukm* (rule), which means rule, command, the absolute, order, judgment, injunction, prescription, and decree.[24] This rule could be a rule of any kind; it is to command one to delegate an order to another whether approval or disapproval. You could say that the moon is rising or the moon is not rising,[25] or that fire burns.

Technically, it is considered a rule of Islamic law. Āmidī (d. 631/1234)[26] defines *adillah* as the science of the proofs of *fiqh* and the indications that they provide with regard to the *aḥkām* of the Sharī'ah. The *ḥukm shar'ī* is therefore defined as: "A communication from God, the Exalted, related to the acts of the subjects through a demand or option, or through a declaration."[27]

The above definition of *al-ḥukm* is found only amongst the *uṣūlī* (juristic scholars). The first point of the definition is that any communication must be from God otherwise it is not accepted and cannot be considered as *a ḥukm*. This communication is related to the actions of the *mukallaf* (subjects). The relationship also enables the *mujtahid* (jurist) to evaluate the requirements, and to judge whether it is for the command for the act or the prohibition. God says "O you who believe! Observe *ṣawm* (fasting)"(2:183). This contains *a ḥukm* which demands obedience. "And come not near to the unlawful sexual intercourse"(17:32). This verse contains *a ḥukm* which requires prohibition.

The *ḥukm* (rule) is clarified through a request (*ṭalab* or *iqtiḍā'*). The request in this case is communicated in the form of a command of an act or its prohibition. The request may or may not be binding. When the request is binding, it creates *wujūb* (an obligation) or *taḥrīm* (prohibition), which are established by *dalīl qaṭ'ī* (definite proof).

When the request is not binding, then the ruling creates *nadb* (recommendation) or *makrūh* (discouraged), which are established without definitive proof. God says "O you who believe! Fulfil (your) obligations"(5:1). This verse is addressed to the *mukallaf* (subject), and consists of a particular demand. And "O you who believe! Let not a group scoff at another group, it may be that the latter are better than the former..." (49:11). This Qur'anic text conveys a prohibition to the *mukallaf*. The freedom of choice is given to the *mukallaf* (subject) a choice to commit the act or avoid it.

On the other hand if the subject is free to perform the act it is known as *mubaḥ* (permissible). For example "But when you finish the *iḥram* pilgrimage (of *ḥajj* or *'umrah*), you may hunt..." (5:2). This *ḥukm* conveys an option for the *mukallaf* (subject) and he has the freedom to act or not to. As a final point of the definition, the communication may be clarified through an enactment or declaration; this is neither a demand nor an option. However, it is in relation to an act which is connected to another act by reason of *sabab* (cause), *sharṭ* (condition) or *māni'* (impediment). "...and *ḥajj* to the House is a duty that mankind owe to God for those who can afford the expenses..." (3:97). Financial ability is the condition for the application of the rule.[28]

The identification of *ḥukm shar'ī* is perceived differently between the *uṣūlīs* (juristic scholars) and the *fuqahā*. For instance God says "And perform *al-ṣalāt*"[29] which is a *ḥukm shar'ī* itself according to the *uṣūlīs*. However, according to the *fuqahā'*, it is the effect or the result of the demand in this verse, namely the *wujūb* (obligation), which represents the *ḥukm shar'ī*.[30]

Basically, *ḥukm shar'ī* (legal rule) is divided into two main categories: the first is *ḥukm taklīfī* (the obligation, creating rule, defining law) and the other is *ḥukm waḍ'ī* (declaratory law). In contemporary common law, Hart has divided it into primary and secondary rules. The only difference is that the rules of Islamic law are based on religious law.

The Muslim jurists designate the category of primary rules as *ḥukm taklīfī* (defining law). The category of secondary rules is designated as the *ḥukm waḍ'ī*.[31] *Ḥukm taklīfī* (defining law) is a communication from God, the exalted, related to the acts of the *mukallaf* (subjects), which consists of a demand or an option; it arises in the five categories of *wājīb* or *farḍ* (obligatory), *mandūb* (recommended), *makrūh* (adversity), *ḥarām* (prohibited) and *mubāḥ* (permissible). In addition, the Ḥanafī school deduces seven varieties from the same definition: 1. *farḍ* (obligatory) 2. *wājīb* (obligatory) 3. *mandūb* (recommended) 4. *makrūh karāḥat al-taḥrīm* (strongly disapproved) 5. *makrūh karāḥat al-tanzīh* (disapproval) 6. *ḥarām* (prohibited) 7. *mubāḥ* (permissible).

Ḥukm waḍ'ī is a communication from God which is related to the acts of the *mukallaf* (subject) in a manner that is declaratory, in another word it is explanatory component for *al-ḥukm al-taklīfīyya* through its fundamental tools which consist of 1. *sabab* (cause) 2. *sharṭ* (condition) 3. *māni'*(impediment).[32]

Shar'īyyah

Shar'īyyah derived from "*sh-r-'a* (legal); *ta-sh rr-'a*" (legislation), it excludes *aḥkām ḥissiyyah* (law of sense perception: for instance fire burns, wood floats on water, the sun shines), *aḥkām 'aqliyyah* (rational rules, for instance one is half of two, etc.), *aḥkām lughawiyyah* (linguistic rules, like the doer of an act is called the subject) and *aḥkām waḍ'īyyah* (declaratory rules).[33]

'Amalīyyah

Aḥkām 'amaliyyah are divided into three types: *fi'lī* (physically), *qalbī* (which takes place in the heart) and *qawlī* (relating to speech). The physical acts as the acts of prayer, murder, homicide; the *qalbī* acts as intention, love, hate, etc.; and *qawlī* acts as recitation during prayers, offer and acceptance in a contract, etc.

According to Imām al-Rāzī (d. 606) the meaning of the term *al-'amaliyyah* does not contain all of *aḥkām fiqhiyyah*, since *aḥkām fiqhiyyah* contains also *naẓarī* (theoretical) rules.[34] Some sources of law such as *ijmā'* (consensus), *qiyās* (analogy) are considered to be *naẓarī* (theoretical). *Aḥkām 'amaliyyah* excludes *aḥkām i'tiqādiyyah*, which is belief in the existence of God, His oneness, His qualities, the truth of the mission of the Prophet (ṣ), belief in the Day of Judgment etc.

Adillah

Is a plural of *dalīl*, which contains the meanings of *ishārah* (indication, sign, token, and symptom), *murshid* (guide, conductor), *burhān* (proof, evidence), and *shāhid* (witness). It also means "*kitābun yustarshad bihī*" (guide book, itinerary), or *fihrist* (index).[35] Linguistically *dalīl* means that which leads or guides to anything sensible or moral. The term means in a literal sense a proof, evidence, indication or guide.

Technically *al-dalīl* means a proof or evidence of a practical *ḥukm* (rule) of the Sharī'ah which is inferred. It is also defined as something which guides one to the practical rule of the Sharī'ah by the correct understanding.[36]

One of the main features of the Islamic Sharī'ah is that it is based on evidence or proof deduced from the Qur'an or the *Sunnah* through *ijtihād* which conforms to these two sources of Islamic law. Consequently, it can be stated that the sources of Islamic Law are mainly either revelation or non-revelation:[37]

Revelation is considered to be of two types:

1. *Al-waḥy al-matlū* or *waḥy ẓāhir* (recited or manifest revelation), which is defined as communication from God to the Prophet Muḥammad (ṣ), conveyed by the angel Gabriel, i.e. the Qur'an.
2. *Al-waḥy ghair al-matlū* or *waḥy bāṭin* (un-recited or internal revelation). This consists of the inspiration (*ilhām*) of concepts only: God inspired the Prophet (ṣ) and the latter conveyed the concepts in his own words, i.e. the *Sunnah,* which comprises the sayings *aḥādith* of the Prophet (ṣ).[38]

Non-revelation refers to *ijmā‘* (consensus of *mujtahidīn* of the Muslim community), *qiyās* (analogy) or *istidlāl* (inference). In addition, Imām al-Shāṭibī (d. 790/1388) divided the sources of the Sharī‘ah into two types: either pure transmitted (*al-naql al-maḥḍ*) or pure opinion (*al-ra'y al-maḥḍ*). Opinion (*ra'y*) is not considered as a source of Sharī‘ah unless it is based on transmitted proof.[39]

Another classification of *adillah* Sharī‘ah is the *qaṭ‘ī* (definitive) and the *ẓannī* (speculative).[40]

The *adillah* Sharī‘ah have also been categorized into transmitted (*naqlī*) and rational (*‘aqlī*). The transmitted proofs, *adillah naqliyyah,* are the Qur'an, the *Sunnah,* and *ijmā‘*. Two other transmitted proofs are the rulings of the Companions and the laws revealed prior to the advent of Islām (*shar‘ man qablanā*). Rational proofs are *adillah ‘aqlīyyah* namely *qiyās, istiṣḥāb,* etc.[41] *Adillah* is further classified by al-Āmidī (d. 631/1233) into *mustaqil* (independent)—such as the first three sources of the Sharī‘ah—and *muqayyad* (dependent).[42]

The sources of the Sharī‘ah (*al-maṣāder* al-Sharī‘ah) are further divided into two types:

Unanimously accepted sources:

1. The Qur'an, 2. The *Sunnah*, 3. *Ijmā‘* (consensus), 4. *Qiyās* (analogy).

Controversial sources:

1. *istiḥsān* (juristic preference), which is the main subject of this research, 2. *maṣlaḥah mursalah* (consideration of public interest), 3. *istiṣḥāb* (presumption of continuity), 4. *qawl al-ṣāḥābī* (the sayings of a companion of the Prophet), 5. *‘urf* (custom), 6. *sadd al-dharā'i‘* (blocking the means), 7. *shar‘ man*

qablanā (revealed laws preceding to the Sharī'ah of Islām) and 8. *istiqrā'* (induction).[43]

The sources of Sharī'ah are identified in the Qur'an as follows: "O you who believe! Obey God and obey the Messenger (Muḥammad) and those of you (Muslims) who are in authority. (And) if you differ in anything amongst yourselves refer it to God and His Messenger"(4:59). The reference to Qur'an is pointed out in the verse as "Obey God" and the reference to the *Sunnah* as "Obey the Messenger". *Ijmā'* is also referred to in the idea of obedience to "Those of you who are in authority" and the last part of the verse "If you differ in anything amongst yourselves refer it to God and His Messenger" which requires the referral of disagreement to God and His Messenger, is in effect a clear authorisation for the principle of *qiyās*.[44]

Muktasabah

Means that which is obtained, thus, any type of knowledge which are not obtained are not considered as *fiqh*.[45] The obtained knowledge is the knowledge of the jurist (*faqīh*) and the follower (*muqallid*). The term *al-muktasabah* excludes the knowledge of the *shar'ī aḥkām* (legal rules) which pertains to man's knowledge of God. This knowledge is not granted by the way of performing *ijtihād* but only by way of divine revelations concerning God's angels and prophets etc.[46] Finally, *adillah tafṣīliyyah* (specific evidences) which is excluded from the definition of *fiqh*, thus the knowledge of the *muqallid* (one who follows the opinion of another) is different from the knowledge of jurists and the knowledge of the leaders of the schools of thought.[47] It is not permitted for the *muqallid* to obtain his knowledge of *fiqh* directly from the Qur'an and the *Sunnah*. However, a *faqīh* can obtain his knowledge from the Qur'an and the *Sunnah* directly.

UNANIMOUS SOURCES OF ISLAMIC LAW

The Qur'an

The first unanimously accepted source of Islamic law is the Qur'an which is not only the first source of Islamic law but also, as far as it is concerned, is the only source and all other sources are explanatory to the Qur'an. Alternatively, all other sources are dependant on the Qur'an in respect of the focal principle of Islamic law.

Definition of the Qur'an

The Qur'an in 'ilm al-uṣūl al-fiqh

The theologians when discussing the attributes of God, define Qur'an as the meaning of the essence of God expressed in utterances or words, yet the *'ulamā' al-uṣūl* treat the Qur'an as a connection of utterances from which *aḥkām* (practical rules) may be derived. Here the utterances are Arabic words. Consequently, they define Qur'an as Arabic utterance or words indicating or explaining the meaning of the speech of God sent down to the Prophet (ṣ), conveyed by the Angel Gabriel and written in the book, transmitted to us by *tawātur* (continuous testimony). It is a proof of the prophecy of Muḥammad (ṣ), the most authoritative guide for Muslims and the first source of the Sharī'ah.[48] It should be noted that some words of non-Arabic origin occur in the Qur'an but this usage is confined to odd words. A phrase or a sentence of non-Arabic origin does not occur in the Qur'an.[49]

Characteristics of the Qur'an

The definition of the Qur'an reveals the following obvious characteristics:

1. Any speech other than that of God is excluded.

2. Any non-Arabic speech of the previously revealed books is excluded.
3. Any Arabic non-revealed speech including the *Sunnah* and *ḥadīth qudsī*[50] is excluded.
4. Any part that is not established by continuous testimony, such as variant readings, is excluded.
5. Any revelation sent down without the challenge of *i'jāz* (inimitability) such as previous revelations and the *Sunnah* is excluded.[51]

Aḥkām (ordinances) of the Qur'an

The Qur'an ordinance /legislation cover several aspects of the life of the *mukallaf* (the subject). The *aḥkām* include the following types:

1. *Aḥkām i'tiqādīyyah* (creed/ convictional).
2. *Aḥkām khuluqīyyah* (ethical and moral).
3. *Aḥkām 'amalīyyah* (practical): This type of *aḥkām* is related to sayings, actions, contracts and behaviour of the *mukallaf* (the subject). *Aḥkām 'amalīyyah* is the *fiqh* of the Qur'an and is the aim of *'ilm uṣūl al-fiqh* (principles of jurisprudence). They are classified into two types:
   i. *Aḥkām al-'ibādāt* (worship or devotional matters) which regulate the relationship between the *mukallaf* and his God such as prayers, fasting, *zakāh* (alms), *ḥajj* (pilgrimage).

The *aḥkām* in the Qur'an about *'ibādāt* (worshipping) consists of approximately 90 verses.[52]

   ii. *Aḥkām al-mu'āmalāt* (transactions) which regulate the dealings of the *mukallaf* with others as individuals or groups, such as commercial, civil, criminal, constitutional, international, economical and financial legislations.[53] Of

> these, family matrimonial law accounts for 70 verses; law of contracts and torts accounts for 70 verses; judiciary 13 verses; criminal law 30 verses; administrative law 10 verses; international law 25 verses and fiscal law about public revenues, public expenditures altogether are 317 verses.[54]

The *Sunnah*

The concept of the *Sunnah* is also unanimously accepted as the second source of Islamic law (Sharī'ah). The *Sunnah* of the Prophet (ṣ) is a proof of Islamic law, and attests to the Qur'an's authority. As the Qur'an indicates the Prophet's teachings are also divinely inspired. "Nor does he speak of (his own) desire. It is only a revelation revealed" (53:3-4). Therefore, the Prophet's words are *ḥujjah* (*dalīl*, evidence, proof) for Muslims; and may have power like that of the Qur'an. The Qur'an commands submission to the Prophet (ṣ) and makes it a sense of duty for Muslims to bow to its judgment and its authority without question. As is indicated in the Qur'an: "And whatever the Messenger (Muḥammad) gives you, take it and whatsoever he forbids you, abstain" (59:7). "He who obeys the Messenger (Muḥammad), has indeed obeyed God" (4:80).

The word *Sunnah* is derived from the root verb *s-n-n*, which the Arabs used to describe the continuous and gentle flow of water; the water flows so gently it appears as one cohesive body.[55] The literal meaning was used by Arabs to describe a clear path or to imply a customary practice, or an established route of conduct whether good or bad; this conduct was set by an individual or a community. The opposite of the *Sunnah* is *bid'ah* (innovation), which is characterised by lack of precedent or continuity with the past. Azharī (d. 370/980) maintains that *Sunnah* is the good path only, hence the term *ahl al-sunnah* which means those who follow the *Sunnah* correctly.[56] It also means "The trodden path and was used by the pre-Islamic Arabs to denote the model behaviour established by the forefathers of a tribe."[57] As a general legislative term, the *Sunnah* is used to imply the practical reality of Islamic Sharī'ah and its concepts, whether it came from the Qur'an, *ḥadīth* or was deduced from these two sources. In this manner, the *Sunnah* includes *khabar* (news or report) and *athar* about the Prophet (ṣ) and the precedent of the Companions.

The Muḥaddithīn (narrators)

Refer to the *Sunnah* as all that is narrated from the Prophet (ṣ), his acts, his sayings and whatever he has tacitly approved, in addition, all of the reports describing his physical attributes and characters before and after the revelation.[58] Suyūṭī (d. 911/1505) reports Ibn Ḥanbal (d. 241/855) as saying "For us the *Sunnah* refers to *athar* (impressions, impacts) of the Prophet (ṣ), the *Sunnah* is the *tafsīr* (interpretation) of the Qur'an and it is the *dalā'il* (indications or proofs) of the Qur'an".[59]

'Ulamā' of *fiqh*

The main concern for these scholars is to search for the *ḥukm* (ruling) of Sharī'ah with regard to the acts of an individual or group. For these *'ulamā'*, the *Sunnah* primarily refers to "*Al-ṭarīqah al-muttaba'ah* (the path followed or the way shown) in the religion, excluding *farḍ/ wājib* (obligatory)". Laknawī (d. 1304/1886) defines the *Sunnah* as an act which, when it is performed results in *thawāb* (reward) and when it is not performed, results in *'itāb* (blame) but not in *'iqāb* (punishment).[60] According to Baiḍāwī (d. 685/1286), the *Sunnah* refers to the *mandūb* (commendable), which he defines as any act that will gain praise for the dutiful person and will not lay blame on the one who abandons the duty; such an act is called both *Sunnah* and *nāfilah*.[61]

'Ulamā' of uṣūl al-fiqh

The main concern for the *'ulamā'* of *uṣūl al-fiqh* is to search for a *dalīl shar'ī* (legal proof) with regards to the *aḥkām al-shar'īyyah* (juristic rulings). Their search into the life of the Prophet (ṣ) is based on his position as messenger of God conveying the laws that govern the lives of people. The Prophet (ṣ) set the principles for *mujtahidīn* (competent jurists) after him.

Consequently their interest in the life of the Prophet (ṣ) is in his *aqwāl* (sayings), *af'āl* (acts) and tacit *taqrīr* (approval) of the acts or sayings of the Companions. They believe that the *aḥkām* legislate them as the second source of Sharī'ah next to the Qur'an. For the *'ulamā' of uṣūl al-fiqh*, the *Sunnah* refers to whatever came from the Prophet (ṣ) in the form of a saying, act or tacit approval, other than the Qur'an.[62]

The juristic usage of the *Sunnah* has two different meanings. According to the *'ulamā' of uṣūl al-fiqh*, *Sunnah* refers to a source of the Sharī'ah (Islamic law) where legal proofs accompany the Qur'an. According to the *'ulamā' of fiqh* (juristic scholars), the *Sunnah* primarily refers to a legal value, which falls under the category of *mandūb*.

***Ijmā'* (consensus)**

The Qur'an and the *Sunnah* are the main sources of Islamic law as mentioned above. *Ijmā'* is, in reality, subsidiary to them and applied when the original sources are silent on a certain problem. *Ijmā'* plays a very important role and undertakes the most essential role in the development of Islamic law in the history.

Ijmāʿ is the third source of Sharīʿah as the following verses and *ḥadīth* indicate.

The Qur'an: "O who believe! Obey God and obey the Messenger (Muḥammad) and those of you (Muslims) who are in authority. If you differ in anything amongst yourselves refer it to God and His Messenger, if you believe in God and in the Last Day. That is better and more suitable for final determination" (4:59).

There are different interpretations of *'ulū al-amr* (those in authority). They can be leaders, commanders of an expedition, scholars, jurists, the Companions of the Prophet (ṣ), Abū Bakr and 'Umar, and the Sulṭān.[63] *'ulū al-amr*, according to Fakhr al-Dīn al-Rāzī (d. 606/1210), means the scholars.[64] Shāfiʿī quotes the following *āyāh* (verse) to support the authority for *ijmāʿ*.[65] "And hold fast all of you together the Rope of God (Qur'an), and be not divided amongst yourselves" (3:113).

In addition, here are some ḥadīth:

"My community shall never agree on an error."[66] "God will not let my community agree upon an error." "I beseeched Almighty God not to bring my community to the point of agreeing on *ḍalālah* (error) and He granted me this." "The hand of God is with the community and (its safety) is not endangered by isolated oppositions." "Whoever leaves the community or separates himself from it by the length of a span is breaking his bond with Islām." "Whatever the Muslims deem to be good is good in the eyes of God."[67]

Definition of ijmāʿ

Ijmāʿ is the verbal noun of the Arabic word *ajmaʿa* , which is derived from (*j-m-aʿ, ajmaʿa, ijmāʿ*). The root meaning of *ijmāʿ* is "to collect, to gather up, assemble, and congregate".[68]

Ijmāʿ has another meaning "composing and settling a thing that has been unsettled, as an opinion which one determines, resolves or decides upon." Therefore, it stands for determining, resolving or deciding an affair so as to make it firmly settled (after it had been unsettled in the mind). Alternatively after considering what might be its issues or result, and saying at one time 'I shall do this', and at another time, 'I shall do that'. Hence the phrase, (*ajmaʿtu ʿalā al-amr* or *ajmaʿtu al-amr*) which means I determined, resolved and decided whom the affair.[69] The word *ajmaʿa* has another meaning, which is, to reach unanimous agreement. As an example: "*ajmaʿa al-qawm ʿalā kadhā*" which means the people reached a unanimous agreement on such and such.[70]

Technical Definition

Ijmāʿ is a unanimous agreement of the jurists of the Community of a particular era on a certain issue.[71] Āmidī (d. 631/1233) defines it as: the unanimous agreement of the *mujtahidīn* (competent scholars) of the Muslim community of any period following the demise of the Prophet Muḥammad (ṣ) on any matter.[72] Ghazālī's view on *ijmāʿ* is an agreement of the community of Muḥammad on a religious point.[73] Briefly *ijmāʿ* is defined as the "agreement of the scholars".[74] *Ijmāʿ* applies to all the religious legal questions and agreements on any point whatsoever (*amr* or *amrun mā*).[75] All problems relating to the Sharīʿah are covered by *ijmāʿ*.

Types of ijmāʿ

Based on the way it is formed, *ijmāʿ* may be divided into two types:

- *ijmāʿ ṣarīḥ*
- *ijmāʿ sukūtī*.[76]

1. *Ijmāʿ ṣarīḥ* (explicit *ijmāʿ ʿaẓīmah*): occurs when all *mujtahīds* (jurists) are united on a specific issue and express opinions which are unanimous. *ʿAẓīmah* in the context of *ijmāʿ* means the agreement of Muslims on the essentials of Islām. It contains the fundamentals of religion over which there is no dispute, such as the necessity of prayer, fasting during *Ramaḍān*, the *ḥajj* (pilgrimage), prohibition of adultery, of usury, and of marrying one's own mother or sister, etc.

2. *Ijmāʿ sukūtī* (tacit *ijmāʿ rukhṣah*): This occurs when some of the *mujtahidīn* (jurists) of the community express an opinion on disputed issue and others, after examining the expressed opinion remain silent. The silence is a sign of acceptance.[77] This kind of *ijmāʿ* is a presumptive *ijmāʿ*, which only creates a probability (*ẓann*).

Sarakhsī (d. 483/1090) states that God has not put the community in hardship, therefore the silence of scholars over an opinion will be considered sufficient for the validity of *ijmāʿ*.[78] Bazdawī (482/1089) indicates that *ijmāʿ* by silence is valid on two conditions: the opinion of a single scholar or a group of scholars should reach all the remaining scholars; and that the time of consideration of the disputed problem should lapse.[79] Ghazālī (d. 505/1111) rejected the validity of *ijmāʿ sukūtī* saying that tacit agreement was neither an *ijmāʿ* nor an authority.[80]

Ijmāʿ is also sub-divided into the following categories:

3. religious-legal (*sharʿī*),
4. worldly (*dunyawī or ghayr sharʿī*),
5. intellectual (*ʿaqlī*),
6. sensory (*ḥissī*)
7. customary (*ʿurfī*),
8. etymological (*lughawī*).[81]

Arkān (essential requirements) of ijmāʿ

It is obvious from the definition of *ijmāʿ* that the pillar or prerequisite of *ijmāʿ* is the consensus of the competent scholars (*ittifāq al-mujtahidīn*) and without a unanimous agreement no *ijmāʿ* will materialise. Similarly, the condition that all *mujtahidīn* should be from the Muslim community is in fact a condition that the *mujtahidīn* themselves have to fulfil and does not constitute an independent *rukn* (condition) of the agreement.

Also, where there is only one *mujtahid* in the Muslim community or *mujtahidīn* of a certain locality, race, colour, school or following, no *ijmāʿ* is expected to materialise; nor does it constitute an essential requirement (*rukn*) of the agreement in question. They are merely conditions and controlling factors to achieve the agreement which is the pillar of *ijmāʿ*.[82]

Ghazālī [83] maintained that the layman's opinion should be taken into account because of the *ḥadīth* "My community does not agree on error", which includes both laymen and *mujtahid*. *Iṣmah* (infallibility, immunity from making errors) is a grace of God bestowed on the whole community and is the doctrinal basis of *ijmāʿ*.[84] Bazdawī (482/1089)[85]suggested that no discrimination should be made between the laymen and the jurists regarding the essentials of the faith; *ijmāʿ* is confined to the *mujtahidīn* only with regard to matters which require expert knowledge.

Qiyās (analogical deduction)

The fourth unanimous principle of Islamic law is analogy (*qiyās*) which is the developed version of opinion (*ra'y*). The tradition of Muʿādh Ibn Jabal, which I have touched upon at the beginning of the thesis, is that the jurist was permitted to give his own opinion, and act upon it as a source of law for a solution.

Definition of qiyās

Qiyās and *qā'is* are verbal nouns, which have the same meaning; measuring or ascertaining the amount, value or quality of something. It is derived from root *q-y-s* and that is why the scales are called *miqyās*. An Arabic idiom "*qāsat al-thawba bi al-dhirā'*" means the cloth was measured by the yardstick.[86]

Qiyās also means similarity, with a view to suggesting equality or similarity between two things whether sensible or moral. For example 'I have compared this book with this book', 'Zayd compares with Khālid in intelligence and descent', 'this person is not evaluated with that person' which means they are not the same value. As the term *qiyās* is used for measuring and comparing, disagreement among *'ulamā'* emerged as to whether *qiyās* in both of the meanings are real or whether one is real and the other is metaphorical.[87]

In the *uṣūlī* (juristic) definition, technically, the *qiyās* is the extension or application of Sharī'ah value from an original case (*aṣl*), to a new case (*far'*), where the latter has the same effective cause (*'illah*) as the former. The original case is regulated by a given text (the Qur'an and the *Sunnah*), and *qiyās* seeks to extend the same textual ruling to a new case.[88]

Āmidī (d. 631/1233) gives some definitions of *qiyās* as follows: a. *qiyās* means attaining the truth, b. *qiyās* is the use of effort to derive the truth, c. *qiyās* stands for similitude, d. *qiyās* is an indication leading to the truth, e. *qiyās* is a knowledge acquired through reflection on a known case.[89]

Baqillānī (d. 403/1013) defines *qiyās* as: "To arrive at a judgement on (*ḥaml*) a known, using a precedent set with a previous, by establishing or rejecting a law on the basis of a connecting link (*amr jām'*)."[90] The Ḥanafī jurist, Ṣadr al-Sharī'ah ('Ubayd Allah bin Mas'ūd [d. 747/1346]) defines *qiyās* as "extending the Sharī'ah value from the original case (*aṣl*) over to the subsidiary (*far'*) by reason of an effective cause (*'illah*) which is common to both cases and which cannot be understood from the expression (concerning the original case) alone."[91] Abū Bakr al-Jaṣṣāṣ (370/955) gave his own definition, stating "*Qiyās* is nothing but the return of the parallel case (*far'*) to the original (*aṣl*) on the bases of the idea or reason (*ma'nā'*) which combines both cases and necessitates equality between the rules of law about them".[92] The main sphere for the operation of human judgement in *qiyās* is identification of a common *'illah* between the original and the new case. Once *'illah* is identified the rules of analogy necessitate the ruling of the text be followed without any interference or change.

Arkān of qiyās

The essential requirements (*arkān*) of *qiyās* as indicated in the above definitions are summarized with the following explanation.

The main requirement is the original case (*aṣl*), namely a ruling given in the text, and which the analogy seeks to extend to a new case. The second requirement is the new case (*far'*) where a ruling is needed. The new case must not be covered by the text or *ijmā'* and must not result in altering the law of the text; this would mean over-ruling the text by *qiyās*. The third essential is the effective cause (*'illah*), which is an attribute (*waṣf*) of the *aṣl* and is found to be in common between the original and the new case. The final element is the rule (*hukm*) governing the original case, which is extended to the new case.

An example of *qiyās* is as follows:

> *"O you who believe! Intoxicants (all kinds of alcoholic drinks), and gambling, and al-anṣāb, and azlām (arrows for seeking luck or decision) are an abomination of Satan's*

handiwork. So avoid (strictly all) that (abomination) in order that you may be successful" (5:90).

In this verse, the drinking of wine is clearly forbidden. If this prohibition is extended by analogy to *nabīdh*, the original case (*aṣl*) would be wine that is forbidden by the Qur'an; the parallel case (*far'*) is *nabidh;* the cause (*'illah*) is intoxication, which is common to both cases, and the rule of law of the original case (*hukm*) is prohibition. *Nabīdh* is also forbidden because of the same cause (*'illah*), which is intoxication, according to the *naṣṣ* (text) "Every intoxicant is *khamr* and every *khamr* is forbidden."[93]

The Ḥanafī jurist Bazdawi (d. 482/1088) confined the essential requirements of *qiyās* to the common effective cause (*'illah*) alone. Both Bazdawi and Āmidī (d. 631/1233) are of the view that the result of *qiyās*, namely the *hukm al-far'* (ruling extended to the new case), should not be included in the essential requirements (*arkān*) of *qiyās*. Isnawī has, on the other hand, included the *hukm al-far'* in the essential requirements of *qiyās*.[94]

Variety of qiyās

Qiyās is divided into three categories based on the strength or weakness of *'illah* (cause).[95] Its types will be briefly illustrated.

1. *Qiyās awlā* (analogy of the superior). This is when the effective cause is more evident in the parallel case than the original case; it is then called *qiyās awlā*. Giving an example we can illustrate the Qur'an text in respect of parents "Say not to them (parents) a word of disrespect, nor shout at them but address them in terms of honour" (17:23). From this one may understand that rebuking or beating them is prohibited too, and in fact is even more obvious than verbal abuse—a deduction made based on analogy.

2. *Qiyās musāwāh* (analogy of equals): This is when the *'illah* is common to both the parallel case and the original case, as deduced by analogy. An example is: "If they commit illegal sexual intercourse, their punishment is half that of free women"(4:25). The text of the Qur'an prescribes half the punishment for the bondswoman (slave women) if they are guilty of adultery. This rule will also apply to a male slave by analogy if they commit illegal sexual intercourse (*zinā*); the punishment is fifty lashes. Making analogy over the bondman (slave) is the same punishment as that of bondswomen.

3. *Qiyās adnā* (analogy of the inferior): This is when the effective cause is less evident in the parallel case than in the original case. The prohibition of *nabīdh* on the analogy of prohibition of wine and inflicting the same punishment for the drinking of *nabīdh* fall under the category of *qiyās*. In this example the intoxication of *nabīdh* is less in severity than that of wine.

   Qiyās has been divided into a further two categories:[96]

   i. *Qiyās jalīy* (obvious analogy): This type of *qiyās* is one where the inability to differentiate (*nafy al-fāriq*) between the original case and the parallel case is certain, or one where the possibility of differentiation is weak. It has been illustrated in the tradition of the Prophet (ṣ) by the analogy of a female slave with a male slave therefore the equation between the *aṣl* (original case) and *far'* (parallel case) is obvious and the disagreement between them is removed by clear evidence.

   ii. *Qiyās khafī* (latent, hidden analogy) is one where the possibility of differentiating between the original and the parallel case is strong, or uncertain. Shawkānī illustrates this with a reference to the two types of wine, namely *nabīdh*, and *khamr*. *Nabīdh* is obtained from dates and *khamr* is obtained from grapes. The rule of prohibition is analogically extended to *nabīdh* despite some difference that might exist between the two.[97] In other words, the removal of uncertainty in the *qiyās khafī*, between the *aṣl* (original case) and *far‘* (parallel case) is by means of presumption (*ẓann*). *Qiyās khafī* and *qiyās adnā* are significantly parallel. Consequently, according to Ḥanafī jurists, *qiyās khafī* is actually considered to be *istiḥsān*.[98]

Various views over qiyās

The *‘ulamā’ al-uṣūl* (juristic scholars) are in agreement on the necessity of *qiyās* in affairs of life (*al-’umūr al-dunyawīyyah*) such as medicine and food. The *‘ulamā’* are also in agreement on *qiyās* which came from the Prophet (ṣ). However, regarding *shar‘ī* affairs (legal matters), the *‘ulamā’* are not united. Is *qiyās* approved by Sharī‘ah? There are five views:[99]

1. The majority of jurists believe that *qiyās* is a source of legislation in Sharī‘ah and practical *aḥkām*. According to Subkī (771/1369)[100] *qiyās* suits the religious communal requirement, and accords with the Qur’anic verse: “Consider, O you possessors of eyes” (59:2)! Consideration in this context means attention to similitude and comparison between similar things.
2. Both reason (*‘aql*) and transmitted evidence (*dalīl naqlī*) indicate that acting according to *qiyās* is *wājib* (obligatory). This is the view of Qaffal (d. 365) and *Ḥasan* al-Baṣrī (d. 436/1044).
3. *Qiyās* is *wājib* for only two situations otherwise it is prohibited to act according to *qiyās*, this is the view of Qāshānī (d. 427), Nahrawānī (d. 390/999) and Dāwūd al-Isfaḥānī (d. 270/884):

i. The *'illah* (cause) of the *aṣl* (original cause) should either be clearly stated or hinted at.
ii. The *'illah* (cause) of the *far'* (parallel case) is more evident than in the original case.

Their view is that *'aql* has nothing to do with these two forms, neither with *wājib* nor with *taḥrīm* of *qiyās,* because the *'illah* is evidently clear (*thābitah bi yaqīn*).

4. Ẓāhirī School and Shawkānī (d. 1250/1834) held the view that *qiyās* is rationally permitted. However, they do not consider that it works in Sharī'ah. Ibn Ḥazm's claim is based mainly on two points: first one is that the *naṣṣ* (texts, verses) of the Qur'an and the *Sunnah* accommodate all incidents. The second one is that *qiyās* is an unnecessary addition to the *naṣṣ*, therefore the *qiyās* abuses the integrity of the text.[101]
5. Shī'ah Imāmīyah and Naẓẓām (d. 221/836) from among the Mu'tazilah hold the view that to perform *qiyās* through reasoning in Sharī'ah is impossible.[102] They concluded that the two different *qiyās* will lead to contradictions for one *ḥukm*. These *'ulamā'* do not consider *qiyās* as a proof of Sharī'ah.

Dihlawī (d. 1762) expresses the following statement stating the necessity of taking into consideration *maṣlaḥah* while performing *qiyās*:

> "When God had revealed to His Prophet a statute of the Sharī'ah and had demonstrated the wisdom and good reason for it, the latter was then qualified to operate with the consideration of expediency (*maṣlaḥah*) set out to him, and to take the *maṣlaḥah* as the effective cause (*'illah*) and pivot of the stature. This was the *qiyās* practiced by the Prophet (ṣ). The *qiyās* left to the community (*ummah*) is to find out the effective cause underlying a stature and to take that as its pivot".[103]

Given Dihlawī's acceptance of *qiyās*, his rejection of the use of *ra'y* and *istiḥsān* comes as a surprise, "For *ra'y* in connection with the Sharī'ah leads to *taḥrīf* (distortion).[104] Hence the Prophetic tradition: "He who inserts into our religion something that is foreign is to be repulsed". This also has a bearing on anybody who makes use of *istiḥsān* advancing a discretionary opinion contrary to strict analogy for reasons of public convenience".[105]

It is obvious that *istiḥsān* does nothing more than prefer the principle of *maṣlaḥah* to *qiyās*.[106] In reality the principle of *istiḥsān* is not a judgment that is merely based on *ra'y* and personal *maṣlaḥah* (benefit) but in contrast it is a method of activating the application of Sharī'ah and the general purposes (*maqāṣid al-'āmmah*), because one who performs *istiḥsān* must consider the Sharī'ah's purpose in any matter. For example performing *qiyās* in a case would cause one to avoid *maṣlaḥah* and bring about *mafsadah* (harm) from a different angle.[107] In unexpected situations eventually *istiḥsān* replaces *qiyās*.[108]

Controversial sources of Islamic law

In addition to the unanimous sources mentioned above, the *Sunnī* schools consider other sources for Islamic law. These sources are somewhat controversial and not universally accepted by all Islamic schools of thought.

This section focus on these further sources, with special emphasis on *istiḥsān*.

The main controversial sources of Islamic law are as follows:

1. *Istiḥsān* (juristic preference), 2. *Maṣlaḥah mursalah* (consideration of public interest), 3. *Istiṣḥāb* (presumption of continuity), 4. *Qawl ṣaḥābī* (the saying of the Companion of the Prophet), 5.*'Urf* (customary law), 6. *Sadd al-Dharā'i'* (blocking

the means), 7. *Shar' man Qablanā* (revealed laws preceding to the Sharī'ah of Islam) and 8. *Istiqrā'* (induction).

These concepts are briefly outlined as below:

- ***Istiḥsān* (juristic preference):** The concept of *istiḥsān* is the main topic of my research and I will cover it in greater detail later.
- ***Istiṣḥāb* (presumption of continuity):** Like the other controversial sources, it is secondary to the Qur'an, the *Sunnah*, *ijmā'* and *qiyās*. *Istiṣḥāb* is validated by the Shāfi'īs, the Ḥanbalis, the Ẓahirīs, and the Shī'ah schools, but the Ḥanafīs, the Mālikīs and the Mutakallimūn, including Abū al-Ḥasan al-Baṣrī, do not consider it as a source of Sharī'ah.[109]

DEFINITION OF *ISTIṢḤĀB*

Literally, the word *istiṣḥāb* comes from the root (*ṣ-ḥ-b*), from which verbs such as to accompany, to remain along with as opposed to separating or departing from, for example, the action of taking a book or a friend along whilst travelling is called *istiṣḥāb*.[110]

Technically, the jurists define *istiṣḥāb* as "a ruling presuming that the present or future status of an issue continues to remain invariably the same as it was in the past, owing to the unavailability of a reason (evidence) to warrant the establishment of any changes of that status".[111] A similar definition considers *istiṣḥāb* as "believing that the existence of something in the past or present renders it obligatory to presume the variability of that existence in the present and future".[112] A third definition given by the jurists is as follows: *istiṣḥāb* means to adhere to a well-established ruling due to the unavailability of any evidence to warrant any change".[113] When a doubt is raised in regard to any issue in existence, the ruling of *istiṣḥāb* states that the issue can continue to exist as before. The same ruling of *istiṣḥāb* is also applied to non-existent issues. For example, when a property is transferred from one owner to another, the ownership of the property continues to remain the right of the first owner until it is transferred to the second owner and the transfer is confirmed by evidence.

Status of istiṣḥāb as a source of Islamic law

The status of *istiṣḥāb* among other sources of Sharī'ah is well explained in the statement of al-Khawārizmī (d. 665/1267) as quoted by Shawkānī, namely that *istiṣḥāb* is the last resort of *muftī* (judge). If the *muftī* is asked about an issue he should pursue the ruling first from the Book, then the *Sunnah*, then *ijmā'*, then *qiyās*. If he fails to find the ruling in these sources, he takes the ruling on that issue from *istiṣḥāb* whether the status is positive or negative. If the jurist has any hesitation regarding a ruling then the ruling continues as it was originally established. If, however, the hesitation was in order to prove the ruling, and no proof is established, then the principle to follow is that there is no evidence to prove the ruling and the status should be changed".[114]

Types of istiṣḥāb (presumption of continuity)

With regard to the existence of a ruling, *istiṣḥāb* is divided into the following types:

1. *Istiṣḥāb al-ibāḥah al-aṣlīyyah lil ashyā'* (presumption of original permissibility for objects): This means that one is to presume the continuation of its permissibility until the contrary is proven. When there is no ruling, then it is presumed to be permissible. All objects, contracts, and services which are beneficial to man are lawful on the grounds

of original permissibility. In the case of legal prohibition, *istiṣḥāb* presumes the continuity of this prohibition until evidence is established to suggest that it is no longer prohibited. The principle of permissibility (*ibāḥah*) begins in the Qur'an: "It is He who has created for you all that is on the earth" (2:29) and "God has subjugated to you all that is in the heavens and on the earth" (45:13). These verses indicate that man should be able to use the resources of the world around him for his benefit unless he has been clearly prohibited.[115]

2. *Istiṣḥāb al-barā'ah al-aṣlīyyah* (presumption of original freedom from responsibility): It is a fundamental principle, according to Islamic law, that a person is free from obligations unless there is evidence to the contrary. For example, no one is required to perform a sixth *salat* (prayer) in one day.[116] According to *al-Majallah* "If one person destroys the property of another and a dispute ensues as to the amount thereof the statement of the person causing such destruction shall be heard, and the requirement of the proof as to any amount in excess thereof is upon the owner of such property."[117]

3. *Istiṣḥāb al-waṣf* (presumption of attributes). This means that everything remains as it was until evidence warranting any changes are established. This was formulated in *al-Majallah* as: "It is a fundamental principle that a thing shall remain as it was originally".[118] For example, the "*mafqūd*" (missing person) is assumed to be alive until evidence is established to prove his death. The Jurists agreed by consensus that his heirs cannot inherit his property until his death has been established. According to most jurists, no one can benefit from any property bequeathed to the missing person until his status is established; the condition of inheritance is fulfilled by proving that the heir (missing person) is alive at the time of the deceased's death. As opposed to other schools of thought,

the Ḥanafī school maintains that a missing person cannot inherit from anyone.[119]

Maṣlaḥah Mursalah (public interest) or *al-istiṣlāḥ*

Another controversial source of Islamic law is *maṣlaḥah* which is based on benefit and avoiding harm. After the unanimous sources, *istiṣlaḥ* is a legitimate basis for legislation. When the *maṣlaḥah* is identified and the *mujtahid* does not find an explicit ruling in the main four sources, then the jurist can resort to further steps to protect social benefit and to prevent corruption in the earth.[120] However, *maṣlaḥah* should not contradict the Sharī'ah and its general objectives.

In this context, Shāṭibī (d. 790/1388) indicates[121] that the purpose of the Sharī'ah is to promote people's welfare and to prevent corruption and hardship; it is clearly explained in the Qur'an that "We have not sent you but as a mercy for all creatures" (21:107), and "God never intends to impose hardship on people" (22:78).

Definitions of maṣlaḥah

Linguistically, *maṣlaḥah* means: benefit/beneficial, appropriate/suitable, convenient and so on. Literally, *maṣlaḥah* is the opposite of *fasād* (evil) according to *Lisān al-'Arab*. In *al-Mu'jam al-Wasīṭ*, *maṣlaḥah* is the removal of evil. The word *maṣlaḥah* is derived from the root (*ṣ-l-ḥ*). Its plural form is *maṣāliḥ* and it is synonymous with *istiṣlāḥ*. *Mafsadah* is its precise antonym. The verb "*ṣaluḥa*" means something which has become beneficial or suitable. When someone "*aṣlaḥa*", he removes the evil and when something is "*iṣṭalaḥah*" it becomes ready to expel the evil in it.[122]

Mursalah means unrestricted. According to *Lisān al-'Arab*, the verb "*arsala*" means to remove the restriction or to ignore it.[123]

Technically, *maṣlaḥah mursalah* is defined by Shāṭibī as that which concerns the subsistence of human life, the completion of man's livelihood, and the acquisition of what his emotional and intellectual qualities require of him, in an absolute sense[124]

It is more technically defined as: a consideration which is proper and harmonious (*waṣf munāsib mulā'im*) with the objectives of the lawgiver; it secures a benefit or prevents a harm, when the Qur'an or the *Sunnah* provides no indication as to its validity or otherwise.[125]

It is obvious that the concept of *maṣlaḥah* has a very close relationship with *maqāsid al-Sharī'ah* (objectives of the Sharī'ah), as *maqāsid* are defined briefly as obtaining *maṣlaḥah* (benefit) and preventing *mafsadah* (evil).

These two concepts (*maṣlaḥah* and *maqāsid*) may sometimes be used interchangeably. The first significant work in this was done by Ghazālī (d. 505/1111) who wrote: "In a real sense *maṣlaḥah* consists of obtaining *manfa'ah* (benefit) and preventing *maḍarrāt* (evil). However, we do not use that meaning... for the term of *maṣlaḥah*, we mean, to protect the objectives of the Sharī'ah (*maṣlaḥah al-Sharī'ah*) which consist of five essential values, namely religion, life, intellect, lineage and property."[126]

Types of maṣlaḥah

Ibn 'Āshūr (d. 1973) divides *maṣlaḥah* into two types: 1. *al-maṣlaḥah al-'āmmah* (public benefit), which is a benefit that is useful to all, or to the majority of the community; and 2. *al-maṣlaḥah al-khāṣṣah* (specific benefit), which is individual consideration of the benefits for people.[127] With regard to the social order, it is divided into three categories:

1. *Ḍarūriyyāt* (essentials),

2. *Ḥājiyyāt* (complementary),
3. *Taḥsīniyyāt* (embellishment).

Regarding the whole community, its groups and individuals *maṣlaḥah* is either 1. *kullī* (whole) or 2. *juz'ī* (partial). There are also three types of *maṣlaḥah* in respect of the people's situations: 1. q*aṭ'ī* (definite), 2. *ẓannī* (speculative), 3. *wahmī* (imaginary).[128] Briefly the main divisions of *maṣlaḥah* are as follows:

Ḍarūriyyāt (*essentials*)

These are things on which the lives of people depend, and the neglect of which causes total disruption and anarchy. Ibn al-Ḥājib, Qarafī, and Shāṭibī consider these to be the five essential values, namely religion, life, intellect, lineage and property. Qarafī adds a sixth essential, protecting honour; this is attributed to Ṭūfī.[129] The first five essentials must not only be upheld but also protected against any real or unexpected threat to their safety. Destroying one of the five essential values is *ḥarām* according to Ghazālī.[130] The five values would be protected in two ways: 1. maintaining the subsistence, 2. removing the disruptions.[131]

Ḥājiyyāt

These are those things which, if neglected, many cause hardship to the community, but not its collapse. Shāṭibī (d. 790/1388) says that *ḥājiyyāt* are those things which are needed to enhance comfort and avoid hardship. If they are not taken into consideration, people would face harm and difficulties. However, those difficulties are not as dangerous as neglect of the essentials."[132] In the field of *'ibādāt* (worship), *ḥājiyyāt* includes the concessions (*rukhaṣ*) that the Sharī'ah grants to the sick and to travellers, permitting them to forego the fast and to shorten the prayers (*salāt*), in order to avoid hardship.

Taḥsīniyyāt

These are also known as *kamāliyyāt* (embellishments) and are supplementary to the previous types. This category represents the interest and awareness of the *mukallaf*. Shāṭibī says that it may be summarized as part of social and moral etiquette in the field of *'ibādāt*, such as eliminating dirt, considering all types of cleanness; or in the field of customary matters, such as good conduct in eating, avoiding wastefulness in consumption; in the field of transactions, such as not selling something which is impure; and in the field of *jināyah* (criminal offence), such as the prohibition on the killing of women, children and scholars whilst on *jihād*.[133] Therefore *sadd al-dharāi'* (blocking the means) is considered as a kind of *taḥsīniyyāt*.

Shurūt (conditions) of maṣlaḥah mursalah

Some strict and indisputable conditions have been set in order that *maṣlaḥah* be considered a valid source.

A vital condition of *maṣlaḥah* is that it must be appropriate to the objectives of the *Shār'* (Lawgiver). Ghazālī says that "Interpreting the *maṣlaḥah* as protecting the *maqāṣid al-Sharī'ah* (objectives of the lawgiver), nobody would oppose obeying the *maṣlaḥah* unless they could produce positive evidence".[134] He adds "We occasionally consider *maṣlaḥah* and rulings when indications interchangeably reflected one another."[135] The following conditions are intended to ensure that the concept of *maṣlaḥah* is not established arbitrarily or by individual whim.

1. *Maṣlaḥah* must not be in conflict with a principle or value which is sustained by a *naṣṣ* (text) or *ijmā'*.[136]
2. *Maṣlaḥah* must be genuine (*haqīqīyyah*) as opposed to imaginary (*wahmīyyah*), which is an improper ground for

legislation. For example the recording of marriages in the court and the issue of marriage certificates or the recording of contracts in the registry department prevents *shahādāh al-zur* (false testimony) and stabilizes the *mu'āmalāt* (contracts).[137]

3. *Maṣlaḥah* must be *kullīyyah* (general) so as to secure its benefits and prevent harm as a whole, not to a particular person or group of people.[138] Besides these conditions, Imām Mālik (d. 179/795) considers further two other conditions:
4. The *maṣlaḥah* must be *ma'qūlah* (rational) and acceptable.
5. *Maṣlaḥah* must prevent or eradicate hardship, which the Qur'an expresses in the *sūrah al-mā'idah* (5:6) "God never intends to impose hardship upon people",[139] yet Ghazālī (d. 505/1111) maintained that *maṣlaḥah* must involve *ḍarūriyyāt* (essentials) for its validation.[140]

Consequently, the main purpose of the law is to obtain benefit (*jalb al-ṣalāḥ*) and avoid evil (*daf' al-fasād*). *Maṣlaḥah* would be obtained by improving man's situation and removing evil, because man is the vicegerent on earth and holder of His truth; therefore making him peaceful would reflect in world peace too.[141] If the evaluation of the *maṣlaḥah* and *mafsadah* were the responsibility of mankind, the Lawgiver's objectives would be in jeopardy.

In this context, Shāṭibī says "In the religious context the aim of obtaining benefit (*jalb al-ṣalāḥ*) and avoiding evil (*daf' al-fasād*) is to provide the needs of this world for the sake of the hereafter, and not to provide personal desires or avoid personal hatreds. Religion prevents people from following their desires and guides them to be a servant of God".[142] God clearly indicates this in the Qur'an: "And if the truth had been in accordance with their desires, verily, the heavens and the earth, and whosever is therein would have been corrupted" (23:71).

'*Urf* (customary law)

The concept of *'urf* is also considered to be one of the controversial sources of Islamic law amongst the jurists.

Definition of 'urf

'Urf as a noun derived from its Arabic root *'a-r-f* (to know). According to *Lisān al-'Arab*, *'urf*, *'irfān* and *'ārifah* all have the same meaning, i.e. anything that the people know as good (*khayr*) as opposed to *munkar* (evil), or any effort you make by speech or action to help others.

Recognizing someone's service or help offered to another to enable them to achieve an ambition is also covered by this concept. Generally, the word is mostly used for a higher level of feelings and a good and dignified expression.[143]

'Urf (custom) and its derivative *ma'rūf* appears in the Qur'an in *sūrah al-Ā'rāf* (7:199) "Keep to forgiveness, enjoin *'urf* (*wa'mur bil 'urf*) and turn away from the ignorant". Zamakhsharī (d. 538/1144) in his commentary on this verse states that: "*'Urf* is known as a beautiful (nice or good) deed".[144] Another word largely synonymous with *'urf* is *'ādah* (habit—plural *'ādah* or *'awāi'd*) which means repetition or recurrent practice of an individual or a group.[145]Technically, *'urf* is defined as "Habitual practices which are acceptable to people of sound nature".[146] *'Ādah* is defined as "habitual practices without a rational relationship".[147]

Types of 'urf

'Urf is primarily divided into two types: *qawlī* (verbal) and *fi'lī* or *'amalī* (actual or practical). An example of verbal *'urf* is the word *walad* which means the offspring, whether a son or daughter,

although in its common usage *walad* is used to denote a son only. It occurs in the Qur'an: "God commands you as regards your children's (inheritance): to the male, a portion equal to that of two females..." (4:11). An example of actual *'urf* is the *bay' al-ṭa'āṭī* (give-and-take sale) which is normally concluded without utterance of offer and acceptance.[148] These *'urf*, either *qawlī* or *'amalī*, eventually are divided into two types: *al-'urf al-'āmm* general custom and *'urf khāṣ*" (special custom).[149]

Conditions of the validity of 'urf

1. *'Urf* must not contradict a *naṣṣ*, or definitive principles of the Islamic law.[150]
2. *'Urf* must be continual or prevalent in most cases. The practice of that *'urf* by a few individuals or of a limited number of people among a large community will not be authoritative.[151]
3. The existence of *'urf* (custom) must be established at the time of the transaction.[152]
4. *'Urf* (custom) must not contravene the clear requirements of an agreement.[153]

Consequently, the following principles, mentioned in *al-majallah*, point out the prevalence of *'urf* in legislation:

- Custom is an arbitrator; that is to say, custom, whether public or private, may be invoked to justify the giving of judgment.[154]
- In the presence of custom, no regard is paid to the literal meaning of a thing.[155]
- Effect is only given to custom where it is of regular occurrence or when universally prevailing.[156]
- A matter recognized by custom is regarded as though it was a contractual obligation.[157]

- A matter established by *'urf* (custom) is like a matter established by law.[158]
- To change *'urf* without consideration for the harm that this may cause is clearly unacceptable.[159]

Sadd al-Dharā'i' (blocking the means)

The validity of this concept amongst the jurists is considered controversial; the Ḥanafī, Shāfi'ī and Ẓāhirī jurists do not recognize it as a source of Islamic jurisprudence, yet Mālikī and Ḥanbalī jurists have validated it as a principle of Sharī'ah.[160]

Definition of sadd al-dharā'i'

Sadd al-dharā'i' (blocking the means) consists of two terms; first, *sadd* (blocking) and second, *dharī'ah,* plural *dharā'i'* (means). Blocking the means implies blocking the means of evil but not blocking the means of good. In juridical application, the concept of *sadd al-dharā'i'* also extends to "Opening the means to beneficence". For this reason some jurists use the term *dharā'i'* (means) alone as a title for the doctrine. The literal meaning of each term will clear this point. According to *Mu'jam Maqāyīs al-Lughah* and *Mukhtār al-Siḥāḥ,*[161] the term *sadd* literally means a barrier between two things, for example a mountain. It also means blocking a gap with landfill to level it; *dharī'a'h* are the means or the causes used to achieve or obtain a certain thing or end.[162]

Shāṭibī (d. 790/1388) defines *dharī'a'h* as "That means by which a prohibited end or thing (containing evil) is obtained."[163] It is obvious that this definition refers exclusively to meaning evil, evil that must be blocked. Other jurists such as Ibn al-Qayyīm (d. 751/1350) define *dharī'a'h* as that which is a means or a way to something.[164] Here (something) implies juridical obedience or disobedience to God. Qarafī (d. 684/1285) considers *dharī'a'h* to be the means to beneficence or evil: the former must be embraced whilst the latter must be blocked. He states that "As the means to evil is prohibited (and must be blocked), the means to *wājib* (obligatory action) is obligatory. The bases regulating the rulings on affairs are two parts. The first part is *maqāṣid* (objectives), which contains the beneficence and evil each in itself. Second, *wasā'il* (means) which are the ways leading to them. The ruling on the ways to obtain the objective or end is the same as the ruling on the objective itself".[165]

Types of dharā'ī ' (means)

Its types are considered from two perspectives: the result discovered by Ibn al-Qayyīm in *"I'lām al-Muwaqqi'īn"*;[166] and the degree of probability, or otherwise, of leading to an evil as discussed by Shāṭibī in *"Al-Muwāfaqāt"*.[167]

First: An example of means which leads to evil or harm is the digging of a deep pit next to the entrance to a public place which is not lit at night; thus anyone who enters the door is very likely to fall into it. That action is completely forbidden as it might cause harm to someone.[168]

Second: Means which are rarely expected to lead to evil and are likely to lead to a benefit. An example is digging a water hole situated in a place which is unlikely to harm anyone.[169]

Third: Means which are most likely (*al-ẓann al-ghālib*) to lead to evil. For example selling weapons during warfare or selling grapes to a wine maker. However, Shāṭibī says that these transactions are invalid according to the consensus of the *'ulamā'*. Briefly, when there is a strong likelihood that they would lead to evil, the means may be declared forbidden.[170]

Fourth: Means which frequently lead to evil. An example is deferred sales (*buyūʿ al-ajal*), which mostly leads to usury (*ribāʾ*).[171]

Consequently, the main understanding of the whole concept of *sadd al-dharāʾiʿ* was founded on the idea of preventing evil before it happens. When the result is expected to be good or commendable, then the means will be acceptable. However when the result is expected to be blameworthy then the means will be considered as being blocked, regardless of the intention of the perpetrator, or the actual recognition of the result itself.

Additionally, if the act performed leads to the situation where the evil is either equal to or bigger than the benefit, then the means must be blocked too, according to the general principle "repelling an evil is preferable to securing a benefit".[172]

Qawl ṣaḥābī (the saying of a Companion of the Prophet)

Many disputes have occurred over the validity of *qawl al-ṣaḥābī*. Briefly the Ḥanafī Mālikī, and Ḥanbalī schools in general have validated the concept as a source of Sharīʿah, but Shāfiʿī does not consider it thus.[173]

Definition of the Term

The word *ṣaḥābī* is derived from the root "*s-ḥ-b*" and the verb *ṣaḥībah* or *ṣaḥābah* (to accompany) and *ṣuḥbah* (companionship), which imply continuity of contact and narration of *ḥadīth* from the Prophet (ṣ). *Qawl ṣaḥābī* consists of two words; "*qawl*" (saying) and "*ṣaḥābī—*plural—*ṣaḥābah*" the Companions. According to most jurists[174] anyone who met the Prophet (ṣ), while believing in him, even for a moment, and died as a believer, is considered as "*ṣaḥābī*" (Companion) regardless of whether he or she narrated any *ḥadīth* from the Prophet (ṣ) or not.

Jurists agree that the *ijmā'* (consensus) of the Companions of the Prophet (ṣ) is a binding proof, and represents the most authoritative form of *ijmā'*. The question arises, however, as to whether the saying or *fatwā* of a single Companion should also be recognized as a source of law and should take precedence over other sources such as *qiyās* or the *fatwā* of other *mujtahidūn*.

There is no disagreement among the jurists that the saying of a Companion is a proof, which commands obedience if it is not opposed by other Companions. Rulings on which the Companions were known to be in agreement are binding. The jurists are however in disagreement with regard to rulings which were based on opinion (*ra'y*) and *ijtihād*, and also in those matters where the Companions differed among themselves.

There is a general agreement among jurists that the ruling of one Companion is not a binding proof over another Companion, regardless of whether the ruling in question was issued by one of the Caliphs, a Judge or a leading *mujtahid* among their number. The jurists did differ as to whether the rulings of a Companion are binding on Successors (*Tābi'ūn*) and the succeeding generations of *mujtahidīn*. There are four views on this,[175] which are briefly summarized as follows:

1. The *ijtihād* of the Companions is not a proof and is not binding on the succeeding generations of *mujtahidūn* or anyone else. This view is held by the Ash'arīs, Mu'tazilīs, Imām Aḥmad, and al-Karkhī.[176]

2. The *fatwā* of the Companions takes priority over *qiyās*, regardless of whether it was in agreement with *qiyās* or not. This was the view of Imām Mālik, Imām Shāfi'ī, Imām Aḥmād, and some of the Ḥanafī jurists.[177]

3. It is acceptable when it is in agreement with *qiyās*. In such a case, *qiyās* comes before the ruling of the Companion. This is a later view of Imām Shāfi'ī.[178]
4. It is acceptable when it is in a conflict with *qiyās* but not when it agrees with *qiyās*. This is the view of Imām Abū Ḥanīfah.[179]

Shar' man qablanā (revealed laws preceding to the Sharī'ah)

This subject represents the extent to which the Sharī'ah of Islām is related to the laws of previous revelations. The Qur'an and the *Sunnah* have chronicled the lives of previous Prophets and some of the rulings of the revelations they received.[180] The Qur'an confirms the essence of believing in the oneness of God and the need for divine authority and guidance to maintain good conduct and the principles of morality and justice that represent ordinary reason and the matter of all divine religions.[181] The same religion has been ordained from the previous prophets and nations, as is indicated in the Qur'an: "He (God) has ordained for you the same religion (Islamic Monotheism) which He ordained for Nuḥ (Noah), and that which We have revealed to you (O Muḥammad), and that which We ordained for Ibrāhīm (Ibraham), Mūsā (Moses) and 'Īsā (Jesus) saying you should establish religion (i.e. to do what it orders you to do practically), and make no divisions" (42:13).

For example, several rulings (*aḥkām*) such as fasting and law of retaliation have been ordained before in previous revelations, "O believers, fasting is prescribed for you as it was prescribed for those who came before you" (2:183), "And we ordained therein for them life for life, eye for eye, nose for nose, ear for ear, tooth for tooth and wounds equal for equal" (5:48).

Istiqrā' (induction)

Istiqrā' is a *ḥujjah* (proof) according to the Shāfi'ī, Mālikī and Ḥanbalī schools, however, the Ḥanafī school does not accept *istiqrā'* as an independent *dalīl* (proof) in proving a *ḥukm shar'ī*.[182]

Istiqrā' (induction) is a process of reasoning by which a general ruling for a certain issue is drawn from a set of principles constituting that issue, based on the fact that the ruling applied to the premise must apply to the whole issue or some of the issues. The general ruling goes beyond the information contained in the principles and does not necessarily follow from them. *Istiqrā'* is divided into two types:

1. *Istiqrā' tāmm* (complete induction) is arrived at by exploring the entire premise with the exception of the premise of disagreement. These results give a definitive (*qaṭ'ī*) ruling.
2. *Istiqrā' nāqiṣ* (incomplete induction) is achieved by following the point of disagreement comparing it with other point. The ruling in this case is mostly probable (*ẓanni ghālib*). Jurists of *uṣūl* use complete *istiqrā'*.[183]

Conclusion

A brief introduction to the legal theory (*uṣūl al-fiqh*) behind the general principles of Islamic law is now concluded and the basis for my research has been established.

The majority of jurists agree that the four fundamental principles are unanimously accepted. There are also other principles that are activated when fundamental principles are silent and unable to help the law for its continuity.

However, while there is unanimity on the four main sources of law, there are considerable differences of opinion on the validity and application of the controversial sources.

Notes

1. The Qur'an and the Sunnah are the two main sources of Islamic Legal Theory. However, the majority of jurists are of the view that Islamic law is based on four sources. It took the jurists considerable time to prove through the texts of the Qur'an and the Sunnah that ijmāʿ is a valid source of law, and any that ḥukm (ruling) based on it should be accorded the status of the ḥukm of God. And qiyās was also successfully used to deduce the law from the Qur'an and the Sunnah. The law deduced by Qiyās and ijmāʿ are actually dependent on evidence from the two main sources.
2. Imran Ahsan Khan Nyazee, "*Theories of Islamic Law*", (Delhi: 1996), p. 131.
3. See Abū Dāwud, "*Sunan*", trans. Aḥmad Ḥasan (Lahore: edt. Muḥammad Ashraf, 1984 iii. 1019 ḥadīth no: 3585.
4. Ibn al-Qayyīm Muḥammad b. Abū Bakr b. Ayūb b. Sa'd Shams al-Dīn Dimishqī (d. 751/1350), "*I'lām al-Muwaqqi'īn min Rabb al-'Ālamīn*", edt: 'Abd al-Raḥmān al-Wakīl, (Cairo: n.d.), vol. 1, p. 51; Zaydān 'Abd al-Karīm, ibid., p. 143.
5. Wahbah Zuhaylī, "*Uṣul al-Fiqh al-Islāmi*", (Beirut: Dār al-Fikr al-Muʿāsir, 1406/1986), vol. 1 p. 418.
6. Mollah Husraw, Muḥammad bin Firāmūz (885/1480), "*Mir'āt al-Uṣūl Sharḥ Mirkāt al-Wusūl*", (Istanbul: Matba'ah al-Amīrah, 1309), vol. 1 p. 56; Laknawī, 'Abd al-'Alī Muḥammad bin Nizām al-Dīn Anṣārī, Baḥr al-'Ulūm, Abu al-'Abbās, Ḥanafī (d. 1180/1767), "*Fawātiḥ al-Raḥamūt sharḥ Musallam al-Subūt fī Uṣūl al-Fiqh*", (Cairo, Bulāq: Matba'ah al-Amīriyyah, 1906), vol. 1, p. 8; Anṣārī, Abū Zakarīyyah Shaikh al-Islām "*Ghāyāt al-Wuṣūl sharḥ lub al-Uṣūl*", (Cairo: Muṣṭafā bāb al-Ḥalabī wa awlāduh, 1360/1941), vol. 1, p. 18.
7. See Elias: ibid.; Joseph Catafago, ibid.; Hans Wehr, ibid.; Nyazee, ibid., pp. 26-7.
8. Ibn Amīr al-Ḥajj Muḥammad bin Muḥammad Shams al-Dīn (d. 879) "*Al-Taqrīr wa al-Takhbīr 'alā Taḥrīr al-Kamāl ibn al-Humām fī 'Ilm al-Uṣūl*", (Bulāq, Cairo: Maṭba'ah al-Amīriyyah, , 1316), vol. 1 p. 17; See Nyazee, ibid., pp. 27-8.
9. Abū Dāwūd Sulaymān bin al-Ash'ās (d. 275/888) "*Sunnan*", trans. Aḥmad Ḥasan, (Lahore: Muḥammad Ashraf, 1984). ḥadīth no. 3672, vol. 3, p. 1043,
10. See Nyazee, p. 27.
11. Ibn Mājah Abū 'Abd Allah Muḥammad (d. 273/886), "*Sunan*", (Istanbul: 1981), ḥadīth no. 2340, vol. 2, p. 784.

12. See Laknawī, ibid., vol. 1, p. 8; Jamāl al-Dīn 'Abd al-Raḥīm al-Ḥusayn Isnawī Shāfi'ī (d. 772/1370), "*Nihāyāt al-Sūl fī Sharḥ al-Minhāj al-Uṣūl*", (Beirut: 1982), vol. 1, p. 18.

13. 'Abd al-'Azīz bin Aḥmad bin Muḥammed, 'Alā al-Dīn al-Bukhārī. (d. 730/1329), "*Sharḥ Kashf al-Asrār 'Alā Uṣūl al-Bazdawī*", (Beirut: Dār al Kutūb al-'Arabi, 1394), p. 1086.

14. Āmidī, ibid., vol. 1, p. 9.

15. Taqīy al-Dīn Abū al-'Abbās Aḥmad b. 'Abd al-Ḥalīm Ibn Taymiyyah (d. 728/1328), "*Al-Musawwadah fī Uṣūl al-Fiqh*", (Cairo: Al-Maṭba'ah al-Madani, 1964), p. 573.

16. Abū 'Alī Badr al-Dīn Muḥammad bin 'Alī Shawkānī (d. 1250/1834), "*Irshād al-Fuḥūl ilā Taḥqīq al-Ḥaq min 'Ilm al-Uṣūl*", (Cairo: 1937), p. 3; Ibn Amīr al-Ḥajj, ibid., vol. 1, p. 17.

17. For the transformation of the Muslim understanding of the concept of fiqh in the last two centuries, see: Murteza Bedir, "Fikih to Law: Secularization Through Curriculum", in *Islamic Law and Society* 11, 3, Leiden, 2004, pp. 378-401.

18. Muslim. Ibid., Kitāb al-Amārah.

19. Muḥammad Ibn Sa'd (d. 230/844), "*Al-Ṭabaqāṭ al-Kubrā*", (Beirut: 1957), vol. 2, p. 363.

20. 'Ubayd Allah Ibn Mas'ūd bin Tāj Al-Sharī'ah al-Ḥanafī, Ṣadr al-Sharī'ah (d. 747/1346), "*Al-Tawdīḥ fī Ḥall Jawāmid al-Tanqīḥ*", (Karachi: 1979), pp. 22-25. Explaining the definition given by Abū Ḥanīfah, he says that it includes three things: 1-knowledge of the teneth of faith, 2-knowledge of ethics and mysticism (Sufism), 3-knowledge pertaining to acts. The first is covered by "'ilm kalām", the second by ethics and mysticism and the third by fiqh. Therefore, he says if you wish to confine the definition to fiqh alone, that is, "Al-fiqh al-Aṣghar", you must add at the end of the definition the word "'amalan" (with respect to acts).

21. Aḥmad Ḥasan, "*The Early Development of Islamic Jurisprudence*", (Islamabad: Islamic Research Institute, International Islamic University, 1994), p. 3.

22. 'Abd al-Raḥmān bin Jād Allah al-Bannānī, al-Maghribī (d. 1198/1784), "*Ḥāshiah 'alā Sharḥ Jalāl al-Dīn al-Maḥallī 'alā Jam' al-Jawāmī' li Ibn Subkī*", (Cairo: 1937), vol. 1 p. 32; Molla Husraw, "*Mir'at al-Uṣūl*", vol. 1 p. 50; Ṣadr al-Sharī'ah, "*Al-Tawdīḥ*", vol. 1, p. 26. He did not use the word "al-muktasabah".

23. ʻUthmān b. ʻAmr b. Abū-Bakr b. Yūnus Abū ʻAmr Jamāl al-Dīn Ibn Ḥājib (d. 646/1249), "*Mukhtaṣar Muntahā' al-Sūl wa al-ʻĀmal*", (Constantinople: Al-Maktabah al-Islāmiyyah, 1310), vol.1 p. 4.
24. See: Elias, ibid.; Joseph Catafago, ibid.; Hans Wehr, ibid.
25. Zuhaylī, ibid., vol. 1, p. 21.
26. Āmidī, ibid., vol. 1, p. 7.
27. Ṣadr al-Sharīʻah, ibid., vol.1, p. 13; Bannānī, "*Ḥāshiah*", vol. 1 p. 32; Nyazee, ibid., p. 64.
28. Abu Ḥāmid Muḥammad ibn Muḥammad Ghazālī (d. 505/1111), "*Al-Mustaṣfā' min ʻIlm al-Uṣūl*", (Cairo Al-Maktabah al-Tijāriyyah, 1356/1937), vol. 1 p. 42; Shawkānī, "*Irshād*" p. 6; Zuhaylī, "*Uṣūl*", pp. 37-43.
29. Qur'an: 2:43
30. Ṣadr al-Sharīʻah, "*Al-Tawdīḥ*" vol. 1, p. 13; Isnawī, "*Sallam al-Wuṣūl*" vol. 1, p. 24.
31. Herbert Lionel Adolphus Hart, "*The Concept of Law*", pp. 77-96 quoted from Nyazee, ibid., pp. 57-8.
32. Zuhaylī, ibid., vol. 1, p. 37; Khallāf, ʻAbd al-Wahhāb (d. 1376/1956), "*ʻIlm Uṣūl al-Fiqh*", 12th ed., (Kuwait: Dār al-Qalām, 1398/1978). See for the use of English terminology: Nyazee, ibid.; Muḥammad Hāshim Kamālī, "*Principles of Islamic Jurisprudence*", (Cambridge: Islamic Text Society, 1997), pp. 321-353.
33. Bannānī, ibid, vol. 1 p. 33, Isnawī, "*Sallam al-Wuṣūl*", vol. 1, p. 25. For more about Sharī'ah see: ʻAbd al-Raḥmān I. Doi, "*Shariʻah the Islamic Law*", (London: Ta Ha Publishers, 1997).
34. Isnawi, "*Sallam al-Wuṣul*", vol. 1, p. 26; Molla Husraw, "*Mar'at al-Uṣul*", vol. 1, pp. 48-54.
35. Elias A. Elias,"*Elias Modern Dictionary*", 5th edition, (Cairo: 1950); Joseph Catafago "*English and Arabic Dictionary*", (London: 1958); Hans Wehr, "*A Dictionary of Modern Written Arabic*", edited by J. Milton Cowan, 4th edition, (Germany: 1979).
36. Zuhaylī, ibid., vol. 1, p. 417.
37. Ismaʻīl Shaʻbān Muḥammad, "*Uṣūl al-Fiqh al-Muyassar*", (Cairo: Kitāb al-Jāmīʻ Tawfīqiyyah), 1994, vol. 1, p. 47.
38. Zuhaylī, ibid., vol. 1, p. 417.
39. Abū Isḥāq Ibrāhīm bin Mūsa al-Ghirnāṭī Shāṭibī (d. 790/1388), "*Al Muwāfaqāt fī-Uṣūl al-Sharīʻah*", edt. ʻAbd-Allah Diraz, (Beirut: Dār al-Maʻrifah, n.d), vol. 3 p. 36.

40. Abū 'Alī Badr al-Dīn Muḥammad bin 'Alī Shawkānī (d. 1250/1834), "*Irshād al-Fuḥul ilā Taḥqīq al-Ḥaq min 'Ilm al-Uṣūl*", (Cairo 1937), p. 47; Abū al-'Aynayn Badrān, "*Uṣūl al-Fiqh al-Islāmi*", (Alaxandria: Muassasah Shabāb al-Jāmi'ah, 1404/1984), p. 53.

41. Badrān, "*Uṣūl al-Fiqh al-Islāmi*", pp. 54-5.

42. 'Alī bin Abī 'Alī Muḥammad bin Sālim Al-Tha'labī, Sayf al-Dīn Al-Āmidī (d. 631/1233), "*Al-Ihkām fī Uṣūl al-Aḥkām*", edt. 'Abd al-Razzāq 'Afīfī, 2nd edt, (Beirut: Maktabah al-Islāmi, 1402/1982), vol. 1, p. 260.

43. Controversial sources number as many as 45. (See Ṭūfī, "*Risalah al-Maṣlaḥah*") 19 of them, as Qāsimi indicated, were dalāil quoted from Qarafī (d. 684/1285); Qāsimī then discovered 26 more by the way of induction (istiqrā). See: Kasif Hamdi Okur "*Maqāṣid ve Ictiḥād*", in Islamic Legal Philosophy Researches, (Konya: Yediveren, 2002), p. 275.

44. Kamālī, "*Principles*", p. 10.

45. Ṣadr al-Sharī'ah, "*Al-Tawdīḥ*", vol. 1 p. 26.

46. Ibn al-Ḥājīb, "*Mukhtaṣar*" vol. 1, p. 25; Ibn Amīr al-Ḥajj, "*Al-Taqrīr wa al-Takhbīr*", vol. 1 p. 20.

47. Mollah Husraw, "*Mir'āt al-Uṣūl*", vo. 1 p. 56; Isnawī, "*Sallam al-Wuṣūl*", vol. 1 p. 27.

48. Bannānī, "*Ḥāshiah*", vol. 1, p. 223.

49. Maḥmūt Shaltūt, "*Al-Islām 'Aqīdah wa Sharī'ah*", (Kuwait: Maktabi Dār al-Qalam, 1966), p. 23.

50. Ḥadīth qudsī or holy ḥadīth is a sub-category of ḥadīth which is saying of the Prophet (ṣ). It is considered to be the word of God, repeated by the Prophet (ṣ) and recorded on the condition of an isnad (chain of verification by authorities who heard from the Prophet) but this report is not part of the Qur'an.

51. Ghazālī, "*Al-Mustaṣfā*", (Cairo: Al-Maktabah al-Tijāriyyah 1356/1937), vol. 1, p. 68; Abū Muḥammad Muwaffiq al-Dīn, 'Abd Allah bin Aḥmad bin Muḥammad bin Qudāmah, Al-Maqdisī (d. 620/1223), "*Rawḍah al-Nāẓir wa Jannat al-Manāẓir*", (Cairo: Matba'ah al-Salafīyyah, 1342), vol. 1 p. 184; Imām Abī 'Abd Allah Muḥammad bin Idrīs Shafi'ī (d. 204/819), "*Al-Risālah*", edt., Muḥammad Sayyīd Kīlāni, 2nd edtn, (Cairo: Muṣṭafā al-Bābi al-Ḥalabī, 1983), p. 41.

52. M. Muṣṭafā Azami, "*Al-Mustashriq Schacht wa al-Sunnah al-Nabawīyyah*", (Riyad: 1985), p. 77.

53. Khallāf, "*'Ilm*", p. 33; Zuhailī, ibid., vol. 1 p. 438; Zakīy al-Dīn Sha'bān, "*Uṣūl*", p. 42.

54. Khallāf, ibid., pp. 32-3; Zaydān, "*Al-Wajiz fī Uṣūl al-Fiqh*", pp. 126-127; Fahrettin Atar, "*Fıkıh Uṣulü*", MÜİFY, (İstanbul: 1996), pp. 33-4; See: M. Muṣṭafā Azami, "*Al Mustashriq*", pp. 74-77. According to him aḥkām verses reaches up to 393.

55. Ibn Manẓūr, ibid., vol. 17, p. 92.

56. Abū Manṣūr Muḥammad b. Aḥmad Al-Azharī (d. 370/980), "*Tahdhib Al-Lughah*", (Cairo: Al-Dār al-Misriyyah, 1966), vol. 4, p. 298.

57. Fazlur Raḥmān "*Islām*", (London: 1966), p. 44.

58. Shawkānī, "*Irshād*", p. 33.

59. Jalāl al-Dīn 'Abd al-Raḥmān bin abī Bakr bin Muḥammad bin Sābiq al-Din al-Khudayrī al-Suyūtī (d. 911/1505), "*Muftāh al-Jannah fī al-Ihtijāj bi al-Sunnah*", (Beirut: 1987), p. 46.

60. Laknawī, "*Tuhfat al-Akhbār fī Ihyā' Sunnah Sayyid al-Abrār*", "Al Bid'ah", p. 119-120. See in M. Ismā'īl Sha'bān, "*Uṣūl al-Fiqh al-Muyassar*", vol. 1 p. 176.

61. Naṣr al-Dīn 'Abd Allah bin 'Umar bin Muḥammed bin 'Alī Al-Shīyrazī Baidhāwī (d. 685/1286), "*Al-Ibhāj fī Sharh Al-Minhāj 'alā' Minhāj al-Wuṣūl ilā 'Ilm al-Uṣūl*", (Beirut: n.d.), vol. 1, p. 56.

62. Āmidī, "*Al-Iḥkām*", vol. 1, p. 169; Baidhāwī, ibid., vol. 2, p. 170; Shawkānī, "*Irshād*", p. 33.

63. Abū Ja'far Muḥammad b. Jarīr Tabarī (d. 310/922), "*Jāmi' al-Bayān Ta'wīl al-Qur'an*", (Cairo, Bulāq: 1329), vol. 8, pp. 486-490.

64. Muḥammad b. 'Umar b. al-Ḥusayn Abū 'Abd Allah Fakhr al-Dīn Rāzī (d. 606/1210), "*Mafātīḥ al-Ghayb: Al-mushtahar bi-al-Tafsīr al-Kabīr*", (Cairo: Al-Matba'ah al-Āmirah al-Sharafīyah, 1324-1327), vol. 3, pp. 242-3.

65. Ghazālī, "*Al-Mustaṣfā*"', vol. 1, p. 111.

66. Abū 'Abd Allah Muḥammad Ibn Mājah (d. 273/886), "*Sunan*", ḥadīth no: 3950, (Istanbul: 1981), vol. 2, p. 1303.

67. Ghazālī, "*Al-Mustaṣfā*"', vol. 1, p. 111; Āmidī "*Iḥkām*", vol. 1, p. 220-1.

68. E.W. Lane "*Arabic English Lexicon*" (London: 1863); Ibn Manẓūr, ibid.

69. E.W. Lane, ibid.; Aḥmad Ḥasan, "*The Doctrine of Ijmā' in Islām*", (Islamabad: Islamic Research Institute, 1992), p.15.

70. Āmidī,"Al-Iḥkām", vol. 1, p. 101; Mas'ūd bin 'Umar bin 'Abd Allah Sa'd al-Dīn Taftazānī (d. 793/1390), "*Al-Talwīḥ 'alā Al-Tawḍīḥ*" on the margin of 'Ubayd Allah bin Mas'ūd Ṣadr al-Sharī'ah", (Cairo: 'Īsā al-Bābi al-Ḥalabī, 1327/1957), vol. 2, p. 41; Bukhārī, "*Kashf*", vol.

1, p. 946; Shawkānī, "*Irshād*", p. 63; Ibn 'Abd al-Shakūr, Muḥib Allah al-Baḥarī al-Hindīy (d. 1119/1707) "*Musallam al-Thubūt ma'a Fawātiḥ al-Raḥamūt fī Uṣūl al-Fiqh*", (Cairo: 1906), vol. 2, p. 166.

71. Bukhārī, "*Kashf*", vol. 3, p. 227.
72. Āmidī, "*Iḥkām*", vol. 1, p. 196.
73. Ghazālī, "*Muṣtaṣfā*"', vol. 1, p. 110.
74. Aḥmad bin Idrīs bin 'Abd al-Raḥmān, Abū 'Abbās Sha'b al-Dīn al-Sanhājī al-Mālikī Qarafī (d. 684/1285), "*Sharḥ Tanqīḥ al-Fuṣūl fī Ikhtisār al-Mahṣūl fī al-Uṣūl*", edt: Tāhā 'Abd al-Raūf Sa'd, (Cairo: Maktabah al-Azharīyyah, n.d.), p. 141.
75. 'Ubayd Allah Ibn Mas'ūd bin Tāj al-Sharī'ah al-Ḥanafī Ṣadr al-Sharī'ah (d. 747/1346), "*Al-Tawdīḥ fī Ḥall Jawāmid al-Tanqīḥ*", (Cairo: Maṭba'ah Muḥammad 'Alī Ṣabīh, n.d.), vol. 2, p. 41.
76. Sha'bān, "*Uṣūl*", p. 45.
77. Ghazālī, "*Al-Mustaṣfā*"', vol.1, p. 121; Āmidī, "*Al-Iḥkām*", vol. 1, p. 129; Shawkānī, "*Irshād*", p. 74; Molla Husraw, "*Mar'āt al-Uṣūl*", vol. 2 p. 259; Laknawī, "*Fawātiḥ al-Raḥamūt*", vol. 2, p. 232; Ibn Amīr al-Ḥajj, "*al-Taqrīr*", vol. 3, p. 101; Bukhārī, "*Kashf*", vol. 2 p. 948; Isnawī, "*Sallam al-Wuṣūl*", vol. 2, p. 375; Bannānī "*Ḥāshiah*", vol. 2 p. 163.
78. Muḥammad bin Aḥmad bin Sahl Abū Bakr Shams al-Aimmah al-Ḥanafī Sarakhsī (d. 483/1090), "*Al-Uṣūl*", edt: Abu al-Wafā' al-Afghānī, (Beirut: Dār al-Fiqr, 1991), vol. 1, pp. 305-6.
79. 'Alī bin Muḥammed bin 'Abd al-Karīm Abū al-Ḥasan Fakhr al-Islām al-Bazdawī al-Ḥanafī (482/1089), "*Uṣūl Al-Bazdawī on the margin of 'Abd al-'Azīz al-Bukhārī Khashf al-Asrār*", (Istanbul: 1308, Reprint, Beirut Dār al-Kitāb al-Arabi 1394/1974), p. 339.
80. Ghazālī, "*Al-Musṭaṣfā*"', vol.1 pp. 121-2.
81. Aḥmad Ḥasan, "*The Doctrine of Ijmā' in Islām*", p. 104.
82. Zuhaylī, "*Uṣūl*", vol. 1, pp. 536-7.
83. Ghazālī, "*Al-Mustaṣfā*", vol. 1 p. 101.
84. Āmidī, "*Al-Ihkām*", vol. 1, p. 226.
85. Bazdawī, ibid., vol. 3, p. 239.
86. Āmidī, "*Ihkām*", vol. 3, p. 183
87. Āmidī, "*Al-Iḥkām*", vol. 1, p. 183; Ibn 'Abd al-Shakūr, "*Musallam al-Thubūt*", vol. 2, p. 246.

88. Āmidī, "*Al-Iḥkām*", vol. 3, p. 186; Shawkānī, "*Irshād*", p. 198; Kamālī "*Principles*", p. 198.

89. Āmidī, ibidl., vol. 3, pp. 262-65.

90. Āmidī, ibid., vol: 3, p. 273. See in Aḥmad Ḥasan, "*Analogical Reasoning in Islamic Jurisprudence*", (Islamabad: Islamic research Institute, 1986), p. 101.

91. Kamālī "*Principles*", p. 200.

92. Abū Bakr Aḥmad b. 'Alī al-Rāzī Jaṣṣāṣ (d. 370/981), "*Al-Fuṣūl fī al-Uṣūl*", edt. Ājil Jasīm al-Nashmī, (Kuwait: Wazārāh al-Awkāf wa al-Shu'ūn al-Islāmiyyah, 1988), Quoted from Aḥmad Ḥasan "*Analogical reasoning*", p. 100.

93. Sulaymān bin al-Ash'ās Abū Dāwūd (d. 275/888), "*Sunnan*", trans. Aḥmad Ḥasan, (Lahore: Muḥammad Ashraf, 1984), ḥadīth no: 3672, vol. 3, p. 1043.

94. Āmidī, "*Al-Iḥkām*", vol. 3, p. 193; Bukhārī, "*Uṣūl*", vol. 3, p. 344; Isnawī, "*Nihāyāt*", vol. 4, p. 53; Kamālī, "*Principles*", pp. 200-216.

95. Isnawī, "*Nihāyāt*", vol. 3, p. 33; Āmidī, "*Al-Iḥkām*", vol. 3, p. 22; Ibn Abd al-Shakūr, "*Musallam*", vol. 2, p. 320; Ibn 'Amīr al-Ḥajj, "*Al-Taqrīr*", vol. 3, p. 221; Baidhawī, "*Al-Ibḥāj*", vol. 3, p.18.

96. Āmidī, "*Al-Iḥkām*", vol. 3, p. 63; Taftazānī, "*Ḥāshiyah*", vol. 2, p. 247; Ibn 'Abd al Shakūr, "*Musallam*", vol. 2, p. 320; Molla Ḥusraw, "*Mir'āt al-Uṣūl*", vol. 2 p. 336; Ṣadr al-Sharī'ah, "*Al-Tawḍīḥ*", vol. 2, p. 82; Ibn 'Amīyr al-Ḥajj, "*Al-Taqrīr*", vol. 3, p. 222; Aḥmad Ḥasan, "*Analogical Reasoning*", p. 83.

97. Shawkānī, "*Irshād*", p. 222; Ibn Qayyīm, "*I'lām*", vol. 1, p. 178. See in Kamālī "*Principles*", p. 215, and Aḥmad Ḥasan, ibid., p. 83.

98. Bukhārī, "*Kashf*", vol. 2, p. 1122; Taftazānī, "*Talwīḥ*", vol. 2, p. 81; Ibn 'Abd al-Shakūr, "*Musallam*", vol. 2, p. 320.

99. Ghazālī, "*Al-Mustaṣfā*", vol. 2, pp. 56,59, 70; Āmidī, "*Al-Iḥkām*", vol. 3 p. 64; Shāshī Isḥāq bin Ibrāhīm Abū Ya'qūp al-Khorasānī al-Shāshī (d. 325/937), "*Uṣūl al-Shāshī with 'Umdah al-Ḥawāshī*", (Delhi: 1303), p. 91; Taftazānī, "*Talwīḥ*", vol. 2, p. 53; Bukhārī, "*Uṣūl*", vol. 2, p. 990.

100. Subkī, 'Abd al-Wahhāb bin 'Alī bin 'Abd al-Kāfī Tājj al-Dīn al-Subkī (d. 771/1370), "*Jam' al-Sharḥ al-Jalāl al-Maḥallī 'Alā' Jam' al-Jawāmī'*", (Cairo: Maktabah al-Tijārīyyah), vol. 2 p. 177.

101. Abū Zahrah, Muḥammad (d. 1395/1974), "*Uṣūl al-Fiqh*", (Cairo: Dār al-Fikr al-'Arabi, 1958), pp. 179-180. See in Kamālī, "*Principles*", p. 220.

102. 'Alī Taqīy Ḥaydarī, "*Uṣūl al-Istinbāt*", (Baghdat: Matba'ah al-Rābitah, 1959), pp. 259-73; Hāshim Maghrūf Ḥusaynī, "*Mabadi' al-'Āmmah li*

al-Fiqh al-Jaghfarī", (Baghdat: Dār al-Nashr li al-Jam'īyyīyn Maktabah al-Naḥḍah), p. 290.

103. Shaḥ Walī Allah Dihlawī (d. 1176/1776), "*Ḥujjah Allah al-Bālighah*", (Delhi: 1954-5), vol. 1, p. 130. Quoted from J M S Baljon, "*Religion and thought of Shah Wali Allah Dihlawi*", (Leiden, Netherlands: E. J. Brill, 1986), p. 169.

104. Dihlawī, "*Tafhīmati Ilāhiyyah*", (Dabhel: 1936), vol. 1, p. 40; vol. 2, p. 133. Quoted from Baljon, ibid., p. 170.

105. Dihlawī, "*Ḥujjat Allah*", vol. 1, p. 169. Quoted from Baljon, ibid., p. 170.

106. Shāṭibī, "*Al-Muwāfaqāt*", vol. 1, p. 40.

107. Ibid., vol. 2, p. 233.

108. Ibid., vol. 4, p. 206.

109. Abū Muḥammad 'Alī al-Andalūsī al-Ẓāhirī Ibn Ḥazm (d. 456/1064), "*Al-Iḥkām fī Uṣūl al-Aḥkām*", (Beirut: Dār al-Kutup al-'Ilmīyyah, n.d.), vol. 5, p. 590; Ibn al-Ḥājib (d. 646/1249), "*Mukhtaṣar al-Muntaha' al-Sūl wa al-'Amal*", (Constantinople: al-Maktabah al-Islāmiyyah, 1310), p. 217; Baiḍāwī, "*Al-Ibhāj*", vol. 3, p. 111; Bukhārī, "*Kashf*", vol. 2, p. 1098; Molla Ḥusraw "*Mar'āt al-Uṣūl*", vol. 2 p. 367; Sarakhsī, "*Uṣūl*", vol. 2, p. 225; Bannānī, "*Ḥāshiah*", vol. 2, p. 285; Abū Zahrah, "*Uṣūl*", p. 286.

110. Al-'Ālim Aḥmad b. Muḥammad b. 'Alī al-Fayyūmī Muqrī, (d. 770), "*Missbāḥ al-Munīr fī Gharīb al-Sharkh al-Kabīr li al-Rāfī*'", edt. Abd al-'Aẓīm al-Shannāwī, (Cairo: Dār al-Ma'ārif, n.d.).

111. Isnawī "*Nihāyat*", vol. 3, p. 131.

112. Qarafī, "*Tanqīḥ*", p. 199.

113. Bazdawī, "*Kashf*", vol. 3, p. 377.

114. Shawkānī, "*Irshād*" p. 237.

115. Sha'bān Zakīy al-Dīn "*İslam Hukuk İlminin Esasları*", trans. Ibrāhīm Kāfī Dönmez, (Ankara: 1990), p. 189; Abu Zahrah, "*Uṣūl*", p. 236; Khudari, "*Uṣūl*", pp. 354-5.

116. Shawkānī, "*Irshād*", p. 238.

117. Al-Majallah: clause: 8

118. Suyūṭī, "*Al-Ashbāh*", p. 47; Majallah al-Aḥkām al-'Adlīyyah: clause: 5.

119. Abū Zahrah, "*Uṣūl*", p. 236; Shawkānī, "*Irshād*", p. 238; Kamālī, "*Principle*", pp. 301-2.

120. Kamālī, "*Principle*", p. 268.

121. Al-Shāṭibī, "*Al-Muwāfaqāt*", vol. 2, p. 3.

122. Haçkalı 'Abd al-Raḥman, "Islam Hukuk Tarihinde Maşlaḥat Tanımları ve Bunların Analizi", in *İslami Araştırmalar Magazine*, 2000, vol. 13, no: 1, p. 47-61.

123. Ibn Manẓūr, ibid.

124. Al-Shāṭibī, "*Al-Muwāfaqāt*", vol. 2, p. 25.

125. Badrān, Abū al-'Aynāyn Badrān, "*Uṣūl al-Fiqh al-Islāmī*", (Alaxandria: Muassasah Shabāb al-Jāmi'ah, 1404/1984), p. 210.

126. See Ghazālī, "*Al-Mustaṣfā*", pp. 174-179.

127. Ibn 'Āshūr, Muḥammad Ṭāhir (d. 1973), "*Maqāsid al-Sharī'ah al-Islāmīyyah*" (İslam Hukuk Felsefesi, Gaye Problemi), translated by Vecdi Akyüz, Mehmet Erdoğan, (İstanbul: Rağbet, 1999), p. 123.

128. Ibn 'Āshūr, ibid., p. 138.

129. Ibn 'Āshūr, ibid., p. 139.

130. Ghazālī, "*Al-Mustaṣfā*", vol. 1, p. 288.

131. Shāṭibī, "*Al-Muwāfaqāt*", vol. 2, p. 8.

132. Ibid, vol. 2, pp. 10-1.

133. Shāṭibī, "*Al-Muwāfaqāt*", vol. 2, p. 327.

134. Ghazālī, ibid., vol. 1, p. 311.

135. Ghazālī, "*Al-Mankhūl min Ta'līqāt al-Uṣūl*", Al-Ṭab'ah al-Thāniyah, (Damascus: Dār al-Fikr al-Arabi), p. 355.

136. Ḥasan bin Muḥammad bin Maḥmūd Aṭṭār (d. 1250/1835), "*Ḥāshiyah 'Alā Sharḥ Jalāl al-Maḥallī 'Alā Jam' al-Jawāmi'*", (Egypt Maṭba'ah 'Ilmīyyah, h.1316), vol. 2, p. 339.

137. Zuhaylī, "*Uṣūl*", vol. 2, p. 799.

138. Khallāf, "*'Ilm*", p. 87; Badrān, "*Uṣūl*", p. 214.

139. Shāṭibī, "*Al-I'tisām*", vol. 2, pp. 307-314.

140. Ghazāli, "*Al-Mustaṣfa*", vol. 1, p. 141.

141. Ibn 'Āshur, "*Maqāṣid*", p. 121.

142. Shāṭibī, "*Al-Muwāfaqāt*", vol. 2, pp. 29-30.

143. Ibn Manẓūr, "*Lisān*", vol. 11, p. 144.

144. Zamakhsharī, jār Allah Maḥmūd bin 'Umar (d. 538/1144), "*Al-Kashshāf al-Ḥaqā'iq Ghawāmiḍ al-Tanẓī wa 'Uyūn al-Aqāwīl fī Wujūh al-Ta'wīl*", (Beirut: Dār al-Kitāb al-'Arabi, 1366), vol. 2, p. 138.

145. Ibn Manẓūr, "*Lisān*", vol. 4, p. 311.

146. 'Abd Allah bin Aḥmad bin Maḥmūd, Ḥāfiz al-Din Abu al-Baraqāt al-Ḥanafī Nasafī (d. 710/1310), "*Al-Mustaṣfā Sharḥ al-Fikh al-Nāfī*" quoted from Zuhaylī, "*Uṣūl*", vol. 2 p. 828.

147. .Kamāl Muḥammed bin 'Abd al-Waḥīd bin 'Abd al-Ḥamīd bin Mas'ūd al-Ḥanafī Ibn al-Humām (d. 861/1457), "*Al-Taysīr Sharḥ al-Tahrīr fī Uṣūl al-Fiqh*", (Cairo, Bulāq: al-Amīyrīyyah, 1317), vol. 1, pp. 317.

148. Sha'bān, "*İslam Hukuku*", p. 175.

149. Abū Zahrah, "*Uṣūl*", p. 217; Sha'bān, ibid., p. 176; Faḥreddīn Atar, "*Fıkıh Uṣulü*", MUIFY, (İstanbul, 1996), p. 88; Zuhaylī, "*Uṣūl*", vol. 2, p. 829; Ismā'īl, Muḥammad Sha'bān,"*Uṣūl al-Fiqh al-Muyassar*", (Cairo, Tawfīqīyyah: Dār al-Kitāb al-Jāmī', 1994), vol. 2, p. 285.

150. Kamālī, "*Principles*", p. 286; Ismā'īl, "*Uṣul*", vol. 2, p. 289; Atar, "*Fıkıh Uṣulü*", p. 89.

151. Ismā'īl, "*Uṣūl*", vol. 2, p. 289; Kamālī, "*Prenciples*", p. 286; Atar, ibid.

152. Ismā'īl, ibid.; Kamālī, ibid.

153. Ibid.

154. Al-Majallah: clause: 36.

155. Ibid., 40.

156. Ibid., 41.

157. Ibid., 43.

158. Ibid., 45.

159. See Majmā' al-Fiqh al-Islāmī, "Karārāt wa al-Tawsīyyāt", (Kuwait: 1988), in 9. For more about custom and its applications, see Chapter Four.

160. Ismā'īl Hakkı Izmirlī (d. 1946), "*'Ilm al-Khilāf*", (Istanbul: 1330), p. 130; Shāfi'ī, "*Al-Ūmm*", (Beirut: 1983), vol. 3, p. 272; Muḥammad Muṣṭafā Shalabī, "*Uṣūl al-Fiqh al-Islāmī*", (Beirut: 1986), p. 304.

161. Ibn Fares, Aḥmad (d. 395/1004), "*Mu'ājam Maqāyīs al-Lughah*", (Beirut: Dār Iḥyā' al-Turāth al-'Arabi), vol. 3, p. 66; Al-Rāzī, Muḥammad b. Abī Bakr (d. 660), "*Mukhtār al-ṣiḥaḥ*", (Beirut Dār al-Ma'rifah, n.d.), p. 113.

162. Ibn Manẓūr, "*Lisān*", vol. 8, p. 96; Anees Ibrahīm, "*Al-Mu'jam al-Wasīṭ*", (Cairo: Dār al-Ma'ārif, 1973), vol. 1, p. 310.

163. Shāṭibī, "*Al-Muwāfaqāt*", vol. 4, p. 198.

164. Ibn al-Qayyīm, "*I'lām al-Muwaqqi'īn*", vol. 3, p. 147.

165. Qarafī, "*Kitāb Anwār*", vol. 2, p. 33.

166. Ibn al-Qayyīm, "*I'lam*", vol. 3, p. 147.

167. Shaṭibi "*Al-Muwāfaqāt*", vol. 2, pp. 358-361.

168. Ibid., vol. 2, p. 358.

169. Ibid., vol. 2, p. 359.

170. Abū Zahrah, "*Uṣūl*", p. 231; Shāṭibī, ibid., vol. 2, p. 361.

171. Ibid., see them in detail in Kamālī, "*Principles*", pp. 310-320.

172. Al-Majallah: clause: 30.

173. Shawkānī, "*Irshād*", p. 213; Ghazāli, "*Al-Mustaṣfā*", vol. 1, p. 135; Āmidī, "*Al-Iḥkām*", vol. 3, p. 133; Shīrāzī, "*Sharḥ al-Luma*", p. 50; Molla Husrāw, "*Mar'āt al-Uṣūl*", vol. 2, p. 250; Bannānī, "*Ḥāshīah*", vol. 2, p. 288.

174. Ibn 'Abd al-Shakūr, "*Musallam*", vol. 2, p. 120; Bannānī, "*Ḥāshiah*", vol. 2, p. 146.

175. Shawkānī, "*Irshād*", p. 213; Isnawī, "*Nihāyat*", vol. 3, p. 173; Ghazālī, "*Al-Mustaṣfā*"', vol. 1, p. 135; Āmidī, "*Al-Iḥkām*", vol. 3, p. 133; Banānī, "*Ḥāshiah*", vol. 2, p. 288; Maḥmūd bin Aḥmad bin Maḥmūd Abū al-Manāqib Sha'b al-Dīn, Zanjānī min al-Shāfi'ī (d. 656/1258), "*Takhrīj al-Furū' 'Alā al-Uṣūl*", edt. Muḥammad Adīb Ṣālīḥ Muassasah al-Risālah, (Dimishq: 1962), p. 82.

176. Muḥammad bin Aḥmad bin 'Alī al-Idrīsi, al-Sharif Tilmisānī al-Mālikī (d. 771/1370), "*Muftāḥ al-Wuṣūl Ilā Binā, al-Furū' 'alā al-Uṣūl*", (Cairo: Jāmi'ah al-Azhar, Kullīyah al-Sharī'ah), reg.no: 72, p. 120.

177. Bukhāri, "*Kashf*", vol. 2, p. 937; Ibn al-Qayyīm, "*I'lām*", vol. 1, p. 30 and vol. 4, p. 156.

178. Banānī, "*Ḥāshiah*", vol. 2, p. 289.

179. Bukhārī, "*Kashf*", vol. 2, p. 938.

180. Zuhaylī, "*Uṣūl*", vol. 2, p. 838.

181. Kamālī, "*Principles*", p. 229.

182. Ghazālī, "*Al-Mustaṣfā*"', vol. 1, p. 33; Shāṭibī, "*Al-Muwāfaqāt*", vol. 3, pp. 298- 304.

183. Ibid.

2

Development of *Ijtihād* by *Ra'y*

Following the end of the period of the revelation, Islamic law was developed with great effort by those who had the authority and expertise, despite the rapid changes in social, economical and political life. It is undeniable that the jurists' contributions had added to the great enhancement of Islamic law in its ability to manoeuvre and its skill to be flexible; therefore Islamic law is described as a law made by jurists.[1]

In order to assess the concept of *istiḥsān* (juristic preference) it is necessary to first consider its basis, for it is possible that the main source of inspiration behind *istiḥsān* is the concept of *ra'y* (personal opinion in juridical judgment). The criteria of personal judgment in *istiḥsān* indicate a direct relationship between *istiḥsān* and *ijtihād by ra'y* which is a personal judgment. Moreover, it is viewed that *istiḥsān* is a product of *ijtihād*. In fact, Abū Ḥanīfah performed *ijtihād* from his personal opinions (conforming to the Qur'an and the *Sunnah*) by saying, "*Qiyās* rules this, but we "*nastaḥsinū*" (prefer) that, or we proved this by *istiḥsān* contrary to *qiyās*, or the *qiyās* of this is so and so and the *ijtihād* of this is so and so, and the *ijtihād* we take".[2]

Concept of ra'y (opinion)

The word *ra'y* is derived from the verb *r'ā* which means to see something or somebody; later it was used as a verbal noun. It may also denote a dream or vision; a view; or that which is known only by heart but cannot be seen with the eye i.e. an opinion.[3] It can also mean *i'tiqād* (faith, belief), *ẓann* (assumption), *'ilm* (knowledge, science), *'aql* (reason, intellect, mentality), *tadbīr* (precaution), and *iṣābah* (target).[4]

Ibn al-Qayyīm (d. 751/1350) points out that one aspect of *ra'y* is "after considering a subject and making a judgment from the heart, a search through the evidence and inferences, both which have their own considerations, is made to implement the truth, reality".[5] Rāghib al-Iṣfaḥānī (d. 502/1109) defines the word "*ru'yah*" as "To perceive an object which is seen"; this perception is divided into the following parts: 1. the five senses and that which replaces the senses in a similar activity. 2.*wahm* (illusion—false impression) and *taḥayyul* (imagination) 3. *tafakkur* (contemplation), 4. *'aql* (intellectual faculty), *idrāk* (perception).[6]

Historical perspective of ra'y

Studying the concept of *ra'y* from the historical perspective shows that there have been different views as to when it was first used. It is the view of the majority of scholars that the use of *ra'y* began during the period of the Prophet's (ṣ) life time. The *ṣaḥābah* (Companions) applied *ijtihād* by *ra'y* according to their perception of an action of the Prophet (ṣ).[7]

An alternative point of view with regard to the ruling based on *ra'y* suggests that the practice of *ra'y* was used only after the death of the Prophet (ṣ). The practice was used when the Companions were faced with issues that had not been detailed in the Qur'an and the *Sunnah.* This view is disputed by scholars such as Ibn Khaldūn (d. 808/1405) and Ibn Ḥazm (d. 456/1064). According to Ibn Khaldūn: "The *aḥkām* had been taught either during the time of the Prophet (ṣ) through revelation, which was sent to the Prophet (ṣ), or his direct speeches and attitudes; therefore it was unnecessary to apply intellectual reasoning or analogy (*qiyās*)".[8] Ibn Ḥazm says "The claim that *ra'y* appeared at the time of the Companions had nothing to do with Companion's actions, contrary to the report that the Companions used *ra'y* (opinion); the validity of such reports and narrations is uncertain."[9] According to those scholars, the sources of Islamic law at the time of Prophet (ṣ) are confined only to the Qur'an and the *Sunnah.* The *ijmā'* took form at a later period than the time of the Companions. The application of analogy was used when a ruling on a matter did not have a textual (*naṣṣ*) reference in the main sources of guidance.[10]

It is well documented that the use of *ijtihād* by *ra'y* has been practiced from the time of the Prophet (ṣ); this is evident from several narrations. For example when the Prophet (ṣ) saw the people of Madīnah fertilizing palm trees, the Prophet (ṣ) forbade it; when he heard the account that the trees had become barren he said, "I'm a human, if I order you to do something in the name of your religion then conform to it. However, if I order something which depends on my personal *ra'y* (opinion), I am only a human".[11] In the famous tradition of Mu'adh Ibn Jabal (d. 18/640), the Prophet (ṣ) asked: "How will you judge when the occasion of deciding a case arises"? He replied: "I shall judge in accordance with God's book". The Prophet asked: "(What will you do) if you do not find guidance in God's book"? He replied: "(I will act) in accordance with the *Sunnah* of the Messenger of God". The Prophet (ṣ) asked: "(What will you do) if you do not find guidance in the *Sunnah* of the Messenger of God and in

God's book?" He replied: "I shall do my best to form an opinion and spare no pains". The Messenger of God then patted him on the chest and said: "Praise be to God who helped the messenger of the Messenger of God to find a thing which pleases the Messenger of God".[12] In support of this view, it is well known that the Companions practiced *ra'y* to achieve solutions on issues pertaining to juristic affairs.

It is obvious that the Prophet (ṣ) applied and practised *ijtihād* by *ra'y* in his lifetime. He taught and encouraged the companions to perform *ijtihād* by *ra'y* with regard to various issues.

Ra'y in terms of a judicial meaning

The scholars of *uṣūl* have called the practice of inference to arrive at a ruling *ijtihād*, *qiyās* (analogy) or *ra'y* (opinion).[13] There are different views on whether *ra'y* is a kind of *ijtihād* or *qiyās*.

Shāfi'ī (d. 204/819) says that *ra'y* is not based on a validated source of Sharī'ah. He considered it to be only a performance of inferences that depends purely on intellectual reasoning and inclination. Therefore, he was critical of scholars who used *ra'y* in their *ijtihād*. He also distinguished between *ra'y* and *qiyās*, and considered them opposed to one another.[14] Ghazālī (d. 5005/1111) considers *ra'y* and *qiyās* as synonyms saying "*Ra'y* consists of comparing and representing any *ḥukm* (ruling) to itself".[15]

It is also the view of some Jurists, particularly the Shāfi'ī scholars that the concept of *ra'y* is synonymous with *qiyās* (analogy). Also taking into consideration the practice of the Companions (*ṣaḥābāh*) and the Successors (*Tābi'īn*), some other scholars have considered it to be a kind of a comprehensive method of *ijtihād* as well as consisting of *qiyās* (analogy), *istiḥsān* (juristic preference), *al-maṣāliḥ al-mursalah* (consideration of public interest), and *sadd al-dharā'ī'* (blocking the means).[16]

Sarakhsī (d: 483/1090) is one of the jurists who believe that *ra'y* is more extensive than *qiyās*. In an interpretation of the verse "Then take admonition, O you with eyes (to see)" (59:2) he explains that *i'tibār* (admonition) means practising *ra'y* in place of that which has no *naṣṣ* (text) and *qiyās*".[17] 'Abd al-Wahhāb Khallāf (d. 1956) says that *ra'y* is more comprehensive than *qiyās*. He defines it as "Analogising and thinking in order to reach the right *ḥukm* (ruling) in a field where no *naṣṣ* (text) is available by the Sharī'ah provided for the purpose of inference.[18]

Shawkānī (d. 1250/1834) points out that *ra'y* could have been applied to the explanation and interpretation of the *naṣṣ* (text), saying that "*Ijtihād* by *ra'y* can be the way of inference from Qur'an and the *Sunnah*. It was originally permitted in Sharī'ah for the consideration of benefit and in cases of necessity."[19] Fatḥī Dīrīnī believes that the confinement of *ijtihād* to *ra'y* on issues which have no *naṣṣ* (text) is incorrect. He says that the Companions' interpretations of the *naṣṣ* (text) should also be included in the circle of *ijtihād* by *ra'y*. For example, when Abū Bakr was questioned on "*kalālah*",[20] his response was "I will express my point of view on this issue; if it is correct and rightly done then it is from God, if I fall into error it is from me and from Satan".[21]

Accordingly, we can see that *ra'y* has virtually the same meaning as *ijtihād*. Technically *ijtihād* is defined as "Maximum effort made by jurists to ascertain, in a given problem or issue, the *shar'ī* rulings deduced from the general principles with the injunction of Islam and its real intent".[22] At first glance, there is a very close relationship between *ijtihād* and *ra'y*. However, it is clear that *ijtihād* is more comprehensive than *ra'y*. At the time of Companions and Successors, the constituent parts of *ra'y* were clear and extensive, as opposed to the *naṣṣ*, which is not obviously clarified and defined. Following that period, some jurists continued to use *ra'y* in the meaning of *ijtihād* in a wider range. At the same time, the majority of jurists confined the use of inference to issues where there were no *naṣṣ* (text) to reach a right and just *ḥukm* (ruling). In addition to *qiyās* (analogy), they also used *istiḥsān* (juristic preference), *al-maṣāliḥ al-mursalah* (consideration of public interests), *sadd al-dharā'ī'* (blocking the means), and *'urf* (customary law) which agreed with the general aim of Sharī'ah and its spirit. Hence, the field of *ra'y* is narrow as compared to that of *ijtihād*, but it is more comprehensive than *qiyās* and consequently it is called "*ijtihād* by *ra'y*".[23]

Types of ra'y (juristic opinion)

Many narrations have been reported by the Companions and the Successors over the validity of *ra'y*, as was the case with *istiḥsān*.[24]

Generally, Ibn al-Qayyīm (d. 751/1350) has divided *ra'y* into three types: *ra'y saḥīḥ* (valid, authentic), *ra'y bāṭil* (invalid; null, and void), and *ra'y mashkūk* (doubtful, uncertain).[25]

1. *Ra'y saḥīḥ* (valid, authentic): This is *ra'y* which does not contradict the textural evidence (*naṣṣ*) but rather supports and confirms it; therefore it is true and valid.[26]
2. *Ra'y bāṭil* ((invalid, null, and void): This is rejected since it contains elements that are harmful and dangerous to the religion.[27] The following are included in this category: *ra'y* that is rejected because it is against *naṣṣ* (text), which confirms that it is invalid and void,[28] *ra'y* which relies on pure *'aql* (intellect and reason); *ra'y* which causes changes to the *Sunnah* of Prophet (ṣ) or can lead to heresy.[29]
3. *Ra'y mashkūk* (doubtful, uncertain): The early scholars gave permission to perform *ra'y mashkūk* to give *fatwā* (formal legal opinion) and *ḥukm* (ruling). However, there has to be

sufficient grounds to justify this and only then when there is no other option to arrive at a solution. No one is forced to perform *ra'y mashkūk,* nor is opposition considered to be *ḥarām* (unlawful); no one who follows it is considered to be against religion or those who oppose it to be following the religion. Hence, one has the freedom to choose between accepting and rejecting this type of *ra'y.*[30]

Concept of *ijtihād*

Ijtihād is one of the most important key words of Sharīʻah (Islamic Law) and the aim to comprehend the purpose of the Qur'an and the *Sunnah.* The main purpose of law is to maintain the continuity of answering people's needs. A legal system which answers questions of its era while offering solutions for future generations can be realized by constantly renewing itself. In this sense, *ijtihād* has very important functions in keeping the law alive, which is one of the main dynamics of the Sharīʻah.

Exigency of ijtihād (performing personal judgment)

The use of *ijtihād* to derive Sharīʻah rulings is crucial for everyday life. Today's Muslims actually need two types of *ijtihād*: the first is to understand its nature by preferring and choosing *ijtihād* to select the main objectives of the Sharīʻah rules. The most basic of Sharīʻah rules is to accommodate the benefit of people and the most suitable opinions for modern life's circumstances. These rules have been handed down from former jurists. The second type is the derivation of new rulings in law using legal methods such as *qiyās, istiḥsān, maṣlaḥah, istiṣlaḥ, 'urf,* and so on, where the jurists' performance of *ijtihād* has room for manoeuvre, according to Qaradāwī.[31]

Ijtihād is a very demanding requirement in modern day life, and therefore it is sometimes an individual duty (*farḍ ʿaynī*) and sometimes a collective duty (*farḍ kifāyah*) for Muslims.[32] If the requirement of *ijtihād* is ignored then the whole Muslim community will be considered sinful. The scholars unanimously agree that *ijtihād* is included in the scope of the following verses: "So keep your duty to God and fear Him as much as you can" (64:16) and "Then take admonition, O you with eyes (to see)" (59:2). Qarafī expresses his anxiety, saying "God save us if there is not an available competent *mujtahid*."[33]

The Qur'an indicates that the use of *ijtihād* is a religious duty and encourages Muslims to avoid disagreements amongst themselves. When they differ, the Qur'an refers them to the Messenger of God or the one who is in authority amongst Muslims (*ʿulul amr*): "O you who have believed, obey God and obey the Messenger and those in authority among you. If you differ in anything amongst yourselves, refer it to God and His Messenger. If you believe in God and in the Last Day. That is better and more suitable for final determination" (4:59). Referring the disagreements to God and His Messenger is an effort made to find solutions according to *naṣṣ*; this is an example of *ijtihād*[34] and an encouragement to Muslims to perform *ijtihād* in the future.

The *Sunnah* of the Prophet (ṣ) encourages the use of *ijtihād*.[35] "When a judge exercises *ijtihād* and gives a right judgment, he will have two rewards, but if he errs in his judgment, he will still have earned one reward."[36] Another example of this concept is the case of the *ḥadīth* of Muʿādh.[37]

Shāfiʿī (d. 204/819) believes that the rulings inferred by *ijtihād* have a divine character: "The rulings which are inferred by *qiyās* are considered to have a divine quality".[38] "The rulings of many cases where there are no direct indications in the Book or the *Sunnah* have to be deduced by means of *qiyās* (analogy) and interpretations of the *naṣṣ*".[39] Juwaynī (d. 478/1085) says that, "When there is no direct trace within the *naṣṣ*, nine out of ten rulings and legal opinions (*fatwā*) are deduced by way of personal opinions (*ra'y*) and inferences."[40]

According to Fazlur Raḥman, the Qur'an should be our guidance and the Qur'an's general principles, values, long term purposes must be determined and systemized; it is important that these principles and purposes are to be formulated and conveyed into the present time. They could become applicable for recent issues pertaining to humankind; in other words, determined principles and purposes should be rationally integrated into present circumstances.[41]

In his model, the principle of *ijtihād* would be performed as a 'double movement': "the process of interpretation proposed here consist of double movements, from the present situation to the Qur'an times, and then back to the present."[42] First, travelling to the time of the revelation of the *naṣṣ*; verses must be investigated, the wisdom behind them discovered, and the purpose of the revelation considered along with their historical circumstances. It is necessary to discover and comprehend the Qur'an's purpose in its entirety and its detailed response to particular circumstances. Generalizing the individual responses sets the precedent for future ethical and social structures. Secondly, returning to the present and pertaining the general systemized principles to issues. This requires from us that the present circumstances be analyzed in detail with its various constitutive components. Historians, sociologists, moralists, should co-operate in the *ijtihād* of the double movement.[43]

If people do not consult the Qur'an and give credence to its fixed ideas, the double movement process would be the sole hope for an ideal technique for a successful interpretation.[44]

Shahristānī (d. 548/1153) believes that performing *ijtihād* is an obligatory duty: "Definitely we know that either *'ibādāt* (worshiping) or *taṣarrufāt* (transactions) are numerous and can not be calculated. We also have to realise that every single matter has not been revealed in the *naṣṣ* (*text*), for it would not be practical. Therefore in respect of the unlimited matters, performing *ijtihād* is an obligatory duty."[45]

Ibn Ṣiddīq indicated that a *mujtahīd* has two ways to obtain the objectives of the lawgiver in the *naṣṣ*. These are as follows:

1. Linguistically investigating *naṣṣ*: While doing this investigation, the general principles become a part of an activity and if the general principles and particular principles are not in harmony then the general principles are preferred.
2. Investigating *naṣṣ* in the context of the objectives of the Sharī'ah.[46]

Generally, the main sources of *sharī'ah* are first divided into two parts:

- Al-Qur'an
- Al-Sunnah

Ijtihād is the main method of making new rulings in Islamic law relying on the two main sources.

The Qur'an has pointed to such issues in *sūrah al-Nisā'*: "O you who believe! Obey God and obey the Messenger (Muḥammad), and those of you (Muslims) who are in authority. (And) if you differ in anything amongst yourselves, refer it to God and His Messenger, if you believe in God and in the Last Day. That is better and more suitable for final determination" (4:59).

The Prophet taught the Companions how to practice *ijtihād*. When the Prophet intended to send Mu'ādh Ibn-Jabal (d. 18/640) to Yemen, the Prophet (ṣ) asked him: "How will you judge when the occasion of deciding a case arises?" He replied: "I shall judge in accordance with God's book." The prophet asked: "(What will you do) if you do not find guidance in God's Book?" He replied: "(I will act) in accordance with the *Sunnah* of the Messenger of God." The Prophet (ṣ) asked: "(What will you do) if you do not find guidance in the *Sunnah* of the Messenger of God and in God's Book?" He replied: "I shall do my best to form an opinion and spare no pains." The Messenger of God then patted him on the chest and said: Praise be to God who helped the messenger of the Messenger of God to find a thing which pleases the Messenger of God".[47]

Sa'īd Ibn al-Musayyib narrated a *ḥadīth* and said: "I asked the Messenger of God. O! Messenger of God what shall we do when we face a problem, which has no answer in the Qur'an and the *Sunnah*?" The Messenger of God said: "Your scholars (*'ulama'*) come together, or worshippers come together from among the believers, and make consultation among yourselves; do not judge on the basis of only one opinion."[48]

As we can see, the Prophet (ṣ) encouraged the Companions to perform *ijtihād* during his life time. The encouragement of people to perform *ijtihād* gave them the ability to find answers to their problems, and to open doors that would never be closed.[49] When 'Umar ibn Khattāb appointed Shurayḥ as a judge to Kūfah, he said to him: "First of all look into the Qur'an as though it was revealed to you without asking anyone, then rule with it. If you cannot find what you are looking for in the Qur'an then follow the Prophet's *Sunnah*. If you cannot find the right guidance in the *Sunnah* then perform *ijtihād* by *ra'y* with your personal opinion and consult the people of righteousness (virtuousness, justness) and honesty."[50]

Definition of ijtihād

Linguistically

Ijtihād is derived from two words; the word *juhd* which means exertion of effort or energy; and *jahd* which means the forbearance of hardship, that is striving and self-exertion in any activity which entails a measure of hardship. It would thus be suitable in order to use *jahada* in respect of one who carries a heavy load, but not so if he carries a trivial weight. *Ijtihād* is the expenditure of efforts to arrive at righteous judgement; it could be either physical such as walking, working or intellectual such as inference of a ruling, or juristic and linguistic theory.[51]

Technically

The juristic meaning of *ijtihād* has several definitions according to the scholars of *uṣūl*. Some define *ijtihād* in accordance with the action and activity exerted by the jurist to arrive at a solution. Ghazālī (d. 505/1111) defines it as "Total expenditure of effort made by a jurist for the purpose of obtaining the religious rulings."[52]

Āmidī (d. 631/1233) defines *ijtihād* as the expenditure of the total efforts in search of *ẓann* (probability), to the extent that the jurist feels obliged to exert himself further in proving the ruling being correct. Āmidī's definition of *ijtihād* implies that it is not enough to exert efforts only; the jurist should feel that he has spared no effort to ensure he could pursue the issue further. According to Āmidī, "*ijtihād* is the application of the jurist using all of his faculties either in inferring the practical rules of Sharī'ah from the sources, or implementing such rules and applying them to a particular issue."[53] The definitive rulings of Sharī'ah that are known by necessity are therefore excluded from *ijtihād*, such as the five pillars of Islām, rulings related to Islamic 'a*qīdah* (belief) and realization of the attributions of God; all these are determined by explicit textual statements. There is only one correct view in regard to these matters and anyone who differs is wrong.[54]

Qarafī (d. 684/1285) defines it as "The expenditure of total effort while considering a case which is condemned by religion."[55]

Isnawī (d. 772/1370) defines *ijtihād* as, "Expenditure of effort to arrive at and realize the rulings of Sharī'ah, whether definitive (*qaṭ'ī*) or probable (*ẓannī*)".[56]

Kamāl Ibn Al-Humām (d. 861/1457) defines *ijtihād* as the expenditure of efforts by the *faqīh* to arrive at a juristic ruling, such ruling being either rational (*'aqlī*) or transmitted (*naqlī*), definitive (*qaṭ'ī*)or speculative (*ẓannī*).[57] Ibn Ḥazm (d. 456/1064) differs and defines *ijtihād* as "Investigating the rules of God solely in the Qur'an and in the *Sunnah*".[58]

Fazlur Raḥmān defines *ijtihād* technically as "The effort to understand the meaning of a relevant text or precedent in the past, containing a rule, and to alter that rule by extending, restricting or otherwise modifying it in such a manner that a new situation can be subsumed by a new solution."[59]

Validity of *ijtihād*

There are many verses which appear to validate *ijtihād* in the Qur'an: "Verily, in these things, there are *āyāt* (proof, evidences, lessons, signs, etc.) for people who reflect" (13:3). "Verily, in these things, there are *āyāt* for the people who understand." (13:4), "Surely, We have sent down to you (O Muḥammad) the book (this Qur'an) in truth that you might judge between men by that which God has shown you" (4:105). These verses support the use of *ijtihād* by way of *qiyās* (analogy).[60] The following verses obviously indicate the validity of *ijtihād:* "...and consult them in the affair." (3:159), "... and who (conduct) their affairs by mutual consultation." (42:38)

In addition, many *ḥadīth* also validate *ijtihād*: It is narrated that 'Amr Ibn al-'Āṣ heard the Prophet (*ṣ*) say: "If a jurist exerts efforts and arrives at a correct ruling he will be rewarded twice, and if he arrives at a ruling which is in error he will be rewarded once".[61]

The *ḥadīth* of Mu'ādh Ibn Jabal, as mentioned above, is a very good example of validation. "I shall spare no pains to do my best to form an opinion."[62]

According to Dasūqī, *ijtihād* which is valid and unanimously accepted is to be used by all jurists. The practice of *ijtihād* is a key to the progress of the development of Islamic law, and opens a gate to Islamic *fiqh* that will develop the law when dealing with new issues. Muḥammad Al-Dasūqī says that the use of *ijtihād* is a kind of revelation of Islamic *fiqh*.[63]

Types of ijtihād

After considering the divisions of *ijtihād* based on the *maqāṣid* (objectives of the Sharī'ah), we should assess its classical typology. As for *ijtihād* based on the *maqāṣid*, Muḥammad Tahir b. 'Āshūr (d. 1973) says that it has five main divisions.[64]

1. Comprehending the commands of the Sharī'ah and its *naṣṣ*, which must be in the context of linguistic meanings and *shar'ī* (legal) meanings.
2. Cases which are contradictory to *naṣṣ* must be examined with a view to *naskh* (abrogation), *takhṣīṣ* (specifying the general), and *rājiḥ* (preference).

3. To perform analogy based on the effective cause, which is obtained from the rulings.
4. Creating a rule in an area where there is no availability of *naṣṣ* (text) and analogy.
5. The *ta'abbudī* (worship) rulings would be accepted as they are.

In performing *ijtihād* the jurist is to consider these five divisions; a jurist needs to know the objectives of the Sharī'ah (*maqāṣid al-Sharī'ah*).

Ijtihād with regard to the amount of effort exerted by the *mujtahid* is divided into two types:

1. Full or Complete *ijtihād*: The *mujtahid* exerts all efforts possible in searching and investigating until he feels that he is incapable of further efforts. This is what Mu'ādh Ibn Jabal indicated in the *ḥadīth* stated above "I shall spare no pains to do my best to form an opinion."[65]
2. Imperfect (Incomplete) *ijtihād:* when there is a lack of effort in searching and investigating. This type of *ijtihād* is not considered as *shar'ī ijtihād.*[66]

Ghazālī (d. 505/111) was the first to divide *ijtihād* into two categories in general:[67]

1. Absolute (*muṭlaq*) *ijtihād*: This is where the *mujtahid* is unrestricted by the rules of a particular *madhhab*. This level of *ijtihād* is for those who have fulfilled all the requirements of *ijtihād*, and also deduced the *aḥkām* from the evidence in the sources.
2. Limited (*muqayyad*) *ijtihād*: This is where the *mujtahid* expounds the law within the confines of a particular school while adhering to the principles laid down by their *imāms.*[68]

Ijtihād is also divided into the general and the specific:

1. General (*'ām*) *ijtihād:* deals with all sections of Islamic *fiqh.*
2. Specific, individual (*khaṣ*) *ijtihād*: deals with a particular section of *fiqh* or evidence such as *ijmā'* and *qiyās.*[69]

Further classifications are individual and collective as follows:

1. Individual *ijtihād:* is when a person fulfils the conditions or requirements of a *mujtahid* without any contribution or participation by another *mujtahid.* Alternatively, it is an *ijtihād* performed by several *mujtahids* on an issue in which there is no evidence of agreement on an opinion. The above type of *ijtihād* is that which the *ḥadīth* of Mu'ādh Ibn Jabal has indicated.
2. Collective (*jamā'ī*) *ijtihād*: This is the *ijtihād* where consultations take place amongst scholars and jurists regarding current issues of importance to the general public. This type of *ijtihād* has been proven by the textual statement of the Qur'an and the *Sunnah* as well as the works of the Companions and their Successors.[70]

Conditions of ijtihād

The aims of the conditions are to ensure the ability of a person to perform *ijtihād.* The earliest complete account of the qualifications of a *mujtahid* was given in Abū al-Ḥusayn al-Baṣrī's (d. 436/1044) *"Al-Mu'tamad fī Uṣūl al-Fiqh"*. Shīrāzī (d. 467/1083), Ghazālī (d. 505/1111) and Āmidī (d. 632/1234) later accepted the broad outline of Baṣrī's exposition, with minor changes. This does not mean that the requirements of *ijtihād* received no attention from the *'ulamā'* who came before Baṣrī'.[71]

The first condition is "to perceive the *maqāṣid* (objectives) of the Lawgiver. The second condition, in the same context, is to have the ability to infer rules based on awareness of the *maqāṣid*."[72] *Uṣūlī* scholars for many centuries prepared extensive lists of the abilities jurists must possess to enable them to perform *ijtihād*. Some increased and others decreased the conditions. An outstanding scholar, Shāṭibī, ignored these lists[73] and reduced the conditions of *ijtihād* to one comprehensive point: the precise comprehension of the *maqāṣid* and in the light of this comprehension the ability to deduce rules from the sources.[74]

Ibn al-Subkī (d. 771/1370) mentions the conditions of *ijtihād* in his book "*Jam' al-Jawāmī'*".[75] In the explanation of "*Minhāj*", Ibn al-Subkī stated that one of the conditions of *ijtihād* is "to know the objectives of the Lawgiver before specializing in that field".[76]

Ṣuyūtī (d. 911/1505) quotes from "*Al-Tanqīḥ*" of Amīnuddīn b. Muḥammad Tabrīzī (d. 621/1224) the following statement: "Knowledge of providing evidence of rulings is obtained by investigating every single word of the main sources (the Qur'an and *Sunnah*) in the context of the *maqāṣid*".[77]

Shāṭibī believes that there are some who think that they are competent in the concept of *ijtihād* but who are unable to perceive the objectives of the Lawgiver. Their self-belief in their ability to arrive at a just ruling undermines Islamic law.

Shāṭibī says: "the incorrect use of partial ruling destroys the general principles. Without realizing their lack of knowledge in understanding the *maqāṣid al-Sharī'ah* questions are never asked, and the ruling is established with the first thought that comes to mind, with no further investigation deemed necessary..."[78]

If a ruling relating to people's needs is adequate and the mufti does not possess the ability to comprehend God's purposes the ruling may cause problems and therefore it is necessary for the mufti to understand the *maqāṣid al-Sharī'ah*.[79]

Status of the gate of ijtihād

The conditions of *ijtihād* stated above are the criteria for anyone who wants to qualify in practicing *ijtihād*, irrespective of the era in which the person may live. In later centuries, restrictions were imposed on *ijtihād* which, by the end of the third century, led to the allegation that the Gate of *ijtihād* was closed. The closure of the gate of *ijtihād* arose in order to prevent those who were incapable of practicing *ijtihād*—yet who claimed to do so—from bringing the concept into disrepute. To those who are capable, the doors to the gate of *ijtihād* remained opened.[80]

Furthermore, recent western scholars, in particular Wael Hallaq, and W. Montgomery Watt, have indicated that the door of *ijtihād* is still open and the term "The closing of the door of *ijtihād*"is a myth.[81] In reality, the door of *ijtihād* was never completely closed, as properly qualified scholars must have the right to perform *ijtihād* continuously. *Ijtihād* is not confined to the four schools of law and can be performed by all capable scholars. Consequently, the gate of *ijtihād*, in my personal opinion, is still and must remain open.

Dihlawī (1703/1762) strongly criticizes those who claimed that the door of *ijtihād* was closed. He calls them: "The simpletons of our time" who are, "totally averse to *ijtihād*. Like she-camels, in the nose of which a piece of wood is put to guide them, they do not know where they are going". *Ijtihād* is actually a *farḍ kifāyah* (a collective duty, the fulfilment of which by a sufficient number of individuals excuses the other individuals from fulfilling it) for every epoch since "every age has its own countless specific problems, and cognisance of the divine decisions with respect to them is essential".[82] He continues: "The occupant of this office is qualified to exercise *ijtihād* whenever an affair arises for which he does not find an unequivocal judgement of the founder (*imām*) of the *madhhab*; he has the right to elicit judgements in the same manner and by preceding analogously the verdicts of the *imām*."[83]

I shall elaborate about this study further in the final chapter.

Implementations of *ijtihād* at the time of the Prophet

At the time of the Prophet (ṣ) many *aḥkām* (rulings) and legislations were determined by *waḥy* (revelation). The solution of an issue or problem encountered during the life of the Prophet was either by revelation or by the Prophet (ṣ) through inspirations. Even in situations where there was no revelation, the Prophet used his knowledge based on experience and the use of *ra'y* (opinion) to perform *ijtihād*. The Prophet (ṣ) is reported to have said, "When I do not receive a revelation I adjudicate among you on the basis of my opinion.[84]

If the Prophet (ṣ) made a mistake, it was corrected through subsequent revelations.[85] Revelation was brought down to the Prophet (ṣ) revealing the messages to give general rules of guidance for issues pertaining to social life during his time and thereafter, ensuring that Muslims could carry out their affairs.[86] However, according to Ash'arīs, Mu'tazilah, Ibn Ḥazm al-Ẓāhirī and some Ḥanbalī and Shāfi'ī scholars the Qur'an provides clear evidence that every utterance of the Prophet (ṣ) partakes of *waḥy*. A specific reference is made to the verse, which provides: "He says nothing of his own desire; it is nothing other than revelation sent down to him" (53:3). This verse is quite categorical on the point that the Prophet (ṣ) is guided by divine revelation and that all his utterances are to be seen in this light. This would mean that all the rulings of the Prophet (ṣ) consist of divine revelations and are not considered to be *ijtihād*.[87]

Another view is that we can not judge the situation of the Prophet (ṣ), owing to the conflicting nature of the evidence.

This view is attributed to Shāfi'ī (d. 204/819) and upheld by Baqillānī (d. 403 AH) and Ghazālī (d. 505/1111). Shawkānī (d. 1250/1834) however rejects this saying that the Qur'an gives us clear indications not only to the effect that *ijtihād* was permissible for the Prophet but also that he was capable of making errors.[88] On the other hand the *'ulamā'* who have supported this view say that such errors were not sustained, meaning that any errors the Prophet might have made were rectified by the Prophet himself or through subsequent revelation.[89] To give an example on this point, the Prophet (ṣ) was blamed in the Qur'an for his errors. In 8:67 we read that "It is not fitting for a Prophet that he should have prisoners (of war) until he has thoroughly subdued the earth" (8:67).

This verse was revealed concerning the captives of the Battle of Badr. It was reported that seventy people were taken prisoner. The Prophet first consulted Abū Bakr asking, what they should do with the prisoners? He suggested that they should be ransomed, whereas 'Umar bin al-Khaṭṭāb held the view that they should be executed. The Prophet approved of Abū Bakr's view but then the verse was revealed, disapproving of taking ransom for the captives' release. Elsewhere, in *sūrah al-tauba* in an address to the Prophet (ṣ), we read: "God granted you pardon, but why did you permit them to do so before it became clear to you who was telling the truth" (9:43)? This verse shows that the Prophet (ṣ) granted a pardon to those who did not participate in the Battle of Tabuk. These passages in the Qur'an indicate that the Prophet had on some occasions acted on his own *ijtihād*; had he acted in pursuance of a divine command there would have been no cause for a reprimand, or the granting of divine pardon for his mistakes.

The subject of whether or not *ijtihād* was used by the Prophet (ṣ) has been, from a very early period, discussed and disagreed upon by the scholars.

Muslim scholars disagree as to whether the Prophet (ṣ) performed *ijtihād* by his personal opinion on issues such as daily maintenance, war and peace rules, rules relating to attack and defence, the solutions of disputes, or juridical and political issues.[90] According to Ibn al-Humām some jurists of the Ḥanafī School have confined the *ijtihād* of the Prophet by *ra'y* to *qiyās* in situations where there was no revelation.[91]

The Prophet performed *ijtihād* by his own *ra'y* on several occasions and he educated the Companions to follow his examples; his instruction of the companions was practical rather than theoretical. The Prophet's (ṣ) practice of *ijtihād by ra'y* provided the example for *qiyās* (analogy), *istiḥsān* (juristic preference), *maṣlaḥah* (consideration of public interest), *sadd al-dharā'ī'* (blocking the means), and *'urf* (customary law).

For example a woman from Juhaynā came to the Prophet (ṣ) and asked: 'My mother vowed to make a pilgrimage, but she died before she could fulfil the vow. Can I do it in her name? The Prophet (ṣ) said: "Yes, fulfil the pilgrimage instead of her; if your mother had a debt, would you not pay it? Pay your debts (fulfil your promises) because God fulfils promises to."[92] Here the Prophet (ṣ) has made a comparison between two similar things: he wanted to show that to fulfil a promise to God is the same as fulfilling a promise made to a human being. This type of analogy is called *awlā'*.[93]

Another example of an analogy is as follows. A nomad tried to reject his ancestors by telling the Prophet (ṣ): 'My wife gave birth to a black baby'. The Prophet (ṣ) asked him "Do you have grey camels among your red ones?" When the nomad said that he did the Prophet (ṣ) asked him "Where did they come from?" The nomad said 'They presumably look like his ancestors.' The Prophet (ṣ) then told him: "Your child presumably also looks like his ancestors."[94]

The Prophet allowed most of the pre-Islamic Arab customs to be preserved, although a few were changed, such as trade, pawn, rent, *salam* (contract of purchase of goods with pre-payment), marriage, the equality between husband and wife and murder cases.[95] When the Prophet (ṣ) came to Madīnah, he saw that the people there had made *salam* (forward sale) agreements for 1 or 2 years. To emphasise this he said: "Anyone who makes *salam* agreements should do this according to specific measurements and for determined periods."[96] This practice, which was common among the Arabs, was practiced freely after a few amendments.[97]

The practices of ijtihād in terms of istiḥsān

Abū al-Ḥasan al-Karkhī (d. 340/952) defines *istiḥsān* as "The principle which authorizes departure from an established ruling to similar cases and authorizes applying an alternative established ruling to cases similar to those which set the precedent." The departure is authorised only when there is enough reason to justify that departure.[98] The departure from a ruling on a certain issue—one that has been applied to a similar case previously—to another ruling, must be based on clear evidence. The evidence which necessitates this departure, as viewed by the jurist, should be established by *naṣṣ*, or *ijmā'* (consensus), *ḍarūrah* (necessity), *'urf* (custom), *maṣlaḥah* (benefit), *qiyās khafīy* (Implicit analogy), or other sources, irrespective of the methods which the earlier, similar ruling depended on, such as *dalīl 'ām* (general evidence), *qā'idah fiqhiyyah* (jurisprudence rule) or *qiyās ẓāhir jaliyy* (apparent clear analogy). This meaning of *istiḥsān* is according to Ḥanafī jurists; other jurists, especially Mālikī scholars, also applied this definition.[99]

Sometimes an issue is included within the range of a settled general rule with the common characteristic of *naṣṣ* or in the light of some evidence. However regarding the issue, another specific evidence is to be found which can be a *naṣṣ, ḍarūrah, 'urf* or *maṣlaḥah* that can be used to judge in opposition to the common *naṣṣ* or the common rule. The *mujtahid* (competent jurist) must be convinced that this specific evidence is to be preferred before abandoning the practice of the common *naṣṣ* or common rule judgements that are used in such issues, and judging according to the specific evidence.

Sometimes when an issue is not within the range of a *naṣṣ*, *qiyās* is then used to judge. Here we come across two different possibilities, apparent clear analogy and implicit analogy. If the *mujtahid* finds that the second one is stronger (*khafī qiyās*) the judgment given accordingly is called *istiḥsān.*[100]

Through *istiḥsān* some issues within the range of common *naṣṣ,* and criteria such as difficulty, complexity, necessity, and need are removed because of their specific nature and a new judgement is given to this special situation to implement *maṣlaḥah.*

If one studies *naṣṣ* from the Qur'an and the *Sunnah,* it is possible to find many examples on this issue. The principle of *istiḥsān* is used to remove the common *naṣṣ* or a settled rule from its area application. The *mujtahid* who applies this principle applies the essence of what the *Shārī'* wants for the people in any given situation or place in order to remove harm or discomfort, and establish *maṣlaḥah.*[101] *Istiḥsān* is in the general sense concerned with the public interest and the *mujtahid* uses his judgement in the context of general rules by proving stronger evidence pertaining to the particular situation. The basis for the *mujtahid's* judgment could be *ḍarūrah* (necessity), *maṣlaḥah, 'urf* (custom), *ijmā'* or the *naṣṣ* of the Qur'an or the *Sunnah.*

When this evidence is *naṣṣ* from the Qur'an or the *Sunnah*, God becomes the one who actually gives this exceptional judgement, the one who makes *istiḥsān*, and it is by His announcement that this *istiḥsān* becomes legal.[102]

As such it is the *Shārī'* who considers the special situations and circumstances with specific conditions, and who abolishes the difficulty, complexity and harm. This provides an ideal guide for the *mujtahid*. On this issue Muṣṭafā Zarqā' says: "The Qur'an and the *Sunnah* are both *istiḥsān*, which is the creation of the *Shārī'*. The concept of *istiḥsān* is to guide the *mujtahid* when applying the *naṣṣ* of the *Shārī'* to issues of life. The *mujtahid* makes *istiḥsān* inspired by the method that the *Shārī'* applies and in this way, the *mujtahid* implements the *Shārī''s* purpose and intentions.[103]

The messenger and the explorer of the Qur'an is the Prophet who applied the method, taught by the Qur'an, from the general *naṣṣ* and established rules to exceptional conditions and circumstances. There are a lot of examples on this issue to be found in the Prophet's *Sunnah*. Before we examine these issues, I shall give a few examples mentioned in the Qur'an:

Verse 4 of the *sūrah an-Nūr* says: "And those who accuse chaste women, and produce not four witnesses, flog them with eighty stripes and reject their testimony forever". As seen in this verse, the accusation of adultery has a more damaging effect on society than the action itself. The 'general sentence' for a man that has seen a woman commit adultery is flogging. However, if the man who sees the woman commit adultery is her husband, then, according to the general sentence, the husband should stay silent or bring forward four witnesses; failure to produce these witnesses will result in his facing the sentence of flogging for *qadhf* (slander, accusation). This sentence obviously causes the husband to suffer. Therefore, in the case of a husband who accuses his wife of committing adultery but is unable to produce four witnesses to substantiate his claim, the court can, according to verse 6 of the same *sūrah* and the following *sūrah*, declare their marriage dissolved and the husband will not be punished for *qadhf*.[104]

According to the general rules, fasting during Ramaḍān is an obligatory duty for every adult Muslim. It is a condition that the Ramaḍān fast should be fulfilled during the month of Ramaḍān with the exception of those who are sick or travelling,

"And whoever is ill or on a journey, the same number—of days which one did not fast must be made up—from other days. God intends for you ease, and He does not want to make things difficult for you" (2:185).

This is prescribed because of the special circumstances; a ruling is passed for difficulties that may arise.[105] If the general sentence of the obligation of fasting applied to the sick and the travellers, such difficulties and sufferings might only delay the healing process or lead to death of the sick. This would be in total contradiction to the *Shārī'*'s general aims, among which are 'to protect human life'.

Among the Prophet's *Sunnah* based on *istiḥsān*, some of the *ijtihād* by *ra'y* practices are these:

The contract known as *salaf* or *salam* (forward sale), is to sell something in return for cash and to show a commitment to deliver it in the future.[106] There are two *naṣṣ* concerning this issue. One is general and concerns the invalidity of the contract. The Prophet told Ḥakīm b. Ḥiẓam: "Do not sell something that you don't own."[107]

The second *naṣṣ* is more specific and concerns the validity of the contract. When the Prophet (ṣ) came to Madīnah, he saw that the people of Madīnah made *salam* (forward sale) for one and two years regarding the fruits of their labour. On this issue, the Prophet (ṣ) said "Those of you who sell goods with *salam* should do this according to stated measurements, scales and time."[108] The reason the Prophet (ṣ) changed his ruling on the permissibility of *salam* contracts was the present needs of the people.[109]

The general sentence for theft in the Qur'an is: "Cut off (from the wrist joint) the (right) hand of the thief, male or female, as a recompense for that which they committed, a punishment by way of example from God" (5:39).

During a war, a man was caught stealing, and was brought to the commander Busr bin Artāī. The commander ordered him to be beaten and not have his hand cut off. He explained: "The Prophet (ṣ) prohibited us from severing hands during wartime."[110] The Prophet (ṣ) did not want the severing of the hand. The general ruling of the *naṣṣ* was leniency shown to the thief therefore lessening the possibility the thief might join the enemy. The thief joining the enemy would cause serious problems; therefore, the leniency was justified.[111] When two problems occur, the lesser of two evils is to be preferred.[112] This principle is taken from the general *naṣṣ* of the *Shārī'*.

During the Battle of Badr, Ḥabāb b. Mundhīr asked the Prophet (ṣ) about the first place picked for the camp: "O, Messenger of God! Is this a place that God has disclosed and we have to accept, or is it a *ra'y* or a war strategy? When the Prophet (ṣ) answered; "No, it is a *ra'y* and a war strategy", Ḥabbāb said; "This is not an appropriate place. I suggest that we set up camp by the water, make ourselves a pond, fill it with water and close all of the other wells. This will deprive the enemy of water." The Prophet (ṣ) accepted Ḥabbāb's suggestion and changed the place.[113] The Prophet (ṣ) by comparing the enemy to other living beings might have made the analogy. "You can't deprive them of water just as you can't deprive these of water." However, Ḥabbāb, considering it was a time of war and that the enemy did not have the right to live, came to a different conclusion.[114] At the end, the opinion that Ḥabbāb suggested was chosen and applied above the others, as it was more likely to further the cause of the Muslims.

The Prophet (ṣ) consulted his friends on the day of the Battle of Khandaq. They discussed coming to an agreement with the Gatafan polytheists, offering them one third of the fruits of Madīnah in exchange for leaving the battlefield. Sa'd bin Mu'adh and Sa'd bin 'Ubādah stood up and said: 'If this is the will of God we will listen and obey God's order. If this is not a revelation but a *ra'y* we will only give them swords, because during 'the age of ignorance', when neither of us had a religion, they could only get the fruits of Madīnah by buying them from us or if we treated them. Now when God has honoured us with His religion, we refuse to offer them anything except disparagement, and we swear that we can only give them our swords'. After this, the Prophet (ṣ) said: "I saw that the Arabs came together to be one against you and I wanted to send them away. You have the right not to accept it, there is no problem"[115] and they insisted on their views.

The examples I have given are *naṣṣ* from the Qur'an and the *Sunnah* and show that in special circumstances, it is one of the *Shārī''s* common goals to remove difficulties and complexities and thus confirm the principles of public need and interest. These rulings show that it is important to note the differences between similar events. One should not always look at events categorically, generally or prescriptively. If there are differences between events, it is necessary to give the ruling on merit. It would be apparently wrong to apply to analogy to events that appear to be in the scope of general rules and then attempt to include it as a general rule when in fact it is an exceptional one. In circumstances like these, the right way is to evaluate events with special features on merit, namely to apply *istiḥsān.*[116]

The Prophet (ṣ) rejected an application to fix the price of goods, as it might be unfair to the seller.[117] However Sa'īd b. al-

Musayyab (d. 94), Rabī'a b. Abī 'Abd al-Raḥmān (d. 136/753) Yaḥyā b. Saī'd al-Anṣārī (d. 147/760) and other jurists made a juridical decision regarding the pricing of goods based on their personal opinions regarding the economic climate of the day.[118] Those scholars believed that an understanding of public interest is crucial in order to protect people from incorrect *aḥkām.*[119]

According to Shaybānī, Ibrahīm al-Nakhā'ī said: "Supposing someone murdered someone else at his front door and alleged that he committed the crime in order to protect his goods and honour. To be able to give a verdict an investigation is carried out. The case may have two possible outcomes. In the first scenario, the law of retaliation is not applied, but the blood-money has to be paid even if the victim is guilty of stealing. However if the victim is known to be a respectable man, then the law of retaliation must come into effect. In the second scenario, the law of retaliation is also dropped, but the blood-money is paid, even if the victim is guilty of adultery and/or fornication. However, the murderer will be prosecuted if the victim is known as a person who is chaste and virtuous."[120] Ibrahīm al-Nakhā'ī gives more consideration to the spirit of the *naṣṣ* rather than the literal meaning, neither rejecting nor applying the law of retaliation based on false testimony but supporting his claims with evidence, thus avoiding incorrect judgements. Nakhā'ī, with this legal opinion, considers nothing other than the public good.[121]

In the view of some Iraqi scholars, the law of retaliation with regard to stolen goods comes into effect only when the value of the goods stolen exceeds a certain amount. For them, this minimum was set at five *dirham* (silver coin), although the generally accepted minimum is usually ten. The minimum value of stolen goods is extrapolated by analogy from the minimum value of the marriage dowry. The Iraqi scholars, however, disagreed saying: "We are surprised that entering into a sexual relationship is allowed by so little an amount." In addition, Ibrahīm al-Nakhā'ī did not take a favourable view of the dowry being less than forty *dirhams* and resorted instead to *istiḥsān* which yielded more useful results than analogy.[122]

At the time of the Companions and the Followers, to be a witness in court for the defence of close relatives—for one's father, say, or one's child—was allowed in accordance with the belief that "everybody's testimony is valid if he is Muslim and righteous".[123] However, with the passage of time and the inevitable weakening of faith which occurred among the Muslim populace as a whole, jurists concluded that this ruling might no longer serve the needs of society, since the possibility of bias and injustice would bring untold harm to the social fabric. They rejected the testimony of relatives in order to prevent corruption and to preserve justice and social harmony. The juristic decision was confined to offspring, fathers, brothers and spouses.[124]

It is a rule of Islamic Law when a woman is widowed that her mourning period should last for four months and ten days, during this which time she should not use *kohl* or perfume. A woman applied to the Prophet (ṣ) asking whether or not her widowed daughter could use *kohl* to aid her painful eyes. In spite of her insistence, the Prophet (ṣ) said "No" three times.[125] However, Imām Mālik (d. 179), Sālim b. 'Abd Allāh (d. 106/724) and Sulaymān b. Yasār (d. 107/725) rule that a woman in such a situation may cure her eyes with *kohl* or another medicine.[126] While there is no possibility that these followers would oppose the saying of the Prophet (ṣ), they considered his prohibition as applying only to that particular woman, as her condition did not necessitate the use of *kohl*. Their judgement was correct, based on their consideration of the avoidance of hardship (*raf' al-ḥarāj*) and the attainment of benefit.[127]

Ijtihād by ra'y of the Companions at the time of the Prophet

At the time of the Prophet (ṣ) there is evidence that the Companions performed *ijtihād* by *ra'y*; these happened in the presence of the Prophet (ṣ) and during his absence.[128] During this time, the concept of *ijtihād* dealt with *adhān* (call to prayer), *ghusl* (ritual ablution of the whole body) and the postponement of the prayer. The Prophet (ṣ) included rulings pertaining to law within the range of *ijtihād.*[129] During the time of revelation and as long as there were no explanations or prohibitions from God, the Companions considered *ijtihād* to be permissible.[130]

When an issue arose and no relevant verses could be found in the Qur'an the Prophet (ṣ) performed *ijtihād* by his *ra'y* (opinion); he authorized the companions to use the same method under the same circumstances.[131] The Companions Mu'adh (d. 18 AH), 'Amr b. al-'Āṣ (d. 65 AH) and 'Uqbah bin 'Āmir (d. 58 AH) performed *ijtihād* in the presence of the Prophet (ṣ).[132]

Examples of this are as follow: During the battle of Dhāt thalāsī 'Amr b. al-'Āṣ was the head of a group of soldiers. During the war he became *junub* (a state requiring a ritual ablution of the whole body). His opinion was that if he washed himself as required the severe cold might kill him; consequently he made *tayammum* (to wash with clean sand or earth where water is unavailable) and led the prayer in front of his friends, saying: 'God says in the Qur'an "Do not kill yourselves". When he returned he recalled this incident to the Prophet (ṣ) and the Prophet (ṣ) approved of it.[133] Because of his fear that the severity of the weather might cause death, 'Amr applied a practice which was permissible when there was no water or when the person was too ill to use water. I agree that 'Amr has implemented a form of *istiḥsān* by taking ease as the basis in accordance with the spirit of the Sharī'ah, but contrary to the general rule.

When 'Alī was a *qāḍī* (Muslim judge) in Yemen he gave a ruling with *ijtihād* by *ra'y*. Three men had intercourse with the same woman over a certain period of time, the result of which was that, the woman gave birth to a child. 'Alī asked the men to draw straws whoever drew the short straw would have the child acknowledged as his, and would pay two *diyah* (monetary compensation of blood) to the other two men. When this incident was narrated to the Prophet (ṣ), he acknowledged it.[134] Muḥammad bin Ḥasan al-Ḥajawī (d. 1956), evaluates this ruling during the Prophet's (ṣ) lifetime as a form of *istiḥsān*.[135] If this or any similar issues arose today modern technology would be the vehicle used to confirm paternity, therefore using technology can be a method of *istiḥsān* which is based on *maṣlaḥah*.

During the Prophet's (ṣ) lifetime *ijtihād* was performed either by the Prophet (ṣ) or, with the permission of the Prophet (ṣ), the companions, who were responsible for the concept of *ijtihād*. Performing *ijtihād* in this period was under the control of the *Shārī'*. Accordingly, personal judgment and human contributions were integrated into the life of Islamic law. This integration into the revelation is not regarded as strange. The corner stone, which is the *maqāṣid al-Shārī'* (objectives of the Lawgiver), has to be taken into consideration when performing *ijtihād*.

Ijtihād at the time of Companions

It is difficult to distinguish between the Prophet's (ṣ) lifetime and the beginning of the era of the Companions. Basically we have the period of the Companions (11-40/632-660); the period of the Successors (40-120/660-738); the period of the Successors of the Successors; and the *mujtahid* imāms (120-160/738-777). An alternative break down would be political, the Companions' period occurs during the Rāshidīn caliphate, the Followers period would be during the Umayyad dynasty (40-132/660-750); and the last period spans both the Umayyad and 'Abbāsīds dynasty.[136]

After the time of the Prophet the Muslims invaded other countries with the intention to convince them to embrace the Islamic way of life. The borderlines of the Islamic countries stretched from Iran to Central Asia in the east, to Syria in the north, to Egypt in the west and later to other North African countries. These were the first contacts and relationships sprung up between the nations and the Muslims who settled there. Consequently, Madīnah and the surrounding areas were populated by foreigners. Muslims visited Makkah for *ḥajj* (pilgrimage) and umrah.[137] All these factors created mutual influences between Arabs and the visitors in every aspect of life. The traditions and customs of the people of Iran and Byzantium became mixed with those of the 'Arab Muslims', and the Islamic norm and systems of law based on the Qur'an and the *Sunnah* were challenged.[138]

When Muslims became aware of the events and traditions of the cities they visited, they recognised the values and the wisdoms to incorporate them into the Islamic law. This was the beginning of new developments within *fiqh* (Islamic law).[139]

Concept of ra'y at the time of Companions

The Companions from time to time used the name *ra'y* and, according to Shāfi'ī, *qiyās* and *ijtihād* have the same meaning.[140] Most of the *Shāfi'īs* have adopted their *imām's* view.[141] Al-Isnawī (d. 772/1310), alleges that *ijmā'* and *ra'y* are *qiyās*.[142] Muḥammad Khudari (d. 1927) defends the view that the Companions used *qiyās* as a reference for new issues where no *naṣṣ* was evident, and called this *ra'y*.[143]

Most of the jurists are of the view that the *ra'y* that the Companions employed was more extensive than *qiyās*, but was an *ijtihād* that also included *qiyās*. When a Ḥanafī jurist 'Abd al-'Azīz al-Bukhārī (d. 730/1330) was answering the objections to the *ḥadīth* of Mu'adh he made this statement: 'I'm making *ijtihād* according to the *ra'y* of Mu'adh. The Prophet (ṣ) confirmed this through his silence. The reason for his silence was that he knew that *ijtihād* was sufficient for all rulings. If *ijtihād* was confined only to a *qiyās* with a known reason it would not be sufficient for even one in a hundred rulings. A prime example is the exchange between the Prophet and Mu'adh. When Mu'adh replied, "I act by the Book and the *Sunnah*", the Prophet (ṣ) asked: "And then with what!"".[144] Consequently, *ra'y* is a general term that includes analogy and other inferences. At that time, *ra'y* included an explanation of the *naṣṣ*, and a comparison of similar cases, which in time led to the establishment of methods of inference such as *istiḥsān, maṣlaḥah* (benefit), *'urf* (custom) and *sadd al-dharā'ī'* (blocking the means).[145]

Analogy among the Companions

During the time of the Companions, methods of *ijtihād* had not yet been codified. *Ra'y* is the given name for the rulings found through *ijtihād* for issues where *naṣṣ* could not be found. Analogy came under the name of 'understanding' (*fahm*), *ra'y* or *ijtihād*.[146] There were of course principles that they regarded when they made *ijtihād*. One example is as follows: 'Umar wrote a letter to Abū Mūsā al-Ash'arī (d. 44 AH) whom he had appointed as *qāḍī* to Basra: "On cases where you are not satisfied, you should think very carefully. Research them and try to find the similarities between two things. When you find similarities that effect the rulings then apply the method of analogy."[147] These words conveyed the fact that he wanted Abū Mūsā to use analogy. Jaṣṣāṣ

(d. 370) says the first generations used the same method, making analogies to establish rulings.[148]

When the Companions chose Abū Bakr to be caliph they said: "Just as the Prophet (ṣ) chose him to be prayer leader, why do we not choose him to be political leader?"[149] Thus the Companions made an analogy between the Prophet's (ṣ) choice of Abū Bakr as *imām* and their election of him as Caliph.

'Umar was told: "Samrā' took wine from Jewish merchants as a tithe (*'ushr*)"[150] from which vinegar was made and sold', 'Umar replied: 'God will give Samrā' what he deserves. Does he not know that the Prophet says: 'God has damned the Jews because, despite it being forbidden, they took the inner fat of animals, changed its appearance, sold it and spent the money."[151] In this incident, 'Umar makes an analogy between the prohibited fat of animals and wine. In both cases, the prohibition includes the selling and spending of the money.[152]

Istiḥsān among the Companions

Even though the term *istiḥsān* had not been used in the technical sense before the Iraqi school, it existed in practice during the time of the Companions and was widely applied.[153] An allusion to the kind of *istiḥsān* that existed in the periods following the Companions can be found in the letter that 'Umar wrote to Abū Mūsā al-Ash'arī: "...Research similar cases and when you find similarities that effect the ruling, apply the method of analogy. Using the results of the analogy select the ruling that adheres to the Islamic principles and ensures your conscience is satisfied that justice has been served."[154] According to the first part of his sentence, 'Umar wanted the analogy applied as soon as the similarities are found and the result is deemed just. However, in the second part of his sentence he says that if this is not possible then a ruling that is in accordance with the basic principles of justice and equity should be given. In other words, if the analogy is not in keeping with the spirit of the Sharī'ah, then the ruling of similarities should be abandoned in order to give a ruling according to the special evidence that is justice and equity (*istiḥsān*).[155]

Some examples of *istiḥsān* as applied by the Companions:

1. Muslim men are allowed to marry women from among the people of the Book (Christian and Jewish women), as stated in the Qur'an (5:6). 'Umar (d. 23 AH) accepts this in principle, but he prohibited it because he believed it would be detrimental to Muslim women.[156] In this example, we see conformity to *maṣlaḥah*, together with the principle of understanding and applying verses and *ḥadīth* by considering all the *naṣṣ*. 'Umar has given a ruling that is in opposition to the general ruling of the *naṣṣ* in this special situation, according to the objective and spirit of the Sharī'ah.[157]

2. According to the general ruling of *naṣṣ* those who inherit through *'aṣabah* (agnates) inherit what remains when those who are entitled (*ashḥābi furūḍ*) have first received their shares. If nothing remains then they will be deprived of an inheritance.[158] In one particular case 'Umar acted according to the general basic rule;[159] the wife, the mother, siblings from the same maternal mother but from a different father, full brothers and half brothers from *'aṣabah* all acted according to its basic rule. Full brothers share by virtue of having the same mother. It is called "shared" (*mushtarik*) because the brothers share in the third, and is every question in which there is a husband and mother or grandmother, and two or more of the mother's offspring, and *'aṣabah* in the form of full siblings. This is also known as the *ḥimāriyyah* case. That is because the case was presented to 'Umar, and he wanted to judge the

exclusion of the full brothers. Despite they are full brothers of *'aṣabah, they* were not entitled for the share. The full brothers objected to this judgment and said, "Consider if our father was a donkey (*ḥimār*), do we not have the same mother?" So 'Umar studied the case again and judged a third for all of them equally, full and uterine siblings, the portion of the man the same as the portion of the female.[160]

In this matter the full brothers should, according to the general ruling of the *naṣṣ,* be deprived of inheritance as mentioned above. However, when 'Umar understood that this was not in accordance with the general objective and spirit of the Sharī'ah, and did not accord with justice and equity, he changed his opinion and gave sentence in accordance with the principle of *istiḥsān.*

3. The general ruling of Islām regarding conquered land and war booty is that it should be divided between the war veterans:

"And know that whatever of war booty that you may gain, verily one fifth of it is assigned to God, and to the Messenger, (Muḥammad), (and also) the orphans, the poor who beg and the wayfarer, if you have believed in God and in that which We sent down to Our slave (Muḥammad) on the Day of criterion (between right and wrong), the Day when the two forces met (the battle of *Badr*) and God is able to do all things" (8:41). "And what God gave as booty to his Messenger (Muḥammad) from them, for which you made no expedition with either cavalry or camelry." "What God gave as booty to His Messenger (Muḥammad) from the people of the townships, it is for God, His Messenger (Muḥammad), the kindred (of Messenger Muḥammad), the orphans, the poor who beg, and the wayfarer, in order that it may not become a fortune used by the rich among you" (59:6-7).

Nevertheless, this general ruling was not applied to the conquest of Iraq and Syria during the time of 'Umar. On the contrary, 'Umar thought that it would be more convenient to make this land the common property of Muslims. The land was to be left in the hands of its owners and taxes would be levied which would be used to pay the wages of judges, officials and soldiers. The taxes would also be used to help widows, orphans and those in need; in this 'Umar was forward thinking, believing that these taxes would be for the benefit of future generations.[161] In this example of *ijtihād* 'Umar has abandoned the general ruling and adopted a ruling that would implement the *maṣlaḥah* for the future of the Muslims.[162]

4. A women from Ṣanā' plotted with her lover to kill her husband. The incident was reported to 'Umar by the governor of the city, Yā'lā bin 'Umayyah. 'Umar's view was the same as the general ruling of the *naṣṣ* namely that two people should not be executed for the killing of one. 'Alī defended the judgement to have them both executed in accordance with the spirit of the law of retaliation. Eventually 'Umar was persuaded and wrote to Yā'lā: 'Execute them both. If, by any chance, the whole city of Ṣanā' were involved in this murder I would have had them all killed.'".[163] By this example of *ijtihād* 'Umar and 'Alī have given a ruling that is not in accordance with the Qur'anic verses which deal with of equity in punishment:

"O you who believe! *Al-qiṣāṣ* (the law of equality in punishment) is prescribed for you in the case of a murder: the free for the free, the slave for the slave, and the female for the female. But if the relatives (or one of them) of the murdered (person) forgive their brother (the killer) something (i.e. not to kill the killer by accepting the blood-money in intentional murders), then the relatives (of the victim) should demand blood money in a reasonable manner, and the killer must pay with handsome, gratitude. This is alleviation and a mercy from your Lord. So after this whoever transgresses the limits he shall have a painful torment (2:178), "And We ordained therein for them: Life for life, eye for eye, nose for nose, ear for ear, tooth for tooth, and wounds equal for equal" (5:45).

'Umar considered this in the beginning and was why he didn't want to apply the *qiṣāṣ* (retaliation) punishment. However with 'Alī's contribution, the incident was studied in greater detail, which led to the view that the punishment of *qiṣāṣ* should be applied in keeping with the demands of *maṣlaḥah*, and the goal and spirit of the *shar'īah*. The basis of *qiṣāṣ* is to implement justice and prevent further injustice. In this way if *istiḥsān* had not been applied to this case, then justice would not have been implemented and it would have opened the door for people with evil intentions.[164]

As seen the *ijtihād* of the Companions is covered by the term *istiḥsān*: in all of these examples the rule of law is changed when conditions change and a fresh situation emerges.[165] The Companions, when performing their *ijtihād,* have not acted in accordance with the given rules; instead, they have acted according to their own initiatives and principles, in keeping with the demands of *maṣlaḥah* and the removal of harm.[166]

Consequently, as has been indicated, the work of *ijtihād* never stops; it continues progressively.

Thus we see that the Companions actually practiced *ijtihād*. Their method of *ijtihād* was mostly based on the *shūrah* (consultation), with there being no written juristic principles on which to base their rulings. In this period, the *mujtahid* (competent jurists) and the *muqallid* (the close and faithful followers of established rules) are indistinguishable from each other. *Ijtihād* was not restricted to any one individual or school of thought. Where *naṣṣ* was silent or not clearly identified, the Companions applied their personal opinions, and anyone had the liberty to perform *ijtihād*.[167]

Ijtihād at the time of the Successors and after

The Successors and the Successors of the Successors were the generation following the Companions. They also used *ra'y* in cases where *naṣṣ* was silent.

The term *ra'y* was not limited to *qiyās* (analogy) during the period of the Companions; it also meant to understand and comment on the *naṣṣ*. One of the Successors of the Successors, 'Abd Allah b. Mubārak (d. 181/797) said: "So long as it does not contradict it, use your personal opinion to interpret the *ḥadīth*."[168] This emphasizes the role of *ra'y* in commenting on the *naṣṣ* and the objectives of the Sharī'ah.

Ra'y is also used in areas where there is no *naṣṣ*. When *Ḥasan* al-Baṣrī (d. 110/728) was asked if the *fatwās* he uttered were rulings based on *ḥadīth* or based on his *ra'y*?, he answered: "All the *fatwās* I utter are based on the narrations of *ḥadīth*, however our *ra'y* is more beneficial to them than their own *ra'y*."[169] It is possible to understand that the Successors used *ra'y* in the way the Companions understood and applied it. It is understood that they used *ra'y* to understand the *naṣṣ*. They also used other forms of *ra'y* such as *qiyās*, *istiḥsān*, and *maṣlaḥah* where there was no *naṣṣ*.[170]

To the end of the period of the Successors, *ra'y* was used particularly in the areas of belief, regarding 'the superstitious beliefs of foreigners' [171] and in the areas of *fiqh* to define *qiyās*. In the *Ṭabaqāṭ* of Abū Isḥāq Ibrāhīm al-Shīrāzī (d. 476/1083), first, he was with those who applied *ḥadīth*, later he was with those who applied *ra'y*; *ra'y* is the *qiyās* of Abū Ḥanīfah (d. 150/767); by this he meant *ra'y* is the last meaning.[172]

We can see the practice of *ijtihād* by *ra'y* at the time of the Successors and after them. The jurists among the Successors, as their predecessors the Companions did, used *ijtihād* by *ra'y* to give a ruling only when they could not find a ruling in the Book, the *Sunnah* and the *fatwā* of the Companions.[173] The use of this method can clearly be seen in the letter that 'Umar wrote to *Qāḍī* Shurāyḥ[174] and in Shā'bī (d. 103/712) answer to the question: "When giving a ruling in court there are three principles: the *Sunnah* followed by *ra'y* and then *ijtihād*".[175] The *ra'y* they used included methods such as *qiyās, istiḥsān, maṣlaḥah,* and *'urf.*[176] Even though methods were unnamed they were used widely and were in accordance with the spirit, meaning and efficiency of the *shar'īah.*[177] In their *ijtihād* they observed the changing of social conditions, the needs of people and their *maṣlaḥah.*[178] Muḥammad Khudarī describes the way the Companions and the Successors used *ra'y*: "When the Companions and the Successors could not find a *naṣṣ* in the Book of God or in the *Sunnah* of the Prophet (ṣ) they used a method they would eventually call *ra'y*. They practiced *ra'y* based on the general rules of the religion such as "Removing harm"[179] and "Abandoning that which is doubtful".[180]

Khudarī goes on to say:

"The experts of *ra'y* and *qiyās* consider the meaning and the true nature of the ruling of the *Shārī'*. According to them the *shar'īah* has general rules which the Qur'an states and the *Sunnah* confirms. Accordingly there are principles which were taken from the Book and the *Sunnah* belonging to every part of *fiqh* and where there is no *naṣṣ* on a certain case, jurists still attempt to produce a ruling. Their attitudes toward the *Sunnah* were such that so long as they were satisfied that a *ḥadīth* did not contradict the main principles, they would use it as the basis of *istiḥsān*.

Amongst the predecessors of those who made *istiḥsān* with this *qiyās* are 'Umar who was among the Companions in the first period; in the second period there was Ibn 'Abbās (d. 68) and later Ibrahīm al-Nakhā'ī (d. 95) who was among the Successors".[181]

Ḥammād b. Abū Sulaymān (d. 120/738), the *muftī* of Kūfa and one of Nakhā'ī's better students, was an authority in *fiqh;* he was also the teacher of Abū Ḥanīfah who followed in the footsteps of his teacher in *ijtihād* by *ra'y*. Ḥammād was the bridge between Nakhā'ī and Abū Ḥanīfah. The knowledge he acquired from his teacher he passed to his student particularly on the importance of thorough research when faced with complex cases, the goals of *Shār'ī*, and interpretations of the Qur'an and *ḥadīth*.[182]

Zayd b. 'Alī (d. 122/740), and his contemporary Abū Ḥanīfah used *ijtihād* by *ra'y* to understand and comment on *naṣṣ*, and where there was no *naṣṣ*, methods such as *qiyās* and *istiḥsān* were implemented.[183] For example, when a pregnant woman dies, but the child in her womb is still alive, then a caesarean section is performed in order to save the baby, because God prescribes: "The one who saves one's life is seen as have saved all human beings" (5:32). In this *ijtihād* of Imām Zayd, a meaning of *istiḥsān* based on *maṣlaḥah* and need can be seen. Abū Ḥanīfah gave the same *fatwā* in similar cases.

Another contemporary of Abū Ḥanīfah is Ibn Abī Laylā (d. 148/765) a *faqīh* who based his opinions on *ijtihād* by *ra'y* when giving fatwa.[184] The Ḥanafī jurist Abū Zayd al-Dabbūsī (d. 430/1039) is one of the first of those who laid out the differences, based on *ijtihād*, between Abū Ḥanīfah, his followers and Ibn Abī Laylā. Amongst the *ijtihād* by *ra'y* methods that Ibn Abī Laylā' uses are *qiyās, istiḥsān, 'urf, sadd al-dharā'ī'*, and *istiṣḥab*.[185] Sarakhsī records that Ibn Abī Laylā practiced 'rational *qiyās*' which is a kind of *istiḥsān*. This practice was abandoned because of some of the practices of the Companions. Ibn Abī Laylā uses this method in the case of terminally ill men who divorced their wives to deprive them of their inheritance. According to 'rational *qiyās*' the husband's intentions were deemed to be vindictive and their wives were permitted to inherit on the understanding that they would not re-marry.[186] Ibn Abī Laylā has applied this *istiḥsān* based on *'urf.*[187]

Was it Ibn Abī Laylā himself who called *istiḥsān* the 'abandoning of *qiyās*' he himself preserving to have his rulings on *'urf* and the utterances of the Companions, or was it the Ḥanafī jurists who came after him who called *istiḥsān* Ibn Abī Laylā's *ijtihād*'? There is no doubt that *istiḥsān* was Ibn Abī Laylā's *ijtihād.*[188] However, the method that the Ḥanafīs called *istiḥsān* is something that Ibn Abī Laylā practiced in his *ijtihād.* Another contemporary of Abū Ḥanīfah, 'Abd Allah b. al-Muqaffā'[189](d. 139/756) was also well known for his opinion on *ra'y, qiyās* and *istiḥsān.* Ibn al-Muqaffā' notes that *qiyās* might cause discrepancies between rulings, and commented on how *qiyās* should be practised.

As Schacht (d. 1969) indicates, the personal use of *ra'y* and *istiḥsān* can achieve unwanted results of *qiyās.*[190] According to Ibn al-Muqaffā', *qiyās* should be practised as long as it leads to *maṣlaḥah*, and applied if a positive result is achieved; however, if the result is negative then *qiyās* should be abandoned and the case with legal evidence should be used.[191]

There are parallels between the thoughts of Ibn al-Muqaffā' and Abū Ḥanīfah, who both abandoned *qiyās* for *istiḥsān.* However, it is not apparent whether there has been interaction between these two, although it can be said that Ibn al-Muqaffā' shares similar thoughts to those of Abū Ḥanīfah, who became known for his teachings on *qiyās* and *istiḥsān.*[192]

Conclusion

The source of law in the first period was the Qur'an and the *Sunnah.* The growth of the Muslim society engendered different social issues and problems, which meant that the established law based on the Qur'an and the *Sunnah* needed to be re-considered, expanded and re-interpreted to give adequate answers to new questions. As a result, Islamic law made improvements according to the circumstances of the era, and this practice is ongoing.

The independent re-considering and interpretation of the law was known as *ijtihād.* Personal opinion (*ra'y*) was the main element in *ijtihād* and become widespread, gradually paving the way for the development of *qiyās* (analogy) and *istiḥsān.*[193]

For many years, it was the belief that only those with outstanding intellectual ability could be involved in the process of rational rule-making. The Qur'an strongly encourages people to contemplate every single Qur'anic verse, and then use their intellect and personal opinions on the legal issues.[194] The Prophet is a good example, for he always considered the opinions of the Companions on issues where the *naṣṣ* was silent.[195]

The problems faced by the Muslim community during the period of the Prophet Muḥammad were easily and effectively solved, as he was the supreme authority to make comment on the verses and explain them to the people. Following the death of the Prophet (ṣ), the problems increased and were of a more complex nature. The Companions had the Qur'an and the *Sunnah* to decide on the new obstacles stemming from the social life.[196] They also needed to use their own opinion to decide upon which verse or *ḥadīth* could be applied to a case. Thus, the Companions employed their own opinion not only to understand the verses correctly and apply them to new problems, but also to achieve a solution for the more problematic cases on which no verses were directly available. The most striking example of this could be seen from the interpretation of 'Umar, the second caliph: his abrogation of the share from the *zakāh* given for *muallafah al-qulūb* (conciliation of hearts) can be seen as an example of this.[197] Although, this practice apparently seems to be conflicting with the holy Qur'an, 'Umar considered the practical conditions along with the spirit of the holy Qur'an for his judgment. He decided upon this matter by assuming that if the Prophet (ṣ) were still alive, he would also seek the solution in the same manner.[198] The land of Iraq and Syria was not distributed among the Companions; rather, it was left to the original owners who were forced to pay taxes, which were used where required.[199] This appears to be in opposition to the traditional applications and rules in which the land is confiscated and shared along with other properties obtained through war. However, 'Umar preferred the common benefits of the community to those of the individual. Social justice necessitated that those lands should not be shared amongst the soldiers. This outstanding example symbolizes the fact that the general rules can be ignored for the sake of the supreme interest of society. This is known as *istiḥsān* in Islamic law.[200]

As can be seen, the opinion of the Companions appeared to be another type of *istiḥsān*. This unique method was often preferred over the common practice, general rules and obvious analogy, especially where the justice, equality and the benefit to the society were concerned. *Istiḥsān* is preferable to an established ruling in a certain scenario or a decision based on absolute reasoning rather than on analogical reasoning. A jurist may have to abandon a compulsory decision and, in fact, relies upon the person's sagacity to differentiate whether a rule should be applied or otherwise. *Istiḥsān* is not an arbitrary, despotic or capricious personal opinion; rather it is the way of making a proper decision by considering the specific nature of the individual cases.[201]

The Successors of the Companions and the Successors of the Successors also used their own opinions widely to solve the problems through resorting to *istiḥsān*. However, during this period two different approaches emerged: one of them prioritized the *ḥadīth;* the other employed the scholars' opinions (*ra'y*). Aḥmad Ḥasan has claimed that these two groups—the *ahl al-ḥadīth* (the traditionalist group) and *ahl al-ra'y* (the rationalist group) did not regard their own approaches as the only methods. This is due to the fact that the *ḥadīth* scholars of that period also used their opinions alongside the *ḥadīth* for their juristic inference, while the *ahl al-ra'y* scholars often prioritized *ḥadīth*.[202] This is because Muslim jurists were committed to reinterpreting the verses in the light of the current needs of society.

Although analogy (*qiyās*) may be regarded as one form of *ra'y*, there is a difference between them. *Ra'y* is flexible and dynamic in nature and the cases are decided upon in the light of the spirit, justice and the wisdom of Islam.[203] Ibn al-Qayyim states that *ra'y* is the decision of a scholar to find the right solution after making a sincere research where the evidence conflicts.[204] In other words, the person who uses *ra'y* trusts that he is making the same kind of decision on a case that the Prophet (ṣ) would have made were he still alive.[205] Analogy is the comparison of two different cases to obtain a solution for the new case. The scope of *qiyās* is narrower than that of *ra'y*, while the emphasis in *ra'y* is on the current situation or the specific conditions of the problem; the emphasis in *qiyās* is on the intangible (abstract) similarities. As stated by Ibn al-Muqaffā, results may not be satisfying in *qiyās* due to the narrowness of its coverage.[206] As can be seen from the time of the Companions and the Successors, the decision is reached through *istiḥsān* by focusing on common interests and consideration of justice. On the other hand, especially in the Iraqi schools, *qiyās* was practiced in a more comprehensive way by hiding the meaning of *ra'y*.[207]

In later years, the scholars of Iraq narrowed the scope of *qiyās* by developing *istiḥsān*, which was a new method in the coverage of *qiyās*.[208] The main reason for this was to avoid the inconsistency in *qiyās*.

Like the Companions, Muslim jurists produced many new legal rulings regarding the current problems of the society. They justified their decisions on the grounds that the new cases must be tackled by considering new conditions and situations.[209] Sometimes they found that it was satisfactory to act according to absolute verses by taking into consideration the general interest and benefit (*maṣlaḥah*) of the society. They were prepared to apply those decisions which were much more in harmony with society's requirements.[210]

Notes

1. Joseph Schacht, "*An Introduction to Islamic Law*", (Oxford: Clarendom Press, 1964), p. 212; See also Sawa Pāshā, "*Islam Hukuku Nazariyatı*", trans. by Baha Arıkan, (Ankara: 1965), vol. 2, p. 354.
2. Muḥammad Muṣṭafā Shalabī, "*Uṣūl al-Fiqh al-Islāmī*", (Beirut: 1986), p. 258.
3. Ibn Manẓūr, Jamāl al-Dīn Muḥammad ibn Mukarram al-Anṣārī (d. 711/1311), "*Lisān al-'Arab*", (Cairo, Mansūrah: Ṭaba'ah Bulāq), vol. 14, pp. 291, 295, 297, 299; Ibn al-Qayyīm Muḥammad b. Abū Bakr b. Ayyūb b. Sa'd Shams al-Dīn Dimishqī (d. 751/1350), "*I'lām al-Muwaqqi'īn min Rabb al-'Ālamīn*", edt. 'Abd al-Raḥmān al-Wakil, (Cairo: n.d.), vol. 1, p. 113.
4. Ibn Manẓūr, ibid., vol. 14, pp. 300-1
5. Ibn al-Qayyīm, "*I'lām*", vol. 1, p. 113.

6. Rāghib Iṣfahānī, Abū Qāsim Ḥusayin (d. 502/1108), "*Mufradāt fī Gharibi Qur'an*", edt. Muḥammad Ḥusayin Kaylānī, (Beirut: Dār al-Ma'rifah), pp. 208-9.

7. Āmidī, "*Iḥkām*", vol. 4, pp. 398-399; Ibn al-Qayyīm, "*I'lām*", vol. 1, pp. 257-261; Bazdawī, 'Alī bin Muḥammād bin 'Abd al-Karīm Abū al-Ḥasan Fakhr al-Islām al-Bazdawī al-Ḥanafī (482/1089), "*Uṣūl al-Bazdawī on the margin of 'Abd al-'Azīz al-Bukhārī Khashf al-Asrār*", (Beirut: Dār al-Kitāb al-'Arabi, reprint 1394/1974), (Istanbul: 1308), vol. 2, p. 205.

8. Ibn Khaldūn 'Abd al-Raḥmān bin Muḥammad (d. 808/1405), "*Muqaddimah*", edt. 'Alī Abd al-Wāḥid Wāfī, (Cairo: Naḥḍat al-Miṣr, n.d.), vol. 3, pp. 1061-2.

9. Ibn Ḥazm Abū Muḥammad 'Alī al-Andalūsī al-Ẓāhirī (d. 456/1064), "*Mulakhkhaṣ ibṭāl al-Qiyās wa al-Ra'y wa al-Istiḥsān wa al-Taqlīd wa al-Ta'līl*", edt. Saīd al-Afghānī (Dimishq: Maṭba'ah al-Jāmi'at al-Dimishq, 1960), p. 4.

10. Bashīr Idrīs Jum'ah, "*Al-Ra'y wa Atharuh fī al-Fiqh al-Islāmī*", p. 24.

11. Muslim, Abū al-Ḥusyn Muslim bin Ḥajjāj (d. 261/874), "*Al-Jāmi' al-Ṣaḥīḥ*", (Istanbul: 1981), p. 140.

12. Abū Dāwūd, "*Sunnan*", vol. 3, no. 3585, p. 1019; Ibn 'Abd al-Bār, 'Umar Yūsuf (d: 463/1071), "*Jāmi' Bayān al-'Ilm*", edt. Muḥammad 'Abd al-Qādir Aṭā, (Beirut: Mu'assasat Kutub al-Saqafiyyah, 1997), vol. 2, pp. 275-6.

13. Bashīr Idrīs Jum'ah "*Al-Ra'y wa Asaruh fī Fiqh al-Islāmī*", (Cairo: n.d.), p. 10.

14. Shāfī'ī Imām Abī 'Abd Allah Muḥammad bin Idrīs (d. 204/819), "*Jimā' al-'Ilm*", edt, Muḥammad Aḥmad 'Abd al-'Azīz, (Beirut: Dār al-Kutub al-'Ilmīyyah, n.d.), pp. 51-2.

15. Ghazālī, "*Al-Mustaṣfā*", vol. 2, p. 255.

16. Khallāf, 'Abd al-Wahhāb (d. 1376/1956), "*Maṣāder al-Tashrī' al-Islāmī fī mā lā Naṣṣah fīhī*", (Kuwait: Dār al-Qalam li al-Nashr wa al-Tawḍī', 1993), p. 8; Shalabī Muḥammad Muṣṭafā, "*Al-Madkhal fi al-Tā'rīfi al-Fiqh al-Islāmī*", (Beirut: Dār an-Nahḍat al-'Arabiyyah, 1985), p.108; Abū Zahrah, Muḥammad (d. 1395/1974), "*Tarīkh Mazāhib al-Islāmiyyah*", (Beirut: Dār al-Fiqr al-Arabi, n.d.), p. 244.

17. Sarakhsī, "*Uṣūl*", vol. 2, p. 106.

18. Khallaf, "*Maṣāder* ", p. 7.

19. Shawkānī, "*Irshād*", p. 202.

20. Kalālah are those who inherit from the deceased who dies leaving neither ascendants nor descendants.

21. Ibn al-Qayyīm, "*I'lām*", vol. 1, p. 122; Fathī Dīrīnī, "*Al-Manāhij al-Uṣūlīyyah fī al-Ijtihād bi al-Ra'y fī al-Tashrī' al-Islāmī*", (Dimishq: al-Sharikat al-Muttaḥidah, 1985), pp. 12-14.

22. Sha'bān, "*İslam Hukuk İlminin Esasları*", p. 373; Khallāf, "*Ilm*", p. 257.

23. Muḥammas Sallām Madkūr, "*Al-Ijtihād fī al-Tashrī' al-Islāmī*", (Cairo: Dār al-Nahḍat al-'Arabiyya, 1984), pp. 40-41. For more information see Bashīr Idrīs Jum'ah, "*Al-Ra'y wa Asaruh fī al-Fiqh al-Islāmī*", pp. 16-18.

24. Ibn 'Abd al-Bār, "*Jāmi' al-Bayān*", pp.248, 276-7, 362-369; Ibn al-Qayyīm, "*I'lām*", vol. 1, pp. 87-99, 104-106, 111-114, 119-126, 270-279; Ḥatīp, Abū Bakr Aḥmad bin 'Alī al-Baghdādī (d: 463/1071), "*Al-Faqīh wa al-Mutafaqqih*", (Makkah: 1975), vol.1, p. 179-186, 200.

25. Ibn al-Qayyīm, "*I'lām*", vol. 1, p. 103.

26. Ibn al-Qayyīm, "*Ighāsat al-Lahfān min Masāyid al-Shayṭān*", edt. Majdī Fathī al-Sayyīd, (Cairo: 1310), vol. 1, p. 334; and "*I'lām*", vol. 1, pp. 118-125.

27. Ibn al-Qayyīm "*I'lām*", vol. 1, p. 104.

28. Ibn al-Qayyīm, "*Ighāsat al-Lahfān*", vol. 1, p. 334.

29. Ibn al-Qayyīm, "*I'lām*", vol. 1, pp. 105-106.

30. Ibid., pp.103-104.

31. Yūsuf al-Qaradāwī, "*Islam Hukuku Evrensellik Süreklilik*", trans. by Yusuf Işıcık, Aḥmet Yaman, (İstanbul: Marifet, Ekim, 1999), p. 12.

32. Ḥayreddin Karaman, "*Islam Hukukunda İctihād*", (İstanbul: MUIFV, 1996), p. 29. For further details on ijtihād see. Maudūdī, Abū al-'Alā' "*Islamic Law and Constitution*", trans. by Khurshid Aḥmad, (Lahore: Islamic publications ltd, 1960), pp. 79-96.

33. Qarafī, "*Tanqīh*", 4th chapter of ijmā', quoted from Ibn Āshūr, "*Maqāsid al-Sharī'ah*", pp. 197-198.

34. Shāfi'ī, "*Al-Risālah*", p. 368.

35. Shāfi'ī, "*Al-Ūmm*", vol. 7, p. 272.

36. Abū Dāwūd, "*Sunan*", ḥadīth no. 3567, vol. 3, p. 1013; Bukhārī "*Saḥīḥ*", vol. 8, p. 157.

37. Abū Dāwūd, ḥadīth no. 3585, vol. 3, p. 1019

38. Shafi'ī, "*Al-Risālah*", pp. 81, 368.

39. Ibid., 368; Shafi'ī "*Al-Ūmm*", vol. 3, pp. 85, 278.

40. Sayyid 'Afīfī, "*Uṣūl al-Tashrī'*", vol. 9, p. 344.
41. Fazlur Rahman, "*Islam and Modernity*", (Chicago: The University of Chicago, 1982), p. 13.
42. Ibid., p. 5.
43. Fazlur Raḥmān, "*Islām ve Çağdaşlık*" pp. 73-76, 95; Ḥayreddin Karaman, "*Modernist Proje ve İjtihād*", in (Maqāṣıd ve İjtihād, Ahmed Yaman), p. 433.
44. Fazlur Rahman, "*Islami Çağdaşlaşma*", in Islamic research magazine, p. 318.
45. Shahristānī, Abu al-Fatḥ Muḥammad b. 'Abd al-Karīm b. Abū Bakr (d. 548/1153), "*Al-Milal wa al-Niḥal*", edt. Muḥammad Sayyid Kaylānī, (Cairo: 1976), vol. 1, p. 348.
46. 'Abd al-Ḥay Ibn al-Ṣiddīq, "*Naqdu Maqāl fī Masāilah min 'Ilm al-Ḥadīth wa al-Fiqh wa Uṣūlih wa Tafḍīlih Baghḍ al-Mazāhib*", (Maghrib: 1988), p. 100.
47. Abū Dāwūd, Ḥadīth no. 3585, vol. 3, p. 1019
48. Tabarānī, Sulaymān b. Aḥmad (d. 360/971), "*Al-Mu'jam al-Saghīr wa al-Mū'jam al-Awsāt*", (Beirut: M. Shakūr Maḥmūd al-Ḥajj Amīr, 1985), Narated by Tabarānī in al-Awṣat. See in "*Mujmā' al-Zawā' id*", vol. 1, p. 178.
49. This is my view but also it is still a controversial subject. A more detailed discussion on the "gate of ijtihād" appears in the final chapter of this work.
50. Ibn Taymīyyah, "*Al-Fatāwā al-Kubrā*", (Dār al-Kutub al-'Ilmiyyah), vol. 19, pp. 200-1; Ibn al-Qayyīm "*I'lām*", vol. 1, p. 171.
51. Ibn Manzūr "*Lisān*", subject Juhidah, vol. 2, pp. 133-4.
52. Ghazālī, "*Al-Mustaṣfā*", vol. 2, p. 350.
53. Āmidī, "*Al-Iḥkām*" vol. 3 p. 204
54. Ibid.
55. Qarafī, "*Sharḥ*", p. 189.
56. Isnawī, "*Nihāyāt*", vol. 2, p. 232.
57. Ibn al-Humām, "*Al-Taḥrīr fī al-Uṣūl*", vol. 3, p. 291.
58. Ibn Ḥazm, "Al-Iḥkām", 41, pp. 977, 1155; and "*Ibṭāl al-Qiyās*", p. 42.
59. Fazlur Rahmān, "*Islām and Modernity*", p. 8.
60. Āmidi, "*Al-Iḥkām*" vol. 3, p. 140.

61. Abū Dāwūd, "*Sunan*", ḥadīth no: 3567, vol. 3, p. 1013; Bukhārī, "*Ṣaḥīḥ*", vol. 8, p. 157.
62. Narrated from Tirmīzī, Dārimī, "*Sunan*", Abū Dāwūd, ḥadīth no: 3585, vol. 3, p. 1019
63. Muḥammad Dasūqī, "*Al-Ijtihād wa al-Taqlīd fī al-Sharī'ah al-Islāmiah*", (Doha: Dār al-Thaqāfah, n.d.), p. 39.
64. Ibn 'Āshūr, "*Maqāṣid*", pp. 27-8.
65. Abū Dāwūd, "*sunan*", ḥadīth no: 3585, vol. 3, p. 1019.
66. Ghazāli, "*Al-Mustaṣfā*", vol. 2, p. 350.
67. Wael B. Hallaq, "*The Gate of Ijtihād: A study in Islamic Legal History*", PhD dissertation, University of Washington, p. 18.
68. Ibn al-Qayyīm, "*I'lām*", vol. 4 p. 212.
69. Ibn Taymīyyah, "*Al-Musawwadah*", p. 356.
70. Qaradāwī, "*Al-Ijtihād fī Sharī'ah al-Islāmiah*", (Kuwait: 1989), p. 182.
71. Hallaq, "*The Gate*", pp. 14-17.
72. Shāṭibī, "*Al-Muwāfaqāt*", vol. 4 pp. 105-6.
73. For more about conditions of al-Ijtihād see Shāṭibī, "*Al-Muwāfaqāt*", vol. 4, pp. 60, 105-106, 111, 114, 162, 170; Bannānī, "*Jam' al-Jawāmī'*", vol. 2 p. 832; Isnawī, "*Al-Minhāj*", vol. 3 pp. 175, 200; Ghazālī, "*Al-Mustaṣfā*", vol. 2, pp. 54, 101,102; Shawkānī, "*Irshād*", pp. 250-252; Abū Zahrah, "*Uṣūl*", pp. 302-307; Karadāwī, "*Al-Ijtihād*", p. 47; Badrān, "*Uṣūl*", p. 208; Qarafī, "*Kitāb Anwār al-Burūq fī Anwār al-Furūqh*", (Beirut: Dār al-Mā'rifah, n.d.), vol. 1, p. 78; Qurtūbī, "*Al-Jāmī' li Aḥkām al-Qur'an*", (Beirut: Dār al-Iḥyā' al-Turās al-'Arabi, 1967), vol. 11, pp. 310-1; Zuhayr, Muḥammad Abū al-Nūr, "*Mudhakkarāt fī al-Uṣūl al-Fiqh*", (Cairo: Dār al-Ta'līf, Kullīyyāt al-Sharī'ah, al-Azhar), vol. 4, p. 226.
74. Aḥmad Raysūnī, "*Nazariyyāt al-Maqāṣid 'inda al-Imām al-Shāṭibī*", (Maryland, USA: the IIIT, 1995), p. 353; Wael B. Hallaq, "*The Origins and Evolution of Islamic Law*", (Cambridge: Cambridge University Press, 2005), p. 146,
75. Ibn al-Subkī, "*Jam' al-Jawāmī'*", vol. 2, p. 383.
76. Subkī and Ibn al-Subkī, "*Al-Ibhāj fī Sharḥ al-Minhāj*", (Beirut, 1984), vol. 3, p. 206.
77. Raysūnī, ibid., p. 355.
78. Shāṭibī, "*Al-Muwāfaqāt*", vol. 4, pp. 174-5.

79. Orhan Çeker, "*Ifta ve Bir Fetva Defteri Örneği*", (Konya: Damla offset, 2000).
80. Sha'bān, "*Uṣūl*", pp. 332-3.
81. Wael B. Hallaq, "Was the Gate of Ijtihad Closed?", in *International Journal of Middle East Studies*, xvi, 1, 1984, 3-41; Montgomery Watt, "The closing of the door of ijtihad"in Oriehtakia hispanica, sive studia F M Pareja octogenaria dictata edenda curavit J M Barral, (Leiden: 1974), 1, 675-8.
82. Dihlawī, "*Al-Muṣaffā*", (Delhi), vol.1, p. 11. Quoted from Baljon, "*Religion and thought of Shah Walī Allāh Dihlawī*", p. 167.
83. Dihlawī, "*Iqd*" quoted from Baljon, "*Religion and thought of Shah Walī Allāh Dihlawī*", p. 167.
84. Abū Dāwūd, ḥadīth no: 3578, vol. 3, p. 1017; Kassāb, al-Sayyīd 'Abd al-Laṭīf, "*Aḍwā'*", p. 58.
85. Khallāf, "*Khulāṣat al-Tārīkh al-Tashrī' al-Islāmī*", (Istanbul: al-Maktabat al-Islāmīyyah, 1984), p. 284; Hayreddin Karaman, "*Yeni gelişmeler karşısında İslām Hukuk'u*", (İstanbul: İz yayıncılık), p. 56.
86. Karaman "*Yeni gelişmeler*", p. 56; Zaydān, "*Al-madkhal*" p. 110.
87. Shawkānī, "*Irshād*", p. 255.
88. Ghazālī, "*Mustaṣfā*", vol. 2 p. 104; Shawkānī, "*Irshād*", p. 256.
89. Kassāb, "*Aḍwā'*", p. 61.
90. Bukhārī, "*Kashf*", vol. 3, pp. 205-206; Ibn Ḥazm, "*Al-Iḥkām*", vol. 5, pp. 127-8.
91. Ibn Humām, "*Ṭahrir*", vol. 4, p. 183; Ibn 'Abd al-Shakūr, "*Musallam*", vol. 2, p. 366.
92. Bukhārī, "*Waṣāyā*", 19; Muslim, "*Nadhr*", 1.
93. Ibn al-Qayyim, "*I'lām*", vol. 1, p. 258.
94. Bukhāri, "*I'tisām*", 12; Muslim, "*Liān*", 18.
95. Sha'bān, "*İslam Hukuk İlminin Esasları*", pp. 176-7.
96. Bukhārī, "*Salam*", 1, 2; Muslim, "*Musāqāt*", 25; Tirmīzī, "*Buyū'*", 70; Abū Dāwūt, "*Buyū'*", 57; Nasāī, "*Buyū'*", 63.
97. Khayyāṭ, 'Abd al-'Azīz, "*Nazariyyāt al-'Urf*", (Amman Maktabat al-Aqṣā', 1997), pp. 116-7.
98. Bukhārī, "*Kashf*", vol. 4 p. 3.
99. Sha'bān, "*İslam Hukuk İlminin Esasları*", pp. 162-3.

100. Ibid., pp. 162-3.

101. Usāmah Ḥamawī, "*Naẓarīyyāt al-Istiḥsān*", MA dissertation at the Faculty of Sharī'ah at the Dimashq University, (Beirut: Dār al-Khayr, 1992), p. 123.

102. Ibid.

103. Zarqā', "*Matkhal*", vol. 1, p. 86.

104. Hamza Aktan, "*Ticaret Hukukunun Yeni Bazı Problemleri Üzerine Islam Hukuku Açısından Bir Değerlendirme*", in I. Uluslararası Islam Ticaret Hukukunun Günümüzdeki Meseleleri Kongresi, (Konya: 1996), p. 210.

105. Aktan, "*Ticaret*", p. 211. For more examples see Hamawī "*Naẓariyyāt al-Istiḥsān*" pp. 125-131; Muḥammad Farfūr, "*Naẓariyyāt al-Istiḥsān fi al-Tashri'ī al-Islāmī wa Ṣilatuhā bi al-Maṣlaḥat al-Mursalah*", (Sham: Dār al-Dimīshq, 1987), pp. 26-36.

106. M. Rawās Kal'ajī, Kanībī Ḥāmid Ṣādık, "*Mujām al-Lughat al-Fuqahā'*", (Beirut: Dār an-Nafāis, 1988), p. 248.

107. Abū Dāwūd, "*Buyū'*", no. 70; Tirmīzī, "*Buyū'*", no. 19; Nasāi, "*Buyū'*", no. 60.

108. Bukhārī, "*Salam*", no. 1, 2; Muslim, "*Musākāt*" 25; Abū Dāwūd, "*Buyū*", 57.

109. Sha'bān, "*İslam Hukuk İlminin Esasları*", pp. 163-4; Ḥamawī, "*Naẓariyyāt*", pp. 135-6

110. Aḥmad, "*Musnad*", vol. 4, p. 181; Abū Dāwūd, "*Ḥudūd*" 19.

111; Ḥamawī, "*Naẓariyyāt*" pp. 138-9.

112. Ibn Nujāym, Zayn al-'Abidīn b. Ibrāhīm al-Shāhir (d. 970/1562), "*Al-Ashbāh wa al-Naẓāir*", (Beirut: Dār al-Kutub al-'Ilmiyyah, 1985), p. 89.

113. Ibn Hishām, 'Abd al-Malik, "*Al-Sīrat al-Nabaviyyah*", edt. Muṣṭafā al-Saqā, Ibrāhīm al-Abyārī, 'Abd al-Ḥāfiẓ Shalabī, (Beirut: Dār al-Khayr, 1992), vol. 2, pp. 197-8; Sarakhsī, "*Uṣūl*", vol. 2, p. 91; Bukhārī, "*Kashf*", vol. 3, p. 210.

114. Karaman, "*İslam Hukuk Tarihi*", (İstanbul: İz Yayıncılık, 1999), p. 71.

115. Sarakhsī, "*Uṣūl*", vol. 2, pp. 91-92; Bukhārī, "*Kashf*", vol. 3, p. 210.

116. Aktan, "*Ticaret*", pp. 211-2; Ḥamawi, "*Naẓariyyāt*", p. 140.

117. Abū Dāwūd, "*Buyū'*", 51; Tirmīzī, "*Buyū'*", 73.

118. Bājī, "*Al-Muntaqā*", vol. 5, p. 18.

119. Shalabī, "*Ta'līl*", p. 79; Sha'bān, "*Islam Hukuk İlminin Esasları*", p. 108.

120. Shaybānī Muḥammad b. Ḥasan (d. 189), "*Kitāb al-Āthār*", (Lahore, 1329), p. 102.

121. Shalabī, "*Ta'līl*", pp. 80-81; Karaman, "*İctihād*", p. 89.

122. Schacht, "*Introduction*", pp. 48-49.

123. Ibn al-Qayyīm, "*I'lām*", vol. 1, pp. 158-159.

124. Ibn al-Qayyīm, "*I'lām*", vol. 1, p. 158; Shalabī, "*Ta'līl*", p. 75; Sha'bān, "*Islam Hukuk İlminin Esasları*" p. 109.

125. Buhkārī, "*Ṭalāq*", 47; Muslim, "*Ṭalāq*", 9; Bājī, "*al-Muntaqā*", vol. 6, pp. 143-144; Mālik, "*Muwaṭṭā*'" vol. 2, p. 597.

126. Bājī, "*Al-Muntaqā*", vol. 6, p. 145.

127. Shalabī, "*Ta'līl*", p. 77; Karaman, "*İctihād*" p. 87.

128. Ghazālī, "*Mustaṣfā*", vol. 2, p. 354; Āmidī, "*Al-Iḥkām*", vo. 4, p. 407; Amīr Bādishāḥ, "*Taysir*", vol. 4, p. 193.

129. Sarakhsi, "*Uṣūl*", vol. 2, pp. 93-94, 130-1; Shawkānī, "*Irshād*", p. 257.

130. Ibn al-Qayyīm, "*I'lām*", vol. 1, pp. 281-2.

131. Ḥamid Allāh, Muḥammad, "Al-Ijtihād fī 'Aṣr al-Ṣaḥābah", *Majallah al-Kulliyāh al-Dirāsāh al-Islāmiyyah wa al-'Arabiyyah*, 1984, vol. 3, issue: 4, p. 23.

132. Amīr Bādishāḥ, "*Taysīr*", vol. 4, p. 195; Āmidī, "*Al-Iḥkām*", vol. 4, p. 408; Ghazālī, "*Mustaṣfā*", vol. 2, p. 355; Shawhānī, "*Irshād*", p. 257.

133. Bukhārī, "*Tayammum*", no. 7; Abū Dāwūd, "*Ṭahārat*", no. 124.

134. Aḥmad, "*Musnad*", vol. 4, pp. 373-4; Abū Dāwūd, "*Ṭalāq*", 32; Ibn Mājah, "*Aḥkām*", no. 20.

135. Ḥajawī, Muḥammad b. Ḥassan, "*Al-Fiqh al-Sāmī fī Tārikh al-Fiqh al-Islāmī*", (Cairo: Dār al-Turās, 1396), vol. 1, p. 94.

136. Karaman, "*İjtihād*", p. 47.

137. Amīn, "*Fajr al-Islām*", pp. 92-3; Karaman, "*İslam Hukuk Tarihi*", p. 101.

138. Abū Bakr Ismā'īl Mik'a, "*Al-Ra'y wa Asaruh fī Madrasah al-Madīnah*", (Beirut: Muassasah al-Risālah, 1985), pp. 69-70; Amīn, "*Fajr al-Islām*" pp. 92-93.

139. 'Abd al-Qadīr, 'Alī Ḥassan, "*Naẓariyāt al-'Āmmah fī Tārikh al-fiqh al-Islāmī*", (Cairo: Dār al-Kutub al-Ḥādisah, 1965), pp. 54-5; Khallaf, "*Tarīkh al-Tashrī*", p. 297; Zarkā, "*Madkhal*", vol. 1, pp. 142-3.

140. Shāfi'ī, "*Al-Risālah*", p. 477.

141. Isnawī, "*Niḥāyat*", vol. 4, p. 16; Rāḍi, "*Al-Maḥṣūl*", vol. 2, p. 265; Subkī, "*Al-Ibḥāj*", vol. 3, p. 16.

142. Isnawī, "*Niḥāyat*", vol. 4, pp. 16-7.

143. Khudarī, "*Tārikh*", p. 88.

144. Bukhārī, "*Kashf*", vol. 3, p. 279.

145. Mik'a, "*Al-Ra'y*", p. 83; Khallaf, "*Maṣādir*", p. 8; Karaman, "*İctihad*", pp. 73, 74.

146. Zarqā, "*Madkhal*", vol. 1, p. 139.

147. Ibn al-Qayyīm, "*I'lām*", vol. 1, p. 126.

148. Jaṣṣāṣ, "*Al-Fuṣūl*", p. 23.

149. Ibn al-Qayyīm, "*I'lām*", vol. 1 p. 270.

150. This is a kind of tax which is taken from non-Muslim traders to allow them access to Muslim countries.

151. Bukhāri, "*Buyū'*", no. 103, 112; Muslim, "*Musāqāt*", 12, 13; Abū Dāwūd, "*Buyū'*", 64; Aḥmad, "*Musnad*", vol. 3, p. 324, Abd al-Razzāq, "*Muṣannaf*", vol.6, p. 75.

152. Sha'bān, "*Islam Hukuk İlminin Esasları*", p. 117.

153. Shalabī, "*Uṣūl*", vol.1, p. 267; Aḥmad Ḥasan, "*The early*", p. 145. See Muḥarrem Önder, "*Ḥanefi Mezhebinde Istiḥsān anlayışı ve uygulaması*", Unpublished PhD dissertation, (Konya: The University of Selçuk, 2000).

154. Ḥaṭib, "*Al-Faqih*", vol.1, p. 200; Ibn al-Qayyīm, "*I'lam*", vol. 1, p. 126.

155. Abu Sulaymān, "*Al Fikr*", p. 32.

156. Ibn Abī Shaybah, "*Musannaf*", vol. 3, p. 474; 'Abd al-Razzāq, "*Muṣannaf*", vol. 7, pp. 176-178.

157. Karaman, "*İctihād*", pp. 67-8; Shalabī, "*Ta'līl*", pp. 44-5.

158. See Bukhārī, "*Farāiḍ*", 3; Muslim, "*Farāiḍ*", 1, 2; Abū Dāwūd, "*Farāiḍ*", 7; Ibn Mājah, "*Farāiḍ*", 10. For more on inheritance and its terms; 'aṣabah, asḥābi furūḍ etc, see: 'Abd al-Raḥmān I. Doi, "*Sharī'ah the Islamic Law*", pp. 271-327, (London: Tā Hā Publishers, 1997).

159. The situation of full and consanguine brothers is as follows. If a man has no brothers, he inherits everything. If he has a full brother or a half brother with the same father the consanguine brother is excluded by the full brother if the latter is considered one of the 'aṣabah, when there is no full brother a consanguine brother has this judgment. If there is a full brother, he excludes the half brother. If nothing remains, they

receive nothing unless there are uterine brothers among the heirs who inherit a third. Then any full siblings, male and female, share equally with the uterine brothers in their third. This portion is called «shared» (mushtarik). Consanguine brothers do not share with the uterine brothers because they do not have the same mother. The rest of the heirs—Males only, or females only, or both—inherit two-thirds, like the wife, mother or grandfather, and this completes the estate.

160. Shalabī, "*Uṣūl*", vol. 1, p. 267; Farrūr, "*Naẓariyyāt*", p. 51; for further details on this see: Yasin Dutton, "*The Origins*", pp. 108-109.

161. Abū Yūsuf, Yāqub Ibrāhim, (d. 182), "*Kitāb al-Kharāj*", (Beirut: Dār al-Ma'rifah, 1970), p. 24-27.

162. Shalabī, "*Ta'līl*" p. 48-56.

163. Mālik, "*Muwaṭṭā*'" vol. 1, p. 871; Ibn Abī Shaybah, "*Muṣannaf*", vo. 5, pp. 410,429.

164. Nadiyah Sharīf'Umarī, "*Ijtihād al-Rasūl*", (Beirut: 1987), pp. 293-296; Ghālib 'Abd al-Kāfī Qurashī, "*Awwaliyyāt al-Fāruq al-Siyāsiyyah*", (Egypt, Manṣūrah: Dār al-Wafā, 1990), pp. 402-408.

165. Ḥasan, "*The Early*", p. 145.

166. Shalabī, "*Al-Madkhal*", p. 218; Karaman, "*İctihād*", pp. 63-73.

167. Karaman, "*İctihād*", pp. 73-4.

168. Jamāl al-Dīn Yūsuf b. 'Abd Allah Zayla'ī (d. 762/1360), "*Nasb al-Rā'yah fī Tashri'ī Aḥādīs al-Hidāyah*", edt. Muḥammad Yūsuf al-Bannūri (Egypt: 135), vol. 4, p. 64; Ibn Qayyīm, "*I'lām*", vol. 1, p. 121; Ibn 'Abd al-Bār, "*Jāmi'*", vol. 2, pp. 251, 367.

169. Ibn 'Abd al-Bār "*Jāmi'*", vol. 2, p. 280; Ibn al-Qayyīm, "*I'lām*", vol. 1, p. 102.

170. Zarqā, "*Madhkal*", vol. 1, p. 168; Muḥammad Anīs'Ubādah, "*Tārikh al-Fiqh al-Islāmī*", (Cairo: 1980), p. 274.

171. Muḥammad Zāhid Kawtharī (d. 1952), "*Fiqh Ahli Iraq wa Ḥadīthuhum*", edt. 'Abd al-Fattāh 'Abū Ghuddah, (Beirut: n.d.), p. 23.

172. Karaman, "*İctihād*", p. 102.

173. Karaman, "*İctihād*", pp. 82-3.

174. Khatīb, "*Al-Faqīh*", vol. 1, pp. 199-200; Ibn al-Qayyīm, "*I'lām*", vol. 1, p. 124.

175. Jaṣṣāṣ, "*Fuṣūl*", vol. 4, p. 67.

176. 'Abd al-Qādir, "*Naẓrāt al-'Āmmah*", p. 167.

177. Karaman, "*İctihād*", pp. 101-2, 108
178. Karaman, "*İctihād*", p. 85.
179. Mālik, "*Muwaṭṭā*", vol. 2, pp. 745, 805.
180. Ibn Nujāym, "*Al-Ashbāh*", p. 85.
181. Khudarī, "*Tārīkh al-Tashrī'*", pp. 147-8.
182. M. Özgü Aras, "Ḥammād b. Abū Sulaymān", *Türkiye Diyanet Vakfı İslam Ansiklopedisi*), p. 485.
183. Baltajī, "*Manāhij al-Tashrī'*", vol. 1, pp. 154, 158.
184. Baltajī, "*Manāhij*", vol. 1, p. 246.
185. Ibid, vol. 1, pp. 249-257.
186. Sarakhsi, "*Al-Mabsuṭ*", vol. 4, p. 154.
187. See further examples: Sarakhsi, "*Al-Mabsuṭ*", vol. 30, pp. 137-150.
188. Baltajī, "*Manāhij*", vol. 1, p 254.
189. On Ibn al-Muqaffā, see 'Alī Sāmī Nashshār, "*Nash'at al-Fikr al-Falsafī*", (Cairo: Dār al-Ma'ārif, 1977), vol. 1, p. 204; Ibn Nadīm, "*Fihrist*", p. 172; Özen, "*Akilleşme Süreci*", p. 362.
190. Schacht, "*The Origins*", p. 103.
191. Amīn, "*Duhāl al-Islām*", vol. 1, p. 210; Özen, "*Akilleşme Süreci*", p. 370.
192. Özen, ibid.
193. Ḥasan, "*The early*", p. 115
194. Qur'an: 47:24.
195. Ḥasan, "*The early*", p. 117
196. Ibid.
197. Jaṣṣāṣ, "*Aḥkām*", vol. 3, pp. 123-4.
198. Ḥasan, "*The early*", p. 119.
199. Abū Yūsuf ,"*Al-Kharāj*", pp. 13-15
200. Ḥasan, ibid.
201. Ibid., p. 145.
202. Ibid., p.126.
203. Ibid., p. 146.
204. Ibn al-Qayyīm, "*I'lām*", vol. 1, p. 103.
205. Ḥasan, "*The early*", p. 146.

206. Ibid.

207. Ibid., p. 147.

208. Ibid., p. 149.

209. Muḥammad Yūsuf Mūsā, "*Tārīkh al-Fiqh al-Islāmī*", (Kuwait: Maktabah al-Sundus, n.d.), vol. 2, p. 9; Karaman, "*İctihād*", pp. 86-89, 93.

210. Mūsa, "*Tārikh*", vol. 2, p. 10.

3

Definition of *Istiḥsān* and Analysis

As I have previously stated the concept of *istiḥsān* is the main theme of my research and the two definitions—the linguistic and technical—are very important parts of the concept and will be elaborated in the usage of its various aspects.

The technical (iṣṭilāḥī) definition of istiḥsān

No technical definitions of *istiḥsān* have reached us from the early Islamic period, simply because there was no reason for *istiḥsān* to be defined. Abū Ḥanīfah and other early Ḥanafī jurists such as Abū Yūsuf (d. 182) and Shaybānī (d. 189) have directly given rulings using the concept of *istiḥsān* without giving any specific definitions or explanations. Their judgments were based on the fundamental principles of securing ease and avoiding hardship: "God intends facility and ease for you, He does not intend to put you to hardship" (2:185).

The fact that the Ḥanafīs were attacked by the Shāfi'ī jurists, and especially by Shāfi'ī himself, shows that the Shāfi'ī schools did not recognize *istiḥsān* as a basis of Islamic Law. They dismissed it as "Arbitrary law-making in religion". Indeed, Shāfi'ī jurists did not understand what the Ḥanafīs meant by *istiḥsān*. Ḥanafī jurists spent much time defending their position and trying to show that *istiḥsān* is a valid source of law, and not merely an ad hoc method.

However, among the jurists there was no consensus as to the precise meaning and definition of *istiḥsān*. Yet in spite of all the different definitions, the meanings are very close. In fact all the definitions may be derived from that of Karkhī which is arguably more comprehensive than the others, as we shall see.

Among the Ḥanafī jurists definitions were given by Karkhī, Sarakhsī, Jaṣṣāṣ, Bazdawī, Nasafī, and Ibn Humām; jurists from the other schools remained flexible, as will be seen later.

It is of course that the jurists living in the 9th century had been influenced by the jurists from the earlier centuries. The jurists in my examples are widely spread over six or seven centuries: Karkhī lived in the 4th century AH and Ibn Humam lived in 9th century AH.

The definitions of the Ḥanafī jurists will be presented in chronological order, and then investigated to discover whether these definitions changed over time. The position of the Shāfi'ī jurists will also be elaborated accordingly.

Other jurists who recognize *istiḥsān* will also be covered, and their definitions may help to throw more light on the subject.

Istiḥsān—a historical perspective

In the early period of Islamic legislation, the sources of the Sharī'ah were confined to the Qur'an, the *Sunnah*, and the use of personal opinion (*ra'y*), with the permission of a competent authority. It is pointless to debate whether *istiḥsān* was applied at the time of the Prophet (ṣ) as a source of law, since both the

Prophet (ṣ) himself and the Qur'an—the actual sources of the Sharī'ah—were all that was needed. Although the terminology of *Uṣūl al-Fiqh* had not been systemized yet, some Companions such as caliph 'Umar, 'Alī, Ibn 'Abbās and Ibn Mas'ūd applied the spirit of *Istiḥsān*, if not the technical method itself.

According to Khudarī (d. 1927) whoever uses *istiḥsān* as a method of legislation is not doing anything new or innovative, and jurists merely codified a method which had been used from the early times of the Islamic period. During the formative period, there were many important leaders who applied this unnamed method. These leaders were appointed to solve obstacles and to eliminate obstructions to legislation which the community encountered. Examples include 'Umar (d. 23 AH) at the first stage; and Ibn 'Abbās (d. 68 AH) Rabī'ah (d. 136 AH) and Ibrāhim al-Nakhā'ī (d. 96 AH) at the second stage.[1] The fundamental sources of Islamic law for them were the Qur'an and the *Sunnah*, which were developed by using personal judgment by competent, guided and intellectual jurists, interpreting in accordance with the needs of the age. Serious consideration of the fundamental sources can produce new meanings, which in turn give rise to new obstacles and different circumstances, thus enabling the jurists to arrive at a solution.

The concept of *istiḥsān* is a developed form of *ra'y*. One could extend the fundamental basis of *istiḥsān* to the time of the Prophet (ṣ), given his advice to Mu'adh (d. 18). This actually advocates a defining role for the community, teaching the people how to use their own discretion and understanding; in this context, if the Prophet (ṣ) had not persuaded Mu'adh to use his own judgment after considering the main sources, the development of Islamic law would not have been successful, and would have remained stagnant. The Prophet's (ṣ) question "What will you do if you do not find guidance in the *Sunnah* of the Messenger of God and in

God's Book?"[2] and Mu'adh's response, "I shall do my best to form an opinion and spare no pains",[3] contains the key to the evolution and dynamism of Islamic law.

In the early periods of Islām the rules of Sharī'ah were never rigidly applied but the main objective was to ensure that the spirit of the action conformed to the Sharī'ah. As we saw in the event of the battle of Banū Qurayzah, some companions of the Prophet (ṣ) were despatched to the enemy's territory and were instructed to perform the *Aṣr* prayer on arrival at their destination. The *Aṣr* prayer time arrived during their journey and an argument ensued: some of the Companions chose to pray on time, believing that the Prophet (ṣ) had not meant for the prayers to be delayed, while others went on, taking the Prophet's (ṣ) command literally, and performed the prayer on their arrival at the place of destination at sunset.

They reported this incident to the Prophet (ṣ), who said nothing. His silence was taken as tacit approval of both sides, indicating that no-one was in the wrong.[4] An important lesson may be learned from his case: it teaches the community not to be rigid, so long as their actions do not conflict with the spirit of the Sharī'ah obedience to divine commands. Both sides were seeking the aim of the Sharī'ah, one party abiding by the command literally and the other abiding by the spirit of the command in order to demonstrate their allegiance to God and to the Prophet (ṣ).

Hence, personal interpretations were given credence at a very early time, and these examples inspired jurists to develop or formulate their understanding of religion and express their feelings without any fear or obstruction. The Battle of Badr yields another example of the use of personal opinion (*ra'y*) by the Companions. The Prophet (ṣ) had chosen a particular battle position for the Muslim army. However, Hubbāb ibn al-Mundhīr considered the place unsuitable and wanted to know whether the Prophet (ṣ) had chosen that place by revelation from God or by his own judgment (*ra'y*). It soon became clear that the Prophet (ṣ) had used his own judgment. Then Hubbāb suggested a more suitable place whereupon the Prophet (ṣ) said: "You have made a suggestion with your opinion (*laqad asharta bi al-ra'y*)".[5] The examples given here indicate that the use of personal opinion became a basis for the use of *istiḥsān* later on.

After the demise of the Prophet (ṣ), the same doctrine continued amongst the Companions, as can be seen in the decision of 'Umar ibn Khattāb regarding the inheritance of two half brothers. The case concerned a woman who died and left behind her husband, her mother, two half brothers, and two full brothers. Initially the Caliph applied the usual ruling, based on an established precedent, as laid out by the Prophet (ṣ). This involved two categories: the *ahl al-farā'iḍ* (those portions for heirs designated in the Qur'an)[6] and *ahl al-iṣābah* (the residual heirs).[7] The *ahl al-farā'iḍ* have definite priority over the *ahl al-iṣābah* in the distribution of the property. According to this basis, 'Umar gave one half of the property to the husband of the deceased woman; one sixth to her mother, and one third to the uterine brothers. No portion was given to the half-brothers as they were considered residual heirs. The half-brothers contested the case saying, "Suppose our father was a donkey (*ḥimār*), do we not still have the same mother as the deceased?"

Consequently, 'Umar revised his first decision based on the consideration of equity and justice. Then he found a stronger reason to depart from the already established ruling to a new ruling, which he '*istaḥsana*' (approved as the better judgment): he ordered a new ruling that one third of the property that remained should be distributed equally among both full and half-brothers. This distribution would take place after the deduction of the husband's and mother's portion.[8] The case later came to be known as "The Donkey Case (*al-himariyyah*)".

'Umar's decision appears to be a basic application of *istiḥsān* and brings to mind Karkhī's definition: his decision differs from the established one, and is based on the consideration of justice and equity. 'Umar made *qiyās* (analogy) with regard to the precept of the Prophet (*athar*), and the appeal by half-brothers caused him to change his decision, departing from *qiyās* to *istiḥsān*.

How do we apprise 'Umar's ruling? Was his judgment based solely on personal opinion, or did he endeavour to act in conformity with the spirit of the Sharī'ah?

When 'Umar was faced with such issues, he applied Abū Bakr's methods, looking for the solution first in the Qur'an and the *Sunnah*; if, after much scrutiny and deliberation, no solution was determined, he then gave a ruling from his personal view of what best accorded with the Sharī'ah.

When 'Umar appointed Shurayḥ as judge of Kūfa, he advised him with the following principle: "Seek a clear ruling in the Qur'an, if you find what you are searching for, do not seek advice from another. However, if you could not find any guidance therein, then conform to the *Sunnah*. Should that fail you, and then proceed with your personal judgment."[9] It is obvious that the use of this guidance enables justice to be administered and 'Umar's departure from the set precedent to the new ruling is justified when stronger evidence comes to light.

The basic notion of *istiḥsān* had been exercised since the time of the Companions even if there is no definite evidence that the exact term was used at the time of 'Umar.

Another example is the water conflict between the two Companions Dahhāk b. al-Muzāhim and Muḥammad ibn Maslamah (d. 46). The Caliph 'Umar sided with Dahhāk b.

al-Muzāhim, when Dahhāk asked for permission to extend a water canal through Maslamah's property. Maslamah objected. The Caliph granted Dahhāk his request on the grounds that it was unlikely to cause any harm to Maslamah, as indicated in the Prophet's (ṣ) saying, "Harm is to be neither inflicted nor reciprocated in Islām".[10] The Caliph did not base this decision on any source or compare it to any established rule as such; he believed his decision on this case was not contradictory to the general spirit and purpose of the Sharīʿah.

Another example of the legal practice of the Caliph was to suspend the prescribed punishment for theft of food during the year of the famine.[11] In the *Kitāb al-Kharāj* the example of theft during the year of the famine was explored. A man had stolen something from *bayt al-Māl* (treasury, exchequer) and ʿUmar had not amputated his hand;[12] he suspended the rule of amputation during famine. At first glance, the Caliph's practice seems to contradict the command of the Qur'an "Cut off (from the wrist joint) the (right) hand of the thief, male or female, as a recompense for that which they committed, a punishment" (5:38). However, the Qur'an is silent on the circumstances attending such punishments. In fact, ʿUmar in this case departed from the established rule to a new rule, i.e. not to amputate a thief's hand during the time of famine. Considering the circumstances of the famine to be exceptional, ʿUmar discontinued amputation for all thieves during the time of famine.

A similar example was reported regarding a case of a stolen she-camel. A slave stole a she-camel, slaughtered and ate it. When the incident reached ʿUmar and he investigated the crime, he ordered the thief's hand to be amputated. ʿUmar then departed from his first decision, decided not to amputate the slave's hand and ordered the owner's slave in for questioning. Judging that the slave-owner had probably starved the slave, ʿUmar departed from the precedent to a new ruling not to amputate the thief's hand. However, he penalized his master and ordered him to pay double the price of the she-camel.[13]

According to the Prophet's (ṣ) practice, war booty was distributed among the Companions. However, 'Umar decided not to distribute the lands of Irāq and Syria among the Companions out of consideration for the general public welfare, which dictated that borders and newly conquered lands should be protected. He therefore distributed the lands amongst the Muslims in general. Bilāl and other companions asked him the reason for his decision after 'Abd al-Raḥmān ibn Awf and others apposed him. 'Umar's response was to point out that the distribution of land amongst the new Muslims would ensure that all land would be worked and protected at all times. However, to distribute it among only the army, for example, would expose borders and conquered lands to danger once the army had returned to the homeland. Then they finally gave their consent as "*al-ra'y ra'yuka*" (the opinion to be followed is yours). This case is illustrated in the Qur'an: (59: 6-10) in justification of 'Umar's decision.[14] Thus, 'Umar has departed from an established rule to a different rule in favour of the general benefit of Muslims.

The basis of 'Umar's *ijtihād* was to help the public in their day to day life by removing any difficulties, so that the objectives purpose of the Sharī'ah might be accomplished. When 'Umar's *ijtihād* is studied,[15] it is obvious that his established reforms were recognised by the Sharī'ah; however, 'Umar did not attempt to alter the obligatory (*farḍ*) principles.

The Qur'an and the *Sunnah* are not based only on obligatory commands; some of the rules exist in the form of recommendations and requests. An authorised individual (*'ulu al-amr*) can attempt to alter non-obligatory rules only. However, attempting to alter obligatory rules and prohibitions is considered destructive to religion.

"Any decision taken by the authorised person (*'ulu al-amr*) makes his orders obligatory (*farḍ*) and whatever he decides to ban becomes prohibited (*ḥarām*). However, as the rulings of the *'ulu al-amr* are restricted within the time of his reign those rulings are likely to be temporary. In addition the *'ulu al-amr's* interference in obligatory rulings (*farḍ*) must be continued only to postponing or bringing these forward under certain circumstances."[16]

It is quite difficult to determine the applications of *istiḥsān* in the very early periods. However, 'Umar's decisions provided the means by which researchers have been able to gain some indication of how to implement *istiḥsān* in legal matters. Early *istiḥsān* then, involved making a decision which was a departure from an established rule for the sake of equity and public interest.

At the beginning it was seen that the appearance of *istiḥsān* could affect judicial and legal proceedings, and social or political issues that were possibly influenced by the caliphs during both the Umayyad dynasty (661-750/41-132), and the period of the Abbasid dynasty (750-1258/132-656). The administration of justice was in the hands of provincial governors throughout most of the Umayyad period. They also appointed particular judges, whose task was to act as agents of the governors in various areas.

Mu'āwiyah ibn Abī Sufyān, Marwān Ibn al-Ḥakam, 'Umar ibn al-Abd al-'Azīz of the Umayyad Caliphs and other members of the family were directly or indirectly involved in Umayyad legal practice.[17] For example, normally when divorce happens before the consummation of the marriage, the husband has to pay only half of the fixed dower, whether or not *khalwah* (privacy) has taken place[18].[19] However, during the Umayyad period, the full dower was paid whether consummation and/or *khalwah* had taken place or not. The right to claim the full dowry for divorce which followed an unconsummated marriage was abolished in Umayyad times and this is attributed to Marwān Ibn al-Ḥakam or to the governor.[20] However, in Abbasid times, the judicial system was separated from the political administration.[21]

After the Arab conquests, the Companions of the Prophet (ṣ) spread out in different parts of the Islamic world, and soon faced the problem of finding solutions to various hitherto unencountered problems. As Muslims, including the Companions settled in conquered areas,[22] 'Umar appointed many Companions to take responsibility for legal activities in the different cities. Shurayḥ b. al-Ḥarith (d. 78) was appointed judge of Kūfa under the guidance of Abū Mūsa al-Ash'arī (d. 44), who told him: "Think again and again over a point so long as it remains doubtful in your mind—a point which you do not find in the Qur'an or in the *Sunnah* of the Prophet (ṣ). Get yourself acquainted with precedents and similar cases; then weigh up the matters (*qis al-umūr*). Then adopt the one that is more favourable in the eyes of God and identical with the truth in your opinion."[23] The legal methods and doctrines of the Kūfī jurists were mainly inherited from Ibn Mas'ūd and 'Alī ibn Abī Tālib's thoughts, opinions, and judgments.[24]

The Iraqi jurists claimed that their opinions were likely to coincide with the decisions of the Prophet (ṣ). The following examples illustrate the harmony between the Companions and the Prophet. One-day Ibn Mas'ūd was asked about a matter. He responded by saying "I am not aware of any decision of the Prophet (ṣ) on such a matter". He was then asked to give his personal opinion (*ra'y*), which he did. One of the men in his circle declared that the Prophet (ṣ) had given the same decision, and Ibn Mas'ūd was exceedingly happy that his opinion had coincided with the decision of the Prophet (ṣ).[25] Therefore, the same idea and spirit was held to have transferred from the Prophet (ṣ) to the Successors through the Companions and through the light of traditions.

Later on, the Successors inherited the role of the Companions, with scholars such as Alqamah bin Qays (d. 62), Al-Aswad bin Yazīd (d. 75), Shurayḥ bin Ḥārith (d. 78), Al-Shā'bi Abū 'Amr (d. 103), Ibrāhim al-Nakhā'ī (d. 95), Ḥammad bin Sulaymān al-Ash'arī (d. 120) all of whom lived in Irāq, the scholarly environment in which Abū Ḥanīfah developed. He learned *fiqh* from his teacher Ḥammad b. Sulaymān, student of Ibrāhim al-Nakhā'ī, Ibrāhim learned *fiqh* from the associates of Ibn Mas'ūd, who in turn were students of Companions of the Prophet (ṣ), such as 'Umar, Ibn Mas'ūd and 'Alī.[26] Their opinions were not expressed arbitrarily; rather they were inspired by the Qur'an and the *Sunnah*. For example, 'Umar was reported to have asked a man who had once come to him with a problem, whether his case had yet been solved. The man replied: "'Alī and Zayd b. Thābit have given a ruling". 'Umar said: "I would have given a similar ruling if I had not been able to find a solution in the Qur'an and the *Sunnah*. My opinion is as theirs."[27]

The Companions did, however, always endeavour to make the Qur'an and the *Sunnah* the main source of their decisions, and to ensure that their rulings did not contradict the Qur'an and the Prophet's (ṣ) traditions.

Istiḥsān found a very appropriate atmosphere in Irāq, in which to develop. Irāqi jurists used personal reasoning (*ra'y*) and *qiyās* (analogy), which they saw as an interesting intellectual challenge, given that they were more interested in the theory of the law, unlike the Madīnah School, which focused on the actual practice of the law.[28] According to Aḥmad Ḥassan the term *istiḥsān* was not used in its technical sense with era of the aforementioned *Irāq* scholars.[29] The idea was prevalent in juristic practice, as we shall see when we look at the "application of *istiḥsān* in the early Ḥanafī School". While Irāqī jurists applied the concept of *istiḥsān* by departing from the established ruling, they did not give any reason for their practice.[30] Abd al-Raḥmān b. Hujairah, a judge between the years 69 and 83 AH; Thaubah b. Nimr between 115 and 120 AH; and Khair b. Nu'aym between 120 and 127 AH [31] all gave rulings based on personal reasoning, yet never made any reference to the principle of *istiḥsān* in its strictly technical sense.

I have not been able to discover any authentic source that leads me to believe that the form of *istiḥsān* was used prior to the time of 'Umar ibn 'Abd al-'Azīz. However Iyās b. Mu'āwiyah (d. 122/740) who was the judge of Baṣra between 101 and 102 AH, said: "Use *qiyās* as a basis for judgment so far as it is beneficial to people, but when it leads to undesirable results then use juristic preference (*fastaḥsinū*)."[32] He suggested that if the present juristic rulings are not sufficient to prevent evil, then in order to arrive at rulings which are more effective, the principle of *istiḥsān* would be used. Muwaffaq b. Aḥmad al-Makkī (d. 568/1198) adds: "If *qiyās* leads to undesirable results you should apply the more accurate of the two opinions."[33]

Iyās b. Mu'āwiyah also says "I understand that the judgments given in the courts should be in accordance with *istiḥsān*."[34] This shows that rulings must not contradict the consideration of *maṣlaḥah*, and must provide justice and equity.

The research thus shows that the use of the term of *istiḥsān* came to light before the time of Abū Ḥanīfah and was not confined to him. When Iyās b. Mu'āwiyah's use of the term *istiḥsān* is compared to Abū Ḥanīfah's, much similarity can be seen. For them, the main purpose of applying *istiḥsān* was to avoid the possibility of causing harm to the public interest. The reason for their emphasis on *istiḥsān* was their desire to avoid the negative results that often occurred when *qiyās* was applied incorrectly. However, *istiḥsān* owes its existence to *qiyās,* and would not have superseded it had *qiyās* not proved to be ineffective in some cases.

The use of *istiḥsān* appears in a different guise in the early Abbasīd period, namely as "discretion" (*istiṣwāb*). Ibn al-Muqaffa' (d. 137/756) observed that discretion must be taken into account in cases where there is no established ruling, and where guidance from the Qur'an and the *Sunnah* is not forthcoming. In exceptional circumstances, the guardians of the Sharī'ah should be aware that unfair and unjust results sometimes obtain from performing *qiyās,* and that therefore the use of discretion is necessary in order to ensure justice. He ruled that unreserved adherence to *qiyās* sometimes leads to injustice, and that flexibility was advisable in law in order to prevent an unjust ruling based on analogical deduction.[35]

From the very early days of Islam, the use of the principle of *istiḥsān* was not clear. Its validity was never open to question, as is clear from the rulings of 'Umar and, later on, Iyās b. Mu'āwiyah who declared that analogical deduction is valid so long as it is beneficial to people; if the analogy is not beneficial it is then abandoned. The door of solution is therefore always left open.

It is evident that all the previous critical disputes appeared over *istiḥsān* after Abū Ḥanīfah's famous saying "*qiyās* is such and such but we apply *istiḥsān*". Abū Ḥanīfah did not elaborate the reason why he applied those judgments of his which were based on *istiḥsān.*[36] On the other hand, whenever Ḥanafi jurists realized that a *ḥadīth* they were using was reliable and proven, even if it contradicted the principles of their school, they acted upon the *ḥadīth:* the application of this ruling is called *istiḥsān.*[37] The following statements will demonstrate that Abū Ḥanīfah used to base his rulings on *ḥadīth*, be they the Prophet's (ṣ) *acta* or *dicta.* Apart from Prophetic *ḥadīth*, he also relied on the practices of the

Companions and those who followed them. He said: "If it had not been for precedents (*athar*) I would have judged here according to *qiyās*", or "If it had not been for the sake of *riwāyah* (transmitted *ḥadīth*), I would have judged the case by *qiyās*"[38]

Ibn Ḥazm suggests that the term *istiḥsān* first appears in the third generation.[39] He discovered no proof of *istiḥsān* being used before Abū Ḥanīfah, explaining that the Ḥanafis say, "*Qiyās* is such and such but we apply *istiḥsān*". He adds that even Imām Mālik performed *istiḥsān* on occasion.[40] Schacht (d. 1969) mentions Ibn al-Muqaffa's views, reiterating that the usage of *ra'y* and *istiḥsān* might remove the undesired results of analogical reasoning.[41]

Goldziher (d. 1921) claims that the first use of the term *istiḥsān* was by Abū Ḥanīfah, in spite of the fact that, according to Schacht, a method and concept similar to *istiḥsān* existed before Abū Ḥanīfah. Schacht claims that the first technical use of *Istiḥsān* was by Abū Ḥanīfah's pupil, Abū Yūsuf (d. 182/798).[42]

Although we do not have the works of Abū Ḥanīfah as evidence, we do have the works of his pupils, especially those of Shaybānī, who attributed the term *istiḥsān* to Abū Ḥanīfah.[43] This fact clearly indicates the weakness of Schacht's claims. Hence, contrary to the claim of Schacht, the term *istiḥsān* was not first used by Abū Yūsuf, who attributes the term itself to his master Abū Ḥanīfah.[44]

An alternative view, proposed by Khaddūrī and Liebesny, is that *istiḥsān* was practiced in Mālikī School, although the idea is now more common to the Ḥanafīs.[45]

In short, despite the fact that the concept of *istiḥsān* was used in the very early days of juristic legislation, my research leads me to believe that the term *istiḥsān* was not used in its technical sense before Iyas bin Mu'āwiyah (d. 122/740).

View point of *istiḥsān* amongst the scholars

Istiḥsān—according to the Ḥanafī school

Ḥanafī scholars see *istiḥsān* as a valid source of Sharīʿah and a basis for the formulation of legal rulings. They also see most criticism of *istiḥsān* as the product of misunderstanding, and the imputation to Abū Ḥanīfah this is because of ulterior motives. However, it is difficult to believe that he would have abandoned a ruling that had been established on true *sharīʿ* foundations for his personal preference.[46]

Al-Taqrīr wa al-Taḥbīr" of Ibn Amīr al-Ḥajj mentions Shāfiʿī's famous dictum, "Whoever rules according to personal preference has set himself up as legislator", but goes on to say that Shāfiʿī was unaware of the true meaning of *istiḥsān* and thus had judged the issue rather hastily. This misunderstanding may come about because of the different meanings of the word *istiḥsān*, one of which is indeed connected to the notion of personal desire.[47]

Ḥanafī scholars are adamant that *istiḥsān* is a source of law and not in any way a form of ruling made according to personal desire. For the Ḥanafī school *istiḥsān* means acting according to one of the two forms of *qiyās. Istiḥsān* may also be acted upon based on *athar* (*ḥadīth*), *ijmāʿ* or necessity. Based on this, the denial of *istiḥsān* is unwarranted since, the Ḥanafīs say, cases are resorted to when they come in opposition to *qiyās jalī* (explicit analogy), making the departure from *qiyās* in this situation a priority. This means that *istiḥsān* is agreed upon when it is opposed to *qiyās jalī* and is acted upon if it is stronger than the *qiyās jalī*. Therefore, there is no point in denying it.[48]

In order to explain the Ḥanafī viewpoint, I will try to summarize what Shaykh ʿAbd al-ʿAzīz al-Bukhārī pointed out in his commentary of *Uṣūl al-Bazdawī*.[49]

Bukhārī's view is that those who deny *istiḥsān* as defined by Abū Ḥanīfah do not deny *istiḥsān* if it is based on *athar*, *ijmā‘* or necessity, since departure from *qiyās* that is based on these indications (*dalā'il*) is generally preferred in such cases, and all scholars accept this. Those scholars who refute the *istiḥsān* of Abū Ḥanīfah do so because they believe it is based on personal opinion (*ra'y*) and the arbitrary departure from *qiyās* with the claim that it is stronger than *qiyās*. Abū Ḥanīfa's alleged response to this was to emphasize that that *istiḥsān* that they were contesting is one of the two kinds of *qiyās*, a separate principle invented for the sake of whim and departure from the truth without evidence. This is because it is compulsory to act according to a stronger *qiyās* in a case where two *qiyās* findings are opposed to each other, whenever possible. The stronger *qiyās* is called *istiḥsān* to indicate the priority of the side that should be acted upon, and the fact that it outweighs the other.

According to Bukhārī the opinion of Sarakhsī is that *istiḥsān* is so named in order to distinguish it from apparent *qiyās* that may be wrongly perceived, since *istiḥsān* is a *dalil* opposed to it; when the weaker *qiyās* is abandoned, the stronger *qiyās* is given the name "*istiḥsān*" as an indicator of its superiority.

Ḥanafī scholars used the term *istiḥsān* and *qiyās* with the aim of distinguishing between two pieces of evidence (*dalīl*) which are opposed to one another. They used the term *istiḥsān* because acting upon it is to be preferred compared with the other, which is different to the method followed in the case of apparent *qiyās* (explicit analogy). According to Bukhārī, Sarakhsī's aim was to defend *istiḥsān* against criticism and to show what is meant by the *istiḥsān* that is the subject of disagreement, rather than intend to offer a comprehensive definition of the term.

Bukhārī continues to explain the confusion that may arise. For example, it is permitted to act according to a *qiyās* which contradicts *istiḥsān*, but acting according to *istiḥsān* is better. For example, acting according to *qiyās al-ṭarḍ* (analogy) is permitted, even though acting in accordance with the *athar* of the Prophet (ṣ) and Companions is preferred. Bukhārī counters this by saying that acting according to *istiḥsān* leads to the departure from *qiyās*, and acting according to what has been departed from is invalid since it is weaker than *istiḥsān*. For this reason, acting according to *qiyās* cannot be sustained if there is *istiḥsān:* a ruling based on *qiyās* no longer carries any weight when opposed by *istiḥsān*. This is also the case of the ruling by *qiyās al-ṭarḍ* with the *athar*, since *ṭarḍ* is not a proof while *athar* is, and therefore, how one could allow acting according to *qiyās* as opposed to *istiḥsān*? The general rule is whatever is not a proof (*ḥujjah*) should not be acted upon, while that which is a proof (*ḥujjah*) should.

This leads to the conclusion that when two pieces of evidence (*dalīlān*) happen to oppose each other and one of them exhibits more weight as compared to the other, then the one which has more weight should be the basis for action. Similarly, this is the case of *qiyās* with regard to *istiḥsān*. This means that *istiḥsān* should be the preferred action. Perhaps those who consider *qiyās* to be the course of action that is allowed as opposed to *istiḥsān* mean that ruling in accordance with *qiyās* is valid when it is faced with no opposition by *istiḥsān* which is stronger than *qiyās*.

Bukhārī concludes his comments on the Ḥanafī point of view with the assertion that *istiḥsān* is a source of law that can be used as a basis for the Sharī'ah rulings. Therefore, he adds, there should be no disagreement as to the validity of the principle.

Then *Bukhārī* refers to those who objected not to the principle of *istiḥsān* as such, but to the term itself. They argued that there is no point in giving a specific name to such acting because the whole of Islamic legislation is more or less the result of *istiḥsān* anyway, since it is all about recommending what is better and less burdensome for the people. Bukhārī replies to this objection by saying that there is no point to this disagreement as it is simply a term, and the rule is that there is no value in terms as such (*la mashāḥatah fī al-isṭilāḥ*).

Those who objected to the name *istiḥsān* themselves concocted names for every kind of *qiyās* such as *qiyās al ḍalālah* (indication), *qiyās al 'illah* (cause), and *qiyās al-shabah.*[50] Furthermore, is it not slightly ironic that *mujtahidin* who, as we shall see shortly, used *istiḥsān* in their rulings, should criticise others for giving that method a name?

In his book "*Tashīl al-Wuṣūl ilā 'Ilm al-Uṣūl*", Maḥillāwī states, "We act upon the wisdom of the proof of *istiḥsān* when it is stronger than *qiyās*. The Ḥanafī school's definition of *istiḥsān* is one of the *adillah* (evidences) agreed upon as opposed to explicit analogy (*qiyās jalī*)".[51]

This statement indicates that *Istiḥsān,* according to the Ḥanafī School, is far from being an issue of personal opinion and whim, used in order to rule against that which God has revealed; *istiḥsān* is taking action according to the stronger evidence (*dalīl*), and no one can say that the stronger *dalīl* is not a valid proof.

The following statement has been reported in "*Fawātiḥ al-Raḥamūt bi-Sharḥ Musallam al-Thubūt*":

"To summarise, *istiḥsān* for us is nothing but a *dalīl* opposing *qiyās,* therefore it is simply an opposition; we can say that *istiḥsān* is a kind of *qiyās*—or, better still, a way of revealing the wisdom that lies behind the *qiyās*: *istiḥsān* simply makes this wisdom obvious. Were it otherwise, there would be no need to call it *istiḥsān,* and we would have to make do with *qiyās,* or *naṣṣ* or *ijmā'*.[52]

Both of the above-mentioned statements indicate the validity of what we have presented as the Ḥanafī viewpoint with regard to what is meant by *istiḥsān.*

In spite of the above explanations, we have been unable to find one universal definition for *istiḥsān* among Ḥanafī scholars. They have debated many different definitions and have discussed various objections and criticisms whilst researching the subject. However, before presenting the discussion of these definitions of *istiḥsān*, they should be simplified so that they can be identified.

Whoever investigates this concept may encounter only two types of *istiḥsān* scenario according to Zakiyyuddīn Sha'bān. These are summarised as follows:

1. The jurist departs from a general ruling on an issue to another ruling because of a particular evidence which justifies this departure,
2. Or: The jurist finds an issue with two differing analogies: one is apparently explicit, the other hidden or implicit. He then departs from the ruling necessitated by the explicit analogy to another ruling necessitated by the implicit analogy. This departure was called *istiḥsān* because the jurist acted according to stronger evidence: such a solution is a "*mustaḥsan*" (preferred) affair.[53]

A jurist may encounter cases that have no explicit ruling in the Qur'an, the *Sunnah*, or *ijmā'*. If, for example, there are two similar original cases and rulings which conflict with one another (*aṣlayn*),[54] and one is based on an explicit *'illah* (cause), easily distinguished, and the other is based on an implicit *'illah* which requires closer examination, the adoption by the jurist of the ruling with the implicit *'illah* is called *istiḥsān* or the juristic preference of an implicit analogy over an explicit analogy.

Based on the above *istiḥsān* may be defined as: The departure from a previous ruling on a certain issue, which is applied to similar issues because of particular evidence that necessitates this departure, as viewed by the jurist, regardless of whether this evidence is *naṣṣ* (textual), *ijmā'* (consensus), *ḍarūrah* (necessity), *'urf* (custom), *maṣlaḥah* (benefit), *qiyās khafī* (implicit analogy), or otherwise, and irrespective of whether the method in which the ruling on the similar problem was established by *dalīl 'ām* (general evidence), *qā'idah fiqhiyyah* (jurisprudence rule) or *qiyās ẓāhir jalīy* (apparent clear analogy).[55] This is the meaning of *istiḥsān* according to the Ḥanafī jurists or others who applied it, especially the Mālikī jurists.

The view of Karkhī (d. 340/952)

One definition which generally gives the meaning of istiḥsān as understood by the jurists of *uṣūl* (principles), and also reflects the definition adopted by the Ḥanafī jurists, who consider it accurate and comprehensive, is that of Abū al-Ḥasan al-Karkhī (d. 340/952). He defines *istiḥsān* as follows: "*istiḥsān* is when one takes a decision on a certain case different from that on which similar cases have been decided on the basis of its precedents, for a reason which is stronger than the one found in similar cases and which requires departure from those cases".[56] This definition has been espoused and accepted by many jurists such as Ṭūfī (d. 716/1317), Shīrāzī (d. 476/1083), Ghazālī (d. 505/1111), and the contemporary jurist Abū Zahrah (d. 1974). It contains all types of *istiḥsān* in general.[57]

Abū Zahrah (d. 1974) comments on the definition, saying that "This definition is the clearest one in which the true nature of *istiḥsān* is expressed by the Ḥanafī jurists, highlighting its aspects, its principle and its essence. The basis of *istiḥsān* is, instead of conforming to one rule, to find a solution with a ruling on the evidence that is presented; this evidence could be against the general principle but in keeping with the aim of the Sharī'ah. In respect of the new solution regarding the problem, the evidence is stronger than the analogy."[58] Another contemporary scholar

'Abd al-Wahhāb Khallāf, considers Karhkī's definition as "the best", saying that "in my view the definition is the definition of Karhkī from Ḥanafīs, Ibn Rushd (d. 595) from among the Mālikīs and Tūfī (d. 716) from among the Ḥanbalīs".[59] The clearest and most comprehensive definition of *istiḥsān* that the researcher has found is that of Khallāf: "In the view of the jurists the technical definition of *istiḥsān* is the authorisation to depart from an established ruling to a different ruling when legal evidence is presented. The legal evidence which is presented is known as the authority of *istiḥsān*."[60]

To summarise, *istiḥsān* is evidence which is preferred over an accepted established ruling after ensuring that this evidence does not contravene the Islamic legal ruling. In fact, Khallāf's definition is not a new one; the only difference is its expression, and thus the meanings of the two definitions are similar.

According to Karhkī, "departure" must be based on particular evidence which warrants a move from an established ruing to a different ruling on a similar case. The purpose of the stronger reason or evidence requires the departure; the jurist (mujtahid) departs from the established ruling because of the stronger reason. I shall illustrate this statement by giving an example:

> If a group of people gain unlawful entry into a house, steal goods and decide to load the goods on to one person's back and that person carries the goods outside while the others carry nothing, what would happen?

According to *qiyās*, the punishment applies only to the person who carries the goods. However, according to "*istiḥsān*" the punishment is applied to all of those who are involved in the robbery.[61] Here, there are two contradictory *aṣl* (original cases):

The first case is: a group of people encourage one of the group to rape a woman; in this case there is no conflict among the jurists, who agree that the penalty is only applied to the rapist. This is a ruling of analogy which is opposite to the ruling of *istiḥsān*. The second case is: a group of people gather with the intent to attack and kill people robbing them of their goods; here the penalty of highway robbery is applied to all. In this case, there is no conflict amongst the jurists; they all agree that the punishment is applied to all who are involved in highway robbery.

According to the Qur'an:

The recompense of those who wage war against God and His Messenger and do mischief in the land is only that they shall be killed or crucified or their hands and their feet be cut off from opposite sides, or be exiled from the land. That is their disgrace in this world, and a great torment is theirs in the Hereafter. Except for those who (having fled away and then) came back (as Muslims) with repentance before they fall into your power; in that case, know that Allah is Oft-Forgiving, Most Merciful" (5:33).

After careful investigation, we see that comparing the house robbery to highway robbery is a clearer solution than comparing it to rape.[62] The departure from one case (*aṣl*) to another case (*aṣl*) because of the stronger reason is called *istiḥsān*. This definition of *istiḥsān* was chosen by Ibn Qudāmah Al-Maqdisī (d. 620/1223).[63]

Shīrāzī (d. 476/1083), who is a follower of the Shāfi'ī school, says: "If Ḥanafī and Karkhī (d. 340/952) say that "*Istiḥsān* is the giving of a ruling with the stronger reason rather than the weaker reason" then we agree with it, and therefore the dispute between us have been solved."[64] After quoting the definition of Karkhī, Ghazālī (d. 505/1111) says that there is "no dispute against the definition".[65] Ghazālī defines *istiḥsān* as: "A departure from the established ruling to a certain case which is similar to previous cases where this ruling was applied due to particular evidence taken from the Qur'an or the *Sunnah.*[66] Ghazālī's definition differs from that of Karkhī's. None of the jurists among the Shāfi'ī school of thought has defined *istiḥsān* as Ghazālī did, identifying different kinds of *istiḥsān* such as, *istiḥsān* based on "*naṣṣ*" (textual evidences), which is based on the Qur'an and the *Sunnah.* However *istiḥsān* is not confined to these two, and Ghazālī's definition is narrower than that of the Ḥanafīs' view because it is far less comprehensive in its scope.

While citing Karkhī's definition, Sarakhsī says: "the precedent which is set aside by *istiḥsān* normally consists of an established analogy (*qiyās*) which may be abandoned in favour of the superior proof, namely the Qur'an, the *Sunnah*, necessity (*darūrah*) or a stronger analogy (*qiyās*)".[67]

Karkhī's definition has been criticised for involving in *istiḥsān* the particularization of the general (*takhṣīṣ*) and *naskh* (abrogation) in spite of the fact that they do not belong in *istiḥsān.*[68] Muḥammad b. Ḥusayn Baḥit (d. 1354/1935) says that if Karkhī definitely meant such a particularization, then they would have a right to accuse him; however, he continues, it was not actually meant; what was meant in his definition was the particularization of analogy by the evidence of implicit analogy, text, *ijmā'*, etc. *Istiḥsān* might be considered as part of particularization, but the concept of abrogation (*naskh*) is completely different to *istiḥsān.* Abrogation is confined to the time of the revelation, while *istiḥsān* is not. The objective of *istiḥsān* is usually to move from difficulty to ease; however, abrogation is not considered in that context.[69]

The view of Al-Jaṣṣāṣ (d. 370/981)

The definition of *istiḥsān* according to Jaṣṣāṣ is the "Departure from a ruling of *qiyas* (analogy) in favour of another ruling which is considered preferable."[70] According to the translation of Aḥmad Ḥasan: "*Istiḥsān* means to depart from the obvious analogical reasoning (*qiyas jali*) and to adopt that which is better."[71]

Jaṣṣāṣ points out that *istiḥsān* is performed in two ways:

The first: a parallel case (*far'*)[72] which has similarity with two original cases (*aṣl*), where the rulings in those cases are different. *Istiḥsān* involves abandoning one of the original cases and taking the other as a basis because of the preference of the jurists.

The second: is the particularization of a ruling with an existing legal cause (*'illah*).[73] This is achieved by considering the text, *ḥadīth*, *ijmā'* (consensus), another analogy or custom.[74] Jaṣṣāṣ has considered *istiḥsān* in the second type as a particularization of ruling (*ḥukm*) with the legal cause; however it is not a particularization of a ruling (*ḥukm*). Sarakhsī and Bazdawī and most of the Ḥanafī jurists do not accept this theory.[75]

The view of Bazdawī (d. 482/1089)

Bazdawī defines *istiḥsān* as, "It is one of the two *qiyās*".[76] 'Abd al-'Azīz al-Bukhāri, who interprets *Uṣūl* al-Bazdawī, points out that, "it is a particularization of *qiyās* (analogy) due to stronger evidence."[77] Al-Izmīrī (d. 1102 AH) agrees with this.[78] Khallāf and others cite Bukhāri's definition as though it was Bazdawi's,[79] however, it is not. The mistake was made when Bukhāri (d. 730 AH) quoted the definition without stating the originator, saying that "as the master pointed out".[80]

The following example, concerning the issue of prepaid sale (*salam*), serves as an illustration of Bazdawī's definition, and the "particularization of *qiyās*". In a normal sale, the good should be available at the time of purchase, as stated in the *ḥadīth*. The Prophet (ṣ) explained to a Companion, Ḥakīm b. Hizām, when asked whether he could sell a commodity prior to purchasing it himself, "Sell not what is not with you".[81] According to *qiyās*, this *ḥadīth* means that the *salam* contract is invalid. Nevertheless, *salam* has been validated by the express terms of other *ḥadīth* in spite of the non-existence of the goods at the time of purchase. Furthermore, a contract cannot be attributed to the future existence of usufruct because monetary compensations are not open to attribution to something in the future. *Qiyās* invalidates *salam* but the *Sunnah* approves it, for the Prophet says: "Whoever concludes *salam*, let him do so over a specified measure, specified weight and specified period of time."[82] Eventually, *salam* has been validated by way of *istiḥsān*, which is contrary to *qiyās*.

When we reconsider Bazdawī's definition we see that there are two kinds of *qiyās*: the obvious (*jalī*), and the hidden or assumed (*khafī*). *Jalī* is the one which is easily intelligible to the mind while *khafī* requires deep consideration and pondering. *khafī* is stronger in effect than *jalī*, thus *khafī* is called *istiḥsān* or *qiyās mustaḥsan* (approved analogy).[83] In certain situations, *qiyās* is called *istiḥsān* owing to the power of its evidence.[84] Shaybānī says, "Some of the *qiyās* involves *istiḥsān*".[85] There are minor differences between the two. *Istiḥsān* is more general than *qiyās khafī*, because the former applies to things other than *qiyās khafī*. Sadr al-Sharī'ah (d. 747 AH) observes that when the word *qiyās* is used absolutely, it means *qiyās jalī*; when the word *istiḥsān* is used it means *qiyās khafī*.[86] Bazdawī says that the *qiyās* which has a weak effect is called *qiyās*, and the *qiyās* which has a strong effect is called *istiḥsān*.[87]

The view of Sarakhsī (d. 483/1090)

Sarakhsī defines *istiḥsān* in a way that is different to other Ḥanafī scholars; he looks at the nature of *istiḥsān*, the wisdom behind the ideas of *istiḥsān*, and the wisdom of its use. *Istiḥsān* represents simplicity, ease and the lifting of difficulties.

Sarakhsī defines *istiḥsān* as "abandonment of an opinion to which *qiyās* would lead in favour of a different opinion when supported by stronger evidence and adapted to what is acceptable to the public." Sarakhsī has mentioned four other definitions. These definitions have been quoted by 'Abd al-'Azīz al-Ḥulwānī (d. 448/1050):[88]

1. "it means to seek ease and convenience in legal injunctions whether *al-khās* (the specific) or *al-'ām* (the general)",
2. "to depart from *qiyās* (analogy) and adopt what is more suitable for the people",
3. "to adopt what is accommodating and to seek mildness",
4. "to adopt tolerance and to seek what gives comfort".

These definitions indicate the general idea of deviating from a law which causes hardship and adopting or creating a law which provides ease and comfort.

One of the main objections levelled against Sarakhsī and his definitions is this: is the departure from one ruling to another, on the ground of ease, really based on evidence, or is it merely a reflection of personal taste or whim? Sarakhsī himself does not explain satisfactorily. He says that, "briefly, those expressions mean that abandoning hardship for the sake of ease is the base of the religion" quoting the Qur'an: "God intends for you ease, and He does not want to make things difficult for you" (2:185). The purpose of the divine injunction is to provide ease and comfort.

Sarakhsī looks at *istiḥsān* from a different perspective and categorises it in two types: the first one is called: "*ijtihād taqdīrī*", which allows jurists all to give rulings and on which there is no cause for disagreement amongst the scholars. The second one is the evidence (*dalīl*), which is in the mind and is set against the explicit analogy. According to Sarakhsī, evidence which opposes the established ruling appears stronger after considering evidence concerning similar cases; therefore ruling with evidence at hand is called *istiḥsān.*[89]

The view of Nasafī (d. 710/1310)

Abū al-Barakāt al-Nasafī has defined *istiḥsān* as: "Evidence which takes the opposite side to *qiyās jalī* (obvious analogy), or it is the opposing evidence to the obvious analogy (*qiyās jalī*)".[90] It would appear that the differences between the previous definitions and this one are slight; the meanings of the two definitions are for all intents and purposes the same. As I explained regarding the issue of forward sale (*salam*), the obvious analogy (*qiyās jalī*) requires invalidating the sale, and then the departure comes owing to hidden analogy (*khafī qiyās*), which validates the *salam*, for the simple reason that the effective cause is obvious and visible. However, other evidence, which is stronger, affects the ruling and became opposite to the established evidence. Therefore jurists practise *istiḥsān* with the stronger evidence that naturally is going to be the opposite of the *qiyās*. The evidence has to be *naṣṣ* (from the Qur'an or the *Sunnah*) or consensus or necessity and hidden analogy.

The view of Ibn Humām (d. 861/1457)

The Ḥanafī jurist Ibn Humām defines *istiḥsān* as "An evidence which is agreed upon textually or consensually, by necessity and by hidden analogy, if it happens to be opposed to a *qiyas* which leads to its understanding." A similar definition is: "The evidence which contradicts the apparent analogy and which needs to be understood through contemplation."[91] In addition, a similar definition was reported in Raḥawī's (d. 774 AH) footnotes;

however the commentator did not mention the term "necessity", and this is explained in the following statement. "The general opinion settled on evidence whether agreed upon, textually, consensually, or by hidden *qiyās*. If it happens to be the opposite of *qiyās*, which understanding leads to, this name will not be given to the same evidence without opposition."[92] With a closer look at this definition, and in addition to what Raḥawī mentioned, despite the fact that the words used differ substantially, the meaning remains more or less the same as the previous one. The term *istiḥsān* which is used in *fiqh* (jurisprudence) books is mostly considered to be *qiyās khafī* (hidden analogy).[93] It has been pointed out in works such as "*Talwīḥ*",[94] "*Fatḥ al-Ghaffār*",[95] "*Mirāt al-Uṣūl*",[96] and "*Ḥāshiyat al-Nasamāt al-Asḥār*"[97] that the technical meaning of *istiḥsān* as used by jurists is "hidden analogy", or *istiḥsān* which was based on evidence such as *naṣṣ* (text), *ijmāʿ* (consensus), *ḍarūrah* (necessity), which opposed explicit analogy.

One of the outstanding scholars of the Ottoman Empire in the last period ʿAlī Ḥaydar Afandī (d. 1936), also held the view that *istiḥsān* is hidden analogy, saying: "There are two types of *qiyās*: one is explicit analogy, known technically as "*qiyās*"; the other is "hidden analogy" (*qiyās khafī*), known as *istiḥsān*".[98]

The view of istiḥsān among the Shāfiʿī jurists

The Shāfiʿī School definitely rejects the principle of *istiḥsān* as a source of Islamic law. Imām Shāfiʿī[99] (d. 204) wrote a book titled "*Ibṭāl al-Istiḥsān*" (Invalidating Juristic Preference) and declared famously: "Whoever approves of juristic preference is making himself the lawmaker ".[100] However, Shāfiʿī jurists have given some definitions of *istiḥsān*, but the definitions that they provided are not their own, and they have taken what they have understood about *istiḥsān* and attributed those definitions to the Ḥanafī School.

In order to explain the opinions of the *'ulamā'* who reject *istiḥsān*, we will present some of the statements from Shāfi'ī's "*Al-Umm and al-Risālah*".

In the chapter entitled "*Invalidating Istiḥsān*" in "*Kitāb al-Umm*", Shāfi'ī says: Any qualified Governor or *muftī* is not permitted to rule or issue *fatwā* unless it is supported by an obligatory report from a source such as the Qur'an, and then the *Sunnah*, and then what the "people of knowledge" agree upon, or from *qiyās* that is based on some of these sources. He is also not permitted to rule or issue *fatwā* by way of *istiḥsān* since *istiḥsān* is not obligatory in any of these meanings.

He then quotes the Qur'an, citing 75:36 "Does man think that he will be left uncontrolled, (without purpose) *sudan*" The people of knowledge never disagreed over the Qur'an, as I know, that *sudan* is the one who neither is instructed to act nor prohibited from taking action. According to Shāfi'ī, the word *sudan*, which Yusuf Alī translates as "uncontrolled", denotes someone who is neither commanded to perform an action nor prohibited from carrying it out. Whoever gives a *fatwa* or rules in a manner opposing God's commands will fall under the category of *sudan.* God makes it known to him that He has left him as *sudan*, and that if whatever he says is opposed to what the Qur'an has revealed, he has therefore opposed the path of the Prophet (ṣ) and the general rule of the group of scholars who narrated the Prophet's (ṣ) words. Shāfi'ī says that if anyone were to ask, "Where in the Qur'an, or the practice of the Prophet (ṣ), do you find authority for rulings?"

He should be shown 6:106 and 5:49: "Follow what thou art taught by inspiration from thy Lord: there is no god but He: and turn aside from those who join gods with Allah."[101] And "And this (He commands): judge thou between them by what Allah hath revealed, and follow not their vain desires, but beware of them lest they beguile thee from any of that (teaching) which Allah hath sent down to thee. And if they turn away, be assured that for some of their crimes it is Allah's purpose to punish them. And truly most men are rebellious."[102]

Shāfi'ī then relates how a group of people asked the Prophet (ṣ) certain questions about the 'People of the Cave' (*ahl al-kahf*), and how the Prophet (ṣ) replied that he would respond to their questions as soon as he had received revelations concerning them via the angel Gabriel; God then revealed verse 22 and 23 of the *sura* entitled *al-Kahf*. Similarly, when the wife of Aws ibn al-Sāmit came to Muḥammad with complaints against her husband, the Prophet (ṣ) did not reply until the first verse of the *sura* entitled *al-Mujādila* had been revealed. Another example was when al-Ajlāni came to the Prophet (ṣ) with the allegation that his wife had committed adultery. Muḥammad replied that nothing had yet been revealed concerning the issue of adultery; when verses were eventually revealed, the Prophet (ṣ) called both of them to bear witness, in accordance with the dictates of the Qur'an: "O David! We did indeed make thee a vicegerent on earth: so judge thou between men in truth (and justice): nor follow thou the lust (of thy heart), for it will mislead thee from the Path" (38:26).

According to Shāfi'ī, nobody is ordered to rule according to *ḥaq* (truth) unless he knows what *ḥaq* is and *ḥaq* cannot become known unless it is from God either as text or by indication, as God made *ḥaq* in his Book and in the *Sunnah* of his Prophet (ṣ). Hence, there is no problem that one faces for which the Book has not given an indication of a solution, either in the form of text or in general. Shāfi'ī adds that if one asks, "what is the text and what is the generality?", text is what God has prohibited or permitted textually, such as marriage with mothers, sisters, grandmothers, aunts and all others mentioned; all other women are permitted. He had also prohibited carrion, blood, pork and *fawāḥish* (corruption) hidden or explicit, as well as other things. These are all clear in the text. As for generally, this is whatever God has ordained concerning *salāt*, *zakāt* and *ḥajj* (pilgrimage), and in a general sense; it was down to the Prophet (ṣ) to show how to perform the ritual prayers, the numbers of prayers, and its times and the actions performed during prayers. He also introduced *zakāt* and specified the kind of money, time and amount, and he also explained *ḥajj* and its requirements".[103]

In the same manner Shāfi'ī continues:

> "I am not aware of any knowledgeable people who can give accreditation to any thinkers and literate people to issue a *fatwā* or rule according to his own opinion, if he is not equipped in the field of *qiyās* which revolves around the book (Qur'an) or the *Sunnah* or *ijmā'* and *'aql*, which explains the similar cases. If they claim they are capable of issuing a *fatwā* or ruling, we would ask them why thinkers who are more capable than many of those who are knowledgeable in the Qur'an, the *Sunnah* and *fatwā*, were not permitted to have a say on issues that were revealed, since both groups know that *Istiḥsān* is not from the Qur'an, the *Sunnah*, or *ijmā'*, and they are more intellectual and more capable of explaining than their public. If it is said those who reject *Istiḥsān* have inadequate knowledge of *uṣūl*, then you will be asked, "What evidence do you have in your knowledge of *uṣūl* if you rule without any base of *uṣūl* or *qiyās* based on *uṣūl*? Do you think that the scholars who have no command of *'ilm al-uṣūl* will not be able to effect *qiyās* in what they do not know, and that your knowledge of *uṣūl* will enable you to perform *qiyās* or permit you to depart from such *qiyās* based on such *uṣūl*? If you are permitted to depart from these *uṣūl*, then they are permitted to rule as you do; then they will depart from *qiyās* based on this *uṣūl* or they will get it wrong".[104]

Shāfi'ī continues:

> "If a ruler or a *muftī* in an issue in which there is neither a text reported or *qiyās* says "I prefer", then he has no choice but to accept others who pass rulings opposed to his on the same issue. Then different rulers (*muftī*) in different places rule according to what each of them prefers, resulting in various rulings on one issue. If this is permitted, they will ignore the others and rule as they wish, and if it is not permitted then they are not allowed to rule as they wish. If the one amongst them who departs from *qiyās* says that people should follow what he says, then he will be asked: "Who ordained that you should obey others or that others should obey you? If any one claims the similar, will you follow him? For my part, I will only follow the one I have been asked to pursue. Similarly, no one is obliged to follow you because obedience is only to the one that God and His Prophet ordained. The *ḥaq* to follow is only what God and His Prophet (ṣ) ordained. God and His Prophet (ṣ) indicate textually or by indications: if God enjoins prayers on one who is incapable of locating the direction of the Ka'ba. He makes it possible for him to discover it by the way of *ijtihād* by seeking the indication to that direction".[105]

These are some of the arguments that Shāfi'ī mentioned in the chapter "*Invalidating istiḥsān*" in the book "*Al-Umm*".

Anyone following the statements of Shāfi'ī will observe that he does not recognize *istiḥsān* in any form whatsoever. As he explained, the rulings can only be deduced from the Qur'an, the *Sunnah, ijmā', qiyās.*

As far as *istiḥsān* is concerned, Shāfi'ī does not recognize it as a basis to issue a ruling. He says that acting according to *istiḥsān* leads to situations where human beings are left in a state of lawlessness (*sudan*), that is, what ever his desire dictates to him and is naturally at odds with the above quoted *āyāh* (verse).

Actually, everybody, including those who recognize *istiḥsān*, reject *istiḥsān* that is based on personal desire. Shāfi'ī said, with regards to the case of the thinkers and the literate, that if they were allowed to rule by *istiḥsān* it would be in contradiction to the use of *istiḥsān,* as those who recognize *istiḥsān* understand that its meaning is the departure from *qiyās* to a stronger *dalīl.* The situations are such that the *dalīl* can only be expected from a *mujtahīd* who is competent in the Sharī'ah rulings and the *dalīl,* while it is unacceptable from thinkers and the literate who are not qualified.

As for the allegation of adultery against the wife of Aws, the Prophet (ṣ) waited for a revelation so that he could issue a ruling. It is generally accepted that during the period of ongoing revelation, there was no need for the application of *istiḥsān, qiyās* or *ijtihād.* With the death of the Prophet (ṣ), the revelation ceased, and so some form of *ijtihād*, and *istiḥsān,* was needed. This is discussed in the section on "invalidating *istiḥsān*". As we have seen, Shāfi'ī does not recognize *istiḥsān* completely, as is mentioned in the book of "*al-Umm*". In his *Risālah,* in the section "*taḥrīm al-istiḥsān*" Shāfi'ī regards *istiḥsān* as *taladhdhudh* (deriving pleasure).[106] This does not differ too much from what is reported in "*al-Umm*", except in the formulation of the words. As far as invalidating *istiḥsān* is concerned, the statements in both books are the same; however, the statement in the "*Risālah*" mentions that it is prohibited (*ḥarām*) for anyone to act according to *istiḥsān.* The "*Risālah*" statement rules in effect that acting according to *istiḥsān* is *ḥarām* (prohibited).

The view of Shīrāzī (d. 476/1083)

Another definition of *istiḥsān*, which is attributed to Ḥanafīs, is one given by a Shāfi'ī jurist, Shīrāzī, as: "Something which is considered good by the faculty of reason (*'aql*) and depends on assumption rather than evidence."[107] However, according to Zarkashī (d. 794/1392), this definition is not quoted directly from Abū Ḥanīfah, but is simply Shāfi'īs interpretation of what *istiḥsān* meant to Abū Ḥanīfah.[108] According to Shīrāzī and Zarkashī this definition and attribution was rejected by the Ḥanafīs.[109]

The Shāfi'īs considered that the definition attributed to Abū Ḥanīfah was used in conjunction with a case where there was no evidence to support the practice of *istiḥsān*. For example: If a man commits adultery and the four witnesses testify that he has committed the crime, the punishment (*ḥadd*) is to be inflicted on the accused, on the basis of *istiḥsān,* in the opinion of Abū Ḥanīfah. Generally, of course, there should be no punishment if the evidence is doubtful. Abū Ḥanīfah might have interpreted the evidence by saying that each one of the witnesses might have seen him at different moments. This would not constitute the standard evidence according to Shīrāzī, and would save the accused from conviction. Alternatively Abū Ḥanīfah could have argued that the fornicators might have moved around during their act of fornication and, as a result, been seen by four different people, at four different moments, from four different positions, thus explaining the divergence in testimonies. But for Shīrāzī, this cannot be evidence; it might be only an *istiḥsān*, which is not evidence.[110] Ghazālī said that it was a ridiculous law based on *istiḥsān* that condones the shedding of Muslim blood.[111]

There is another definition given by the Shāfi'ī Bishr b. Ghiyās (d. 218/833) which is attributed to Abū Ḥanīfah: "*Istiḥsān* is a departure from analogy that is based on personal opinion, in which case it can be considered valid without the support of evidence."[112]

> Zufar gives a similar example in Sarakhsī's book, *al-Mabsūṭ*: "If a man commits adultery and the four who witnessed the crime

testified that he committed the act but in different corners of the house, the punishment (*ḥadd*) shall not be inflicted on the accused on the basis of *qiyās* (analogy). Since the act is seen from two different sides of the room, it could appear that the act of adultery took place in two different rooms, and, therefore the punishment (*ḥadd*) is applied to the adulterers according to *istiḥsān*; this is the opinion of Abū Ḥanīfah and other *imāms*. The witnesses are unanimous on the adultery and only disagree on what they actually witnessed, and therefore it should be accepted that the crime of adultery was committed and that punishment should be administered, even if it was impossible to describe the dress the woman was wearing at the time or to observe every detail.

The Ḥanafīs opposed this definition, as the evidence was not conclusive in the Ḥanafī *Uṣūl* (methodology) books. This invites doubt about the attribution and the possibility of its accuracy. The doubt caused al-Baṣrī (d. 436/1044) to respond by saying: "the advocators of the concept of the definition know the purpose of their ancestors who evidently stated in many cases 'we approved *istiḥsān* depending on this *athar* (tradition) and evidence'. We understand that they do not approve *istiḥsān* without positive evidence."[113] Therefore, what al-Baṣrī said confirmed that the attribution of the definition to Abū Ḥanīfah may be incorrect.

The view of Ghazālī (d. 505/1111)

Ghazālī gives three different definitions of *istiḥsān*. The first he describes as: "That which the jurist prefers using the intellectual faculty; the Jurist (*al-Mujtahid*) uses his own judgement to arrive at the decision."[114] After giving the definition, he criticizes it. According to him, before the appearance of *istiḥsān*, the Muslim community had unanimously accepted that the *mujtahid* would not give any *fatwā* (ruling) without depending on *adillah* Sharī'ah (proofs of Islamic law) rather than depending on his own desires. Ghazālī rejects the concept by saying, "We approve (*nastahsinu*) the invalidation of *istiḥsān*".[115] Āmidī (d. 631/1233)[116] and Isnawī (d. 772/1370)[117] also have mentioned the same definition.

Scholars other than those of the Shāfi'ī School also mention a similar definition. One such scholar is Shāṭibī, who added the expression "and tends to it by his opinion".[118] Shāṭibī, when discussing the definition, explains that when looking closely at the definition and those who adopt it, it is their custom to use *istiḥsān* to give the people their desires; however, this should not contradict the evidence of Sharī'ah. In such a case, ruling by *istiḥsān* is acceptable as long as it does not contradict Sharī'ah.

Shāṭibī continues, "This definition may apply to certain acts of worship which are the evidence that is the invention of certain people but which have no textual basis in the Book of Allah. Such definition is aimless since it follows that *istiḥsān* has to be divided into the good (*ḥasan*) and the bad (*qabīḥ*), which means that not all of *istiḥsān* is correct. It could be understood that Shāṭibī did not accept this definition; the mind (*'aql*) often accepts that which is incorrect and based on desire, even if it distances one from what is right (*ḥaq*). Shāṭibī mentions a comment that contains a similar meaning to such understanding in "*al-I'tiṣām*". He says: "Scholars agree, if customs and habits lean towards this definition, it is acceptable to have a ruling (*ḥukm*) based on *istiḥsān*, though this ruling must not contradict the Sharī'ah. This shows that some acts of worship can be without textual basis, thus leading to what is known as "*bid'ah*"; consequently it has to be either good or bad since not every *istiḥsān* is right (*ḥaq*)."[119] Shāṭibī states as an objection to this definition that "whatever the *mujtahid* selects by using his mind (*'aql*), leads to another objection which is: "Is it with evidence (*dalīl*) or without evidence?" Scholars in general concur that it should be based on evidence (*dalīl*) but there is nothing in the definition that shows reference to evidence (*dalīl*). Shāṭibī continues: "If the opinion of the scholar is based on evidence of Sharī'ah it could have been more accurate and representative of the case, but since such things are not mentioned in the definition, the definition consequently is no longer valid for *istiḥsān*." It is possible that the scholars who gave a different definition of *istiḥsān* reflected their own point of view without evidence.

The definition that has been criticised and rejected by al-Juwaynī (d. 478/1085), his pupil Ghazālī and other Shāfi'ī scholars such as Āmidī and Isnawī, has not been found in any Ḥanafī *Uṣūl* sources. The reality is that Abū Ḥanīfah and his followers have used *istiḥsān* in their judgements. However, after examination and investigation of the examples of *istiḥsān*, we can clearly see that these examples have been based on a validated proof and its preferred analogy (*qiyās*) with a legal reason.[120]

Consequently, whenever they approve *istiḥsān* it is simply a case of *ijtihād* based on personal desire, because they have performed *istiḥsān* after investigation and hard work. If it is merely based on personal desire, then laborious work is unnecessary.[121]

Nobody can reject the role of *'aql* (intellect) when dealing with matters pertaining to people or the methods of finding evidence to reach a ruling or the reason why it is acceptable since it is not against the aim of Sharī'ah. As al-Ṭūfī (d. 716/1316) explains, "The definition is accepted according to what is generally agreed by scholars, if it concords with Sharī'ah proof; otherwise it is rejected."[122]

The view of Āmidī (d. 631/1233)

Āmidī, a Shāfi'ī jurist, views *istiḥsān* as a proof that action should be based on evidence. He considers that *istiḥsān* is not a subject of disagreement if it is supported by text, or *ijmā'* or others. In such situations there is no disagreement over its validity as a proof, although there can be disagreements over the terminology.

Actually, his opinion is that the disagreement stems from the use of different words to describe *istiḥsān*. Additionally, this disagreement is of no use since the words are used to describe what the *mujtahīd* prefers based on *dalīl* and the public preference (*maṣlaḥah mursalah*) without any proof of Sharī'ah. The meaning here is *istiḥsān* that is based on a *dalīl* thus becomes a proof, and there is no room for disagreement over such an issue.

It can be concluded that Āmidī views *istiḥsān* as a proof so long as the departure from *qiyās* stems from the availability of a stronger *dalīl*.[123]

Āmidī has defined *istiḥsān* as: "An evidence embedded (*yanqadihu*) in the mind of the jurist that words will not assist him to express or show."[124] Ghazālī said much the same in his second definition.[125] Shāṭibī gave the same definition;[126] a similar definition was given by Isnawī, although he applied different words. He defined *istiḥsān* as: "Evidence embedded in the mind of the jurist, but unexpressed by word."[127] Similar definitions were also given by Ibn al-Subkī, Shawkānī, al-Taftazānī, and Shaykh 'Abd Allah Dirāz (d. 1351/1932), who defines *istiḥsān* as: "Evidence embedded in the mind of the jurist who finds difficulties to express it in words".[128]

Criticism has emerged about whether the definition hesitates between acceptance and rejection. The explanation for this is as follows: the first section of the definition "evidence embedded" makes one wonder what is meant by "*embedded*"; it is meant as confirmation of the evidence and it should be applied, which is the general agreement. There is no lack of explanation on the part of the jurist. His explanation may differ to what others understand, but the jurist himself does not have any problems because he understands the evidence. If, however, the "*embedding*" is taken as a knowledge of the evidence, but has been mixed with some doubt, then it will be rejected according to the general agreement of the scholars. A *ḥukm* (ruling) can not be adopted with doubt and probability.[129] These objections, which Ghazālī and 'Aḍuḍ al-Dīn al-Ijī (d. 756 AH) report,[130] show that this definition is not valid for *istiḥsān*.

It is essential for *ḥukm* to be dependent on evidence that is clearly taken from Sharī'ah. This is to enable the jurist to distinguish whether the evidence is true or false. Therefore if the evidence could not be expressed, it follows that *ḥukm* cannot depend on it.

The view of istiḥsān according to the Mālikī school

It is generally accepted that Mālikīs recognize *istiḥsān*, as is clear from the definitions mentioned previously in the first part. It was narrated that Imām Mālik (d. 179 AH) said, "*Istiḥsān* represents nine-tenths of human knowledge".[131] According to Ashba' adopting *istiḥsān* may outweigh *qiyās*.[132]

If this is so, then we can not imagine *istiḥsān* being defined by some as "Whatever is preferred by *mujtahid* rationally and through self inclination based on personal opinion". Nor is it "a proof that emerges (*yanqadihū fī nafs al-mujtahid*) in the mind, but the *mujtahid* could not express it in words". Such *istiḥsān* cannot be viewed as nine-tenths of human knowledge; nor will it outweigh *qiyas* as one of the proofs. Shātibī says, in what could be seen as support for *istiḥsān*, "I used to agree with those scholars and dismiss *istiḥsān;* however, it gained support and was strengthened, since we can find a number of rulings (*fatāwā*) of the Caliphs and the learned Companions and those around them, and so there can be no denial. After that I changed my mind and began to support it."[133]

It was reported in "*Sharḥ al-'Aḍūḍ 'alā al-Muntahā*" that "*istiḥsān,* over which there is disagreement, went unnoticed because they mentioned in its interpretation issues that do not amount to a basis for disagreement. Some of these issues are generally accepted, others lie somewhere between being generally accepted and rejected. As to those who define it as what emerges (*yanqadiḥu fī nafs al-mujtahid*) in the mind of the *mujtahid* but which can not be expressed in words, this constitutes a quandary between acceptance and rejection. Otherwise, what does it mean to say emerges (*yanqadiḥu*)? If it means the realization of confirmation of evidence, then acting according to it becomes obligatory by general agreement, irrespective of the inability to express it in words. If the meaning of it emerges (*yanqadiḥu*) and is difficult to express in words because one has doubts about the *dalīl,* then *istiḥsān* is rejected in this case by general agreement because the rulings are not confirmed by probability and doubt. If *istiḥsān* means that the *mujtahid* prefers rational thinking and is inclined to his own opinion, then this is rejected by general agreement. Since there is no difference between a member of the public and a scholar, this would spring from personal desire. If however, *istiḥsān* means the departure from a ruling on a similar case to a different ruling due to stronger evidence, then this is generally accepted and there is no disagreement."[134]

It can be concluded from both of the above statements that the Māliki School recognize *istiḥsān* and accept it is a proof on which a number of *fiqh* cases have been established.

Shawkānī (d. 1834 AD) says that the view of Qurtūbī (d. 671 AH) is that Imām Mālik denied *istiḥsān* and did not adopt it.

Shawkānī also claims that it was Imām al-Ḥaramayn (d. 478 AH) who attributed the recognition of *istiḥsān* to Imām Mālik. According to Shawkānī: "Imām al-Ḥaramayn attributed *istiḥsān* to Mālik and Qurtūbī denied *istiḥsān* and said it is unknown according to Imām Mālik's madhhab".[135] This statement is in fact at odds with the reports in the books of the Mālikī School.

Perhaps the reader will note, from the statements we have reported that there is no indication anywhere of the denial of *istiḥsān* by Mālik rather than the recognition, by Mālik, as was mentioned earlier.

Consequently, it can be seen that the Mālikī School recognize *istiḥsān* as a proof of *shari'ah;* however, their views of *istiḥsān* are somewhat different from those of the Ḥanafī School. The Mālikī School views *istiḥsān* as departure from *qiyās* due to public interest; *istiḥsān* for them does not go beyond being a *maṣlaḥah* (public interest) that requires the departure from *qiyās*, even though this *maṣlaḥah* depends on a proof of Sharī'ah. The departure from *qiyās* is due to a necessity so that people do not suffer from hardship.

This is explained in the book *al-Muwāfaqāt:* "The one who 'prefers' (i.e. to make *istiḥsān*) does not refer to his own personal taste or desire, but is simply trying to obtain the purpose of the Legislator (i.e. God) which is to discover what are the obligatory duties. For example, in an issue that requires *qiyās,* but in which *qiyās* may leads to missing a *maṣlaḥah* or bringing about *mafsadah,* the application of *qiyās* in absolute terms will inevitably lead to hardship in some of its sources, and therefore the possibility of harm must be avoided."[136]

This statement shows that the previous explanation is correct. Reference to a group of *fiqh* issues will be referred to in the section on the effects of the application of *istiḥsān* on the construction of Islamic *fiqh*. Al-Shāṭibī concludes his sayings by asserting that this is a technique of proof (*dalīl*) that shows the correctness of this rule and is the basis on which Mālik and his followers constructed their views.[137] This would explain the direction of the Mālikī School in recognizing *istiḥsān*, as it is limited to a *maṣlaḥah* (public interest) as opposed to *qiyās*, while the Ḥanafī school says this proof may be *athar*, *ijmā'*, *qiyās khafīy*, necessity, or *maṣlaḥah*.

The view of Abū al-Walīd Al-Bājī (d. 474/1081)

Quoting from Mālikī jurist Ishāq bin Khuwaydh Mindād (d. 390/1000), al-Bājī defines *istiḥsān* as "Acting on a ruling based on a stronger *dalīl* as compared to another",[138] Qarafī (d. 684 AH) comments on this definition saying that "in this manner, it becomes *hujjah* by *ijmā'*, while actually it is not".[139] In fact, this definition, although it agrees with other definitions as far as meaning is concerned, is criticized for the wordings or terms it uses. This definition is general and does not have any limitation because it is based on stronger evidence.

Shāṭibī (d. 790/1388) gives the following explanation: "*Istiḥsān* according to us and the Ḥanafīs is "practising on a ruling based on the stronger of two evidences (*dalīlayn*)".[140] On the other hand, this is also applicable to *nāsikh* (abrogating) with *mansūkh* (abrogated); general (*'ām*) with particular (*khāṣ*), and absolute (*mutlaq*) with *muqayyad* (constrained).

The view of Ibn al-'Arabī (d. 543/1147)

According to Ibn al-'Arabī, *istiḥsān* is "To abandon what is required by the law, when applying the existing law would lead to a departure from some of its own objectives."[141] It is clear that Ibn al-'Arabī indicates that the essence of *istiḥsān* is "to apply a ruling based on the stronger of the two evidences (*dalīlayn*)".

The explanation of this definition is that there would be a *dalīl*, which concerns general principles, and which would be applicable to various cases. In some such cases, a *dalīl* may later emerge which is different—and preferable—to the first. This new dalil necessitates a ruling different to the earlier one. In such situations the *mujtahid* departs from the general ruling based on the first *dalīl* by the way of exception for this case; he acts on the basis of the new *dalīl* to deduce another ruling which departs from the generality of the earlier *dalīl*. The reason for this action of the *mujtahid* is based on the general principle of the jurisprudential maxims, which holds that: "Repelling an evil is preferable to securing a benefit",[142] or to keep away a *mafsadah* rather than obtaining *maṣlaḥah* or to bring about a *maṣlaḥah*, which would otherwise be missed if the *mujtahid* acted on the basis of the first *dalīl*. Shāṭibī comments on this definition, saying: "It is the departure from a ruling for *'urf*, *maṣlaḥah*, or *ijmā'* avoiding the hardship in respect of the preference of ease to facilitate people's affairs.[143]

The view of Ibn Rushd (d. 595/1198)

Ibn Rushd says that "*Istiḥsān's* usage is so common that it exceeds *qiyās;* it is the departure from a *qiyās* that leads to extremity and exaggeration in the ruling of a case which is based on the meaning of an effective cause (*'illah*) and thus influences the ruling of the case.[144] Despite all of these different explanations, the meanings are compatible with Ibn al-'Arabī's definition.

The view of Ibn Al-Abyārī (d. 618/1221)

Shams al-Dīn Abū Ḥusayn al-Abyārī defines *istiḥsān* as "using partial *maṣlaḥah* (in the interest of the public) as opposed to general *qiyās* (analogy)."[145]

Shāṭibī interprets this as: "the implication of using partial *maṣlaḥah* is to bring forward the *mursal* (discontinued) evidence (*istidlāl mursal*) to *qiyās*".[146] To explain this 'Abd Allah Dirāz (d. 1351) gives the example of someone who buys goods of his own free will and on his death leaves his heirs in disagreement as to whether to keep or return the goods. *Istiḥsān,* Dirāz explains, would dictate that if the vendor refuses to take the goods back, then it is acceptable to keep them.[147] Consequently, *istiḥsān* thus defined cannot be expanded, as it is limited to *maṣlaḥah mursalah.* The discussion of this definition shows that it does not succeed in defining *istiḥsān*; it only makes *istiḥsān* applicable where the *dalīl*, particularizing the *qiyās*, is considered as nothing other than *maṣlaḥah mursalah.*

The view of Shāṭibī (d. 790/1388)

Abū Isḥāq Ibrāhīm al-Shāṭibī, a Māliki jurist, is one of the prominent scholars dealing with the concept of *maqaṣid* (objective of the Sharī'ah). He considers *istiḥsān* as a source of Islamic law, but says that the interpretation should not be based on desire, and that the jurists must have a full understanding of the intention of the Lawgiver. When presented with a new problem the jurists will resort to *istiḥsān* if the use of the strict application of analogy will lead to loss of *maṣlaḥah* or the possibility of evil. He defines *istiḥsān* as "An evidence embedded (*yanqadiḥu*) in the mind of the jurist but which words will not allow him to express".[148] The same definition has been given by Āmidī (d. 631) and a similar definition given by Ibn al-Subkī (d. 771), Shawkāni (d. 1250), Taftazānī (d. 793), and Shaykh 'Abd-Allah Dirāz (d. 1351).

The view of istiḥsān amongst the Ḥanbali school

The narrations reported about the Ḥanbalī School's views on *istiḥsān* as a principle of Sharī'ah differ: some narrations reported that Imām Aḥmad (d. 241 AH) recognized *istiḥsān*, while others reported that he did not.

Abū Yā'lā (d. 458/1065) defines *istiḥsān* as "leaving one *ḥukm* (ruling) for another stronger or better *ḥukm* (ruling)." He points out that the Qur'an or the *Sunnah* and *ijmā'* will be reliable proofs while performing *istiḥsān*.[149]

Qaḍi Yā'qūb reports that *istiḥsān* is the way of Imām Aḥmad. It is "The departure from one ruling to another which has priority; no one can deny this. If the name differs there is no point in disagreement over terms when there is an agreement on the meaning."[150] This is based on the statement which Ibn Qudāmah (d. 620/1223) narrates from Qaḍi Ya'qūb, who contended that *istiḥsān* with its meaning is generally agreed upon.

Ibn Taymiyyah narrates from Hulwānī: "Hulwānī interpreted *istiḥsān* in different ways. In my opinion *istiḥsān* is probably the departure from *qiyās jalī* and other proofs to a *dalīl* from the text of a solitary *ḥadīth* (*khabar wāḥid*) or another *dalīl*, or the departure from *qiyās* to a saying of a companion when *qiyās* does not apply. I have noted that al-Fakhr Ismā'īl, in his book, "*Al-Jadal*", reports a similar interpretation of *istiḥsān*. The Ḥanafī School agreed with us in that when a companion said something in which *qiyās* finds its way, then it is taken as if the companion had said that to avoid incorrect interpretation. The Shāfi'īs opposed us on this issue. Similarly, the Ḥanafīs agreed with us on *istiḥsān* whilst Shāfi'īs disagreed with us".[151]

Ibn Taymiyyah's statement shows that recognizing *istiḥsān* in the narration which *Qāḍī* Yā'qūb reported from Imām Aḥmad, and which Hulwānī and al-Fakhr Ismā'īl support, is a proof if it is based on *dalīl*. This means that we depart from *qiyās* based on such a *dalīl* whether this *dalīl* is a solitary *khabar* or another report. If the departure was due to a saying of a Companion, then following this method confirms that *istiḥsān* is a proof for them (Ḥanbalī) and there can be no disagreement over this issue. The narration confirming *istiḥsān* as a proof comes from Maimūnī, and is quoted by Ibn Taymiyyah: "Our *shaykh* said that Aḥmad used *istiḥsān* in many cases". In the Maimūnī narration, Imām Aḥmad is quoted as saying: "I prefer (*astaḥsinū*) *tayammum* for every prayer, and the *qiyās* here is on equal footing with water where the ritual prayer can still be performed until the *wuḍū* (ablution) is invalidated or until the water becomes available".[152] This narration thus shows that *istiḥsān* is a proof for Imām Aḥmad where it can be traced clearly in many *fiqh* issues.

However, Abū Ṭālib reported that Imām Aḥmad did not resort to *istiḥsān*. He says that when the followers of Abū Ḥanīfah encountered an issue opposed to *qiyās*, they then adopted it and departed from *qiyās*. This leads to the conclusion that when faced with an issue which is opposed to *qiyās* the correct thing to do is depart from *qiyās* to *istiḥsān*.[153]

This leads to the conclusion that from the Ḥanbalīs point of view, one cannot depart from one *qiyās* to another *qiyās;* rather, departure from *qiyās* can only be sanctioned by *naṣṣ*, be it a *ḥadīth* or other reports. This could be explained best by Abū al-Khaṭṭāb (d. 510/1116) who is reported in the *Musawwadah* as saying: "For me, he (*imām* Aḥmad) denied the *istiḥsān* without evidence, which is why he said that the Ḥanafīs departed from *qiyās* which they claimed was right (*ḥaqq*). If *istiḥsān* was based on *dalīl*, they adopted it and he (*imām* Aḥmad) did not deny it, because it was right (*ḥaq*). And he said: I follow the *ḥadīth* and I do not perform *qiyās* based on it, this means that I depart from *qiyās* by *khabar*, which is *istiḥsān* by *dalīl*".[154]

Ibn Taymiyyah explains this as meaning that when he sees an indication which is stronger than *qiyās*, the *mujtahid* is led to depart from *qiyās* and to adopt that indication without invalidating *qiyās* itself. This is about departing from *qiyās zāhir* (explicit analogy) to *qiyās khafiy* (implicit analogy) which is stronger and refers to specifying the cause (*takhṣīṣ ʿillah*). Ibn Taymiyyah prohibits the specification of *ʿillah* while he supports the adoption of *istiḥsān,* whatever the reason for the departure from *qiyās* and when it refers to a stronger *dalīl*, be it text or other reports.[155]

Ibn Taymiyyah refers to what *Qāḍī* said in reply to Abū al-Khaṭṭāb's statement. He says that there is a difference between the specification of *ʿillah* and the departure from *qiyās* to *khabar* (report). This is because whoever speaks of the validity of *takhṣīṣ ʿillah* may depart from *qiyās* for a *dalīl* or without a *dalīl;* this prevents its meaning from being subjected to *takhṣīṣ* (specification) with evidence. Ibn Taymiyyah responds by saying: "If we do not adopt *takhṣīṣ ʿillah* this takes away the restriction located in *takhṣīṣ* and makes it a restriction in the *ʿillah* (cause); this explains that the *ʿillah* is incomplete. As explained by the specified (*al-mukhaṣṣaṣ*) that it is not completed, thus there is no difference between the specification and non-specification of *ʿillah.* This is what Abū al-Khaṭṭāb said and it is in agreement with the saying of al-Baṣrī and Ibn Al-Khaṭīb and others."[156]

This leads to the conclusion that *istiṭsān* for Abū al-Khaṭṭāb is an *ʿillah* which is stronger than the *qiyās* and is opposed to *qiyās,* irrespective of whether this *dalīl* is a *khabar* or implicit *qiyās* (*qiyās khafiy*). Thus he supported the departure from one *qiyās* to another; this departure is known as *takhṣīṣ ʿillah.* Thus this Ḥanbalī Scholar has invalidated the report in the second narration.

Al-Hulwanī (d. 448/1050) however, sees *istiḥsān* with the same view as the Ḥanafīs. For him, *istiḥsān* is more general than both Abū al-Khaṭṭāb's definition and what has been reported in the earlier narration. In one case he says that it is the stronger *qiyās* and in another, he says, it is the stronger *dalīl*, and this is more general than the first. This would mean that *istiḥsān* for him may be based on the Qur'an, the *Sunnah*, or *ijmā'*.[157]

For Najmuddīn al-Ṭūfī (d. 716/1316), the definition of *istiḥsān* was similar to that of Ibn Qudāmah. However, his definition was more comprehensive in spite of Ibn Qudāmah confining the evidence to the Qur'an and the *Sunnah*. Al-Ṭūfī expands the meaning of *istiḥsān* to cover all of the *adillah* Sharī'ah (legal proofs). He defines *istiḥsān* as "A departure from the existing precedent, by taking a decision in a certain case different from that on which similar cases have been decided in the light of special *adillah* Sharī'ah (legal proof)."[158]

In conclusion, the Ḥanbalīs recognize *istiḥsān* in spite of their disagreement over the meaning; some interpreted it as the departure from *qiyās* to the saying of a companion or a solitary *ḥadīth* (*khabar wāḥid*), while others saw it as a departure from one *qiyās* for a stronger *dalīl*, or as a departure from one *qiyās* to a stronger one. Only Abū Ṭālib dismisses *istiḥsān* as a ruling based on personal desire.

When we examine the Ḥanbalīs and what they said on the subject of *istiḥsān* the following could be concluded:

1. The majority of the Ḥanbalī Scholars agree that *istiḥsān* is the departure from *qiyās* to a *dalīl* stronger than that *qiyās*, even though they use different expressions. Some of them say that it is the departure from what *qiyās* requires to a *dalīl* which is that which is stronger compared to that *qiyās*. Others say it is the stronger of two *qiyās*, and so on.
2. All of them—based on this definition—accept *istiḥsān*, and consider it to be the way of Imām Aḥmad, whom they portray as resorting to *istiḥsān* based on this definition.

3. Given the above, *istiḥsān* is not an independent proof, but is related to weighing proofs against each other, as Ibn Taymiyyah confirmed earlier.
4. They reject any kind of *istiḥsān* that is based on personal desire without *dalīl,* and consider this to be legislating in Sharī'ah that which God forbids.
5. They are not in disagreement with other scholars, as all scholars recognized *istiḥsān* as long as the departure was from one *dalīl* to a stronger one.
6. The report which claims that Aḥmad denied *istiḥsān* does not convey a clear denial. In spite of this Abū al-Khaṭṭāb (d. 510/1116) interprets this as denial of *istiḥsān* which is not supported by a *dalīl.* In such situations the original rule remains intact. That is Aḥmad recognized *istiḥsān* as long as the departure from *qiyās* is by a *dalīl.*[159]

In short *istiḥsān* is a principle of Sharī'ah for the Ḥanbalīs in spite of their disagreement on how to arrive at *istiḥsān.* As for those who said it is not a principle (e.g. Abū Ṭālib), they were referring to *istiḥsān* without a *dalīl,* which springs from *hawā'* (desire); there was no disagreement over this.

Thus it can be said that the Ḥanafīs, Mālikīs and Ḥanbalīs agreed upon the recognition of *istiḥsān* in spite of the different ways they conceived of the departure from one ruling to another.

The view of istiḥsān amongst the Shī'ah jurists

The Imāmī Shī'ah

The Imāmī Shī'ah do not accept *istiḥsān* at all and rejects the performance of *qiyās* (analogy). It is their belief that *istiḥsān* has been approved without evidence, and thus they do not give any credence to the *istiḥsān* rulings.[160] They claim that *istiḥsān* and *qiyās* are not considered as proof if they are not based on explicit textual or reasonable evidence; furthermore, they are obviously forbidden as they are based on assumption.[161]

Zaydīyyah jurists

The concept of *istiḥsān* among the Zaydiyyah thought is close to the Ḥanafīs. The Zaydiyyah and Ḥanafī jurists consider *istiḥsān* as part of analogy.[162] It is defined as "A departure from one established ruling to a stronger one."[163] The Zaydī definition of *istiḥsān* is very close to the Ḥanafī definitions. While Karkhi's definition and that of the Zaydīs is similar, the meaning is exactly the same even though Karkhi's definition has been criticised because it included the *takhṣīṣ 'illah* (particularization) within the scope of *istiḥsān*.[164]

In the Zaydiyyah school of thought, the condition upon which *istiḥsān* can occur is if the departure is from one speculative proof to another. First, both must fulfil the conditions of eligibility and one of them must be stronger and preferable.[165] If the proofs are both *qiyās*, or one is *qiyās* and the other is a *ḥadīth* (*khabar, athar*), there is nothing to be considered, since *istiḥsān* is based on the principle that "No conflict occurs between two definite proofs". The conflict between two definite proofs is only to be taken into account when considering *naskh* (abrogation), and so it is not an *istiḥsān*.

Indeed, the Zaydiyyah declare that *istiḥsān* can not be based on definite proofs, owing to the jurisprudential principle which accords priority to definite proofs over speculative proofs. Conflict arises only when both proofs are speculative. The Zaydiyyah also point out the conditions of *qiyās*, which is against the *istiḥsān*, must be fulfilled.[166]

The view of istiḥsān amongst the Ẓāhiriyyah jurists

The foundation of Ẓāhiriyyah (Literalists) thought is based on the literal meanings of the Qur'an and the *Sunnah*. The jurist Dawūd Ibn 'Alī (d. 270/884) is the founder of this school; his most famous disciple was the belletrist, poet, historian, theologian, jurist, philosopher, and polemicist Ibn Ḥazm (d. 456/1064).[167] The Literalists instructed their followers in the superficial rather than the deeper meaning of the Qur'an and the *Sunnah*.

According to the Ẓāhiriyyah, the primary source of the Sharī'ah is the text of the Qur'an, in accordance with the verse: "O you who believe! Obey God and obey the Messenger (Muḥammad) and those of you (*Muslims*) who are in authority. (And) if you differ in anything amongst yourselves, refer it to God and His Messenger if you believe in God and in the last day. That is better and more suitable for final determination." (4:59). Citing the verses "...we have neglected nothing in the Book," (6:38), "the Book is an exposition of everything"(16:89). "...I have perfected your religion for you, completed my favour upon you..." (5:3), "and that you may explain clearly to men what is sent down to them..." (16:44), Ibn Ḥazm indicates that every aspect of life and all human needs be they material or spiritual, are provided for in the Qur'an, and therefore no divergence is allowed from the text of the Qur'an except where one verse is abrogated by another.[168]

As indicated in the Qur'an, the second source of the Sharī'ah is the Tradition (*ḥadīth*), which is a record of the Prophet's (ṣ) *acta* and *dicta*. The Prophet (ṣ) is deemed totally trustworthy, as the Qur'an itself confirms: "Nor does he speak of (his own) desire. It is only a Revelation revealed." (53:3-4).[169]

The last source is consensus (*ijmā'*) which for Ibn Ḥazm signifies the general agreement of the Companions of the Prophet (ṣ). However, it is a further condition that they all should be aware of the matter agreed upon and no one should have any disagreement. Beyond this he does not accept any other principle as a source of law; therefore he rejects *qiyās* (analogy).[170]

Accordingly, *istiḥsān* is also rejected on the following grounds: "Those who listen to the Word and follow the best thereof those are the ones whom God has guided and those are men of understanding" (39:18). Ibn Ḥazm says that this verse is evidence against, rather than support of, *istiḥsān* and *qiyās*. God does not say they should follow what they consider best; He says, "Follow what He considers best". Therefore, the best words are those which conform to the Qur'an and the *ḥadīth,* and not to something that man considers best. Also *ijmā'*(consensus) fits in with this, and whoever apposes it, will be considered a non-Muslim. According to Ibn Ḥazm, God explains this with the following verse: "...and if you differ in anything amongst yourselves, refer it to God and His Messenger, if you believe in God and in the Last Day. That is better and more suitable for final determination" (4:59). Here it can be seen that God does not say 'refer it to what *you* consider best' (*mā tastaḥsinū*); in addition it is impossible that the truth (*al-ḥaqq*) will be in what *we* like (*mā nastaḥsinū*) without proof. If it were so, God would have commanded something that he did not wish, in which case textual evidence and proofs would contradict one another. This would also mean that the God had ordered us to differ when He actually prohibits us from doing so. It is impossible that all scholars would like the same thing, taking into consideration the difference in their inclination, nature and objectives, so it is impossible to achieve complete agreement on any one issue. He goes on to say "We see that what the Mālikīs consider good, the Ḥanafīs may consider bad and vice versa. This proves that consideration of *istiḥsān* is wrong because God's religion does not revolve around other people's considerations; it would apply only if the religion were not complete. But the religion is complete without requiring any extension or supplementation. "The truth is the truth (*al-ḥaqqu ḥaqqun*) even if people dislike it, and wrong is wrong (*al-bāṭilu bāṭilun*) even if people like it." He later describes *istiḥsān* as a passion (*shahwah*), an inclination (*hawā*ʾ), and an error (*ḍalāl*).[171]

Ibn Ḥazm believes that the very fact that one accepts a *qiyās* and then departs from it is enough to invalidate *istiḥsān* as a principle. For there would be nothing to favour one jurist's *istiḥsān* over another's. If the religion of Islam were based on *istiḥsān* everyone would have the right to legislate whatever they desire.[172]

It can be concluded from this statement that Ibn Ḥazm categorically objects to *istiḥsān* and believes it is not a principle of law. The invalidity however is not only confined to *istiḥsān* but also is extended to *qiyās*. Those who denied *istiḥsān,* including Ibn Ḥazm, seem somewhat extreme. What is the motive behind their denial? For as we have seen from the views of those who support *istiḥsān*, the principle does not go beyond the departure from a ruling due to a stronger *dalīl.*

Ibn Ḥazm, among others, seems to be lumping the juristic preference of scholars together with the opinion of the layman, implying that a jurist's ruling based on a considered proof is the same as a layman's opinion that is based on personal desire.

In short, the group who denied *istiḥsān* did so to preserve the agreed *dalīl* and to avoid any other rulings. The scholars who are *mujtahid* recognized only the rulings of the Islamic Sharīʿah and considered the abuse of such rulings a remote possibility.

The view of istiḥsān amongst the Muʿtazilah jurists

Bishr b. Ghiyās b. Abī Karīmah ʿAbd al-Raḥmān al-Marīsī (d. 218/833), a follower of the Shāfiʿīs, the Murjiites (Muʿtazilī) and the Ḥanafīs, was also a special disciple of Imām Abū Yūsuf (d.

182/798) and a famous theologian. He attributes to Abū Ḥanīfah the following definition: "*Istiḥsān* is a departure from analogy based on personal opinion which can be considered right without requiring evidence."[173] Al-Baṣrī (d. 436/1044) recognizes *istiḥsān* as a principle of Sharī'ah as long as the departure from *qiyās* depends on a *dalīl.* Al-Baṣrī's view holds more credence than that of others who disagreed with the Ḥanafīs, bearing in mind the fact that he himself was from a different school. His view is also confirmed by other scholars of different jurisprudential persuasions.

In *Al-Mu'tamad*, Al-Baṣrī explains:

"Let it be known that what has been said by the followers of Abū Ḥanīfah is that he recognizes *istiḥsān*, and many of those who rejected *istiḥsān* thought that they (the followers of Abū Ḥanīfah) meant that is it a ruling without *dalil.* In addition, what the later Ḥanafīs stated is "*Istiḥsān* is the departure from one ruling to another that is stronger." This has priority over what those who disagree with them thought; the people of knowledge are more aware of the aims of their predecessors. They stated in many issues: "We preferred this *athar*, for such a reason" and thus we came to know that they did not prefer something without following the proper procedure. That which invalidates such a ruling is either its being a ruling out of desire, or one based on whatever comes to mind first; or *ẓann* (speculations); or an *amārah* (indication) to that ruling. These are as attainable by a child or a member of the public as they are by the scholar. This would mean that we would have to accept all of them equally, and nobody would be blamed for ruling in that way, because these matters deal with *ḥaqq* (right) and *bāṭil* (wrong), and because *ẓann* (speculation) without *amārah* (indications) is not distinguishable from the speculation of a mad man. The talk about *istiḥsān* as explained by the followers of Abū Ḥanīfah concerns both meaning and definition. As for the meaning, some indications (*amārah*) are stronger than others. It is permissible to depart from one *amārah* to another without invalidating the one that has been departed from. This is referred to as *takhṣīṣ ʻillah* (specification of the cause)."[174]

Al-Baṣrī's views afford us the best defence so far of the recognition of *istiḥsān*. As a theologian, al-Baṣrī recognizes *istiḥsān* as a principle whether it is a departure from *qiyās* owing to a *naṣṣ* or *ijmāʻ*, or a departure from *qiyās ẓāhir* (explicit analogy) to a *qiyās khafīy* (implicit analogy) stronger than the first. He defines it clearly with the following words: "*Istiḥsān* is a departure from the established ruling to another ruling, when the reason (*dalīl*) in the second is stronger than the one found in the first, and other fresh evidence is provided (*ḥukm al-ṭārī*) vis-à-vis the previous one."[175]

Al-Baṣrī states that many of those who reject *istiḥsān* assume that it is the derivation of rulings without evidence. However, he believes that the disciples of Abū Ḥanīfah did not perform *istiḥsān* randomly. Rather, they used proper methods and ways of reasoning, as is evidenced by statements such as "we approved *istiḥsān* depending on this *athar* and evidence (*istaḥsannā hādha al-athar, wa liwajhi kadhā*)". This makes it clear that they do not approve *istiḥsān* without depending on evidence.[176]

Al-Baṣrī's view seems entirely logical, for it is unreasonable to assume to that so many scholars from the different schools of jurisprudence were given to producing rulings on a whim and without sufficient evidence.

These are the opinions of the scholars who give their opinion about *istiḥsān* as a principle; I have presented their views separately, since they differ from one *madhhab* to another.

Further evidences of the validity of *istiḥsān*

In the previous section, I discussed the various technical definitions of *istiḥsān* according to various schools and scholars. Anyone who examines these definitions should be able to distinguish between those who consider *istiḥsān* as a principle and those who reject it. The historical development of *istiḥsān* has been traced. Lastly, opinions of the early Ḥanafī scholars and their applications of *istiḥsān* have also been expounded.

I shall now look in greater depth at the ways in which different groups either accepted or rejected *istiḥsān* as a valid principle of Islamic law.

First, *istiḥsān* was defined as a departure from a ruling on an issue to another for a reason that is stronger. Similarly, some scholars consider *istiḥsān* as evidence opposed to *qiyas* or departure from one *qiyas* to a stronger one. Such scholars see *istiḥsān* as a principle of Sharī'ah, the effect of which appears clearly in many issues of *fiqh*. Ḥanafī, Mālikī, Ḥanbalī and Ẓaydī schools of thought followed this path, but for the Mālikīs *istiḥsān* differs from the others.[177]

Secondly, those scholars who consider *istiḥsān* to be whatever the *mujtahid* bases his intellectual judgment on, or judgments judged by personal opinion,[178] do not consider *istiḥsān* as a principle of *sharī'a*. Rather, they see it as a ruling that has been arrived at out of personal desire and whim without any evidence from the Qur'an, the *Sunnah* or *ijmā'*; as such, it constitutes nothing other than a man-made law that has no place in Islamic jurisprudence.[179] Hence the well-known statement of Shafi'ī, who represents the group of scholars who reject *istiḥsān* as a principle of Sharī'ah "*Man istaḥsana faqad sharra'ah*"(whoever approves of juristic preference is making himself the Lawmaker).[180] This will be clearer when we discuss the views of scholars in detail. It is represented by the Shafi'īs, Ẓāhirīs and the Shīʿah. However, Āmidī and Taftazānī, both of whom follow the Shāfiʿī school, recognized *istiḥsān*[181] as did the Mutakallimūn (Theologians) and Abū al-Ḥusayn al-Baṣrī.[182]

Lastly, there are those who took the middle ground between the two sides; they did not view *istiḥsān* as an independent principle, but referred it to the other principles already agreed upon among scholars, namely the Qur'an, the *Sunnah*, *ijmāʿ* and *qiyās*.[183] *Istiḥsān* according to such points of view does not extend beyond these four principles, which have been agreed upon. Thus the holder of this view neither rejects the proof of *istiḥsān*, as Shāfiʿī did, nor does he say that it is an independent principle, as the Ḥanafī, Mālikī and Ḥanbālī jurists did. This group of scholars is represented by Shawkānī (d. 1834).[184] It should be noted that some Mālikī and Ḥanbalī scholars reject *istiḥsān* while other scholars of these two schools accept it, as was discussed in detail earlier when we explored the views of various jurists.

This section will explain the reason behind the disagreement over *istiḥsān* as a principle of law and will be elaborated on, following an overview of the various evidences to justify the claims of those who consider it to be a valid principle of Sharīʿah, and those who do not. Both groups discussed each other's arguments with the aim of invalidating each other's claim while upholding their own. As the discussion was not limited to the opinion of one group, but included the opinion of their opponents and supporters, it gave way to many discussions, which we will discuss separately.

Reason for disagreement over the validity of istiḥsān

Before discussing the views of the *'ulamā'* (jurists) on *istiḥsān*, it is worth exploring the reasons behind the disagreements among them as to whether *istiḥsān* is a principle of Sharīʿah or not.

The opponents of *istiḥsān* are those who see it as "Arbitrary law making within religion", mainly because they did not understand what the supporters of *istiḥsān*—the Ḥanafīs, Mālikīs, and Ḥanbalīs—meant by the term.

In the early Islamic period, the term *istiḥsān* and its exact meaning were not directly defined; it was applied in judgments without any specific definition or explanation being given. Supporters' considerations are based mainly on the fundamental principle of securing ease and avoiding hardship. This procedure of the usage of *istiḥsān* was misunderstood by its opponents.

Shāṭibī is of the view that the point of dispute relates to several issues:

1. *Istiḥsān* relates to "the people of innovation" (*ahl al-bid'ah*) who make statements that are far from the *aḥkām al-dīn* (rulings of religion) and attempt falsely to present it as the form of *istiḥsān* that the scholars have adopted.

This may have been one reason why scholars refused to accept *istiḥsān* as a principle; this refusal might have been because they intended to tighten the noose "around the people of innovation" and thus prevent misguidance wherever possible. These scholars believed that since it is possible for anyone to use *istiḥsān*, it could be used as an excuse to propagate self-opinion and thus lead to the collapse of the principles of religion.

2. *Istiḥsān* does not materialize unless there is a *mustaḥsin* that makes *istiḥsān* valid; such a *mustaḥsin* has to be either the *shar'* (law) or *'aql* (intellect). If it is *shar'* then the issue is already resolved as the evidence in Sharī'ah has shown, and consequently following the *dalīl* (evidence) cannot be called *istiḥsān*. In such situations there is no need for additional interpretations to the Qur'an, the *Sunnah*, *ijmā'* and whatever is derived from them in the form of *qiyās* and *dalīl*.

As for *'aql*, if *istiḥsān* by way of *'aql* is based on a *dalīl* (evidence) then there is no point calling it *istiḥsān*; since the reference here is the *dalīl* and nothing else. If, however, *istiḥsān* is by the way of *'aql* without any *dalīl*, then it is a *bid'ah* (innovation). This might have been the reason why some scholars said that *istiḥsān* is not valid, or the reason that made some refer *istiḥsān* to other sources.

3. Those who differ with the above view do so if the action is based on the stronger of the two *dalīls* (proof) which they state is a proof when the general (*'ām*) continues and when the *qiyās* is directly proportional. Both Abū Ḥanīfah and Mālik specify the general by implicit or explicit *dalīl* (proof). Although Mālik prefers to specify generality by *maṣlaḥah* (public interest) whilst Abū Ḥanīfah prefers to specify by solitary (*aḥād*) *ḥadīth* from the companions when it is opposed to *qiyās*, they both recognize specifying *qiyās* and disqualifying the cause (*'illah*). However once the evidence is established, Shāfi'ī does not accept specifying the *'illah* of *shar'*".[185]

This is what could be understood from Shāṭibī who clarifies the point of disagreement by saying: "As for *istiḥsān*, since the "people of innovation" have links to *istiḥsān* it cannot be without a *mustaḥsin* (recommending), and this can either be *'aql* (reason) or *shar'*. As for *shar'*, to approve or disapprove is immaterial since the issue is already settled; the evidence has already decided the case and calling it *istiḥsān* is of no use, nor is attempting to lay down any extra interpretation. The exception to this rule is that which has been established by the Qur'an, the *Sunnah* and *ijmā'* from *qiyās* or by *istidlāl* (inferences). Only one thing remains—*'aql* (reason)—as the tool of choice. If reasoning is with evidence then there is no point in calling it *istiḥsān*, since as a reference it becomes the *dalīl*. If it is without *dalīl* then it is *bid'ah* (innovation). Mālik and Abū Ḥanīfah recognise that it is worth considering *istiḥsān* in *aḥkām;* this view is opposed by Shāfi'ī who denies it to such an extent that he said: "Whoever gives approval places himself as the Law-giver." What could be concluded from their *madhhab* (i.e. Mālik and Abū Ḥanīfah) is that it refers to acting according to the stronger of two *dalīls.* This is what Ibn al-'Arabī (d. 543/1148) stated: "the general if it continues and *qiyās* if it is directly proportional, and Mālik and Abū Ḥanīfah see *takhṣīṣ* of the general by any *dalīl*, implicit or explicit." He (Ibn al-'Arabī) said; "Mālik prefers to specify with *maṣlaḥah* and Abū Ḥanīfah prefers to specify with the solitary saying of a companion, which is opposed to *qiyās*." He said: "And both specify *qiyās* and reject the cause, whilst Shāfi'ī does not accept any specification of *'illah* (cause) of *shar'* once *shar'* has been proved".[186]

It is possible that the above statement is Shāṭibī's explanation of the disagreement the scholars have over the validity of *istiḥsān* to deduce the Sharī'ah rulings. The reasons of disagreement might be very different; for example, it may refer to the linguistic meaning of *istiḥsān*. Linguistically *istiḥsān* covers all meanings including the *mujtahid's* preference based on evidence (*dalīl*); whatever is preferred by way of personal desire (*tashahhī* and *hawā*); and whatever the public prefer. It is this general linguistic meaning which might have been the reason for some to reject *istiḥsān* as a principle of law. The linguistic terms have already been discussed in previous chapters.

The above summarize the reasons behind the disagreement among the *'ulamā'* of *uṣūl* (jurists of the principles of Islamic law) over the validity of *istiḥsān*. The main point of discussion concerning the validity of *istiḥsān* is, as far as I know, what Shāṭibī stated was a precautionary measure against those who would tighten the noose around the "people of innovation" (*ahl al-bid'ah*), who try to interpret the religion and invent whatever is necessary to suit their own interests and desires. We now turn to the opinions of the *'ulamā'* (jurists) who consider *istiḥsān* as a principle and those who reject it altogether. We will explore the opinions and discuss the evidence they provide to determine whether *istiḥsān* is a valid proof that should be acted upon.

The 'ulamā' who recognize istiḥsān

As we have seen, most scholars confirm that the concept of *istiḥsān* is recognized by the Ḥanafī, Mālīkī, Ḥanbalī and Zaydī schools. However, despite the fact that *'ulamā'* from these different schools recognized the validity of *istiḥsān* as a principle they often disagreed over the meaning of the term.

The cause of the differences of opinions about the way *istiḥsān* is directed towards the deduction of juristic rulings is the technique with which each *madhhab* (school) presents those rulings. Ḥanafī scholars have used two techniques to prove the validation of *istiḥsān*. The first technique is to identify its true nature and framework, then distinguish the types of *istiḥsān*. Following this, they consider the various relationships between types and then relate a particular *istiḥsān* individually in the context of *shar'ī dalīl* (valid sources)[187] which is a recognized proof by the other schools of thought. The second technique is the expending of effort in order to prove the validity of *istiḥsān* as a recognized concept for everyone.[188] The first technique was discussed earlier through in various examples. We now turn to the second technique, which is presenting the evidence needed to prove its validity.

The supporters of the validity of *istiḥsān* resort to proof from the Qur'an, the *Sunnah*, and *ijmā'*. According to Ḥanafī scholars, to perform *istiḥsān* is to comply with Qur'anic verses which command man to follow what is best, good and beautiful.[189] Three verses from the Qur'an are mentioned by this group to support their claims. The first is the verse in which God addresses Moses concerning the Torah: "(and said): Take and hold these with firmness, and enjoin thy people to hold fast by the best in the precepts"(7:145).

The people of Moses were ordained to follow what is best; this is a common-sense given, and leads to the conclusion that acting according to the best is evidence by way of *'aql* and is supported by Sharī'ah. Generally it is accepted that *istiḥsān* is the departure from the good and acting according to the best when it is based on a stronger *dalīl*. It is not possible for any one to raise an objection to the ruling in this verse by claiming that it is a specific commandment for the children of Israel only. And it cannot have been abrogated by the Islamic Sharī'ah since Islamic law states that any ruling for those who came before us is also a ruling for us unless the text explicitly specifies it as abrogated. As will be shown in the following verses, acting according to the best has not been abrogated by the Islamic Sharī'ah; rather, the Sharī'ah supports of it. "Those who listen to the Word (good advice), and follow the best of it" (39:18)

The above verse mentions the praise and appreciation of those who depart from what is good in order to follow the better or the best. Nobody can deny that the praise for taking an action, and the punishment for not acting, implies that acting according to the best is obligatory. But in the case where acting according to the best leads to praise for the action, but not to punishment for inaction, then acting according to *istiḥsān* becomes optional (*mandūb*).

This shows that *istiḥsān* falls between *mandūb* (optional) and *wājib* (obligatory). However, those who validate *istiḥsān* may deem it *wājib* as explained by the following verse; "And follow the best of that which was revealed to you from your Lord"(39:55).

According to Sarakhsī, "The whole of the Qur'an is beautiful, but here it requires following the best".[190] The verses praise the best of those words that were heard and listened to, and command man to follow the best of what is revealed. *Istiḥsān* is included in this and therefore it too is praised indirectly.[191]

The above verse enjoins man to follow the best and to leave the evil. *Istiḥsān* does not by its nature stop the jurist from departing from the good to the best, which is a command; and a command implies obligation, according to *'ulamā'* of *'uṣūl* (jurists of the principles of Islamic law). Therefore, following the best is obligatory and this is what is required as far as *istiḥsān* is concerned. Therefore, what is good should be obtained and what is bad should be avoided.[192]

Such proofs were put forward by those *'ulamā'* (jurists) who recognize *istiḥsān*. They can be referred to in the same references mentioned earlier during the discussion on the views of the *'ulamā'* recognizing the validity of *istiḥsān*. These verses strengthen each other and show the validity of *istiḥsān*.

Denial of the validity of istiḥsān

The group who denied the validity of *istiḥsān* discuss the proofs put forward by the group who recognize *istiḥsān* in the following way:

As far as the first *dalīl* from the Qur'an[193] is concerned, the opponents of *istiḥsān* state that this *dalīl* is contrary to what the supporters of *istiḥsān* claim, and is against rather than for *istiḥsān*. This is because the order (*amr*) in the verse is not aiming at acting according to *istiḥsān* as an obligatory principle; here, God orders the children of Israel to act according to the best that was revealed in the *Torah,* and not the *istiḥsān* claimed by its supporters. God orders the 'children of Israel' to take the best of the texts that were revealed in this divine book. The ruling at hand' then has been deduced from the text rather than from an opinion or a whim. Even if we accept that this text implies permission to act according to *istiḥsān*, then this permission was specific to the Jews rather than the Muslim community, and most of these rulings have been abrogated by the Islamic Sharīʿah.

The opponents of *istiḥsān* criticize the interpreting of verses in this manner by the principle's supporters. Ghazālī claims that the objective of the verse that requires following the best is the evidence: whenever people see something is good by their *ʿaql* (intellect) alone it should not be considered as a *dalīl* (proof).[194]

As for the second evidence from the Qur'an,[195] the opponents of the validity of *istiḥsān* put forward three objections, according to al-Māwardī.[196]

First objection: God ordered him (Moses) to follow the best (*al-aḥsan*) and not what is perceived as the best (*al-mustaḥsan*). *Al-aḥsan* (the best) is that which in itself contains goodness, while *al-mustaḥsan* (what is perceived as best) is what others view or prefer as good, even if it is not. Hence, both types are very different and it becomes obligatory to follow the best (*al-aḥsan*) rather than that which is viewed or preferred as best.

Second objection: It is clear that the best has to be followed, since there are rewards for obedience and punishment for disobedience. This is obvious and has noting to do with *istiḥsān.*

Third objection: As the *qiṣāṣ* verse (2:178) demonstrates, the best is understood as that which man must fulfil in order to do what is right. In the contrast of this verse, for example, forgiveness, while portrayed as better than *qiṣāṣ*, is still optional rather than obligatory.

The group who recognised *istiḥsān* tried to substantiate their claim by resorting to the *Sunnah*, by following the *ḥadīth* narrated from the Prophet (ṣ) which states: "Whatever the Muslim community views as good is also considered by God as good".[197] In the interpretation of this *ḥadīth* it was said, that if it was not a *ḥujjah* (proof) then on the side of God it would not be considered as good.[198]

Whenever Muslims who are knowledgeable in the field of deducing the Sharī'ah ruling, and have the ability to judge the stronger from the weaker, are shown something which is good and stronger than other things that the *mujtahid* approved, it becomes *ḥujjah* (proof) to what God describes as good. *Istiḥsān* is by nature of this sort. The group who recognized the validity of *istiḥsān* based on this *ḥadīth* faced two objections: First objection: Ibn Ḥazm is of the view that this *ḥadīth* was never transmitted from the Prophet (ṣ) in any form whatsoever; there is no doubt that this *ḥadīth* does not exist in any transmitted *ḥadīth*, we only know it from ibn Mas'ūd.[199]

Second objection: If we assume that this *ḥadīth* is valid then it is not its intention to allude to *istiḥsān*, since it does not say "whatever *some* Muslims view", but "Whatever Muslims view". This statement conveys the validity of *ijmā'* and is generally agreed upon among the *mujtahidīn.*[200]

The group who recognise *istiḥsān* also use *ijmā'* to support their claims, particularly on juristic rulings which appear to be at odds with the *dalil* involved. For example, people entering a public bath without specifying the time or the amount of water to be used is contrary to the normal contract of rent (*ijārah*), in which jurists agree that for the contract to be valid it is necessary to specify the period and the due amount of rent. Traditionally, it was also accepted that drinking water without specifying the amount or the value of money to be paid also contradicts the conditions for the contract to be valid. These are considered good (*istiḥsān*) by the *'ulamā*.[201] As the *Sunnah* shows, this is also supported by the generally accepted custom during the life of the Prophet (ṣ), even though it is contrary to the *uṣūl* followed in rent and sales contracts. There is a possibility that it might have also been the custom during the life of the Companions; if this was the case, then the evidence (*dalīl*) becomes *ijmā'* which everyone accepted. The evidence in such cases is the *Sunnah* or *ijmā'* (consensus) and this is the sort of *istiḥsān* that no one would deny.[202]

The arguments based on *ijmā'* face the following objections:

First objection: With regard to the public bath example, the *'ulamā'* did agree that this is permissible and hence the departure from the *aṣl* (base) is constructed on *ijmā'* and not on *istiḥsān*.

Second objection: What people accept and tolerate in these transactions that some claim to be based on *istiḥsān* is simply what they are used to. The public do not object to such transactions so long as they do not lead to indecency. If judgment is required on such matters, we must refer back to the principle rules and not to *istiḥsān*.[203]

These are the arguments that were put forward by the *'ulamā'* who recognized *istiḥsān* together with the objections of its opponents. The *'ulamā'* who rejected *istiḥsān* will be discussed below.

The 'ulamā' who reject istiḥsān

As I have mentioned earlier, the first figure to reject *istiḥsān* was Imām Shāfi'ī (d. 204),[204] whose book "*Ibṭāl al-istiḥsān*" (invalidating juristic preference) contains his famous statement: "*Man istaḥsana faqad sharra'a*" (whoever approves of juristic preference is making himself the Lawmaker).[205] Among those who agreed with him on this issue were:[206] Isnawī (d. 772/1370); Bishr b. Ghiyās (d. 218/833); Shīrāzī (d. 476/1083); Ghazālī (d. 505/1111); Dāwūd al-Zāhīrī (d. 270/884);[207] Ibn Ḥazm;[208] and the Imāmi Shī'ah.[209]

Those who rejected *istiḥsān* put forward both scriptural (*naqlī*) and rational (*'aqlī*) arguments to support their claim.

One example of scriptural evidence is:

"O ye you believe! Obey Allah and obey the Messenger, and those charged with authority among you. If ye differ in anything among yourselves, refer it to Allah and His Messenger, if ye do believe in Allah and the Last Day: That is best and more suitable for final determination" (4:59).

This verse confirms that the best is that which is taken from the Qur'an or the *Sunnah* of the Prophet (ṣ). Rulings are taken only from these two sources, since they are the origin of the Sharī'ah. As for anything taken from other than these two sources, it will evidently lead to dispute, which must be avoided. The verse directed the Muslim community to refer to the Qur'an and the *Sunnah* for rulings; no mention is made of *istiḥsān,* or the community adopting what it prefers. Who is to say that one preference is better than another? If *istiḥsān* and the adoption of personal desire as a criterion for rulings were to be implemented, religion would suffer: *ḥalal* may be deemed *ḥarām*, and *ḥaqq* may be deemed *bāṭil*, and vice-versa. There is no need for this, since the religion is clear enough as it is, and anyone with common sense can understand it.[210]

That the Qur'an and the *Sunnah* are the principle sources of Islamic Sharī'ah is not to be denied. Moreover, whoever opposes them and rules by his own opinion is likely to miss the right path and end up actually opposing the principles of the Sharī'ah.

However, the type of *istiḥsān* that is recognized by its supporters is somewhat different; for them, *istiḥsān* is based on text (*naṣṣ*), *ijmāʿ*, necessity or *maṣlaḥah* (public interest). As such, it should not lead to disagreement, and religion is not in jeopardy: *ḥaqq* will not become *bāṭil*, nor will *ḥalāl* become *ḥarām*. In fact such situations arise only when the source of *istiḥsān* is *hawā* and *tashahhī* (pleasure taking), and nothing as such is accepted by the *ʿulamā'* who recognize the validity of *istiḥsān*.

Another example of scriptural evidence is:

"This day I have perfected your religion for you, completed My Favour upon you, and have chosen for you Islām as your religion." (5:3).

According to the opponents of *istiḥsān*, God is saying here that the religion has been perfected, and therefore adding to the Sharīʿah is not permitted; if the religion had been incomplete, then *istiḥsān* would have been permitted. *Ḥaqq* is *ḥaqq* even if people despise it and *bāṭil* is *bāṭil* even if people prefer it; this is enough to prove that *istiḥsān* means ruling by the way of desire and pleasure as well as misguidance. As far as the Qur'an[211] is concerned, the religion has been perfected and *istiḥsān* is unnecessary.[212]

However, this argument is weak. After all, does anyone who recognizes the validity of *istiḥsān* actually consider the religion to be incomplete, that *istiḥsān* is there for the completion of the religion? Supporters of *istiḥsān* clearly do not subscribe to this view. There is no doubt for them that the religion is complete. However, there are always new issues that arise after the revelation has ceased. The *ʿulamā'* sought for *ijmāʿ* and *qiyās* to give rulings on such issues and *istiḥsān* is one principle on which some rulings are based. To rule *istiḥsān* as invalid is to invalidate *ijtihād per se*. Yet no-one holds this view, since the Prophet (ṣ) approved *ijtihād* as the *ḥadīth* of Muʿadh ibn Jabal[213] confirms.

Another Qur'anic example is:

"And follow that which is inspired in you from your lord. Verily, Allah is Well Acquainted with what you do" (33:2).

According to the opponents of *istiḥsān,* here God is ordering the Prophets to follow revelation, and nothing else, since following anything other than revelation constitutes disobedience to God's command; ruling through desire is nothing but misguidance, which goes against what God asks us to follow. God explicitly prohibits this according to the Qur'an.[214] Ruling according to *istiḥsān* is nothing but ruling by *ẓann* (probability) and through personal desire and whim (*hawā'*). No one is ordered to rule by *ḥaqq* until he becomes aware of what *ḥaqq* is, and *ḥaqq* cannot become known from anyone other than God. God has enshrined *ḥaqq* in the Book (the Qur'an), and then in the *Sunnah* of His prophet (ṣ), and thus there is no solution for any obstacles that one may encounter without the Qur'an indicating this solution either directly or indirectly.[215]

The opponents of *istiḥsān* claim that the principles of the Sharī'ah were generally accepted at the time of the Prophet because revelation was still in progress and nothing else could be followed while the revelation continued. The best evidence that can be put forward for this is that *ijmā'* was not accepted as principle of law during the lifetime of the Prophet (ṣ).

While this writer aggress that there is neither *ijmā'* nor *istiḥsān* nor *qiyās* while revelation is in progress, after the death of the Prophet (ṣ), *ijmā'* became a reality as the Prophet (ṣ) validated *ijtihād* for the companions whom he sent to teach people in certain remote areas.

The best scriptural support for this is the *ḥadīth* of Mu'ādh. When the Prophet (ṣ) intended to send Mu'ādh to Yemen, the Prophet (ṣ) asked him:

"How will you judge when the occasion of deciding a case arises? He replied, I shall judge in accordance with Allāh's book. The Prophet (ṣ) asked, "What will you do if you do not find guidance in Allāh's book?" He replied, "I will act in accordance with the *Sunnah* of the Messenger of Allāh. The Prophet (ṣ) asked, "What will you do if you do not find guidance in the *Sunnah* of the Apostle of Allāh and in Allāh's book?" He replied, "I shall do my best to form an opinion and spare no pains in my search for truth." The apostle of Allāh then patted him on the chest and said: "Praise is to Allāh who helped the messenger of the Apostle of Allāh to find something, which pleases the apostle of Allāh."[216]

From the *ḥadīth* it can be concluded that the Prophet (ṣ) approved *ijtihād* because Mu'ādh was far from the Prophet (ṣ) and thus had less access to revelation than companions who were at the Prophet's (ṣ) side. This *ḥadīth* clearly does not support the argument that when the revelation was still in progress, nothing else should be followed, under any circumstances. And after the death of the Prophet (ṣ), the community was in need of some sort of *ijtihād* supported by a *dalīl;* and *istiḥsān* falls within this category of *ijtihād*.[217]

According to Ibn Ḥazm, the supporters of *istiḥsān* base their claim on the following rational proof: *istiḥsān*, conceived during the era of Abū Ḥanīfah and Mālik, is seen as a precaution there to remove hardship from the people; it is closer to custom, to what people are familiar and feel comfortable with, then it is to true principles of law. God in the Qur'an[218] states that this is *bāṭil*. All of the verses adduced by the supporters actually serve to invalidate their claims. No-one could be more compassionate towards the believers than God the Creator, the Sustainer and the One who sent the prophets for guidance. Precaution means following the order of God and what is despicable is disobedience to Him. Nothing is good except what God has ordered His prophet to permit, and nothing is despicable other than what God has prohibited.[219]

Regarding the evidence which states that *istiḥsān* in the era of Abū Ḥanifa and Mālik was invalid on account of its being based on convenience it is necessary to point out that scholars such as Abū Ḥanīfah and Mālik did not recognize *istiḥsān* according to their desire without any *dalīl;* rather, all cases in which they resorted to *istiḥsān* were based on *dalīl shar'ī.* Therefore, what their opponents claim is nothing more than a false allegation. The supporters of *istiḥsān* never mentioned any *istiḥsān* that was opposed to either the Qur'an or the *Sunnah.*

Opponents of *istiḥsān* counter this by pointing out that the Prophet (ṣ) did not speak out of his own desire; nor did he give a ruling on issues pertaining to the affairs of religion by way of preference. Rather, he followed the revelation, and when he did not receive a revelation he waited for one. If this is the case for the Prophet (ṣ), who was not permitted to say anything other than that which had been revealed to him, or to use means other than analogy, then it becomes a priority for others not to speak on affairs of religion unless they are following the same path as the Prophet (ṣ).[220]

The second rational evidence adduced by its opponents is the assertion that *istiḥsān* was never practiced by the Prophet (ṣ). He never gave any *fatwā* based on what he preferred concerning the affairs of religion, and always waited for revelations. If it is not permitted for the Prophet (ṣ) to rule according to personal opinion, then, it is automatically prohibited for people other than the Prophet (ṣ) to do so.[221]

The supporters of *istiḥsān* respond to this by saying that it is pointless to discuss the application or non-application of *istiḥsān* during the time of the Prophet (ṣ). It is obvious that the Prophet (ṣ) did not perform *istiḥsān*, for the simple reason that revelation was incomplete and ongoing. A *mujtahid* today, however, does not receive revelation, which is why he has to rely on *ijtihād*. If we say that *istiḥsān* is not permitted because of the cessation of the revelation, then we would have to rule out *qiyās* and *ijmāʿ* on the same grounds. Yet the opponents of *istiḥsān*, do not deny *qiyās* or *ijmāʿ*. It is crucial that we recognize that *istiḥsān* depends on *dalīl*. It should be noted that Shāfiʿī denied *istiḥsān* but recognized *qiyās*. How did he differentiate between the two?

The third rational evidence adduced by the opponents of *istiḥsān* is that *qiyās* is stronger than *istiḥsān*, as it is permitted to specify the *ʿāmm* (general) by *qiyās*, but not by *istiḥsān*. Thus it is not permitted to put *istiḥsān* before *qiyās*. If *istiḥsān* had been a *dalīl*, then it would have been permitted to make the departure from *istiḥsān* as an evidence, thus proving *istiḥsān* will lead to its own invalidity.[222]

The supporters of *istiḥsān* respond by saying that *istiḥsān* cannot come before a stronger *qiyās* when the departure from *qiyās* for *istiḥsān* is a weak *qiyās*, and there is no restriction on invalidating the weaker in deducing the *fiqh* rulings. It is confirmed in the books of *ʿulamā'* who recognize *istiḥsān* that they never departed from *qiyās* in favour of *istiḥsān* unless it was stronger. A stronger *qiyās* cannot invalidate *istiḥsān* because *istiḥsān* only invalidates the weaker *qiyās*, and naturally this cannot be a principle of Sharīʿah.[223]

These are the arguments that both sides have put forward, to defend their positions. We now turn to the application of *istiḥsān* by the early Ḥanafī school.

Application of *istiḥsān* in the early Ḥanafi school

In this part of the study I aim to cover the implementation of *istiḥsān* in the early Ḥanafī school. This should provide ample proof that *istiḥsān* was applied in the early period of Islamic legislation. The main scholars covered here will be the shool's eponymous founder, Abū Ḥanīfah (d. 150 AH) together with Zufar (d. 158 AH), Abū Yūsuf (d. 182 AH), and Shaybānī (d. 189 H).

Abū Ḥanīfah and the concept of istiḥsān

The area in which Abū Ḥanīfah lived attracted many scholars and developed into a thriving intellectual milieu.[224] Abū Ḥanīfah's father's occupation as a trader enabled him to associate with those who took an active part in the social and economical activities of their society.[225] Abū Ḥanīfah stood against the government[226] was a staunch supporter of *ahl al-bayt* (the household of the Prophet *ṣ*) and used *qiyās* and *istiḥsān* when asked for guidance in various situations. He had a powerful understanding of *qiyās*, and in the words of Imām Shāfi'ī, was described in terms of great respect: "Many scholars could be considered the heirs of Abū Ḥanīfah in their use of *qiyās* and *istiḥsān*."[227]

The failure of Abū Ḥanīfah to leave any written manuscripts explaining the concept or procedure of *istiḥsān*, or the conditions of its validity, is a source of conflict amongst the jurists, for the lack of written material has led him to be accused of judging cases without depending on any textual evidences. When he made the following statement: "*qiyās* is such and such but we apply *istiḥsān*",[228] he was criticized by many scholars such as Ibn Ḥazm (d. 456/1064)[229] and especially Imām Shāfi'ī, who said "Whoever approves of juristic preference is making himself the Lawmaker".[230]

However, it is not entirely true to say that there is no trace of any reports regarding Abū Ḥanīfah's techniques; in fact he left writings giving indications as to his methods of performing *ijtihād* and his use of the principle of *istiḥsān*. He expressed this method as follows: "I read God's book to obtain guidance. If I am unable to find any guidance in the Qur'an then I resort to the Tradition (*Sunnah*) of the Prophet (*ṣ*) and the true reports (*ḥadīth*) which have been transmitted from generation to generation by trustworthy narrators. If neither the Qur'an nor the *Sunnah* yields any guidance, I then refer to the opinions of the Companions. Consequently, when I make my personal decision then I do not ask others' opinions. However, if a matter has been considered by Ibrāhīm al-Nakhā'ī (d. 96), Shā'bī (d. 103), *Ḥasan* (d. 110), Muḥammad b. Shirīn (d. 110), Sa'īd b. al-Musayyab (d. 94) *et al.* I also act on their *ijtihād*."[231]

Abū Ḥanīfah also seriously considers the issue of abrogated *ḥadīth*. Accordingly, his way of recourse to the Tradition was to research intensively a Tradition and to see whether it had been narrated through trustworthy narrators from the Prophet (*ṣ*) through the Companions; if it had, he would then apply it in his judgments.[232] In addition to his authority in *ḥadīth* and *fiqh*, he was also aware of the customs (*'urf*) and traditions of the people, and how previous *ijtihāds* had been incorporated and practiced.[233] He was also a master in *qiyās*. Abū Ḥanīfah explained his methods when applying *qiyās* as follows: "We make *qiyās* from one matter to another based on the Qur'an or the *Sunnah* or *ijmā'* (consensus) of the Muslim Community. We consider seriously our *ijtihāds* and whether they adhere to certain principles or not."[234] He points out that *qiyās* would not be applied to every case without a reason, saying: "*Qiyās* cannot be applied to everything".[235] The application of *qiyās* is a great responsibility because it may cause unexpected results and bad solutions. In this respect he says "To urinate in a mosque is better than some kinds of *qiyās*".[236]

Abū Yūsuf (d. 182) made a statement regarding his master's method of performing *ijtihād*, saying, "In any case which is presented to Abū Ḥanīfah, his first requirement is information as to whether there are any Traditions (*athar*) regarding this matter. When we show him what there is, he then applies his knowledge after examining the case and ensuring that it is according to procedure. If two opinions are given and the information is stronger in the Tradition then the stronger opinion is chosen to resolve the issue. However if the two opinions are similar, he judges the case on his own personal opinion (*ra'y*). Thirdly, if any Traditions do not exist relating to this issue, he refers it to *qiyās*. Whenever *qiyās* yields an unacceptable result, he eventually abandons it in favour of *istiḥsān*.[237]

Abū Zahrah summarizes Abū Ḥanīfah's method of performing *ijtihād* similarly: "He performs *ijtihād* when he can not find any guidance in the Qur'an, in the *Sunnah* or within the *qawl al-ṣaḥābah* (the saying of the Companions). To ensure a competent judgment, he assesses a case on opinion and investigates it using different aspects of deduction. Sometimes he goes with *qiyās* and occasionally makes *istiḥsān*. He considers people's benefit and obeys the principle which states that "No harm shall be inflicted or reciprocated in Islām".[238] If he decides to use *qiyās* when its results conflict with the custom of the people, he then applies *istiḥsān*. Whatever he chooses to perform, whether *qiyās* or *istiḥsān*, the customs of the people are taken into consideration.[239]

Abū Ḥanīfa's connection with trade life gave him an intensively absorbed knowledge on how to deal with the common practices and needs of the people, and the newly-occurring problems of daily life. This knowledge gave him the flexibility to depart from the unexpected results of analogy and arrive at rulings that might benefit the people, through the principle of *istiḥsān*.[240]

According to Shaybānī, "Abū Ḥanīfah was discussing *qiyās* with his friends who always debated with him fiercely in order to arrive at the truth. When Abū Ḥanīfah said, "I am making *istiḥsān*", nobody could fault him because he had judged so many cases on the grounds of the principle of *istiḥsān*. Eventually everyone abandoned their previous opinions and followed him."[241]

The reason for Abū Ḥanīfah's success is that he automatically recognizes the effective causes (*'illah*), distinguishes between the explicit and implicit, and applies the ruling that is consonant with the people's benefit, thereby obtaining justice and equity.[242] His use of the principle of *istiḥsān* was performed proficiently without contradicting the main principle of religion and the soul of the Sharī'ah. Ibn Shubrumah extols Abū Ḥanīfah's supremacy in the application of *istiḥsān* by saying, "If someone is allowed to present just one opinion in God's religion, it can only be Abū Ḥanīfah's saying, "I approve *istiḥsān*".[243] In addition to this, Abū Ḥanīfah was reported to have said about the validation of this principle "*istiḥsān* is a principle that is necessary for the production of legal rulings in the religion."[244]

Abū Zahrah points out the main factors behind Abū Ḥanīfah's confidence and his success in performing *istiḥsān*: "He used the principle of *istiḥsān* perfectly. Use of this principle, requires deep perception and awareness of the benefits of people, and a knowledge of their current transactions and lifestyles. Besides these, it demands an awareness of God's commands which constitute the main principle of Sharī'ah, the ability to deduce implicit effective causes, and to find appropriate qualities (*waṣf*) and connect rulings to them; to be dexterous in departure from explicit analogy to implicit analogy, and to understand the applicability or non-applicability of different rulings."[245]

As for this statement "*Qiyās* is such and such, but we apply *istiḥsān*",[246] Abū Ḥanīfah did not explain either the meaning of this concept nor its conditions for validation. As we have seen earlier, the reason behind the disagreements amongst the scholars is there that were not enough explanations and definitions available to them. Nevertheless, Abū Ḥanīfah used to refer his judgments to the *athar* (*ḥadīth*)[247] or *riwāyah* (transmitted *ḥadīth*) and rely on its authority that they narrated from the Prophet (ṣ) or approved precedent. This might not have been generally known to others, which is why he made a statement saying: "If it had not been for precedents, I would have decided here according to *qiyās*", or "If it had not been for the sake of *riwāyah* (transmitted *ḥadīth*), I would have decided the case by *qiyās*"[248]

In the writings of his disciples, Abū Yūsuf (d. 182) and Shaibānī (d. 189), the use of the concept of *istiḥsān* by Abū Ḥanīfah and the early Ḥanafis is explained, primarily in the context of the notion of "departure from *qiyās*". Abū Ḥanīfah based his method of judgement on departing from applications of *qiyās* to the principle of *istiḥsān* based on distinctive and specifically valued evidence and prudence.[249] The examples of the practice of *istiḥsān* in the writings of Abū Yūsuf (d. 182) and Shaibāni (d. 189) reveal that the use of the concept could mean the following:

1. Leaving *qiyās* due to the precedents of the Companions:[250]

The sayings of the Companions of the Prophet (*qawl ṣaḥābī*), as mentioned earlier, is a valid yet a controversial principle of Sharī'ah.[251] For example, if a man grants his wife the authority to choose whether or not she will remain with him, and she chooses divorce, her right to divorce him is ruled invalid according to *qiyās*: only men, and not women, have the right to instigate divorce proceedings. However, according to 'Umar (d. 23), 'Uthman (d. 35), 'Alī (d. 40), Ibn Mas'ūd (d. 32), Ibn 'Umar (d. 73), Ā'ishah (d. 58), Abū Ḥanīfah and his disciples such a divorce on the authority of the woman is possible, thanks to *istiḥsān*.[252]

Abū Ḥanīfah's departure from *qiyās* is based on the sayings and practices of the Companions. The following example illustrates the comparison between *qiyās* and *istiḥsān*. If someone has pigeon excrement on his clothes, *qiyās* does not allow that person to perform ritual prayers since according to *qiyās*, pigeon excrement is ritually impure and therefore any form of prayers would be considered void. However, *istiḥsān* allows that person to go to prayers based on the practice of Ibn Mas'ūd (d. 32) who once brushed pigeon excrement from his clothes using his fingers before going on to pray. Ibn 'Umar, when faced with the same problem, wiped the bird excrement from his clothes using a piece of stone, then went to pray. According to *qiyās*, since excrement is considered impure it should prevent a person from prayer; however Abū Ḥanīfah and his disciples departed from a ruling in *qiyās* and applied *istiḥsān*, concluding that the bird excrement is considered natural and should not prevent any prayers, based on the practices of the Companions Ibn Mas'ūd and Ibn 'Umar.[253] *Istiḥsān* is preferred over *qiyās* even if it is a practice of only one Companion. One of the Ḥanafi scholars, Abū Sa'īd Aḥmad b. al-Birdāī (d. 317/929) said: "We have understood from our masters that even only one person's *qawl* (word) from among the Companions may be preferred over *qiyās;* on that word, *qiyās* would be left".[254] When there is more than one opinion from the Companions (*qawl ṣaḥābī*) then Abū Ḥanīfah chooses the more preferable one.[255]

2. Leaving *qiyās* owing to the consensus (*ijmā'*)[256] of the Companions:[257] The consensus (*ijmā'*) of the Companions is confined to the time of the first four Caliphs and represents their established practices. The Caliph 'Umar in particular, consulted the Companions on new cases and announced their decisions in open congregations.[258] Sarakhsī reports a case of apostasy (*irtidād*) from Islām, in which a husband and wife apostatise together. According to *qiyās* such a couple must

separate, as apostasy is an obstacle to *nikāḥ* (marriage) and the continuance of a marriage. However, Abū Ḥanīfah and his disciples Abū Yūsuf and Shaibānī departed from the ruling of *qiyās* based on the consensus of the Companions with regard to the case of the Banū Ḥanīfah. It is known that the Banū Ḥanīfah tribe avoided paying obligatory alms and therefore were deemed to have apostatised from the religion.[259] This crisis caused Abū Bakr to announce a war against the rebels unless they agreed to pay *zakāt* (alms), repent and return to Islām. Even when they repented, the Caliph did not ask them to renew their marriages (*nikāḥ*); nor would any other Companions require it[260] as the consensus of the Companions not recognize this as case of apostasy.

3. Leaving *qiyās* in favour of *sadd al-dharā'ī'* (blocking the means):[261] In the case of fornication, if a man is accused of committing adultery and discrepancies are found in the witnesses' evidence, then according to *qiyās* the accusation is doubtful and no *ḥadd* punishment is administered. However, Abū Ḥanīfah disregarded this and gave his opinion based on *istiḥsān*, namely that the *ḥadd* punishment should be administered in order to deter others from committing such criminal acts.[262] Ghazālī opposed Abū Ḥanīfah's ruling, saying that the *ḥadd* punishment should be carried out only when the evidence is indisputable.[263]

4. Leaving *qiyās* due to authentic tradition (*ḥadīth ṣaḥīḥ*):[264]

According to *qiyās,* eating and drinking in *Ramaḍān*, whether consciously or by mistake voids the fast and necessitates expiation. However, Abū Ḥanīfah and his disciples observe that according to *istiḥsān,* eating or drinking by mistake or through forgetfulness does not annul fasting.[265] Accordingly, Abū Ḥanīfah says, "I would have decided according to analogy if there had been no narration"[266] since such incidents are out of one's hands. For example, a fly may be entering a man's mouth and he may swallow it: this should be considered as a kind of eating or drinking by mistake. Abū Ḥanīfah discusses this point, saying that this circumstance is beyond the control of one who is fasting, and compares it to a person swallowing dust whilst speaking.[267]

> Another example regarding this concept is that laughing out loud while praying annuls the ablution. According to *qiyās* ablution is annulled when something is expelled from the body; however laughing cannot be used as a comparison. If laughing invalidated the ablution during the ritual prayer, it stands to reason that it would invalidate ablution outside of the prayer too: laughter is laughter whenever it occurs. Laughing outside of the ritual prayers does not invalidate ablution according to *qiyās*. In spite of the ruling of *qiyās* the rule of *istiḥsān*[268] says that laughing annuls the ablution, based on a report narrated from the Prophet (ṣ), who said "Whoever laughs, let him repeat his prayer and ablution".[269]

Abū Ḥanīfah and his disciples were highly respectful of the Traditions, and used them in their *ijtihād;* even if it was a *ḥadīth ḍaif* (weak tradition) they would prefer it over *qiyās*. Ibn Ḥazm has affirmed that Abū Ḥanīfah and his disciples were united concerning the effectiveness of a weak *ḥadīth* against *qiyās*, considering it to be on a higher level.[270]

Yaḥyā b. Ādam (d. 203/818) comments on Abū Ḥanīfah's method of departing from *qiyās* due to a *ḥadīth ṣaḥīḥ* (authentic tradition): "Whoever says that Abū Ḥanīfah approves *qiyās* over *athar* (*ḥadīth*), is making an unfair accusation. Abū Ḥanīfah's practices and his disciples' writings are full of examples of his departing from *qiyās* and applying the rule of *athar* (*ḥadīth*).[271]

5. Leaving explicit analogy (*qiyās jalī*) for something that is more effective and beneficial:[272]

If a person who performs a supererogatory prayer, begins praying whilst standing and wants to continue the prayer sitting down, without an excuse, then according to Abū Ḥanīfah, this is allowed, based on the principle of *istiḥsān*. However, Abū Yūsuf and Shaibānī do not give permission, based on analogy. They compared it to an obligatory prayer: a person is not allowed to perform two *rak'a* standing and then, without an excuse continue to pray whilst sitting. According to Abū Ḥanīfah, sitting without an excuse in a supererogatory prayer (*nāfilah*) is like sitting with an excuse in an obligatory prayer (*farḍ*); therefore, it is certainly considered the same as an obligatory prayer. There are no differences whether one sits at the beginning of, or during an obligatory prayer.[273]

Abū Ḥanīfah in this case preferred to compare someone who performs a supererogatory prayer to someone who prays sitting, with an excuse. However it is unimaginable to compare this situation with someone who intends to pray two *rak'as*. Someone who intends to pray two *rak'as* of ritual prayer commits himself to fulfill that duty. Someone who begins to perform a supererogatory (*nāfilah*) prayer also commits himself to complete it.[274] At the beginning of the performance of worship, those who intend to perform the supererogatory prayer are free to do so; however once they begin to worship, they are under obligation to complete it.[275]

However, Abū Ḥanīfah did not compare this to the explicit analogy; instead be used *istiḥsān*, through implicit analogy (*qiyās khafī*), even though the first thing which comes to mind is explicit analogy. The reason to give permission for someone with an excuse to sit during obligatory prayer is to alleviate hardship and difficulties. The supererogatory (*nāfilah*) prayer is an optional act of worship and not an obligatory duty; therefore asking someone who is performing the supererogatory prayer to fulfil the duties of obligatory prayer is not alleviating hardship and difficulties.

Sitting during supererogatory prayer has been permitted in order to alleviate hardship and difficulties.[276]

f- Leaving analogy in favour of wide spread common custom (*'urf*).[277]

Example: if someone buys goods on the condition that they be delivered to his home, according to the principle of analogy, that condition is void and the transaction cannot take place. Despite this Abū Ḥanīfah has approved making such a condition, since this was the people's custom.[278]

On the other hand, Abū Ḥanīfah does depart from custom; one example is the custom of marking animals (*ish'ār*). This was one of the Prophet's traditions, applied during the *ḥajj* to indicate that the animal was intended for sacrifice. The Prophet (ṣ), after performing the afternoon prayer at Dhu-l Hulayfa, asked for a camel, which he then marked on the right side of its hump.[279] Despite this, Abū Ḥanīfah disapproved of the custom because of the cruel manner in which the Iraqis branded their animals. Abū Ḥanīfah was not against the *ḥadīth*, because it was clear that the Prophet (ṣ) forbade cruelty to animals.[280]

After an in-depth investigation of Abū Ḥanīfah's works, we can see how and why he used the term *istiḥsān*. In short, *istiḥsān* is to depart from explicit analogy to implicit analogy which is discovered only after very careful consideration. This kind of *istiḥsān* is debated among the scholars. Abū Ḥanīfah was also using *istiḥsān* in the sense of departing from an already established rule or *qiyās,* or from something which caused difficulties for the Muslim community, in favour of Prophetic Traditions, consensus, rulings of the Companions of the Prophet (ṣ), and custom.

This kind of *istiḥsān*—departing from explicit analogy to implicit analogy—is based proofs and evidences which may not be accepted in the viewpoint of others.[281] The use of *istiḥsān* from the viewpoint of Abū Ḥanīfah indicates that he was departing from *qiyās* not only for the sake of the benefit of people, but also with regard to a *ḥadīth* (tradition) or a custom which is common and prevalent among the community. This does not mean that he simply preferred *istiḥsān* to customs or whenever it was in line with traditions: he preferred custom or traditions whenever it was in the people's best interests.[282]

Abū Ḥanīfah also paid attention to matters between individuals where one has a natural priority over the other. For example, if a man tells his wife: "If you are menstruating, consider yourself divorced", and the woman says that she is indeed menstruating, then according to Abū Ḥanīfah,the divorce is valid, even if the husband disbelieves her and claims that she is lying. This is because a woman has natural priority over a man when it comes to being believed with regard to women's issues such as menstruation, pregnancy and so on. However, according to *qiyās,* her statement is not accepted and she is not divorced. Hence, Abū Ḥanīfah departed from *qiyās* on the grounds that only women can be certain in such a matter.[283]

Zufar[284] (d. 158) and the concept of istiḥsān

Zufar was the first of the three students of Abū Ḥanīfah. Later the other two, Abū Yūsuf and Al-Shaybānī, became more famous than Zufar.[285] At the beginning of his academic career Zufar was known for his adherence to the Traditionalist School (*Ahl al-Ḥadīth*). Impressed by Abū Ḥanīfah's teaching, he studied *fiqh* and was thoroughly educated in *ra'y* (opinion) and *qiyās* (analogy). He quickly made a reputation amongst the disciples for his sensitive and sharp analogy.[286] He has been quoted as saying ""We do not approve of opinion (*ra'y*) when there is a Tradition (*athar*) available; whenever an *athar* comes through we depart from opinion."[287]

Zufar's method of practising *ijtihād* is based on the Qur'an, the *Sunnah*, *ijmā'*, *qawl al-ṣaḥābah* (the sayings of the Companions of the Prophet), *qiyās*, *istiḥsān* and *'urf.* As such, it was not so far removed from the methods of his master, Abū Ḥanīfah and his friends, Abū Yūsuf and Shaybānī. These methods were based on the teachings of their master. The other disciples used slightly different methods in many cases and had different points of view when they were implementing these principles.[288]

For example, if a husband gives permission to someone to divorce his wife in accordance with the principle of *ṭalāq raj'ī* ("revocable")[289] but the person who is authorized to give the divorce pronounces the divorce to be absolute (*ṭalāq bā'in*),[290] according to Zufar this divorce is not recognised because he has misused the authority which was given to him. However, Abū Ḥanīfah, Shaybānī and Abū Yūsuf disagree with Zufar on this issue and consider that this is recognised as *ṭalāq raj'ī.*[291]

Zufar's method of approving *istiḥsān* is based on public interest, so long as it is not in contradiction with the principles of Sharī'ah. However, at times he favours *qiyās* where others favour *istiḥsān.* When a matter was being considered the application of *qiyās* was approved if the outcome was not negative and not opposed to the required purpose; where the application of *qiyās* produced negative results, then *istiḥsān* would be approved as it aims to seek the reason why *qiyās* resulted in negativity, thus benefiting the people. Zufar usually prefers to approve the rule of *qiyās* rather than *istiḥsān.* However, if there is a dispute between *qiyās* and *istiḥsān,* he would approve *istiḥsān* in the sense of implicit analogy which is based on *naṣṣ*, *qawl al-ṣaḥābah* (the saying of the Companions of the Prophet) and present *'urf* (custom).[292]

Abū Yūsuf (d. 182 AH) and the concept of istiḥsān

Abū Yūsuf was appointed[293] judge of Baghdād during the time of al-Mahdī (d. 169 AH), al-Hādi (d. 170 AH) and al-Rashīd (d. 193 AH).[294] This position gave him the opportunity to practice Ḥanafī law in order to resolve the problems presented to him, and so his rulings and his practice of *istiḥsān* come from both actual life and juristic theory.[295] Schacht asserts that the first technical user of *istiḥsān* was not Abū Yūsuf,[296] who he claims inherited this method from his master, Abū Ḥanīfah. Abū Yūsuf practiced *istiḥsān* very skilfully in his *ijtihād* thanks to his position as judge, despite his allegiance to Tradition (*Ḥadīth*).[297]

Abū Yūsuf's method of judgment with regard to the principle of *istiḥsān* can be found in his rulings, words and writings. According to the sources, he would pray to God, saying: "O my Lord! As you are aware, whenever I face a problem I look for guidance. First I look in your Book and if I find guidance there then I take it; otherwise I continue, looking in your Prophet's (ṣ) traditions. If the guidance can not be found either in the Book or in the Prophet's (ṣ) traditions, I then take into consideration the Companion's words."[298] Sarakhsī points out that Abū Yūsuf's method considers the saying of the Companions (*qawl ṣaḥābī*) and is preferable to *qiyās*.[299] Karkhī (d. 340/952) was reported as saying "Abū Yūsuf used to say: "*Qiyās* is such and such, but I left it because of *athar* (tradition)".

According to Karkhī the meaning of *athar* here is an opinion of the Companions where no opposing opinion has been recorded. It obviously means that if any of Abū Yūsuf's contemporaries had a conflict of opinion, then applying the Saying of the Companions would be deemed more preferable.[300] Abū Yūsuf followed his master's methods of *ijtihād*, seeking guidance first in the Qur'an, the *Sunnah* and the Sayings of the Companions; the Saying of the

Companions were given priority over *qiyās.*[301] In his use of the principle of *istiḥsān,* he also followed his master, and mainly used it to oppose the rule of *qiyās.*[302]

Abū Yūsuf embraced the principle enshrined in the following quote: "It is an accepted fact that the terms of law vary due to changes of the times".[303] An example is the case of *kharāj* (land tax), which was fixed for a certain amount by the second Caliph 'Umar. Abū Yūsuf, however, did not hesitate to change and reset it according to the circumstances of the times.[304] Abū Yūsuf took the opposite view to Abū Ḥanifah on the matter of usury. If the Prophet (*ṣ*) ruled that goods could be sold in different units of weights and measures, according to Abū Ḥanīfah and Shaybānī, custom (*'urf*) could not be taken into consideration. However, Abū Yūsuf has a different opinion, and rules that since circumstances have now changed, trading should be in accordance with local or popular custom.[305]

Abū Yūsuf sometimes uses the term "I approve" (*astaḥsinū*), to mean "I believe it is the right thing to do", and sometimes uses the opposite term "I disapprove" (*astaqbiḥū*), meaning "I believe it is the wrong thing to do". For example, if a man is attacked by a camel, and the man then kills the camel, according to the opinion of Abū Ḥanīfah and Shaybānī based on *qiyās,* the person who has been attacked must pay compensation to the camel's owner. Despite their opinion, Abū Yūsuf points out that it is the man who is entitled to compensation. This is a kind of *istiḥsān* for he says "I disapprove (*astaqbīḥū*) of him compensating the owner of the camel."[306]

After considering Abū Yūsuf's writings and rulings on the basis of the principle of *istiḥsān,* we can see that he uses *istiḥsān* in the following senses:

1. Leaving the explicit analogy (*qiyās jālī*), which is based on discretion and prudence, in favour of an alternative analogy that has a stronger effective cause (*'illah*):

For example, if someone performs four *rak'as* of supererogatory prayer but does not sit within the required time of *tashahhud*[307] at the first sitting, according to Abū Ḥanīfah and Abū Yūsuf his prayer is valid. This is a type of implicit analogy within *istiḥsān*. They have compared the four *rak'as* of supererogatory prayer to four *rak'a* of obligatory prayer, and have arrived at the logical conclusion that the four *rak'a* supererogatory prayer, despite the fact that the required time of sitting has not been adhered to, is as valid as an obligatory prayer, since it was performed of his own free will.[308]

Next is an unusual example of *istiḥsān* approved by Abū Yūsuf, in favour of the general benefit of Muslims: If a Muslim steals from an infidel who is living in a Muslim country and who abides by the laws of that country and pays tax (*jizyah*) the Muslim will not have his hand amputated. According to *qiyās*, however, a Muslim thief *will* have his hand amputated.[309] This type of legal opinion is a very peculiar example of *istiḥsān* in that it appears to be an unjustified decision. In spite of the difficulties of understanding the judgment of Abū Yūsuf which is not to amputate the hand of the Muslim thief, Aḥmad Ḥasan presumes that it was his intention to discourage the entry of foreigners into Muslim territories in order to keep society immune from their influence.[310]

2. Approving *istiḥsān* based on the text (*naṣṣ*):

The following examples explain Abū Yūsuf's departure from *qiyās* and approval of *istiḥsān* based on *naṣṣ*, which is the authentic Tradition: laughing out loud during prayer negates the ablution;[311] fasting is not invalidated when someone eats or drinks by mistake;[312] and the validation of the agreement of crop sharing (*muzāra'ah*) and share tenancy.[313]

3. Approving *istiḥsān* based on the consensus (*ijmā'*) of the Companions: one example is when a husband and wife apostatise together, their marriage (*nikāḥ*) continues as it is.[314] In a similar case, if a woman apostasizes from Islām during a terminal illness, the husband should inherit her estate; this is based on *istiḥsān* according to Abū Yūsuf and Abū Ḥanīfah. According to *qiyās,* the husband is excluded from the inheritance.[315] In these circumstances Abū Yūsuf gives the explanation that the woman's apostasy during terminal illness must be out of pure malice, as it is clearly her intention to disinherit her husband. Therefore, the circumstances surrounding apostasy should be absolutely clear in the situation of terminal illness. According to *qiyās* the husband does not inherit her estate as it does not distinguish between the different circumstances of normal and terminal illness.[316]

4. Approving *istiḥsān* based on the Saying of the Companions of the Prophet (*qawl al-ṣaḥābi*):[317] For example, if someone in authority—a ruler, say, or a judge—has witnessed a crime of theft, adultery or the consumption of alcohol, they cannot pass judgment based on their personal knowledge; they can only pass judgment when the legal evidence has been established. Abū Yūsuf indicates here that "this is a kind of *istiḥsān* based on a Tradition (*athar*) which is reported from Abū Bakr and 'Umar. However, according to *qiyās*, they are able to execute their judgment on the basis of their personal knowledge.[318] Through *istiḥsān,* justice is established. The authority is powerless to judge without evidence. If the judgment had been allowed by mere personal knowledge, it may be an arbitrary decision as it creates turmoil within society, causing people to lose their trust. However, the

requirement of evidence ensures that the people continue to have faith in the judicial system.

5. Approving *istiḥsān* on the grounds of necessity, the pursuit of ease, and avoidance of hardship or the removal of that which is harmful:[319]

The following are considered as forms of *istiḥsān:* Friday prayer is permitted to be held in more than one mosque in the same town, in order to alleviate any difficulties within the Muslim community;[320] after a successful battle, the booty (*ghanīmah*) is collected and, if it is not possible to forward it to the treasury (*bayt al-māl*), the commander may distribute it among his men;[321] and *muzāraʿah* and *musāqāt* (share tenancy) agreements are deemed valid in order to alleviate hardship.[322]

6. Approving *istiḥsān* on the grounds of custom. For example, a person employs a labourer to dig a well without first asking permission from the ruler. The well is dug beside a path along which Muslims walk, and afterwards someone falls into the well and dies. According to *qiyās* the labourer must accept the responsibility of the death. According to the general custom, an individual must have the ruler's permission before he can have the well dug. Abū Yūsuf says that *qiyās* should not be considered in this case because the labourer had already taken permission from the employer, and therefore, according to *istiḥsān*, it is the employer who has to accept the responsibility for the crime.[323]

According to Abū Yūsuf, another example of the use of *istiḥsān* would be in the case of a husband paying *zakāt al-fitr*[324] on his wife's behalf but without her permission. This is valid according to *istiḥsān* because custom dictates that the husband is responsible her paying *zakāt al-fitr* and therefore his wife's permission is not necessary. According to the rule of *qiyās,* this is not valid.[325]

7. Departing from a ruling of *qiyās* due to doubt and uncertainty over the evidence:

According to *qiyās,* if a man is accused of fornication (*zinā*) by four people, the penalty prescribed by the Qur'an is one hundred lashes.[326] However, what happens if two people give evidence that the accused is married?[327] Will he be punished with the hundred lashes first and then by being stoned?

According to *qiyās,* if the witnesses withdraw the accusation while the accused is being punished, he must still be subjected to the rest of the lashes. However, *istiḥsān* rules that the accused person should be relieved of both the penalty of lashes and stoning.[328] Because of doubts and uncertainty over the evidence, *istiḥsān* overrules *qiyās* in accordance with the Sharī'ah, which dictates that a *ḥadd* punishment should not be established where there is uncertain evidence.[329] Therefore, *istiḥsān* departs from the ruling of *qiyās* on the ground of uncertain evidence in order to secure justice for the people. Also, had *qiyās* been enforced, the accused person would be faced with two different punishments for a single crime; carrying out double punishments for one offence is considered unjust and therefore must be avoided.[330]

Shaybānī (d. 189) and the concept of istiḥsān

Shaybānī[331] is also a Traditionalist and depends on Traditions for his rulings to a greater extent than Abū Yūsuf.[332] He points out the importance of balance between tradition and *ra'y* saying that "Tradition can only work when it is hand in hand with opinion (*ra'y*), and vice versa. Knowledge of *ra'y* or Tradition is not enough to judge or take the place of a *muftī* (the authority of giving *fatwā*-ruling)."[333] In this context, Shaybānī follows Abu Ḥanifah, and is careful not to make any rule arbitrarily without depending on legal evidence. To avoid an arbitrary decision he applies analogy; if no guidance is found in the Qur'an and the *Sunnah*, or results in a bad decision, he departs from *qiyās* and applies *istiḥsān*. He also made the condition that the one eligible to perform *ijtihād* to give a *fatwā* (ruling) will be the one "who knows the Qur'an, the *Sunnah*, the Sayings of the Companions of the Prophet (ṣ), and Muslim jurists' considerations of *istiḥsān*. He must be versed in performing *ra'y* (opinion) *ijtihād* and giving *fatwās*, which are validated rulings on obligatory acts such as praying, fasting, and pilgrimage; and forbidden acts such as drinking alcohol, fornication, and dealing in usury. When he performs *ijtihād*, he uses the faculty of reasoning and compares it to something similar, and even if a mistake is made with the judgment, applying it is permissible."[334]

Shaybānī often uses the following statement "I depart from *qiyās* and approve *istiḥsān*".[335] His definition of the *istiḥsān* that sometimes refers to *athar* (tradition) was called *ra'y* at the time of the Companions.[336] He used *istiḥsān* in the sense of taking an opposite side and departing from *qiyās*.[337] Without giving an explanation that is opposite of *qiyās*, he simply says: "this is *istiḥsān*" or "According to *istiḥsān*, it is as such: Jaṣṣāṣ and Sarakhsī give some quotations from Shaybānī's book called "*Kitāb al-Istiḥsān*".[338]

Shaybānī criticises the kind of *istiḥsān* which is performed against clear evidence and considers it to be an arbitrary decision. He condemned the *ahl al-Medinah* for what he saw as their hypocrisy in their use of *istiḥsān:* he saw them as people who would abandon their Traditions when faced with a problem, and approve *istiḥsān* which was not supported by *athar* (Traditions) and the *Sunnah*, and which went against their own narrations. How, he asks, could they be *ahl al-athar* (Traditionalists) when they depart from their own narrations? This confirms that Shaybānī never approved *istiḥsān* over Tradition.[339] For example, the *ahl al-Medinah* on inserting the *salām* (conclusion of prayer) between every two *rak'a* of canonical prayer. Shaybānī responded saying, "How dare they approve this with *istiḥsān*!" A narration had been reported concerning the Prophet who prayed four *rak'as* at noon without separating them by a *salām*.[340] These examples clearly indicate that Shaybānī was insistent that *istiḥsān* be based on legal evidence.

Shaybānī applied the principle of *istiḥsān* in the following ways:

1. Using *istiḥsān* based on textual *naṣṣ*:

According to Shaybānī, *qiyās* is not a valid principle to be applied when there is textual evidence.[341] Shaybānī opposes the Madīnah jurists and their claim that someone who has eaten by mistake or through forgetfulness during Ramaḍan has to repeat the fast. He says: "Of course the Madīnah jurists are sure that *ra'y* (opinion) would not be applied in the presence of definite proof as Abū Ḥanīfah said, 'I would have ordered the fast to be repeated if there were no narrations'"[342]

In the case of laughing whilst praying, the Madīnah jurists, despite the presence of textual evidence, applied the ruling *qiyās*, saying, 'Laughing out loud whilst praying does not annul ablution; ablution is annulled when some kind of excretion occurs from the body, which cannot be compared with laughing. If laughing had invalidated ablution at prayers it would also have invalidated ablution outside of the prayer: laughter is laughter wherever and whenever it occurs. In spite of the *istiḥsān* ruling which says that laughing invalidates ablution during prayer, according to *qiyās* laughing does not invalidate ablution.[343] This *istiḥsān* ruling is based on a report narrated from the Prophet (ṣ), who said: "Whoever laughs let him repeat his prayer and ablution".[344] Given such clear evidence (*athar*), *qiyās* is not applied. Shaybānī criticizes them, saying "If *athar* (Traditions) were not present when the jurists of Madīnah were considering practising *qiyās,* it would be acceptable, but since they are present, *athar* has to be followed.[345]

2. Using the principle of *istiḥsān* based on the Sayings of the Companions:

   Shaybānī approves the use of *istiḥsān* to validate the continuation of a marriage (*nikāḥ*) of a husband and a wife who have apostatized together, on the basis of the agreement of the Companions.[346]

3. Using the principle of *istiḥsān* based on avoiding hardship:[347]

   If a small piece of animal faeces is dropped into a well, according to *qiyās* the water cannot be consumed, since it is ritually impure. However if very little has contaminated the water, according to *istiḥsān* it is considered pure; as wells are located on open lands it is difficult to prevent the wells from becoming contaminated from the various germs carried by the wind.[348] This ruling is based on the maxim of the Sharī'ah: "Necessity renders prohibited things permissible".[349]

   In the subject of the forward sale (*salam*) one of the requirements is that the goods must be physically present at the time of the contract; if they are not present, then, according to *qiyās*, *salam* is invalid. An example is when one of the Companions, Hakīm b. Hizām, asked the Prophet (ṣ) if he could sell a commodity prior to purchasing it. The Prophet (ṣ) answered: "Sell not what is not with you".[350] Despite *qiyās* invalidating *salam,* another *ḥadīth* approves *salam:* "Whoever concludes *salam,* let him do so with a specified measure, weight and within a specified period of time."[351] Shaybānī uses *istiḥsān* to legitimize forward sale in order to prevent hardship for Muslims.[352] Similar business transactions such as *muḍārabah,*[353] *muzāra'ah,*[354] *musaqāh*[355] are also validated by *istiḥsān*, despite *qiyās* invalidating them.

4. Using the principle of *istiḥsān* based on custom:

The consideration of (*'urf*) plays an important role in the legal thinking of Shaybānī.[356] For example if a certain town and its residents ask Muslims for protection, then according to the ruling of *istiḥsān* the agreement of protection would also cover the belongings of those people mentioned in that agreement. The terms *qal'ah* (fort) or *madīnah* (town) in their common usage (*'urf*) does not simply apply to the buildings but all the contents in the buildings. However, according to *qiyās*, it would only apply to the fort or the town, and it would exclude the contents.[357]

5. Using the principle of *istiḥsān* to explain an ambiguous statement:

If a man says to his wife "Consider yourself divorced if you enter the house" while his wife is in the house," Shaybānī says that according to *istiḥsān*: "the condition would only be fulfilled if the woman re-entered the house after having left it. However, according to *qiyās*, the presence of the wife in the house at the time when the husband pronounces this statement is taken into account, and the very fact that his wife is in the house fulfils the condition of the husband's statement."[358] This statement is unclear: if he applies his condition whilst she is still in the house then he is contradicting his own oath, and therefore it remains ambiguous. *Istiḥsān* explains that the husband's statement is unclear and, rather than applying *qiyās* ambiguously, states that the oath only applies if the wife leaves the house and then re-enters.

Conclusion

As founders of the theory of *istiḥsān*, the Ḥanafī jurists defined the term in various ways. However, the definitions, although explained differently, have the same meaning.

Methodologically the first to define *istiḥsān* was Karkhi who lived in the third and fourth century. The key word in his definition is "departure" (*al-'udūl*), which points to the heart of the objective: simple departure is not enough; there must be a stronger reason for a departure. The word *tark* (departure) and the word "better" (*awlā*) were used by Jaṣṣaṣ (d. 370/981). After one century, the way of expressing *istiḥsān* changed slightly. The different key word given by Bazdawī (d. 482/1089) was "particularization" (*takhṣīṣ*) with a stronger reason. Sarakhsī (d. 483/1090) had four definitions, each with a different perspective, and used the key words, "ease, convenience, suitability, accommodating, seek mildness, tolerance" which appear to be the main goal of *istiḥsān* in departing from *qiyās* (analogy). Nasafī (d. 710/1310) and Ibn Humām's definitions also have more or less the same meaning, and use the key phrase "evidence, opposing *qiyās jalī* (explicit analogy)."

Briefly, the main common point of the Ḥanafī jurists concerning *istiḥsān* is the idea of departure from one ruling to another, or to prefer one decision to another,[359] or to set aside *qiyās jalī* (obvious analogy),[360] or to adopt what is more suitable, easy, convenient and comfortable.[361]

"Whoever approves juristic preference is making himself the lawmaker".[362] Shāf'ī's criticism of *istiḥsān* is based on the above statement, which rejects *istiḥsān* altogether. Nevertheless, the Shāfi'ī scholar Āmidī (d. 631/1233) appeared to recognize *istiḥsān* when giving the definition and using the key phrase "an evidence embedded (*yanqadiḥu*) in the mind of the jurist". Rather than agreeing with Shīrāzī (d. 476/1083), who said, "Depending on assumption rather than evidence", he shares the same idea as Ghazālī (d. 505/1111) who said "Use your own judgment to arrive at a decision". Besides the Shāfi'ī jurists, the Imami Shī'ites also rejected *istiḥsān,* considering it to be assumptions without proof. However, the Zaydīs, despite being an offshoot of Shī'ism, considered *istiḥsān* as a valid principle of Sharī'ah. In addition, the Zaydīs made further conditions that the proof which allows the departure must be eligible for the conditions of *ṣiḥḥat*, which must be stronger or preferable.[363]

As we are aware, the opinions of the Mālikī jurists about the definitions of *istiḥsān* are not far from those of the Ḥanafīs. "Departure from a *qiyās* that would lead to extremity and exaggeration in the ruling," is a quote from Ibn Rushd (d. 595/1198). "Preferring or acting on a ruling based a stronger *dalīl*" is the opinion of al-Bāji. In addition, the basis, while departing from one ruling to another ruling, should be one of the following: *shar'ī dalīl* (legal proof): *'urf* (consensus), *maṣlaḥah* (benefit), or ease, *raf' al-ḥaraj* (removal of hardship).[364]

Ḥanbalī jurists concur with Ḥanafīs on *istiḥsān,* despite different definitions. According to the Ḥanbalīs, departure must be based on consideration of the main principles, (the Qur'an, the *Sunnah* and *ijmā'*). The key words in Ḥanbalī definitions are "leaving, returning and departure" because of stronger or better reasons; "abandoning the *qiyās jalī* (explicit analogy)" are the same as the key phrase given by the Ḥanafī jurist Nasafī.

Ibn Ḥazm and the followers of the Ẓāhirī school rejected *istiḥsān* unconditionally. According to them, everything one needs is available in the Qur'an: "...we have neglected nothing in the Book" (6:38). Ibn Ḥazm likens *istiḥsān* to a passion (*shahwah*), a whim (*hawā'*) and an error (*ḍalāl*).[365] He says that the truth (*al-ḥaqq*) will not be what we like (*mā istaḥsannā*) unless there is proof for it. If it were so, God would have commanded something that is not pronounced; then the realities of things would be invalid, and textual evidence and proof would contradict each other.[366]

Lastly, Basrī (d. 436/1044) considered *istiḥsān* to be a principle of Sharī'ah; he did not believe that the Ḥanafī jurists' use of *istiḥsān* depended on self-opinion and personal judgment without evidence.[367] However, Bishr bin Ghiyās (d. 218/833) despite being a Mu'tazilī, considered it to be self-opinion which does not depend on evidence.[368]

Examining the views of the *'ulamā'* regarding the validity of *istiḥsān,* we conclude the following: *istiḥsān* is a valid principle according to Ḥanafi, Mālikī, Ḥanbalī, Abū Al-Ḥusain Al-Baṣrī from the *mutakallimūn,* and Al-Āmidī who is from the Shāfi'ī scholars. *Istiḥsān* is not a valid principle according to Shāfi'ī, Ghazālī, Isnawī and Ibn Ḥazm al-Ẓāhirī.

As the application of the concept of *istiḥsān* has been elaborated throughout the research, with its varieties of practices and the early period of Islamic law, we have seen that *istiḥsān* has been practiced based not on personal desire but on valid legal evidence. These applications were sometimes based on the text (*naṣṣ*); the sayings of the Companions (*qawl ṣaḥābī*); the consensus of the Companions (*ijmā' al-ṣaḥābah*); authentic tradition (*ḥadīth ṣaḥīḥ*); implicit analogy which is more effective and beneficial; wide spread common custom; necessity and needs that are based on ease, avoiding hardship and removing that which is harmful; and whenever there was doubt due to the uncertainty of the evidence.

On the validity and disagreement over *istiḥsān* the Ḥanafī viewpoint can be summarized as follows: Ḥanafī jurists divided *istiḥsān* mainly into two categories. The first is a kind of *qiyās*, which is based on implicit analogy. The second is based on text (the Qur'an, the *Sunnah*), consensus (*ijmā'*), necessity (*ḍarūrah*) etc. Amongst the schools of thought there is no disagreement on rulings deduced from proofs which are based on the Qur'an, the *Sunnah*, *ijmā'*, *ḍarūrah*, *qawl ṣaḥābī*, *'urf*. However, it is difficult to say that there is no disagreement over *istiḥsān* which is based on an implicit analogy that is preferred to an explicit analogy, because its effective cause is stronger than the explicit effective cause. Shāfiʿī gave much attention to *qiyās,* considering it as a main principle of Sharīʿah; his views on the components of *qiyās* differ to those of Ḥanafīs with regard to the determination of *ʿillah.*[369] In fact, opponents do not contradict Abū Ḥanīfah's view of *istiḥsān* which is based on *naṣṣ*, *ijmāʿ*, and *ḍarūrah* because these are unanimously considered valid amongst the scholars.

However, they did oppose Abū Ḥanīfah when they believed that he was implementing personal opinion (*ra'y*), which is considered to be the abandoning of *qiyās* by whim and personal desire.[370] It is obvious that opponents have criticized Abū Ḥanīfah abandoning the explicit analogy and preferring implicit analogy irrespective of the power of its effective cause; this was considered to be an approval of it without *dalīl* where there was no reliable basis, and his judgment was seen to be based purely on arbitrary opinions inspired by intellectual reasoning. Therefore, Ḥanafī scholars focused on this criticism and tried to prove that their use of *istiḥsān* was valid and legal.

Moreover, the Ḥanafīs sometimes determine the *ʿillah* (effective cause) of the implicit analogy by way of *ijtihād.* The way that the *ʿillah* is determined differs from one scholar to the next, which is unavoidable. Because of this, different approaches occurred amongst the Ḥanafī scholars. In some cases Abū Ḥanīfah approved *istiḥsān* by implicit analogy while Abū Yūsuf and Shaybānī approved *istiḥsān* by explicit analogy; sometimes it would be vice-versa. I would say that if internal conflicts within one *madhhab* are inevitable, then different approaches and interpretations on legal issues between two different schools of thought are entirely to be expected.

When we take into consideration the evidence presented by the group which recognizes the validity of *istiḥsān,* we see that on the whole they are more than enough to refute any objections raised against them. The *istiḥsān* that has been objected to by those *'ulamā'* who refute the principle is somewhat different from the *istiḥsān* described by the groups who recognize its validity. This is because the group supporting *istiḥsān* do not accept it unless it is supported by strongly validated evidence. As for the *istiḥsān* that relies on whim and personal desire, this is not supported by evidence, and since its source is what the person himself prefers rationally (by *'aql*), this *istiḥsān* is not approved by the group that recognize *istiḥsān*.

As it is understood from the evidence which has been proposed, the reason Shāfi'ī and others rejected *istiḥsān* is that they assumed it was the giving of a ruling not based on the Qur'an, the *Sunnah*, *ijmā'* or *qiyās*, but rather solely through *aql* (intellect) and desire.[371] Such *istiḥsān* is to deviate from what is right for the sake of personal pleasure: "*Istiḥsān* is merely doing what is agreeable."[372]

As we have shown in the previous chapters there is a lot of confusion regarding the concept of *istiḥsān*, which is why the scholars' debate on the validation of *istiḥsān* is centred around whether *istiḥsān* could be a principle of Islamic law or not. Debates concentrated mainly on the true relationship between the *lughawī* (linguistic) and the *iṣṭilāḥī* (technical) meanings of *istiḥsān*. Some scholars saw the *lughawī* (linguistic) meanings as positive, others as negative. There are many *iṣṭilāḥī* definitions of *istiḥsān*.

Shīrāzī and Juwaynī from the Shāfi'ī school opposed *istiḥsān* but after citing both the definitions of Karkhī and other recognized definitions they said "If these definitions are what they mean when they say '*istiḥsān*' then there is no dispute."[373] Ghazālī was of a similar opinion. "The principle is not disputable; however, naming it *istiḥsān* will be rejected".[374] Here he was concerned with the terminology rather than the concept.

Later Shafi'ī scholars such as Rāzī, Āmidī, ibn al-Subkī, and Isnawī rejected Ghazālī's approach, claiming that his reasoning did not come from the Qur'an and the *Sunnah,* and was not used by previous scholars in their *ijtihād.*[375]

Taftazānī (d. 792 AH) made the following statement pointing out the disagreement over *istiḥsān:*

"Many arguments have been made on both sides and whoever accepted *istiḥsān* has been criticized. The arguments occurred because no investigation had been undertaken to identify the real facts and neither party understood the others' intentions. Both parties issued hurtful criticisms and they were unkind and insensitive. Advocators of *istiḥsān* believe it is one of the four main principles. The statement "whoever performs *istiḥsān* puts himself in place of the Lawgiver", which means whoever approves a rule from his own personal desire and pleasure without basing their judgment on the proofs approved by the Shārī' put themselves in place of God, has nothing to do with *istiḥsān.* In fact, there is no reason to dispute the concept of *istiḥsān.*"[376]

Taftazānī gives examples explaining that there is no dispute over the term, quoting several definitions of *istiḥsān* which are unanimously accepted as a principle of Sharī'ah.[377]

Shāfi'ī and the disciples who followed him in many cases approved rulings according to *istiḥsān.* Al-Suyūṭī (d. 911/1505) in accordance with the maxim of *fiqh* "Any needs, whether of a public or private nature, are so dealt with as to meet the exigencies of the case",[378] said that on issues involving matters such as rent and transfer of property, for example, *istiḥsān* may be used rather than *qiyās.*[379]

In my opinion the disagreement over the validity of *istiḥsān* is without substance as no-one recognizes *istiḥsān* without the support of evidence. Additionally *istiḥsān* which is based on a stronger *dalīl* and departs from a weaker *dalīl* is accepted by all *'ulamā'*. There are issues based on *istiḥsān* which Shāfi'ī adopted that demonstrate this. These have mentioned by al-Māwardī in his book "*adab al-qāḍī*".[380] Some of these issues are as follows:

For example, Shāfi'ī is reported to have said: "If there was no disagreement presented against a solitary saying of a Companion, the Companion's opinion becomes valid evidence (*hujjah*)". Moreover, Shāfi'ī performed *istiḥbāb* too by saying "I approve this (*astaḥbibu*)".[381] Therefore Sarakhsī claimed that there is no difference between *astaḥsinu* (I approve the preferable) and *astaḥbibu* (I deem the preferable), but the term *istiḥsān* is more clear and preferable then the term *istiḥbāb*.[382]

The right of the claimant to ask for pre-emption (*shuf'ah*) within three days following the sale of the property is according to Shāfi'ī, an example of *istiḥsān* not an *aṣl*.[383] This shows that Shāfi'ī adopted *istiḥsān* although the *aṣl* is the right of the claimant to seek pre-emption immediately. The way of *istiḥsān* here is that people generally agreed to delay the right of pre-emption as near as possible to the pre-emption deadline. If the sale became known to the claimant at night it would be delayed until the next morning; the time allowed includes the time it would take for him to eat and dress. The Qur'an set the 3 day limit.[384] This *istiḥsān* is based on *naṣṣ* and *ijmā'* together. It was Shāfi'ī who said that when governors require an oath it should be taken on the Qur'an; he considered this good (*ḥasan*). Here *istiḥsān* confirms that an oath taken on the Qur'an is binding when applied to various issues relating to money; it also makes the *kaffārah* obligatory, which persuades people to take it seriously.[385] This is *istiḥsān* as the principle rule is that an oath should be taken in God's name only.

Shāfi'ī also ruled that cupping the ears with the hands whilst performing *adhān* (the call to prayers) is good. The reason for this was the precedent set by Bilāl, who was in charge of performing the *adhān* during the Prophet's time and the Prophet (ṣ) tacitly approved (*sunnah taqrīriyyah*) this as basis for this *istiḥsān*.

When a question was asked of Shāfiʿī as to whether *ʿumra* could be performed in the month of *ḥajj*, he said "it is good, I deem it good (*astaḥsinu*)"[386] Al-Māwardī states that Shāfiʿī never adopted *istiḥsān* without an associating *dalīl; istiḥsān* based on *dalīl* is unproblematic, while *istiḥsān* that is not associated with *dalīl* is rejected.[387]

When we study the statements of both early and contemporary scholars, the usage of *istiḥsān* becomes clear. Shāṭibī was in the beginning one of the *ʿulamā'* who denied *istiḥsān* as he thought it was ruling only through desire and personal opinion. He eventually understood that the point of view of those who recognized *istiḥsān* had to be based on *dalīl*. This was mentioned in the rulings (*fatāwā*) of the well known Companions of the Prophet (ṣ). He was motivated to support the view that *istiḥsān* is a valid source of Sharīʿah. Shāṭibī thus states in his book "*Al-Iʿtiṣām*": "I also said the same as those *ʿulamā'* who dropped *istiḥsān* and whatever was based on it, until *istiḥsān*, after being traced through the *fatāwā* of the caliphs, the well known Companions and their followers, and without any objections from other companions, became stronger and firmer. Thus for me, it gathered more strength, it gave my soul tranquillity and my heart trusted in it willingly. I followed the Companions and took them as an example, may God be pleased with them all".[388]

This statement shows that whoever understands and recognizes the real meaning and rationale behind *istiḥsān*, will find that, basically, there is no disagreement between the *ʿulama'*.

Shāikh Maḥillāwī states in his book "*Tashīl al-wuṣūl ilā ʿilm al-uṣūl*": "Actually, no *istiḥsān* over which there is disagreement could be realized, and if it meant simply that which the mind (*'aql*) considers good, no one would ever deem it valid. If it is intended to mean what the Ḥanafīs meant, then it is a valid source for all, and it is a matter that is not worthy of disagreement".[389] This statement shows that there was no real disagreement over the validity of *istiḥsān*. To explain this issue further we refer to the opinions of contemporary scholars:

Khallāf says: "What widened the gap of disagreement in this and similar subjects is that the followers of the four main *imāms* were exaggerated in advocating the view of their individual *imām*, for whenever one of the followers of a particular *imām* catches a statement of another *imām* and such statements appear to have some contradiction, he (the follower) withholds this apparent meaning and starts to reply invalidating the concept of *istiḥsān*. In turn whoever comes after him from the same school also exaggerates, and thus the disagreement is widened farther. Had there been good intentions without suspicion, and had they accepted it with good intentions, there would never have been room for disagreement".[390] Khallāf continues: "Had those who disagreed with each other specified exactly the point of disagreement before exchanging the proofs (*ḥujjah*), Muslims would have been saved the trouble of having to research and clarify many different terminologies."[391]

This view of Khallāf continues what we have uncovered during the research concerning the opinions of the various schools supporting and opposing the validity of *istiḥsān*. Therefore, the view that outweighs other opinions is the view of the group who recognize the validity of *istiḥsān*, on the condition that the departure from the principle rule is in favour of *istiḥsān* and is supported by a *dalīl*. *Istiḥsān* is a valid source as long as it is not based on personal whim and is supported by one of the Sharī'ah proofs.

We can conclude that as long as *istiḥsān* remains the departure from the rule on the grounds of the existence of a stronger *dalīl*, there is sufficient ground for recognizing its validity. In cases where *istiḥsān* is without any *dalīl*, but depends on personal desire, then it is not permitted. This ensures that the doors are closed in the face of those who do not have adequate knowledge of the rules of Islamic Sharī'ah to perform *iftā'* and legislate laws. Consequently, the *'ulamā'* who recognize *istiḥsān* disapprove of *istiḥsān* without *dalīl*. As I elaborated earlier, all of the reported cases in which *istiḥsān* was performed were issued based on a *dalīl*. Ḥanafī, Mālikī and Ḥanbalī scholars have recognized *istiḥsān* as a source of Sharī'ah and have used it to find solutions in circumstances where there is no textual source available.

Notes

1. Khudarī, "Tārīkh", p. 210.
2. Abū Dāwūd, "*Sunan*", ḥadīth no. 3585, vol. 3, p. 1019.
3. Ibid.
4. Muḥammad Ibn Sa'd (d. 230/844), "*Al-Ṭabaqāt al-Kubrā*", (Beirut: 1957), vol. 2 p. 76.
5. 'Abd al-Malik Ibn Hishām, (d. 218/833) "*Al-Sīrat al-Nabawiyyah*", edt. Muṣṭafā al-Saqā, Ibrāhīm al-Abyārī, 'Abd al-Ḥāfiẓ Shalabī, (Beirut: Dār al-Khayr, 1992), vol. 2, pp. 210-1.
6. For details of the heirs see: Qur'an: 4:1-40.
7. 'Aṣabah: those who are entitled to the remainders of the shares. See Doi, "*Sharī'ah*", p. 277.
8. Noel j. Coulson, "*Succession in the Muslim Family*", (London: Cambridge university Press, 1971), pp. 73-4; Abu Zahrah, "*Imām Mālik*", p. 324; Noel J. Coulson, "*Conflicts and tensions in Islamic Jurisprudence*", (Chicago: The University of Chicago press, 1969), p. 17.
9. Khudarī, "*Tārīkh*", pp. 142-3.
10. Ibn Mājah "*Sunan*", ḥadīth no: 2340, vol. 2, p. 784.

11. Abū Zahrah, "*Imām Mālik*", p. 324.
12. Abū Yūsuf, "*Kitāb al-Kharāj*", p. 14.
13. Mālik, "*Al-Muwaṭṭā*'", vol. 2, p. 748.
14. Abū Yūsuf, "*Kitāb al-Kharāj*", pp. 13-15; Fazlur Raḥmān "*Islamic Methodology in History*", (Lahore: 1965), pp. 180-1.
15. Nu'mānī, "*Omar*", vol. 2.
16. Orhan Çeker, verbally given information by him at the University of Selçuk dated on 29.03.04 in Konya/ Turkey.
17. Schacht, "*The Origins*", p. 192.
18. Khalwah: where a man and woman are left alone together.
19. Qur'an: 2:237.
20. See: Schacht, "*The Origins*", p. 193.
21. Tyan E. "*Histoire de l'organisation judiciaire en pays d'Islam*", vol. 1, p. 132, 1938-43; see Schacht, "*The Origins*", p. 191.
22. Khudarī, "*Tārīkh*", p. 135.
23. Abū Uthmān 'Amr b. Baḥr Jāhiz (d. 255/869), "*Al-Bayān wa al-Tabyīn*", (Beirut: 1967), vol. 1, p. 49. Quoted from Ḥasan, "*Analogical Reasoning*", p. 42; Khudarī, "*Tārīkh*", p.143.
24. Ḥasan, "*The Early*", p. 21; Schacht, "*The Origins*", p. 31.
25. Abū Yūsuf, "*Kitāb al-Āthār*", p. 607; Shaybānī, "*Kitāb al-Āthār*", p. 22; Shaybānī, "*Al-Muwaṭṭā*'", p. 244, versions of Māliki's Muwaṭṭā, Lucknow, 1297 and 1306 (Muw, Shaib), with a commentary by 'Abd Allahi Laknawī (d. 1304). See in Schacht, "*The Origins*", p. 29.
26. Schacht, "*The Origins*", p. 32.
27. Khudarī, "*Tārkh*", p. 143.
28. Kamal A. Fārukī, "*Islamic Jurisprudence*", (Pakistan, Karachi: Publishing House, 1962), p. 24.
29. Ḥasan "*The Early*", p. 145.
30. Ibid., p. 146.
31. Schacht, "*The Origins*", pp. 100-1.
32. Abū Sulaymān, "*Al-Fikr al-Uṣūlī*", p. 152; Makkī, "*Manāqib*", vol. 1, p. 84; Jaṣṣāṣ, "*Fuṣūl*", vol. 4, p. 229.
33. Makkī, "*Manāqib*", vol. 1, p. 84.
34. Jaṣṣāṣ, "*Fusūl*", vol. 4, p. 229.

35. Ibn Muqaffā, "*Risālah*", pp. 125-6.
36. Bazdawī, "*Uṣūl*", p. 1125.
37. Khudarī, "*Uṣūl*", p. 210.
38. Bazdawī, "*Kashf*", p. 1126.
39. Ibn Ḥazm, "*Mulakhkhaṣ*", p. 5; Ibn Ḥazm had used the term 'asr'=(one hundred years) to mean 'generation'. See also "*Al-Iḥkām*", vol. 6, p. 289. This term was also used by the Prophet (ṣ) in the famous ḥadīth which is known as 'praising three generations'; see Bukhārī, "*Fadāil al-Ṣaḥābah*", 1; Rikāk , 7; Muslim, "*Fadāil al-Ṣaḥābah*", 52; Abū Dāwūd, "*Sunnan*", 10.
40. Ibn Ḥazm, "*Mulakhkhaṣ*", p. 9.
41. Schacht, "*The Origins*", p. 112.
42. Ibid.
43. Shaybānī, "*Al-Aṣl*", vol. 1, pp. 55, 201-2, 368; vol. 2, pp. 358-9; vol. 4, pp. 465-6, vol. 5, pp. 103-4, 128-9; "*Al-Jāmi' al-Ṣaghīr*", pp. 90, 212, 245, 295, 319.
44. Ḥasan, "*The early*", p. 146.
45. Khaddūrī, Mājid and Liebesny, J. Herbert, "*Law in the Middle East*", (Washington: the Middle East Institute, 1955), vol. 1, p. 101.
46. Bukhārī, "*Kashf*", vol. 4, p. 3.
47. Ibn Amīr al-Ḥajj, "*Al-Taqrīr*", vol. 3, pp. 222-3.
48. Ṣadr al-Sharī'ah, "*Al-Tawdīḥ*", vol. 2, pp. 81-2.
49. This is not the actual statement of Bukhari but rather what could be understood from his statement. A reference to this can be found in "*Sharḥ Uṣūl al-Bazdawī by al-Bukhārī*", vol. 4, pp. 3-5, 13.
50. For more about them and their definitions. See: Aḥmad Ḥasan, "*Analogical Reasoning*", pp. 76-92, 294-302; and Bukhārī, "*Kashf*", vol. 4, pp. 3-5, 13.
51. Al-Mahillāwī, "*Tashīl*", p. 237.
52. Laknawī, "*Fawātiḥ*", vol. 2, p. 321.
53. Sha'bān, "*Uṣūl*", pp. 144-5.
54. The linguistic definition of "*aṣl*" is the foundation or basis on something. It is defined technically in many different aspects. The original case (*aṣl*) is one of the four constituents of qiyās (analogy).

There is, however, a difference of opinion amongst jurists on the definitions of the original case.

55. Sha'bān, "*Uṣul*", pp. 144-5.
56. Bukhārī, "*Kashf*", vol. 4 p. 3.
57. Ghazālī, "*Mustaṣfā*", vol. 1, p. 283; Juwaynī, "*Talkhīṣ*", vol. 3, pp. 311-3.
58. Abū Zahrah, "*Uṣūl*", p. 251.
59. Khallāf, "*Maṣāder*", p. 71.
60. Ibid.
61. Sarakhsī, "*Uṣūl*", vol. 2, p. 201; Jaṣṣāṣ, "*Fusūl*", vol. 4, p. 238.
62. Jaṣṣāṣ, "*Fusūl*", vol. 4, p. 239.
63. Ibn Badrān, "*Sharḥ Rawdat*", vol. 1, p. 497.
64. Shīrāzī, "*Sharḥ al-Luma*", vol. 2, p. 970.
65. Ghazālī, "*Al-Mustaṣfā*", vol. 1, p. 283.
66. Ghazālī, "*Al-Mustaṣfā*", vol. 1, p. 273.
67. Sarakhsī, "*Al-Mabsūṭ*", vol. 10, p. 145.
68. Taftazānī, "*Talwīḥ*", vol. 2, p. 163; Bukhārī, "*Kashf*", vol. 4, p. 3.
69. Bāḥusain, "*Raf' al-Kharāj*", pp. 378-9.
70. Kamālī, "*Istiḥsān*", p. 24; Al-Jaṣṣāṣ, "*Al-Fuṣūl*", vol. 4, p. 234.
71. Ḥasan, "*Analogical Reasoning*", p. 410.
72. Far' (parallel case): This is a parallel or fresh case which is not covered by the text (*naṣṣ*). A jurist finds out a rule of law for this case by the use of qiyās. This is also known as maqīs (the case which is analogically compared with a textual rule); See Aḥmad Ḥasan "*Analogical Reasoning*", p. 16. See also Al-Jaṣṣāṣ, "*Uṣūl*", p. 226; Ghazālī, "*Al-Mustaṣfā*", p. 324; Āmidī, "*Al-Iḥkām*", vol. 3, p. 276; Basrī, "*Al-Mu'tamad*", vol. 2, p. 703; Ibn Amīyr al-Ḥajj, "*Al-Taqrīr*", vol. 3, p. 124.
73. Jaṣṣāṣ, "*Al-Fuṣūl*", vol. 4, p. 234.
74. Ibid, pp. 243-49.
75. For particularization of the cause (*takhṣīṣ 'illah*) see Jaṣṣāṣ, "*Fuṣūl*", vol. 4, pp. 243-249; Sarakhsī, "*Uṣūl*", vol. 2, pp. 204-208; Bazdawī, "*Uṣūl*", vol. 4, pp. 7-32; Bukhārī, "*Kashf*", vol. 4, pp. 8, 32; Nasafī, "*Kashf al-Asrār*", vol. 2, pp. 293-299; Ibn Amīr al-Ḥajj, "*Taqrīr*", vol. 3, p. 177.
76. Bazdawī, "*Uṣūl*", vol. 4, p. 3.

77. Bukhārī, "*Kashf*", vol. 4, p. 3; Taftazānī, "*Talwīḥ*", p. 2, p. 163; Ibn al-Ḥājib, "*Muntahā*", p. 207
78. Izmīrī, "*Mir'āt al-Uṣūl*", vol. 2, p. 335.
79. Khallāf, "*Masāder*", p. 69; Zaydān, "*Al-Wajīz*", p. 217.
80. İbrahim Kafi Dönmez, "*Islām Ḥukuk'unda Kaynak Kavramı*", unpublished PhD dissertation, (Istanbul: 1981), pp. 128-9
81. See Kamali, "*Istiḥsān*", p. 47.
82. Bukhārī, "*Ṣaḥīḥ*", no. 441, vol. 3, p. 243.
83. Sarakhsī, "*Al-Mabsūṭ*", vol. 10, p. 145.
84. Bazdawī, "*Uṣūl*", vol. 4, p. 6; Nasafī, "*Kashf*", vo. 2, pp. 293-204.
85. Jaṣṣāṣ, "*Fusūl*", vol. 4, pp. 234, 237-8.
86. Ṣadr al-Sharī'ah, "*Al-Tawdīḥ*", vol. 2, p. 82.
87. Bazdawī, "*Uṣūl*", vol. 2, p. 84.
88. Önder, "*Hanefi Mezhebinde*", p. 77.
89. Sarakhsī, "*Uṣūl*", vol. 2, p. 200.
90. Nasafī, "*Kashf*", vol. 2, p. 164.
91. Rahawī,"*Ḥāshiyāt*", p. 811.
92. Ibid., p. 812.
93. Ansārī, "*Fawātiḥ*", vol. 2, p. 320.
94. Taftazānī, "*Talwiḥ*", vo. 2, p. 163.
95. Ibn Nujāym, "*Fatḥ al-Ghaffār*", vo. 3, p. 30.
96. Molla Ḥusraw, "*Mirāt al-Uṣūl*", vol. 2, p. 335.
97. Ibn Abidīn, Muḥammad 'Amīn (1252/1836), "*Ḥāshiyāt al-Nasamāt al-Asḥār*", (Cairo: Muṣṭafā Bāb al-Ḥalabī, n.d.), p. 150.
98. 'Alī Ḥaydār, "*Uṣūli Fiqih*", p. 387.
99. For more about Imām al-Shāfi'ī see Abū 'Iyd Ḥasan Muḥammad Salīm, "*Al-Imām al-Shāfi'ī wa Atharuhu fī Uṣūl al-Fiqh*", unpublished PhD dissertation, (Egypt: Faculty of Shar'īah and Qānūn Al-Azhar University, 1976).
100. Anṣārī, "*Ghāyat al-Wuṣūl*", p.139; Alwānī, "*The Ethics*", p. 75; Ghazālī, "*Mustaṣfā*", vol. 1, p. 274, ibid., "*Mankhūl*", p. 374; Isnawī, "*Nihāyat al-Sūl*", vol. 4, p. 399.
101. Qur'an: 6:106

102. Qur'an: 5:49
103. Shāfi'ī, "*Al-Umm*", vol. 7, pp. 298-9.
104. Ibid., vol. 7, p. 300.
105. Ibid., vol. 7, p. 301
106. Shāfi'ī, "*Al-Risālah*", vol. 3, pp. 219-21.
107. Māwardī, "*Adab al-Qāḍī*", vol. 1, p. 651.
108. Zarkashī, "*Al-Baḥr al-Muḥīt*", vol. 6, p. 94.
109. Shīrāzī, "*Sharḥ al-Lumah'* ", vol. 2, p. 969; Zarkashī, "*Al-Baḥr*", vol. 6, p. 93.
110. Shīrāzī, "*Sharḥ*", vol. 2, p. 970.
111. Ghazālī, "*Al-Mankhūl*", p. 377.
112. Zarkashī, "*Al-Baḥr*", vol. 6, p. 93; Shirazi, "*Sharḥ*", vol. 2, p. 970.
113. Baṣrī, "*Al-Mu'tamad*", vol. 2, p. 295.
114. Ghazālī, "*Al-Mustaṣfā*", vol. 1, p. 137.
115. Ghazālī, "*Al-Mustaṣfā*", vol. 1, p. 138
116. Āmidī, "*Al-Iḥkām*", vol. 4, p. 138.
117. Isnawī, "*Minhāj*", vol. 3, p. 141.
118. Shāṭibī "*Al-I'tiṣām*", vol. 2, p. 136
119. Shāṭibī "*Al-I'tiṣām*", vol. 2, p. 136
120. 'Iwaḍ, "*Al-Istiḥsān 'inda 'Ulamā' Uṣūl*", vol. 5, p. 31.
121. Ibid., p. 32.
122. Ṭūfī, "*Sharḥ Mukhtasar al-Rawḍa*", vol. 3, pp. 190-3.
123. Āmidī, "*Al-Iḥkām*", vol. 4, p. 138.
124. Ibid., vol. 4, p. 138.
125. Ghazālī, "*Al-Mustaṣfā*", vol. 1, p. 138.
126. Shāṭibī, "*Al-I'tiṣām*", vol. 2, p. 137.
127. Isnawī, "*Minhāj*", vol. 3, p. 140.
128. Ibn Subkī, "*Sharḥ al-Jalāl al-Maḥallī*", vol. 2, p. 395; Taftazānī, "*Talwīḥ*" vol. 2, p. 81; Dirāz, "*Sharḥ al-Muwāfaqāt*", vol. 4, p. 206.
129. Al-Majallah: clause: 74.
130. Ghazālī, "*Al-Mustaṣfā*", vol. 1, pp. 138-9; Ijī, "*Sharḥ al-Mukhtaṣar*", vol. 2, p. 288.

131. Abū Zahrah, "*Uṣūl*", p. 207; Shāṭibī, "*Al-I'tiṣām*", vol. 2, p. 137.
132. Ibid., vol. 2, p. 138.
133. Ibid., vol. 2, p. 147.
134. Taftazāni, "*Sharḥ al-'Aḍūd*", vol. 2, p. 288.
135. Shawkānī, "*Irshād*", p. 240.
136. Shāṭibī, "*Al-Muwāfaqāt*", vol. 4, pp. 206, 7.
137. Ibid., vol. 4, p. 207
138. Qarafī, "*Sharḥ Tanqīḥ*", p. 451; Bājī, "*Iḥkām al-Fuṣūl*", vol. 2, p. 693.
139. Ibid., p. 451.
140. Shāṭibī, "*Al-Muwāfaqāt*", vol. 4, pp. 117, 8.
141. Shāṭibī, "*Al-I'tisām*", vol. 2, p. 139; Shāṭibī, "*Al-Muwāfaqāt*", vol. 4, p. 207.
142. Majallah: clause 30.
143. Shāṭibī, "*Al-Muwāfaqāt*", vol. 4, p. 208.
144. Shāṭibī, "*I'tiṣām*", vol. 2, p. 139.
145. Shāṭibī, "*Al Muwāfaqāt*", vol. 4, p. 206.
146. Ibid., vol. 4, pp. 205, 6.
147. Ibid., vol. 4, pp. 205, 6.
148. Shāṭibī, "*I'tiṣām*", vol. 2, p. 137.
149. Abū Yā'lā Muḥammad bin al-Ḥusain bin Muḥammad bin Aḥmad bin al-Farrā' Ḥanbalī (d. 458/1065), "*Al-'Uddah fī Uṣūl al-Fiqh*", edt. Aḥmad Sayr al-Mubāraki, Muassasah al-Risālah, Beirut, 1400/1980, vol. 5, p. 1607.
150. Ibn Qudāmah, "*Rawḍat*", p. 85.
151. Ibn Taymiyyah, "*Al-Musawwadah*", p. 451.
152. Ibid., p. 452.
153. Ibid., p. 452
154. Ibid., p. 452.
155. Ibid., p. 453.
156. Ibid., p. 454.
157. Ibid., pp. 454-5.
158. Al-Ṭūfī, "*Sharḥ al-Mukhtaṣar*", vol. 3, p. 197.

159. ʿAbd Allah b. ʿAbd al-Muḥsin Turkī, "*Uṣūl Madhhab al-Imām Aḥmad Ibn Ḥanbal-Dirāsah Uṣūliyyah Muqāranah (Uṣūl comparative studies)*", first print, 1394 H, 1974, (Cairo: ʿAin Shams University Press), p. 515.

160. Abū Zahrah, "*Al-Imām al-Ṣādiq*", pp. 527-9.

161. Ibid., pp. 527-8.

162. Abū Zahrah, "*Al-Imām Zayd, Ḥayātuhū wa ʿAṣruhu-Arāuhu wa Fiqhuhu*", (Beirut: Dār al-Nadwah al-Jādiydah, n.d.), p. 438.

163. Ibid., p. 438.

164. Baṣrī, "*Al-Muʿtamad*", vol. 2, p. 296; Taftazānī, "*Talwīḥ*", vol. 2, p. 162; Ibn al-Ḥājib, "*Muntahā*", p. 207; Bukhārī, "*Kashf al-Asrār*", vol. 4, p. 3.

165. Abū Zahrah, "*Al-Imām Zayd*", p. 439.

166. Ibid., p. 439.

167. A.G. Chejne, "*Ibn Ḥazm*", preface, (Chicago: Kazi Publications inc., 1982), p. 7.

168. Ibn Ḥazm, "*Al-Nubadh*", p. 43.

169. Ibn Ḥazm, "*Al-Iḥkām*", v. 2, p. 253.

170. Ibn Ḥazm, "*Al-Nubadh*", p. 44; Ibn Ḥazm, "*Al-Iḥkām*", v. 2, p. 197.

171. Ibn Ḥazm, "*Al-Iḥkām*", vol. 2, pp. 195-6; Chejne, "*Ibn Ḥazm*", p. 122.

172. Ibn Ḥazm, "*Mulakhkhas*", edt. Said al-Afghāni (Dimishq: 1960), p. 50.

173. Zarkashī, "*Al-Baḥr*", vol. 6, p. 93; Shīrāzī, "*Sharḥ al-Lumaʿ*", vol. 2, p. 969.

174. Baṣrī, "*Al-Muʿtamad*", vol. 2, pp. 838-9.

175. See Ḥasan, "*Analogical Reasoning*", p. 410.

176. Baṣrī, "*Al-Muʿtamad*", vol. 2, p. 295.

177. Bukhārī, "*Kashf*", vol. 4 p. 3; Ḥasan, "*Analogical Reasoning*", p. 410; Bukhārī, "*Sharḥ*" vol. 4, p. 3; Taftazānī, "*Talwīḥ*", vol. 2, p. 163; Ibn al-Ḥajīb, "*Muntahā*", p. 207; Nasafī, "*Kashf*", vol. 2, p. 164.

178. Māwardī, "*Adab al-Qāḍī*", vol. 1, p. 651; Ibn Ḥazm, "*Al-Aḥkām*", vol. 6, p. 757.

179. Shāfiʿī, "*Al-Risālah*", vol. 3, pp. 219-21.

180. Alwāni, "*The Ethics*", p. 75; Ansārī, "*Ghāyat al-Wuṣūl*", p. 139.

181. Āmidī, "*Al-Iḥkām*", vol. 4, p. 136, Al-Taftazānī, "*Al-Talwīḥ*",v. 2, p. 82.

182. Baṣrī, "*Al-Mu'tamad*", vol.2, p. 838; Amīr Pādishah, "*Taysīr*", vol. 4, p. 78; Ibn al-Humām, "*Al-Taqrīr*" vol. 3, p: 222; Iji, "*Sharḥ*", vol. 2, p. 288; Ibn Qudāmah, "*Rawḍat*", p. 85.

183. 'Abd al-Ḥāfiẓ, Madīḥa 'Alī, "*Al-Istiḥsān wa Atharuhū fi-Binā al-Fiqh al-Islāmī*", PhD dissertation at Faculty of Arabic and Islamic study, (Cairo: Al-Azhar University, 1984), p. 76.

184. Shawkānī, "*Irshād*", p. 231.

185. Shāṭibī, "*Al-I'tiṣām*", vol. 2, pp. 136-7

186. Ibid., vol. 2, pp. 136-7.

187. Dönmez, "*Kaynak Kavramı*", p. 168.

188. Jaṣṣāṣ, "*Fusūl*", vol. 4, pp. 227-9; Sarakhsī, "'*Usūl*", vol. 2, pp. 200-1; Bukharī, "*Kashf al-Asrār*", vol. 4, p. 6.

189. Sarakhsī, "*Uṣūl*", vol. 2, pol. 200; Nasafī, "*Kashf al-Asrār*", vol. 2, p. 299.

190. Sarakhsī, "*Al-Mabsūṭ*", vol. 10, p. 145.

191. Āmidī, "*Al-Iḥkām*", vol. 4, p. 393; Bukhārī, "*Kashf*", vol. 4, p. 13.

192. Ijī, "*Sharḥ Mukhtaṣar*", vol. 2, p. 384.

193. Qur'an: 7:145

194. Ghazālī, "*Mustaṣfā*", vol. 1, p. 277.

195. Qur'an: 39:18

196. Māwardī, "*Adab al-Qādī*", vol. 1, pp. 655-6.

197. Ibn Ḥanbal, "*Al-Musnad*", vol. 1, p. 379; Ibn Mājah, "*Sunan*", ḥadīth No: 2340, vol.2, p. 784.

198. Āmidī, "*Al-iḥkām*", vol. 4, p. 394.

199. Ibn Ḥazm, "*Al-Aḥkām*" vol. 6, p. 759.

200. Al-Māwardī, "*Adab al-Qāḍī*", vol. 1, pp. 656-7; Ibn Ḥazm, "*Al-Aḥkām*", vol. 6, pp. 759; Āmidī, "*Al-Iḥkām*", vol. p. 394.

201. Āmidī, "*Al-iḥkām*", vol. 4, p. 393; Ghazālī, "*Mustaṣfā*", vol. 1, p. 279.

202. Māwardī, "*Adab al-Qāḍī*", vol. 1, p. 652; İzmirī, "*Ḥāshiyah*", vol. 2, pp. 335-6.

203. Māwardī, "*Adab al-Qāḍī*", vol. 1, p. 657.

204. Shāfi'ī, "*Al-Risālah*", p. 503; and "*Al-Umm*", vol. 7, p. 309.

205. Anṣārī,"*Ghāyat al-Wuṣūl*", p.139; Alwānī, "*The Ethics*", p. 75; Ghazālī, "Mustaṣfā", vol. 1, p. 274, Ghazālī, "*Mankhūl*", p. 374; Isnawī, "*Nihāyat al-Sūl*", vol. 4, p. 399.

206. Shīrāzī, "*Sharḥ al-Luma*", vol. 2, p. 969; Juwaynī "*Talkhīs*", vol. 3, p. 310; Ghazālī, "*Mustaṣfā*", vol. 1, p. 274; Ghazālī, "*Al-Mankhul*", p. 374; Rāzī, "*Maḥsūl*", vol. 2, p. 559; Āmidī, "*Al-Iḥkām*", vol. 4, p. 390.

207. Shīrāzī, "*Tabaqāt al-Fuqahā*", p. 92-3; Ibn Subkī, "*Tabaqāt*", vol. 2, pp. 284-293.

208. Ibn Ḥazm, "*Al-Iḥkām*", vol. 6, p. 192.

209. Abū Zahrah, "*Al-Imām al-Ṣādiq*", pp. 527-9.

210. Māwardī, "*Adab al-Qāḍī*", vol. 1, p. 653; Ibn Ḥazm, "*Al-Aḥkām*", vol. 6, p. 758.

211. Qur'an: 5:3.

212. Shāfi'ī, "*Al-Umm*", vol. 7, p. 294; Ibn Ḥazm, "*Al-Aḥkām*", vol. 6, p. 758.

213. Abū Dāwud, "*Sunan*", ḥadīth no. 3585.

214. Qur'an: 38:26.

215. Shāfi'ī, "*Al-Umm*", vol. 7, p. 298.

216. Abū Dāwud, "*Sunan*", ḥadīth no. 3585,

217. 'Abd al-Ḥāfiẓ, "*Al-Istiḥsān*", p. 142.

218. Qur'an: 79:40-1; 12:53; 30:29.

219. Ibn Ḥazm, "*Al-Aḥkām*", vol. 6, p. 760.

220. Shāfi'ī, "*Al-Umm*", vol. 7, p. 299.

221. Ibid., pp. 143-4.

222. Māwardī, "*Adab al-Qāḍī*", vol. 1, p. 655.

223. Māwardī, "*Adab*", pp. 144-5.

224. Kūfa was one of the biggest cities of Irāq, consisting of various tribes and communities, and was a center of the ancient civilizations. Before Islam, schools were established there for the teaching of Greek philosophy. It was also later the base for Shī'ah, Mu'tazilah, Khawārij and mujtahid 'Successors' such as: Alqamah b. Qays (d. 62), Masrūq b. al-Ajdā' (d. 63), al-Aswad b. Yazīd (d. 75), Shuraykh b. al-Ḥārith (d. 78), who spread the teaching of the Companions, 'Alī Ibn Abī Ṭālib (d. 40), Ibn Mas'ūd (d. 32), ibn 'Umar (d. 73), ibn 'Abbās (d. 68), of the Prophet (ṣ). See Abū Zahrah, "*Abū Ḥanīfah*", pp. 30-1.

225. Abū Ḥanīfah's father was a silk trader. Abū Ḥanīfah grew up in a wealthy family and took over the business from his father. Shā'bī (d. 110) one day advised him to attend a scholarly gathering, which he did. The rest is history. See Makkī, "*Manāqib*", vol. 2, p. 106.

226. Abū Ḥanīfah lived 52 years of his life in the period of Umayyad dynasty, and the remaining 18 years under the Abbāsīd dynasty. He lived under the rule of the despot governor Hajjāj b. Yūsuf Thaqafī and was witness to the murders of various members of the ahl al-bayt. He was also imprisoned. Later on, he understood that the Abbāsid dynasty was a continuation of the same tyrannical system; he took a stand against them, which caused him to be persecuted. See: Abū Zahrah, "*Abū Ḥanīfah*", pp. 19, 104, 107-8. See also Khatīb Baghdādī, "*Tārīkhi Baghdād*", vol. 13, p. 239.

227. Saymarī Ḥusain b. 'Alī (d. 436/1045), "*Akhbār Abū Ḥanīfah wa Aṣḥābuh*", (Beirut: 1985), p. 26.

228. Bazdawī,"*Kashf*", p. 1125.

229. Ibn Ḥazm, "*Al-Iḥkām*", vol. 2, pp. 195-6; Chejne, "*Ibn Ḥazm*", p. 122.

230. Alwānī, "*The Ethics*", p. 75; Ansārī, "*Ghāyat al-Wusūl*", p. 139.

231. Makkī, "*Manāqib*", vol. 1, p. 80; Saymarī, "*Akhbār*", p. 24; Baghdādī, "*Tarīkh*", vol. 13, p. 368.

232. Muḥammad Qāsim 'Abduh Ḥārithī, "*Makānāt al-Imām Abū Ḥanīfah bayn al-Muḥaddithīyn*", p. 23, PhD dissertation, (Pakistan: the University of Islamic studies), p. 23.

233. Makkī, "*Manāqib*", vol.1, p. 80.

234. Makkī, "*Manāqib*", vol. 1, p. 74.

235. Ibid.

236. Saymarī, "*Akhbār*", p. 27; Makkī, "*Manāqib*", vol. 1, p. 81.

237. Makki, "*Manāqib*", vol. 1, p. 85

238. Ibn Mājah, "*Sunan*", ḥadīth no: 2340, vol. 2, p. 784; Shāṭibī, "*Muwāfaqāt*", vol. 3, p. 17; Khudarī, "*Tārīkh*", p. 199.

239. Abū Zahrah, "*Abū Ḥanīfah*", p. 342, also see Uzunpostalcı, "Ebu Hanife", *Türkiye Diyanet Vakfı İslam Ansiklopedisi*, vol. 10, p. 136.

240. Abū Zahraḥ, "*Abū Ḥanīfah*", p. 75.

241. Saymarī, "*Akhbār*", p. 25; Makkī, "*Manāqib*", vol. 1, p. 81.

242. Abū Zahrah, "*Abū Ḥanifah*", pp. 330, 332, 334; Uzunpostacı, ibid., vol. 10, p. 136.

243. Makkī, "*Manāqib*", vol. 1, p. 84.

244. Māwardi, "*Adab al-Qādi*", pp. 649-50.

245. Abū Zahrah, ibid., p. 364.

246. Bazdawī, "*Kashf al-Asrār*", p. 1125.

247. Athar: impact, trace, vestige; also deeds and precedents of the Companions of the Prophet (ṣ). See Kamali, "*Principle of Islamic Jurisprudence*", pp. 47-8; also see Schacht, "*The Origins*", pp. 78, 119.

248. Bazdawī, "*Kashf*", pp. 1126-1130.

249. Baltacī, "*Manahīj al-Tashrī*", vol. 1, p. 357.

250. Sarakhsī, "*Uṣūl*", vol. 2, pp. 105, 108, 110, 113; Baltacī, "*Manāhij*", vol. 1, p. 359; Abū Zahrah, "*Abū Ḥanifah*", p. 311.

251. Shawkānī, "*Irshād*", p. 213; Ghazālī, "*Al-Mustaṣfā*", vol. 1, p. 135; Āmidī, "*Al Iḥkām*", vol. 3, p. 133; Shīrāzī, "*Al-Luma*'", p. 50; Molla Husraw, "*Mar'āt al-Uṣūl*", vol. 2, p. 250; Bannānī, "*Ḥāshiah*", vol. 2, p. 288.

252. Sarakhsī, "*Al-Mabsūṭ*", vol. 6, pp. 210-1, vol. 13, p. 17; Sarakhsī, "*Uṣūl*", vol. 2, pp. 105-6, 110-1; Makkī, "*Manāqib*", vol. 1, pp. 83-4.

253. Sarakhsī, "*Al-Mabsūṭ*", vol. 1, pp. 56-7.

254. Ibid., vol. 2, p. 105.

255. Ḥaythamī, "*Al-Ḥayāt al-Ḥisān*"; Makkī, "*Manāqib*", vol. 1, p. 74; Saymarī, "*Akhbār*", p. 24.

256. For more about ijmāʿ see in introduction chapter.

257. Baltacī, "*Manāhij al-Tashrī*", vol. 1, p. 359.

258. Shāfiʿī, "*Kitāb al-Umm*", vol. 7, p. 242; Abū Yūsuf, "*Kitāb al-Athar*", p. 192.

259. Bukhari, "*Zakat*", 1; Muslim, "*Imān*", 8.

260. Sarakhsī, "*Al-Mabsūṭ*", vol. 5, p. 49.

261. For more on this, see: introductory chapter.

262. Sarakhsī, ibid., vol. 4, p. 138.

263. Sarakhsī, ibid., vol. 4, pp. 138-140.

264. Sarakhsī, "*Uṣūl*", vol. 1, p. 339; Baltacī, "*Manāhij al-Tashrīʿ*", vol. 1, p. 359; Abū Zahrah, "*Abū Ḥanīfah*", pp. 290-1, 293-4.

265. Jaṣṣāṣ, "*Fuṣūl*", vol. 4, p. 116; Sarakhsī, "*Al-Mabsūṭ*", vol. 3, p. 65.

266. Dihlawī, "*Hujjat Allah*", vol. 1, p. 16; Shaybānī, "*Al-Hujjah ʿalā Ahl al-Madīnah*", vol. 1, p. 392; Haythami, "*Al-Ḥayāt al-Ḥisān*", p. 104.

267. Sarakhsī, "*Al-Mabsūṭ*" vol. 4, p. 93.

268. Jaṣṣāṣ, "*Fuṣūl*", vol. 4, p. 116; Sarakhsī, "*Al-Mabsūṭ*", vol. 1, pp 77-8.

269. Bayḥāqī, "*Al-Sunan*", vol. 1, pp. 146-7; Hawarizmī, "*Jāmi' al-Masānīd*", vol. 1, pp. 247-8.

270. Haytamī, "*Al-Ḥayat al-Ḥisān*", pp. 42, 106.

271. Jaṣṣāṣ, "*Fuṣul*", vol. 4, pp. 116-7; Makkī, "*Manāqib*", vol. 1 p. 83; also for more examples, see Sarakhsī, "*Al-Mabsūṭ*", vol. 1, pp. 53, 169, vol. 13, p. 122, vol. 17, pp. 63-64.

272. Baltajī, "*Manāhij*", vol. 1, p. 361.

273. Sarakhsī, "*Al-Mabsūṭ*", vol. 1, p. 208 and similar examples are vol. 1, pp. 49-50, 183; vol. 7, p. 8; Shaibānī, "*Al-Jāmi' al-Ṣaghīr*", pp. 90, 192-3, 212, 245.

274. Sarakhsī, "*Uṣūl*", vol. 1, pp. 115-6. According to the Ḥanafis, to complete a started supererogatory worship is obligatory (wājib).

275. Baltacī, "*Manāhij*", vol. 1, p. 362.

276. Sarakhsī, "*Uṣūl*", vol. 1, p. 115.

277. For more on the concept of custom see the introductory chapter.

278. Sarakhsī, "*Al-Mabsūṭ*", vol. 12, p. 199, also for more on this concept, see. Makkī, "*Manāqib*", vol. 1, p. 75; and also see Sarakhsī, "*Al Mabsuṭ*", vol. 11, pp. 159, 180-1, 192-3, vol. 12, pp. 84, 159-161.

279. Ibn al-Athīr, "*Jāmi' al-Uṣūl*", vol. 3, pp. 338-9.

280. Mūsa, "*Abū Ḥanīfah*", pp. 76-79.

281. Baltajī, "*Manāhij*", vol. 1, p. 363.

282. Ḥasan, "*The early*", p. 145.

283. Sarakhsī, "*Uṣūl*", vol. 2, p. 202.

284. Imām Zufar: Zufar b. Huzayl b. Qays al-Anbārī, from the Tamim tribe. He was a judge (qaḍi) and one of the best friends of Abū Ḥanīfah. He originated from Iran (Isfahan): his father was an 'Arab and his mother Iranian. He lived in Baṣra and died there in 158h. it is not known whether he has left any work of jurisprudence. See Isma'īl Sha'bān Muḥammad, "*Uṣūl al-Fiqh Tārikhuhu wa Rijāluhu*", p. 46; Abū Zahrah, "*Abū Ḥanīfah*", pp. 244-5.

285. Ibid.

286. Khudarī, "*Tārikh*", p. 240; Saymari, "*Akhbār*", pp. 24, 112-3; Abū Zahrah, "*Abū Ḥanīfah*", p. 244; Khaṭīb, "*Tārikh*", vol. 14, p. 246.

287. Ismā'īl, "*Uṣūl*" p. 46.

288. Baltajī, "*Manāhij*", vol. 1, pp. 400-1.

289. Ṭalāq Raj'ī: A husband has the right to take back his wife, who still menstruates, as long as she has not yet entered her third menstruation in the course of the iddah (waiting period); it is the third in the case of a free woman, and the second menstruation in the case of a slave woman. See: Al-Qayrawānī, "*Risālah*", bāb fi al-nikāḥ wa al-ṭalāq, p. 89-97 quoted from: Doi I. "*Shari'a*", p. 177. The first two pronouncements of divorce followed by the periods of retreat from the wife with whom marriage is consummated are called ṭalaq raj'i. It is based on the following Qur'an: 2:229 "A divorce is only permissible twice after that the party should either hold together on equitable terms or separate with kindness." In this kind of divorce the spouse can still enjoy the usual benefit from each other since the marital relationship is not over. If one of them dies, the other will inherit from him or her, as the case may be. Maintenance will still remain available to the wife and children. The raj'a (return) is the right of the husband. As Qur'an says: 2:228 "And the husband has the better right to take them back in that period if they wish for reconciliation." It will suffice just to utter the words like "I take you back" or the return can be effected through actions such as resuming sexual relations or kissing. See ibid.

290. Ṭalāq Bāin: This is divorce with three pronouncements of divorce before the consummation of marriage. There is no possibility of return to the conjugal relationship when the three divorces are completed. There are two kinds of ṭalaq bāin: Baynūnah ṣughrā and baynuna kubra. The baynūnah ṣughrā decreases the conjugal rights of the husband. In the event of the death of one of the parties, the other will not inherit from him or her as all the conjugal rights cease. The former husband cannot even re-marry the former wife unless she marries another man and he voluntarily divorces her without any intention of taḥlil. See ibid.

291. Ismā'īl, "*Uṣūl*", p. 46.

292. Baltajī, "*Manāhij*", vol. 1, pp. 422-3.

293. He is one of the greatest followers of Abū Ḥanīfah. He was also an Imām in his own right. Abū Yūsuf was a descendand of the Anṣār and Ṣaḥābah, Sa'd b. Sibāt. He was born in Kufah in 113 or 117 h. and passed away in 182 h. He regularly attended Abū Ḥanīfah's circle of lectures and acknowledges of his mastery in fiqh. He was attending Ibn Abī Laila's lecturers at first: "I would attend Ibn Abī Lailā's circle, who recognized my potential, however when some issue would arise, he would apply Abū Ḥanīfah's ijtihāds. Owing to this, I considered that I should go to Abū Ḥanīfah's circle and study and gain more benefit

from him. Eventually, I attended regular circles of Abū Ḥanīfah." He followed his master's method of ijtihād and reached the level of mujtahid mutlaq (absolute independent legal thinker). After the death of his master he moved to Baghdad. In 150 h. was appointed qāḍi (judge) by the caliph al-Mahdi and carried out this duty for 16 years; he was also given the highest legal post in the entire khilafah, namely that of qāḍi al-quḍāt (chief Justice). Abū Ḥanīfah said of him: "If God forbid, this man (Abū Yūsuf) dies, the world will lose one of its great scholars." A narration from Abu Ḥanifa about the participants of his own lecture: "Among the students there are 36 mature men: 28 of them are capable of being judge, 6 of them are good for the position of giving legal opinions, and 2 of them are capable of being both chief justice (raīs al-quḍāt) and giving legal opinions (ifta'), they are AbūYūsuf and Zufar". However, al-Shaybānī was only 18 years old when Abū Ḥanīfah died. He actually became famous after the death of his master. (See ibn Bazzaz, "*Manāqibi Imām 'Āzam*", vol. 2, p. 125., quoted from Abū Zahrah, "*Abū Ḥanīfah*", pp. 222-3). His most famous teachers are A'mash, Hishām b. Urwah, Sulaimān b. Taīmī, Abū Isḥāq al-Shaybānī, Yahyā b. Sa'īd al-Ansārī (d. 146), Mālik b. Anas (d. 179), Sufyān b. Uyaynah, Ḥasan b. Dinār, Hanzalah b. Abū Sufyan. He learned maghazi (military history and siyar (international law) from Muḥammad b. Isḥāq and knowledge of fiqh from Muḥammad Abī Lailā (d. 150). He was endowed with so much intelligence and such a good memory that he learned all these disciplines simultaneously. Abū Yūsuf was ranked so high in Tradition (ḥadīth) as to be considered a ḥāfiẓ in it. Ibn Jarīr Tabarī used to say: "Qāḍi Abū Yūsuf Ya'qūb b. Ibrāhim is a faqih (jurist) and 'alim (scholar). He knows ḥadīth, he is famous for reciting ḥadīth by memory, and he used to visit and attend the lectures of muḥaddithīn and at one sitting learn 50 to 60 traditions. After the lecture he would dictate them". See Ibn 'Abd al-Bār, "*Intiqā*", p. 172; Bilmen, "*Iṣṭilaḥāti Fiqhiyyah*", vol. 1, p. 392.

294. Ismā'īl, "*Uṣūl*", p. 53.

295. Abū Zahrah, "*Abū Ḥanīfah*", p. 225.

296. Schacht, "*The origins*", p. 112.

297. Matlūb, Maḥmūd, "*Abū Yūsuf*", (Iraq: the University of Baghdad, 1972), p. 129.

298. Ibid., p. 129.

299. Sarakhsī, "*Uṣūl*", vol. 2, p. 105.

300. Jaṣṣāṣ, "*Fuṣūl*", vol. 3, p. 361.

301. Salim Öğüt, "Ebu Yusuf", *Türkiye Diyanet Vakfı İslam Ansiklopedisi*, vol. 10, p. 263.

302. Ṭahawī, "*Mukhtaṣar*", pp. 211, 342, 402; Abū Yūsuf, "*Kitāb al-Kharāj*", pp. 178, 182, 189; Sarakhsī, "*Al-Mabsūṭ*", vol. 1, pp. 37-88, 183, vol. 2, pp. 13, 214; vol. 3, p. 105.

303. Matlūb, "*Abū Yūsuf*", p. 130; Majallah: clause: 39.

304. Abū Yūsuf, "*Kitāb al-Kharāj*", p. 84.

305. Ibn al-Humām, "*Sharḥ Fatḥ al-Qadīr*", vol. 7, p. 15.

306. Ṭahawī, "*Al-Mukhtaṣar*", p. 258.

307. To say while sitting: "There is no god but Allah and Muḥammad is Allah's Apostle."

308. Sarakhsī, "*Al-Mabsūṭ*", vol. 1, p. 183, for more examples see: Al-Shaybānī, "*Al-Jāmī' al-ṣaghīr*", pp. 90, 204, 212, 243, 245, 319; Ṭahawī, "*Al-Mukhtaṣar*", pp. 342, 402; Sarakhsī, "*Al-Mabsūṭ*", vol. 2, pp. 13, 214, vol. 6, p. 28, vol. 12, p. 12.

309. Abū Yūsuf, "*Kitāb al-Kharāj*", p. 117.

310. Ḥasan, "*The early*", p. 147.

311. Sarakhsī, "*Al-Mabsūṭ*", vol. 1, pp. 77-8; Jaṣṣāṣ, "*Fuṣūl*", vol. 4, p. 116

312. Jaṣṣāṣ, "*Fuṣūl*", vol.4, pp. 116-7.

313. Sarakhsī, "*Al-Mabsūṭ*", vol. 23, pp. 2, 32.

314. Ibid., vol. 5, p. 49.

315. According to Islamic law, Muslims are prohibited from inheriting from unbelievers and vice-versa. See Bukhārī, "*Hajj*", no. 44; "*Farāiḍ*", no. 25; Muslim "*Farāiḍ*", no. 1, (Lā yarith al-Muslim al-Kāfir wa la al-Kāfir al-Muslim).

316. Abū Yūsuf, "*Al-Jāmi' al-Saghīr*", pp. 182-3.

317. Jaṣṣāṣ, "*Fuṣūl*", vol. 3, p. 361; Sarakhsī, "*Uṣūl*", vol. 2, p. 105.

318. Ḥasan, "*The Early*", p. 146; Abū Yūsuf, "*Al-Kharaj*", p. 178. Also for more examples see Jaṣṣāṣ "*Fuṣūl*", vol. 3, pp. 361-2; Sarakhsī, "*Uṣūl*", vol. 2, pp. 106, 110.

319. Matlūb, "*Abū Yūsuf*", p. 130.

320. Kāsānī, "*Badāi' al-Sanāī'*", vol. 1, p. 260; Sarakhsī, "*Al-Mabsūṭ*", vol. 2, p. 120.

321. Sarakhsī, "*Al-Mabsūṭ*", vol. 10, p. 34.

322. Ibid., vol. 23, pp. 17, 32, 41, 46.

323. Abū Yūsuf, "*Al-Jāmī' al-Ṣaghīr*", p. 182.

324. The charitable donation paid at the and of the month of Ramadan.

325. Sarakhsī, "*Al-Mabsūṭ*", vol. 3, p. 105, for more examples see vol. 5, pp. 194-105, 213, vol. 8, pp. 135, 186, vol. 12, p. 142, vol. 18, p. 190, v. 19, pp. 77-78, 93, 100, 117.

326. Qur'an: 24:2: This verse indicates that one hundred lashes is for an unmarried person who commits illegal sexual intercourse. A narration from Abū Hurairah (d. 59) states that God's Messenger judged that the unmarried person who was guilty of illegal sexual intercourse should be exiled for one year and receive the legal punishment that is one hundred lashes. See *Ṣaḥīḥ al-Bukhārī*, vol. 8, no. 819.

327. A married who commits adultery is stoned according to Sharī'ah: According to a Narration from Jabir b. 'Abd Allah al-Anṣārī, "A man from the tribe of Banī Aslam came to God's Messenger and informed him that he had committed illegal sexual intercourse and he bore witness four times against himself. God's Messenger ordered him to be stoned to death as he was a marred person. See *Ṣaḥiḥ al-Bukhārī*, vol. 8, no. 805.

328. Abū Yūsuf, "*Al-Jāmī' al-Ṣaghīr*", p. 165.

329. See Haskafī, "*Al-Durru al-Mukhtār*", 3:150. It is based on this statement: "Drop the hudud in cases of doubt as far as possible." See Suyūṭī, "*Al-jāmi'u al-Saghīr*", no. 313-4; Tabrīzī, "*Mishkāt al-Maṣābiḥ*", no: 3570, vol. 2, p. 1061; Ibn al-Qayyīm, "*I'lām*", vol. 1, p. 209.

330. Abū Yūsuf, "*Al-Jāmī' al-Ṣaghīr*", p. 165.

331. Shaybānī is also one of the outstanding disciples of Abū Ḥanīfah. He was born in 135 h. and passed away in 189 h. He attended for about 2 yrs the lectures of Imām Abū Ḥanīfah, was 18 years old when his master died, and upon the latter›s death he completed his education under Abu Yūsuf. He also studied for 3 yrs the Muwaṭṭa' under Imām Mālik in Medīna. He has a prodigious knowledge of literature and language. Imām Shāfi'ī said: "Muḥammad b. Ḥasan would fulfil both the heart and the eye; whenever he expounded a point of law, it seemed as if the revealing Angel had descended upon him." Also he took knowledge from Syrian Awzā'ī (d. 176/792), Sufyan b. Uyaynah (d. 198/813), and 'Abd Allah ibn Mubārak (d. 181) from Khorasānian. He synthesized the principle of Ahl al-ḥadīth and the principle of ahl al-ra'y. Despite associating with the caliphs, he did not bow down to them. He was appointed qāḍi (judge) during the time of Hārun al-Rashid. See: Abū Zahrah, "*Abū Ḥanīfah*", pp. 233-4. Al-Shaybānī occupied himself with the narration of traditions (ḥadīth) at first; later

he adopted the principles of the Iragians from Abū Ḥanīfah. Imām Shāfi'ī also met him and studied his books. See: Al-Khudarī, "*Tārikh al-Tashrī' al-Islāmī*", p. 240. He was a judge and a faqih who was famous for giving quick solutions. Because of his post as judge, he had ample opportunity to practice his knowledge of fiqh. In addition, he decreased the disputes and different view points between the Iraqi and Hijaz schools due his knowledge of both groups. See Osman Keskioğlu, "*Fıkıh Tarihi ve Islam Hukuku*", (Ankara: 1980), p. 106.

332. Schacht, "*The Origins*", p. 305.

333. Nasafī, "*Kashf*" vol. 1, p. 11; Sarakhsī, "*Uṣūl*", vol. 2, p. 113.

334. Ibn al-Qayyīm, "*I'lām*", vol. 1, p. 102.

335. Shaybānī, "*Al-Aṣl*", vol. 2, pp. 238, 370, 392, 406, vol. 3, p. 320, vol. 4, pp. 423, 457, vol. 5, pp. 111, 169-70, 190, 206-207; ibid., "*Al-Siyar al-Kabīr*", vol. 1, pp. 447, 521, 552, vol. 3, pp. 850-1, 907, 932, vol. 4, pp. 1217, 1366, 1451, 1573, vol. 5, pp. 1807, 1813, 2125.

336. Khudarī, "*Tarīkh*" p. 210.

337. Shaybānī, "*Al-Jāmi' al-Ṣaghīr*", pp. 90, 192, 212, 243, 245, 332, 410, 411.

338. Ibid., pp. 122, 204, 295, 319, 361, 376; Jaṣṣāṣ, "*Fuṣūl*", vol. 3, pp. 167, 173; Shaybānī, "*Uṣūl*", vol. 1, pp. 328, 332, 336, 338, 370, 372, vol. 2, pp. 22, 24-5.

339. Shaybānī, "*Al-Hujjah*", vol. 1, p. 222.

340. Ibid., vol. 1, p. 272.

341. Ibid., vol. 1, p. 316, v. 2, p. 382.

342. Ibid., vol. 1, p. 392.

343. Jaṣṣāṣ, "*Fuṣūl*", vol. 4, p. 116; Sarakhsī, "*Al-Mabsūṭ*", vol. 1, pp. 77-8.

344. Dāraqutnī, "*Al-Sunan*" vol. 1, pp. 161-171; Bayhāqī, "*Al-Sunan*", vol. 1, pp. 146-7; Hawarizmī, Abū Muayyad Muḥammad b. Maḥmūd (d. 665/1267), "*Jāmi' Masānīd al-Imām*", (Beirut: Dār al-Kutub al-'Ilmiyyah), vol. 1, pp. 247-8.

345. Shaybānī, "*Al-Hujjah*", vol. 1, p. 204; for this example see p. 199 in this book.

346. Sarakhsī, "*Al-Mabsūṭ*", vok. 1, p. 49. For more examples, see ibid., vol. 1, p. 56, ibid., "*Uṣul*", vol. 2, pp. 106, 110, 112. For more about contemporary approach of apostasy, see An-Nāīm, "*Towards*", pp. 9-11, 49, 109, 130, 150, 107-114, 183-187.

347. Ibid., pp. 242-3.

348. Sarakhsī, "*Al-Mabsūṭ*", vol. 4, p. 155, for more examples, see vol. 2, p. 89, vol. 4, pp. 89, 132.

349. Majallah: clause: 21

350. Abū Dāwūd, "*Buyū'*", 70; Nasāī, "*Buyū'*", 60.

351. Bukhārī, "*Ṣaḥīḥ*", ḥadīth no. 441, vol. 3, p. 243.

352. Shaybānī, "*Al-Aṣl*", vol. 1, p. 27.

353. Muḍārabah: This means a contract of co-partnership, in which one of the parties (the proprietor) is entitled to a profit on account of the capital (*ra's al-māl*) he has invested. He is designated as the owner of the capital (*rabb al-māl*). The other party is entitled to profit on account of his labour and is designated as the muḍārib (or the manager) in as much as he derives a benefit from his own labour and endeavours.

354. Muzāra'ah: This is a contract between two persons whereby one party is the landlord and the other the cultivator. They both agree that whatever is produced by cultivation of the land shall be divided between them in specified proportions.

355. Musāqah: This is a contract between two parties whereby one party takes charge of the fruit tree of the other partner on condition that the crops shall be divided between them on specific terms.

356. Muḥammad Dasūkī, "*Al-Imām Muḥammad bin Ḥasan al-Shaybānī*", (Qatar: 1987), p. 242.

357. Shaybanī, "*Al-Siyar al-Kabīr*", vol. 1, p. 270. Sarakhsī, "*Al-Mabsūṭ*", vol. 15, p. 171, vol. 8, pp. 135, 186, vol. 12, p. 46, vol. 15, pp. 170, 172, 174.

358. Al-Shaybānī, "*Al-Jāmi' al-Ṣaghīr*", p. 1310.

359. Sarakhsī, "*Al-Mabsūṭ* ", vol. 10, p. 145.

360. Nasafī, "*Kashf*", vol. 2, p. 164.

361. Khallāf, "*Al-Maṣādir*", p. 75.

362. Alwānī, "*The Ethics*", p. 75; Anṣārī, "*Ghayat al-Wuṣūl*", p. 139.

363. Abū Zahrah, "*Al-Imām Zayd*", p. 439.

364. Shāṭibī, "*Al-Muwāfaqāt*", vol. 4, p. 117; Shāṭibī, "*Al-I'tiṣām*", vol. 2, p. 139.

365. Ibn Ḥazm, "*Al-Iḥkām*" vol. 2, pp. 195-6; see Chejne, "*Ibn Ḥazm*", p. 122.

366. Ibn Ḥazm, "*Al-Iḥkām*", vol. 2, p. 196.

367. Baṣrī, "*Al-Mu'tamad*", vol. 2, p. 295.

368. Zarkashī, "*Al-Baḥr al-Muḥīt*", vol. 6, p. 93; Shīrāzī, "*Sharḥ al-Luma'*", vol. 2, p. 969.

369. Baltajī, "*Manāhij*", vol. 2, pp. 846-7.

370. Bukhārī, "*Kashf*", vol. 4, p. 4.

371. Shāfi'ī, "*Al-Risālah*", p. 25. For English translation of "*Al-Risālah*" see Mājid Khaddūrī, "*Islamic Jurisprudence Shāfi'ī's Risālah*", (Baltimore: The Johns Hopkins Press, 1961), p. 70,

372. Shāfi'ī, "*Al-Risālah*", p. 507.

373. Shīrāzī, "*Sharḥ al-Luma'* ", vol. 2, p. 970; Juwaynī, "*Talkhīs*", vol. 3, p. 313.

374. Ghazālī, "*Mustaṣfā*", vol. 1, p. 283.

375. Rāzī, "*Maḥṣūl*", vol. 2, p. 561; Āmidī, "*Al-Iḥkām*", vol. 4, p. 390; Ibn Subkī, "*Al-Ibhāj*", vol. 3, p. 203.

376. Taftazānī, "*Talwīḥ*", vol. 2, p. 162.

377. Ibid., vol. 2, p. 163.

378. Majallah: clause: 32; Suyūṭī, "*Al-Ashbāh wa al-Nazāir*", p. 62; Ibn Nujaym, "*Al-Ashbāh*", p. 91.

379. Suyūṭī, "*Al-Ashbāh*", p. 62.

380. Māwardī, "*Adab al-Qāḍī*", vol. 1, pp. 658-59-60.

381. Shāfi'ī, "*Al-Umm*", vol. 5, p. 52.

382. Sarakhsī, "*Uṣūl*", vol. 2, p. 201.

383. Ibn Subkī, "*Al-Ibhāj*", vol. 3, p. 204; Āmidī, "*Al-Iḥkām*", vol. 4, p. 391.

384. Qur'an: 11:65

385. Ibn Subkī, ibid., vol. 3, p. 204; Āmidī, ibid., vol. 4, p. 391.

386. Shāfi'ī, "*Al-Umm*", vol. 7, p. 268.

387. Al-Māwārdī, "*Adab al-Qāḍī*", vol. 1, p. 660.

388. Shāṭibī, "*Al-I'tiṣām*", vol. 2, p. 147.

389. Maḥillāwī, "*Tashīl*" p. 237.

390. Khallāf, "*Maṣādir* ", p. 77.

391. Ibid.

4
Various Types of *Istiḥsān*

Scholars divide *istiḥsān* into many types depending on the school of thought and the basis based on which they recognize the validity of the principle. We have touched on this issue in the previous chapter; now we will discuss it in greater detail.

Istiḥsān appears originally as a reaction to the concept of *qiyās*, and mainly when a jurist is faced with a problem for which he can not arrive at a ruling from the definitive sources of law within the Qur'an and the *Sunnah*, and when he then searches for precedent and tries to find a solution by making a comparison with a previous case. His investigation may reveal two different solutions: one of which is based on an explicit (*jalī*) analogy and the other on an implicit (*khafī*) analogy. If they contradict each other, then the jurist may reject the former in the favour of latter. The implicit analogy is considered to be more effective and therefore is preferred over the explicit. Departure from one type of *qiyās*, i.e. *jalī*, to another type of *qiyās*, i.e. *khafī*, is simply called *istiḥsān*.

Despite the controversy over the division of *istiḥsān*, it is divided mainly into two categories **a:** analogical *istiḥsān*, which consists of a departure from *qiyās jalī* to *qiyās khafī* and **b:** exceptional *istiḥsān* (*istiḥsān istithnā'ī*) which consists of making an exception to a general rule of the existing law; it is approved when the jurist is convinced that by making such an exception, justice might be better served.[1] After confirming the division of *qiyās* into two types—the explicit and the implicit—Ṣadr al-Sharī'ah (d. 747/1346) calls the implicit (*khafī*) analogy *istiḥsān*. However, *istiḥsān* is more comprehensive than implicit analogy: while every implicit analogy can be called *istiḥsān,* not every case of *istiḥsān* can be called implicit (*khafī*) analogy. *Istiḥsān* is an evidence (*dalīl*) which is established against explicit analogy. Ṣadr al-Sharī'ah then says that it is divided into several types such as *ijmā'*, *ḍarūrah* (necessity), *athar* etc.[2]

Another jurist Bazdawī (d. 482/1089) also indicates that *istiḥsān* is an implicit analogy, and says that its other types consist of *athar*, *ijmā'* (consensus) and *ḍarūrah* (necessity).[3]

The contemporary scholar Khallāf (d. 1376/1956) divides *istiḥsān* into two main types:[4] 1. *istiḥsān* which is departure from one ruling to another. It includes: a. the requirement that the departure be from *qiyās jalī* to *qiyās khafī*, b. the requirement that the departure be general text (*naṣṣ 'ām*) to a specific ruling (*ḥukm khās*), and c. that the departure be from the general rule of the existing law to an exceptional law. 2. *Istiḥsān* based on *sanad* (evidence), which the departure requires.

The second type of *istiḥsān* is considered by the schools of thought (*madhhabs*) along the following lines. The Ḥanafīs divide *istiḥsān* into four types: a. *istiḥsān* based on *athar*, which is the textual evidences in the Qur'an and *Sunnah*, b. *istiḥsān* based on *ijmā'* (consensus), c. *istiḥsān* based on *ḍarūrah* (necessity), d. *istiḥsān* based on *qiyās khafī* (implicit analogy). Ibn Nujaym (d. 970/1562) has summarised the divisions recognized by the Ḥanafīs as follows: *istiḥsān* is based on *naṣṣ* (*athar*), *ijmā'* (consensus), *ḍarūrah* (necessity) and *qiyās khafī* (implicit analogy).[5]

The Ḥanbalī School has not pronounced officially on the divisions within *istiḥsān*. However, particularly, their *istiḥsān* can be divided into three types: a. departure from a ruling in favour of *naṣṣ*, b. departure from *qiyās* in favour of the saying of the Companions, c. departure from *qiyās* in favour of a stronger one. They have also pointed out that the departure from *qiyās* may be in respect of *naṣṣ* of which *khabar wāḥid* (isolated Tradition), *ḥadīth mashhūr* (well known Tradition), *ḥadīth mutawātir* (widely spread Tradition) and textual evidences from the Qur'an are some examples. Sometimes, the departure occurs in favour of the saying of the Companions, even if it is against *istiḥsān*. These types are agreed upon among the scholars. In spite of this, if the departure applies to another analogy, the scholars on this issue are in disagreement. In addition, departure in favour of a stronger analogy is recognised.

The Mālikīs divide *istiḥsān* into four types: a. *istiḥsān* based on *'urf* so long as it does not contradict textual evidence, b. *istiḥsān* based on *maṣlaḥah* (benefit), c. *istiḥsān* based on *ijmā'* (consensus), d. departure from *qiyās* in order to avoid hardship and secure benefit for man.[6]

In spite of the disagreement over the division of *istiḥsān*, some common issues with regard to the types of *istiḥsān* are generally agreed upon. As Sarakhsī points out, the first type of *istiḥsān*—departure from *jalī* to *khafī*—is agreed upon by all the scholars, and opposition to it is unthinkable. Therefore it is regarded as *ra'y ghālib*.[7]

Ra'y ghālib can be defined as: "The application of *istiḥsān* by interpretation through the most appropriate opinion resembling the ruling whose application the Legislator has entrusted to our opinion".[8] It is illustrated in the example of the fixing of maintenance (*mut'ah*) and alimony (*nafaqah*) as mentioned in the Qur'an "But bestow on them (a suitable gift), the rich according to his means, and the poor according to his means, a gift (*mut'ah*) of reasonable amount is a duty on the doers of good" (2:236). Another example is fixing the cost of the mother's food and clothing as indicated in "The father of the child shall bear the cost of the mother's food and clothing on a reasonable basis" (2:233). and, "For divorced women, maintenance (*mut'ah*) (should be provided) on reasonable (scale)" (2:241). In the Qur'an the maintenance (*mut'ah*) of women, and the cost of their food and clothing has been made obligatory on those, responsible according to their financial capacity. Fixing the exact amounts involved is entrusted to the discretion of the *mujtahid*.[9]

Approving such *ijtihād* based on prevailing opinion is called *ra'y ghālib*, which is the prevailing opinion in *istiḥsān*.[10] Other issues such as the types of punishment for killing an animal in the protected places (*ḥaram*), the evaluating of an animal to be sacrificed, or the evaluation of the blood money in the case of injury have been left to the discretion of the jurists, which is based on the most prevalent opinion (*ra'y ghālib*).[11]

Istiḥsān **in the sense of departing from one ruling to another ruling**

As I have touched on above, this can be divided into three types as follows.[12]

Departure from qiyās jalī to qiyās khafī

Ḥanafīs divide *qiyās* into the *jalī* (explicit) and the *khafī* (implicit). *Jalī* is an analogy where the *'illah* (effective cause) appears at first glance, without careful consideration needing to be given to it. For example, the prohibition of *nabidh* appears to follow on by analogy from the prohibition of wine. However, *qiyās khafī* is one where the effective cause (*'illah*) is understood after careful consideration and reflection.[13] In other words, *qiyās khafī* is preferred over *qiyās jalī* if they are opposed to each other, on account of the effective cause (*'illah*) which is stronger in *khafī*. Therefore, it is called the *qiyās* of juristic preference (*istiḥsān al-qiyās*).[14]

Ḥanafī jurists point out that the *qiyās khafī*, which they called *istiḥsān* is in reality a kind of *qiyās* and therefore, its ruling can be moved referred (*ta'diyah*) to other cases.[15] In order to refer a ruling of *qiyās*, it must be related to an effective cause (*'illah*) that is based on another cause (*'illah*). Every ruling which is based on *'illah* would be referred to other cases (*furū'*) which have a similar *'illah*. This is the ruling of the validated *qiyās*. *Ta'diyah* (referring a ruling to another case) is an indispensable factor of an effective cause (*'illah*) according to the Ḥanafīs.[16]

We can see how *qiyās khafī* is preferred over *qiyās jalī* in the following examples:

1. According to Ḥanafī rulings, when transferring the ownership of agricultural land, all of the ancillary rights (*ḥaqq al-irtifāq*) attached to the property, such as the right of water (*ḥaqq al-shurb*), the right of passage (*ḥaqq al-murūr*) and the right of flow (*ḥaqq al-masīl*), are also transferred. This is indisputable, even if it is not stipulated explicitly in the document. Besides this, in the contract of lease (*ijārah*), even if the ancillary rights are also not explicitly mentioned in the document, the usufruct (*intifā'*) is considered as part of the contract. So, the leaseholder is able to benefit from these rights.

Another transaction, which resembles both contract sales and leases, is called *waqf* (charitable endowment). If it is considered from the point of view of the donor, *waqf* resembles a contract of sale, because the ownership changes hands. Considering it from the side of the donee, *waqf* resembles a contract of lease (*ijārah*), because both involve a transfer of usufruct (*intifāʿ*). However, the ownership is not transferred to the other party.

According to these explanations, the contract faces two different *qiyās* (analogy) rulings when the property is donated as *waqf* (charitable endowment): if it is compared to a contract of sale, what is not included in the contract and is not specified in it, such as the ancillary rights (*haqq al-irtifāq*) will not be included. If it is compared to a contract of lease, the ancillary rights will be included in the scope of *waqf*, even if these are not explicitly mentioned and specified by the donee. Here, the first instinct is to compare *waqf* with a contract of sale; comparing it to a contract of lease comes to mind only after investigation. Therefore, comparing *waqf* to a sale is called an explicit analogy (*qiyās jalī*), while comparing it to a lease is called implicit analogy (*qiyās khafī*).

Consequently, including the ancillary rights in the transaction of the *waqf* without requiring any statement or permission from the donee is a ruling of *istiḥsān*. If, however the ancillary rights are not included it is a ruling of *qiyās* (analogy).[17] The main reason for the preference of *istiḥsān* over analogy is that such analogy would lead to unfair results: the *waqf* of cultivated land without its ancillary rights would frustrate the basic purpose of *waqf*, which is to facilitate the use of the property for charitable purposes. Usufruct is the essential purpose of *ijārah*, and this would enable us to say that *waqf* can be deemed valid even if it does not specify the ancillary rights to the property in detail. Therefore, it is compared to a lease in order to avoid hardship for the people.[18]

As we see, the effective cause of the implicit analogy, which is not contrary to the *Shārīʿs* (Law-maker) purposes, is stronger than the explicit analogy, and therefore it is preferred over explicit analogy so that the benefits of the people will be secured.

2. If a husband tells his wife "Consider yourself divorced if you are menstruating", and his wife says "I am menstruating", according to the rule of *qiyās*, her statement is not accepted unless her husband approves or it is made clear that she is definitely menstruating. However, the wife's statement is considered true and the divorce is actualised based on *istiḥsān*.

The original case (*aṣl*), based on *qiyās*, is when a husband says to his wife "If you enter the house you are divorced" or "If you speak to someone you are divorced", and the wife immediately says "I entered the house after your stipulation" or "I have spoken with someone". After that, if husband denies her word, the wife would not be divorced. However, if she has evidence to verify it, or if her husband has confirmed her claims, she is then divorced, even if another original basis (*aṣl*) is found and its effective cause is stronger. The ruling of *istiḥsān* is therefore based on the new *aṣl* (original case) as mentioned in the Qur'an: "And it is not lawful for them to conceal what God has created in their wombs, if they believe in God and the Last Day" (2:228). In addition, a narration from 'Ubay b. Kāb verifies this: "To trust a woman of her honour is a necessity."[19] The Qur'an and *ḥadīth* advise women that concealing menstruation is forbidden. Therefore, it is necessary to trust women on those issues which can only be recognized by them. The ruling of the Qur'an and *ḥadīth* have become an *aṣl* (original case) for the statement of women on that issue. In addition, if woman says, "my period has ended" then her statement must be taken as true. Therefore, her statement in the issue of divorce when she says "I have a period" is also accepted on the basis of this *aṣl* (original case), according to *istiḥsān*.[20]

3. If a group of people gain unlawful entry into a house, steal collected commodities and load them on one person's back and that person carries the commodities outside while the others are not carrying anything, according to *qiyās*, the punishment is only applied to the person who carried the commodities. However, according to *istiḥsān* the punishment is applied to all of those who were involved in the robbery.[21]

In this case, there are two contradictory *aṣl* (original cases): the first involves a group of people who encourage one of their number to rape a woman. In this case, there is no conflict among the jurists and the penalty is applied only to the rapist. This is a ruling of *qiyās* as opposed to *istiḥsān*. The second case is that of a group of people who congregate with the intention to attack, kill and rob people of their commodities; in this case, the penalty of highway robbery is applied to all. This case is not disputed by jurists because they agree that the punishment must be applied to all who are involved in the highway robbery. According to the Qur'an:

"The recompense of those who wage war against God and His Messenger and do mischief in the land is only that they shall be killed or crucified or their hands and their feet be cut off from opposite sides, or be exiled from the land. That is their disgrace in this world, and a great torment is theirs in the Hereafter. Except for those who (having fled away and then) came back (as Muslims) with repentance before they fall into your power; in that case, know that God is Oft-Forgiving, Most Merciful" (5:33-34).

After investigating carefully, it becomes clear that comparing the house robbery to a highway robbery offers a clearer solution than comparing it to rape.[22] The departure from one original case (*aṣl*) to another because of the stronger reason is a solution sought by *istiḥsān* in order to better protect society.

4. If a man sells goods, such clothes, with a specific weight or measure under a contract of forward sale (*salam*)[23] to someone, but then withdraws the offer of sale before being paid, the transaction becomes null and void. However, if this transaction is completed in the normal way and the seller does not withdraw the offer of sale, the transaction is valid according to *istiḥsān* because the customer is able to take his goods any time he wants and the possibility of illegal action is therefore avoided. This is in spite of the fact that, according to *qiyās* both transactions are similar. As is normal, the goods will be delivered later in the forward sale (*salam*). If the money is not taken in advance, both parties may discontinue the transaction, which then causes harm to either the seller or buyer or both. Paying in advance is preferred as the contract will be more secure. The condition[24] of a forward sale (*salam*) naturally includes guarantee of security.[25]

We can draw a conclusion regarding implicit analogy as follows:

i. Departing from explicit analogy to implicit analogy indicates that the explicit analogy, at the appearance of the effective cause (*'illah*), could not secure the benefit of the people and is thus unable to manifest the wisdom of the Sharī'ah.[26]

ii. To prefer the explicit analogy is to risk the occurrence of unexpected and unwanted results, which would not be conducive to the public good. When *istiḥsān*, which is the implicit analogy, is preferred, the purposes of the *Shārī'* will obviously be achieved.

iii. While rulings based on explicit analogy are suitable for specific issues with textual (*naṣṣ*) evidence, implicit analogy is more suited to non-specific issues with no clear textual evidence to support them. Indeed, implicit analogy may realize the purpose of *naṣṣ* more effectively than explicit analogy.

Departure from naṣṣ to a specific ruling

Under this sub-heading, I will give some information about the *'ām* (general) the *khāṣṣ* (specific) and *takhṣīṣ* (particularization).

The 'ām (general)

This is a term that involves general principles or issues rather than details or particular issues: it is not confined to one particular case or amount and may be generalized to cover a wide range of different issues and people. For example; in "(as for) the thief, the male and the female, amputate their hands in recompense for what they earned (i.e. committed) as a deterrent punishment from God. God is Exalted in Might and Wise" (5:38), the words "*al-sāriqu wa al-sāriqatu*" (the male and the female thief) apply to all who commit that crime, and no-one in particular is specified.

The khāṣṣ (specific)

This is a term that denotes detailed and exact meaning connected with only one specific thing or person. For example, 'Umar, man, woman etc. Besides this, even if it contains plurality, and that plurality is restricted, then the term is considered as *khāṣṣ*, for example; two, three, four, a hundred, two thousand etc.

Scholars unanimously agree that the *khāṣṣ* (specific) definitely indicates a determined meaning, so long as contrary evidence against its specificity does not exist. The specific meaning cannot define the term to be anything other than what it is.[27] For example, in

"God will not impose blame upon you for what is meaningless in your oaths, but He will impose blame upon you for (breaking) what you intended of oaths. Therefore, expiation is the feeding of ten needy people from the average of that which you feed your (own) families or clothing them or the freeing of a slave. But whoever can not find (or afford it) then a fast of three days (is required)" (5:89).

The words "*raqabah*", (neck), "*'ashara*", (ten), and "*thalāthah*", (three) are *khāṣṣ* (specific) and denote the expiation of broken oaths, namely the freeing of a slave, the feeding of ten orphans, or fasting for three days. Indicating these with *khāṣṣ* (specific) terms excludes any possibility of their having other meanings.[28]

Takhṣīṣ (particularization)[29]

The thing or issue which prompts particularization is called *mukhaṣṣiṣ* (particularising agent), while the thing or issue particularised is known as the *mukhaṣṣaṣ* (particularized agent).[30]

Departing from a general ruling to a specific ruling in order to uphold the spirit and purpose of the Sharī'ah is considered a type of *istiḥsān*. In the ruling of *qiyās*, particularization is not recognized under any conditions; however *istiḥsān* allows the particularization of the *'illah* in order for *istiḥsān* itself to be applied. As we know, one of the definitions of *istiḥsān* given by the Ḥanafī jurists is the "abandoning of one judgement in favour of another".[31] For example, according to the general rulings in the Qur'an, Muslims are prohibited to eat unlawful meat (*maytatah*) which has not been slaughtered ritually: "Forbidden to you (for food) are: *al-maytatah* (the dead animals-cattle beast not slaughtered)..." (5:3). Here the word "*al-maytatah*" (dead) is comprehensive and covers sea animals as well as others. However, the Prophet's saying "*Huwa al-ṭahūru māuhu al-ḥillu maytatuhu*",[32] particularizes the word to mean all animals apart from sea animals.[33]

From a different perspective, if someone's life is in danger and there is nothing for him to eat except carrion (*maytatah*), then the general ruling has to be reconsidered and put aside, since protecting the live of Muslims is considered to be one of the five essential values of the Sharī'ah. The *'illah* (cause) of the particularization of the general ruling here is starvation, which may lead to death. Hence, particularization is aimed at securing a better understanding of the general principles of the Sharī'ah and its proper implementation by means of *istiḥsān*.[34] This kind of implementation, according to Ḥanafī thought, is considered part of *istiḥsān*, which is based on the *naṣṣ* of the Qur'an and *Sunnah*.[35]

More examples here will help to further illustrate this. According to the general text of the Qur'an, theft is absolutely forbidden and the thief is punished by the cutting off hands. "And (as for) the male thief and the female thief, cut off (from the wrist joint) their (right) hands as a recompense for that which they committed, a punishment by way of example from God. And God is All Powerful, All wise" (5:38). The *naṣṣ* of the Qur'an requires that the thief's hand be amputated if the condition of stealing is fulfilled. General rulings of Islamic law require the cutting off of the thief's hand even in the year of famine, because of the generalized meaning of the word "*sāriq*" (thief). However, the scholars are in agreement that during a famine, no amputation would take place. As 'Umar practiced such particularization, no one opposes the consensus.[36]

Nevertheless, the consensus is restricted by the condition that the person who steals would not be able to find food to eat. If he has sufficient rations and he survives, he will then be penalized. In spite of the ruling of *qiyās*, which requires amputation because the text does not distinguish between the obligatory or non-obligatory nature of amputation, scholars have said that it is not necessary, based on *istiḥsān*. Ibād b. Shuraḥbil, narrates the following anecdote: During a year of famine, hunger forced me to steal food, which I hid in my clothes. When the owner found out, he thrashed me and took me to the Prophet (ṣ). The Prophet (ṣ) said: "If he is uneducated, educate him; and if he is starving, feed him." He then ordered the owner to return my clothes and gave me a container of food.[37] In the light of this *ḥadīth*, Ibn Qudāmah said that, as narrated from Aḥmad Ibn Ḥanbal, if a needy person steals, his hand will not be amputated during the year of famine. It was also narrated by 'Umar ibn Khaṭṭāb that "amputation will not take place during the year of famine" and according to'Umar's practice, the penalty was avoided.[38] This is because the *ḥadd* penalty was never carried out when there was doubt. Consequently, 'Umar particularized the general text of the Qur'an because of the year of famine and avoided the cutting off of the hand based on the concept of *istiḥsān*.

Departure from the general rule of the existing law to an exceptional law

Exceptional *istiḥsān* is represented here by the example of charitable endowment (*waqf*) made by someone mentally defective (*safih*) who is under the protection of a guardian. This is based on the *istiḥsān* ruling which permits the mentally defective to make such endowments regardless of whether or not they are under someone's guardianship. It is based on the benefits of the people because permitting it by way of *istiḥsān* may encourage people to do charitable and good works. According to *qiyās*, however, a mentally defective person cannot make a charitable endowment (*waqf*) under protection of a guardian. The charitable endowment is a kind of donation (*tabarru'*) and a person under guardianship is not eligible to give donations.[39] *Istiḥsān* departs from the established ruling and thus validates the donation.

However, if the one under guardianship does make a charitable endowment, what is the position?

According to the general rule, which is *qiyās*, this donation is not valid if the mentally defective (*safih*) makes a donation. Al-Khussāf, a Ḥanafī jurist, observes that this donation may cause harm to his self, and therefore is not valid. However, Abū Yūsuf is of the opinion that it is valid. However, all Ḥanafī scholars agreed that if he donates something after he leaves the guardianship, it is valid.[40]

Istiḥsān based on *sanad* in terms of the departure

Under this sub-heading, I am going to discuss the types of *istiḥsān* based on *sanad.* We know that *istiḥsān* is invalid if it is not based on *dalīl,* in which case it would be seen as acting according to one's own wishes and desires. Therefore, relating it to the evidence is vital, otherwise it is not recognised. Jurists divide *istiḥsān* into different types as I have mentioned earlier.

We encounter, in general, three types of *istiḥsān*, which are based on explicit evidences, according to the Ḥanafī sources. These are *istiḥsān* based on *athar* (the Qur'an and the *Sunnah*); on *ijmā'* (consensus); and on necessity (*ḍarūrah*). In addition, they considered implicit analogy as one of the types of *istiḥsān.*[41] Beside this, we also come across kinds of *istiḥsān* based on the sayings of the Companions,[42] on *'urf;* on *maṣlaḥah;*[43] on *raf' al-ḥaraj* (avoiding hardship);[44] on precaution (*iḥtiyājāt*); and on the consideration of current needs.[45]

Ḥanafī Jurists have also used the term *athar* (tradition)[46] more than the term *naṣṣ* (text), and include the sayings of the Companions[47] in this term.[48] They used to say, "We approve *istiḥsān* on the ground of *athar*" which is based on the sayings of the Companions.[49]

As Shāṭibī shows, Mālikī scholars also divide *istiḥsān* into four types;[50] *istiḥsān* based on *'urf* (custom); on *maṣlaḥah* (benefit); on *raf' al-ḥaraj* and *mashaqqah* (avoiding hardship); and *ijmā'* (consensus).[51]

Comparing the Ḥanafī and Mālikī viewpoints, we see that they agree on *istiḥsān* which is based on custom (*'urf*), or on benefit (*maṣlaḥah*). Khallāf adds that benefit (*maṣlaḥah*) contains that which the Ḥanafīs call necessity (*ḍarūrah*), and which the Mālikīs refer to as avoidance of hardship (*raf' al-ḥaraj*). Departure from a ruling inferred by *qiyās* or from a general ruling or established ruling to another ruling on the ground of custom (*'urf*) or benefit (*maṣlaḥah*) which brings ease and avoids hardship is called *istiḥsān* by both schools.[52]

However, they disagree as to what the evidence is based on, and whether it is *naṣṣ* (text) or implicit analogy (*qiyās khafī*). However, to describe something as *istiḥsān* based on *naṣṣ* or implicit analogy does not make sense, since a ruling that is based on *naṣṣ* is established by *naṣṣ* (text) and *qiyās* too. Therefore, *istiḥsān* based on *naṣṣ* is an exception.[53]

Despite this disagreement, the scholars do not reject rulings that are inferred; their disagreement is purely academic.

Consequently, we may consider *istiḥsān* based on *sanad* into five types: 1. *Istiḥsān* based on *athar*, which is the Qur'an, the *Sunnah* and the saying of the Companions. 2. *Istiḥsān* based on *ijmā'* (consensus). 3. *Istiḥsān* based on necessity (*ḍarurah*) and the avoidance of hardship (*raf' al-ḥarāj*). 4. *Istiḥsān* based on benefit or public good (*maṣlaḥah*). 5. *Istiḥsān* based on custom (*'urf*).

The Qur'an, the *Sunnah* and the saying of the Companions will now be considered in the context of textual evidence (*naṣṣ*).

Istiḥsān based on athar

The meaning of *istiḥsān* based on *athar* is the departure from the ruling of *qiyās jālī* (explicit analogy) to a ruling that is proved by *naṣṣ* which opposes the ruling of *qiyās*.[54] The ruling of *naṣṣ* is considered as stronger evidence, whether it is from the Qur'an or the *Sunnah* or from *athar*. The ruling of *qiyās* cannot charge the opposition of *naṣṣ*. Considering many cases based on the general rulings and general texts using analogical reasoning is quite possible; however, it may oppose the Lawgiver's purposes and thus run counter to the public good.[55]

There is no dispute among the scholars that *mutawātir*[56] and *mashhūr ḥadīth* (well-known *ḥadīth*)[57] narrated from the Prophet (ṣ) are preferred over *qiyās*.[58] Isolated traditions (*khabar wāḥid*) are also seen as a valid source of law.[59] However, in the case of a dispute between a *khabar wāḥid* (isolated tradition) and analogy, which is a subject of disagreement among the scholars, the former is usually preferable.[60]

However, Zarqā criticises the kind of *istiḥsān* which is based on *naṣṣ* and *athar*, saying that *istiḥsān* which is based on *naṣṣ* and *ijmā'* could not be called *istiḥsān* because these rulings are already based on *naṣṣ* and *ijmā* and have nothing to do with *istiḥsān* or *qiyās*. He says that *istiḥsān* is the departure from analogy due to the non-existence of written legal rulings. Of course, the Qur'an, the *Sunnah* and *ijmā'* have priority over *qiyās* (analogy).Therefore, neither *qiyās* nor *istiḥsān* is needed and it is incorrect to call this *istiḥsān* because it causes confusion.[61]

Despite Zarqā's comments, his view seems erroneous because *qiyās* would not be approved with the existence of *naṣṣ* and *ijmā'*; only when *naṣṣ* and *ijmā'* are absent may *qiyās* or general rulings be applied.[62] In fact, jurists who approved *istiḥsān* used the statement "We left this *qiyās* because of *athar*"; "If *athar* is not existent we would approve it according to present *qiyās*."

Istiḥsān based on the Qur'an

This kind of *istiḥsān* is illustrated by the following examples:

1. A highway robber repents after stealing goods and after a while recompenses the owner of the goods. According to *qiyās,* he must be prosecuted because of his original crime. This case refers to a thief and a highway robber; and on the basis of *ḥirābah* (highway robbery), punishment is obligatory. However, *istiḥsān* departs from this and no longer considers it highway robbery after repentance. Repentance (*tawbah*) releases the guilty party from the charge of highway robbery and drops the punishment of *ḥadd,* based on *istiḥsān,* as indicated in the Qur'an: "Except for those who return (repenting) before you overcome (i.e. apprehend) them. And know that God is forgiving and Merciful" (5:34). This verse necessitates the departure from the ruling of *qiyās* and the dropping of the *ḥadd.* An example is that of Ḥarith ibn Zayd. He was a highway robber who later repented and was not executed, even though he had committed the crime. 'Alī ibn Abī Ṭālib approved the departure from the ruling of *qiyās* based on the above mentioned *naṣṣ.*[63]

2. An elderly person is incapable of performing the obligatory fast. He is allowed instead to pay a sum of money for each day of the missed obligatory fast, based on *istiḥsān.* However, he is not allowed to do this according to *qiyās* because there is no connection or similarity between fasting and the feeding of poor people. Despite the *qiyās* ruling, God has shown leniency to those who are incapable of fasting: "So whoever among you is ill or on a journey (during them) then an equal number of

days (are to be made up). And upon those who are able (to fast, but with hardship) a ransom (as substitute) of feeding a poor person (each day)" (2:184). Therefore, it is allowed based on the textual *naṣṣ*.[64]

3. A Muslim does not have to pay upkeep to his father if the latter is a non-Muslim, according to analogy based on the fact that they do not inherit from each other after death. However, Ḥanafī jurists base their judgment on the verse "Accompany them in this world with appropriate kindness" (31:15) and approve *istiḥsān* against the ruling of *qiyās,* thus departing from the established ruling to one which says that a Muslim has to pay upkeep to his poor elderly parents who are non-Muslims. In addition, Ḥanafī jurists base their judgements on the following rational reason, namely that rights of upkeep and financial maintenance between parents and a child are a natural matter of birth rights (*wilādah*), and that leaving parents in poverty is an unkind act.[65]

Istiḥsān based on the Sunnah

This kind of *istiḥsān* is illustrated by the following examples:

1. Eating and drinking in *Ramaḍan* by mistake nullifies the fast and requires expiation, according to *qiyās*. However, Abū Ḥanīfah and his disciples observe that according to *istiḥsān*, eating or drinking by mistake do not nullify the fast.[66] Eating and drinking by mistake is compared to cutting short the prayers by mistake, which does not nullify the prayer.[67] According to *istiḥsān,* the eating or drinking is not purposeful and thus does not nullify the fast. Therefore, *istiḥsān* is validated and preferred over the ruling of *qiyās*. It is based on *naṣṣ* for the Prophet (ṣ) says "Whoever eats or drinks by mistakes, let him complete his fasting because it

is a gift from God." And: "If a person who is fasting eats or drinks by mistake, it is a *rizq* which God feeds him with and no compensation is required", similarly "Whoever breaks his fast by mistake in the month of *Ramaḍan* is neither required to repeat the fast nor to pay *kaffārah* (penance, expiation)."[68] Consequently, *qiyās* is departed from on the grounds of *naṣṣ* (*ḥadīth*), and *istiḥsān* is approved. Abū Ḥanīfah says: "I would have used *qiyās* if narrations had not been found".[69] Naturally, eating or drinking by mistake is beyond one's power. Also a fly entering the mouth is considered the same as eating or drinking by mistake. Abū Ḥanīfah says that such incidents are beyond one's control whilst fasting, and dust entering a person's mouth whilst speaking.[70]

2. Forward sale (*salam*), for example, is invalid because of failing to satisfy one of the requirements of a valid sale, which is that the subject matter of the sale must be physically present at the time of contract. According to *qiyās* forward sale is invalid. The Prophet (ṣ) was asked by one of the Companions, Ḥakīm b. Ḥizām, whether he could sell a commodity prior to purchasing it himself. The Prophet (ṣ) replied: "*sell not what is not with you*".[71] Despite the fact that *qiyās* rejects forward sale, the *ḥadīth* approves *salam* with the following statement: "Whoever concludes *salam*, let him do so in a specified measure, specified weight and specified period of time."[72] Based on this *ḥadīth*, Ḥanafī jurists validated forward sale (*salam*) according to *istiḥsān*.[73]

Istiḥsān based on athar

The meaning of *athar*, as I have explained earlier, refers to the *acta* and *dicta* of the Prophet (ṣ) and the Companions.[74] Provided that there was no disagreement concerning it, a Companion's opinion was acceptable by Ḥanafī jurists as a kind of implicit *ijmā'* (*ijmā' sukūtī*) that was preferred to *qiyās*.[75]

Istiḥsān based on *athar* will be illustrated by the following examples;

1. A judge, ruler or political authority who witnesses witness a crime of theft, adultery or the drinking of wine, may not judge or punish on the basis of his own witnessing and must wait until legal evidences are established. This kind of *istiḥsān* is based on a tradition (*athar*) reported from Abū Bakr and 'Umar. However, according to *qiyās* they are able to execute the judgement on the basis of their personal knowledge and witnessing.[76]
2. If a person is unconscious and the time for prayer passes, according to *qiyās* the person should not have to make up the prayer later. However, Ḥanafī jurists departed from the ruling of *qiyās* to the ruling of *istiḥsān* based on the behaviour of 'Ammār, one of the Companions. He was once unconscious for a whole day, then woke up and prayed the prayers he had missed. Therefore, the Ḥanafīs ruled that whoever misses their prayer in such a circumstance should make up that prayer.[77]
3. A group of people attack a person and kill him; according to *qiyās*, retaliation (*qaṣās*) is not required against the whole group. The chief condition in retaliation is equality. Killing more than one person is considered as transgression and oppression. However, Ḥanafī jurists departed from the ruling of *qiyās* based on the practice of the Caliph 'Umar. It is narrated that seven people had killed a person during an attack. 'Umar was reported to have said "I would have ordered retaliation against the whole of the population of San'ā if they had joined in the killing of one person".[78]

Istiḥsān based on consensus (ijmā‘)

Ijmā‘[79] is the unanimous agreement of the *mujtahidūn* of the Muslim community of any period following the demise of the Prophet Muḥammad (ṣ) on a religious issue.[80]

Istiḥsān based on *ijmā‘* is illustrated here by the following examples:

1. Ḥanafī scholars mainly illustrate this kind of *istiḥsān* by the concept of *istiṣnā’* (the contract for manufacturing of goods).[81] For example, if someone places an order with a craftsman for certain goods to be made at a price which is determined at the time of the contract, according to the general rule of Sharī‘ah, it is invalid. This is because the object of the contract does not exist at the time the order was made. Making a transaction for a non-existent object is invalid according to the Prophet's (ṣ) prohibition, "Sell not what is not with you".[82]

However, the Ḥanafīs use *istiḥsān* and depart from the established ruling of *qiyās* on the grounds of the consensus of the Companions. During the time of the Companions, this customary transaction was prevalent and no one scholar rejected it. Dabbūsī (d. 430/1039) says: "They depart from the ruling of *qiyās* because of consensus which is based on the customary transactions, and it is accepted in, and uncontested by, the Muslim community."[83] A similar point has been made by Sarakhsī: "*Qiyās* does not deem this contract valid, yet we left the ruling of *qiyās* on the grounds that the transaction in question has been customary since the time of the Prophet (ṣ)".[84] People were implementing this transaction, and none of the scholars rejected it; custom is a factor that must be considered in social and economic issues such as this. Following custom reflects the Prophetic Tradition: "What the Muslims deem to be good is good in the sight of God"[85] and "My community will not agree on an error. When you see disagreement, you should follow the overwhelming majority."[86]

2. According to Sarakhsī, if a husband and wife apostatize together, they must separate, according to *qiyās*. This is because the situation of apostasy is an obstacle for performing *nikāḥ* (marriage) in the first place; and secondly, it hinders the continuance of *nikāḥ*. However, Abū Ḥanīfah and his disciples, Abū Yūsuf and Shaibānī, depart from the ruling of *qiyās* because of the consensus of the Companions, based on the case of the Banū Ḥanīfah. It is known that the Banū Ḥanīfah tribe had apostatized in order not to pay *zakāt*.[87] Because of this, Abū Bakr declared war on them, while inviting them to repent. After their repentance, the Caliph did not ask them to renew their marriages (*nikāḥ*), and no other Companions required it either.[88]

The example indicates the consensus of the Companions with regard to this case. In fact, not all the Companions gave their opinion on this case, but expressed their tacit approval by not rejecting Abū Bakr's decision. That is why this consensus is considered as a kind of tacit consensus (*ijmā' sukūtī*).[89] Ḥanafī Jurists apply *istiḥsān* based on consensus without indicating that it is a kind of tacit *ijmā'*.

3. A man dressed in *iḥram*[90] points out an animal to another man, who may or may not be dressed in *iḥram*. The second man then slaughters that animal. Given that to slaughter an animal while in the state of *iḥram* is forbidden, who is to be punished: the man who pointed out the animal in the first place, or the one who slaughtered it? According to the rulings of *qiyās*, punishment is not required. However, punishment *is* required according to the consensus of the Companions. *Istiḥsān* departs here from the ruling of *qiyās* based on the Companions' agreement. Someone asked Ibn 'Umar: "I

pointed out a deer while we were in *iḥram*, and then my friend killed the deer. What should I do?" 'Umar then asked 'Abd al-Raḥmān ibn Awf for his opinion. The latter replied that a sheep must be sacrificed as expiation. 'Umar said: "I agree with the opinion". A similar case has been reported from 'Alī and Ibn Abbās.[91]

Istiḥsān based on necessity (ḍarūrah) and the avoidance of hardship (raf' al-ḥarāj)

It is important to point out that Ḥanafī scholars use the term 'necessity' where Mālikī scholars use the term 'avoiding hardship'.[92]

In order to understand the concept of necessity, I shall first explore the meanings of *ḍarūrah*.

Linguistically, the word "*ḍarūrah*" has an opposite meaning to the word *maṣlaḥah* (benefit). It is derived from the root *ḍ-r-r*, one of the derivatives of which is *ḍarar or 'harm'*. Fīrūzabādī (d. 817/1414) explains "*ḍarar*" as 'straits', and then mentions the words *iḍtirār* (harming) and *ḍarūrah* (necessity), which also are included in the meaning of *iḥtiyāj* (need, exigency, necessity) and *muḥtāj* (needing, necessitous).[93] The word "*uḍturra*" also appears in the Qur'an with the meaning of 'forced'.[94] "But whoever is forced (by necessity), neither desiring it nor transgressing (its limit), then indeed, your Lord is Forgiving and Merciful" (6:145).[95]

According to Jaṣṣaṣ, *ḍarūrah* means necessity, and he interprets its meanings which come in the verse "He has explained in detail to you what He has forbidden you, excepting that to which you are compelled" (6:119). The permissibility alluded to in this verse may be adapted to any kind of compulsion during danger. The necessity in that context is because it may cause danger to part of the body. It covers circumstances such as when a starving person cannot find anything to eat except a dead body, or when a person is forced to eat a dead body even though there is edible food present, provided that eating the edible food is riskier than eating the dead body.[96]

Ḥanafī Scholars consider the concept of *ikrāḥ*[97] (coercion) in the field of *ḍarūrah* as a necessity too. If for example someone is threatened to be killed or maimed in order to make him to eat or drink something unlawful, then in that context it becomes necessary to carry out their commands.[98] However, if the person is threatened with jailing for life or beating, then he is not allowed to commit unlawful things; the condition of 'necessity' is that it be life-threatening. To commit unlawful acts in order to avoid non-life threatening consequences is not accepted.[99] These kinds of *ikrāḥ* (coercion) are called light coercion.

However, if a beating with lashes were to reach to limit that would be unbearable, then the condition of necessity (*ḍarūrah*) is fulfilled. The pain threshold of individuals differ and it is at the discretion of the person who is in that situation.[100]

If an act reaches the level of *ḍarūrah* (necessity), it naturally becomes lawful. This is enshrined in *fiqh* maxim: "Necessity renders prohibited things permissible."[101] Anṣārī (d. 1180/1767) indicates that *ḍarūrah* must reach the level of necessity before it becomes valid.[102] According to 'Alī Ḥaydār Afandī (d. 1936) *ḍarūrah* refers to a situation which involves doing something by force or eating things that are forbidden by the religion.[103] Consequently, *ḍarūrah* is generally concerned with fear of destruction and threat to one of the five essential values of human life, namely: religion, life, intellect, lineage and property,[104] which must be protected from harm.[105]

The concept of *ḍarūrah* is closely related to legal concepts such as *iḥtiyāj* (need), *ḍarar* (harm), *raf' al-ḥaraj* (avoiding hardship), *mashaqqah* (hardship, difficulty), and *'umūm al-balwā* (general calamities). Explanation of these terms now follows.

Iḥtiyāj (need)

Technically the term *iḥtiyāj* (need) here means "a situation of facing difficulty and hardship, such as when a hungry person cannot find food to eat." In the "*Fawātiḥ*" it is described as: "a circumstance which does not reach the level of *ḍarūrah*."[106] Zarkā defines it as: "A case which necessitates ease in order to achieve a goal". Need (*iḥtiyāj*) is a less significant than *ḍarūrah*. The reason for this is that whilst rulings approved by need are continual, they are only temporarily accepted in the case of *ḍarūrah*.[107]

Needs are divided into two types: a- General needs, both of the individual and of the whole Muslim community (*Ummah*), irrespective of ethnic group or class distinctions. Examples are: *salam* (forward sale), *bay' wa shirā'* (trading), *ijāra* (leasing), *waṣīyyah* (will, testament) and so on. b- Specific needs, namely those of people who live in a particular country, or of a member of a particular occupational group. Other examples include the use of gold teeth because of illness; the wearing of silk; and a doctor examining the usually clothed parts of a woman's body.[108] The concept of *ḍarūrah* became a law enshrined in the Ottoman court manual: "Any need, whether of a public or private nature, is so dealt with as to meet the exigencies of the case".[109]

Ḍarar (harm)

This term is similar to *ḍarūrah*; however, it is used more comprehensively. Every *ḍarūrah* may be a *ḍarar*, but the opposite is not the case. Sarakhsī says that *ḍarūrah* has a close similarity with *ḍarar*, as the *ḍarūrah* is defined as "Having fear that one may lose life or limb through lack of food." In addition, many such cases are based on the principle of *raf' al-ḍarar* (avoiding the harm) to approve *istiḥsān.*[110]

Suyuṭī considered the term *ḍarūrah* together with the term of *ḍarar* and pointed out that the *fiqh* maxim "Necessity renders prohibited things permissible"[111] was derived from the principle of avoidance of harm.[112] Actually, all these maxims are derived from the Prophet's *ḥadīth*: "Harm must neither be inflicted nor reciprocated".[113] As we see, *ḍarar* and *ḍarūrah* are virtually the same, and are involved in many cases, such as returning goods due to a fault[114] and most contracts involving freedom of choice (*khiyār*).[115] However there is some disagreement as to whether *ḍarar* and *ḍarūrah* covers issues such as fraud, bankruptcy of the buyer, *hijr* (limitation of someone's legal competence), *shuf'ah* (right of pre-emption), retaliation (*qaṣāṣ*),[116] *al-ḥudūd* (punishments) or *kaffarāt* (expiation).[117]

Raf'al-ḥaraj (avoiding hardship)

Linguistically the term "*ḥaraj*" means tight, close, straitened, narrow, sin, prohibition, narrowness, and critical point. Beside those meanings, it is also means 'forest'. The most prevalent of all these meanings is narrowness and closeness.[118]

Technically, it is defined as "A thing which causes immoderate harm to life or any parts of the body or properties, at present or in the future."[119] Therefore, "avoiding hardship" is the effort made to keep away from all kinds of difficulties in the first place, or to try to make it easy and mitigate it, and if it happens, then to seek to halt it.[120]

In the Ḥanafī sources, the term was formulated in order to make things easier and thus facilitate human needs.[121] In addition to the term "*raf' al-ḥaraj*", the terms "*daf' al-ḥaraj*", "*wad' al-ḥaraj*", and "*naf'y al-ḥaraj*" are also used.[122]

The principle of "avoiding hardship" is especially considered by the Lawgiver as a purpose of the general law when rulings are established. Hence the verse: "God intends for you ease and does not intend for you hardship" (2:185).[123] Here the Lawgiver wishes to make things easy and to avoid imposing hardships on people and thus does not obligate anyone more than his or her capacity: "No one is charged with more than his capacity" (2:233).[124]

Accordingly, the Prophet (ṣ) enjoined the Community (*Ummah*) to pursue ease and avoid hardship as far as possible, as seen in his saying, "The best of religion is that which brings ease".[125] Suyūṭī and many jurists have taken this principle into consideration based on the *Shāri's* purposes and have then applied it successfully, in accordance with the maxim "Latitude should be afforded in the case of difficulty, that is to say, upon the appearance of hardship in any particular matter, latitude and indulgence must be shown".[126] Difficulty thus requires ease that is to say in times of hardship, consideration must be shown, and cases which were not permissible by analogy must then be permitted.[127]

Such permission is only allowed during a time of hardship. It is disallowed when the difficulties no longer exist. The original ruling is then restored as soon as the extraordinary situation finishes. This is in accordance with the maxim, "When a prohibition is removed, the thing to which such prohibition attaches reverts to its former status of legality."[128]

Many cases of Islamic jurisprudence, such as the transfer of debts and loans, are derived from this principle; the latitude and indulgence shown by Islamic scholars in their rulings are all based on this rule.[129]

Mashaqqah (hardship)

The dictionary definition of "*al-mashaqqah*" is "hardship, difficulty, trouble, discomfort, inconvenience".[130] In its technical sense, it became a very important norm (*qāidah*) in Islamic law as the basis of many *sharʿī* rulings. This norm is alluded to in the maxim, "Difficulty begets facility".[131] Commenting on this maxim, Alī Ḥaydar Afandī says, "difficulty is the cause of facility and in time of hardship consideration must be shown; in another words, it is necessary to make ease in the time of hardship."[132] It is based originally on the verses: "God intends for your ease, and He does not want to make things difficult for you" (2:185),[133] and "The best of religion is that which brings ease".[134]

Suyūṭī suggests that all ease and latitude in Islamic law can be linked to this norm. The situations in which this principle is involved include such as travelling, illness, oblivion (forgetfulness), illiteracy (ignorance), general calamity (*ʿumūm al-balwā*) and deficiency (*naqṣ*).[135]

Not every difficulty or hardship is considered as a reason for leniency. Therefore, *mashaqqah* (hardship) is divided into different types: Shāṭibī considers *mashaqqah* as having two main categories; a- genuine hardships, b- imaginary hardships.[136] Suyūṭī also divides it into two types, albeit slightly differently. First, he says there are hardships which come from *ʿibādāt* (worship) itself. Examples of these include: making minor or major ablutions with cold water; fasting on long hot days; enduring long journeys to *ḥajj*; *jihād;* and the hardship of punishments such as the stoning of adulterers and the punishing of murderers. Such hardships are seen as an inextricable part of these acts of worship and obedience, and cannot be removed.[137] However, the permissibility of *tayammum*[138] because of fear of possible illness from taking ablutions with very cold water, is an exception.[139]

Secondly, he considers hardships which do not come from *'ibādāt* (worship); these he divides into three:

1. Fear of disaster or loss of life or limb.
2. Insignificant hardships. Examples might include slight headaches, for example, or nausea. Such difficulties are insignificant and cannot be cited as a reason for the relaxation of laws. Gaining the benefits of worship is more important than repelling these kinds of difficulty which are relatively unimportant.
3. Intermediate hardships. For example, a sick person fasts in *Ramaḍān* and worries that the fast may delay his recovery. Under such circumstances, the person is allowed to discontinue the fast. Similarly, someone for whom water may be dangerous is allowed to make *tayammum* even when water is available.[140] This third category of hardship is very difficult to quantify, and so jurists tend to judge each case in the light of the criteria pertaining to the first two categories alone.[141]

The conditions of ḍarūrah (necessity)

To be valid, *ḍarūrah* (necessity) must fulfil certain conditions.

1. There must be absolutely no doubt as to the existence of *ḍarūrah,* or to the impossibility of escaping from the situation which invokes the principle without recourse to a change of ruling. The reason for invoking this principle must be a situation which is life threatening, or which jeopardizes the health or property of an individual.[142] This concept is clearly alluded to in the *Majallah* in the words "No weight is attached to mere supposition".[143]
2. The compelled person must consider the general purposes of the lawgiver (*Shārī'*) while acting on something. The five

essential Sharī'ah values, which are religion, life, intellect, lineage, and property, must be given protection.[144]

3. Avoiding a situation of *ḍarūrah* must not lead to greater evil or harm. In other words, doing something prohibited out of necessity should not bring about a worse situation than the original one.[145] Jurists have added to the maxim "Necessity renders prohibited things permissible"[146] the caveat that the case for *ḍarūrah* has to be a compelling one.

This condition is based on the principle of choosing the lesser evil. (*ahwan al-sharr*). Obviously, if there are two benefits to choose from, the greater and more general good is preferred over the minor and specific one.[147] However, if there is a benefit and a harm; then first the harm must be removed, and then the benefit pursued. The Lawgiver gives more attention to the avoidance of the prohibited than implementation of the obligatory.[148]

An example of choice between evils is as follows. Consider three prohibited things; *kufr* (unbelief); *qatl* (murder); and *zinā* (adultery), all of which are forbidden in Islamic law.[149] However, if someone is forced to deny his belief, he will be forgiven as long as he keeps his belief in his heart. To force others, on the pain of death, to commit murder is prohibited. If such coercion actually leads to murder, *qiṣāṣ* will not be exacted from the killer, but from the one who forced him to kill. And similarly, if someone is coerced into committing adultery, he or she will not be punished by law, despite the fact that the law abhors such a crime and, considering its far-reacting social implications, deems it more destructive than the killing of a single individual under threat.[150]

This concept has been articulated by jurists in the following maxim: "A private injury is tolerated in order to ward off a public injury."[151] The prohibition from practice of an incompetent physician is derived from this principle. Similar maxims include:

"Severe injury is removed by lesser injury",[152] "In the presence of two evils, the greater is avoided by the choosing of the lesser",[153] "The lesser of the two evils is preferred",[154] and "Repelling an evil is preferable to securing a benefit".[155]

4. The limits of *ḍarūrah* should not be exceeded. The person who is in difficulty should be content with a solution that is just enough to rescue him from *ḍarūrah*.[156] For example, if a starving person can find only ritually impure food, he must eat as much as will allow him to survive; exceeding the limits is prohibited, in accordance with the statement "Necessity is estimated by the extent thereof".[157]

When the circumstances of *ḍarūrah* are over, the permission to benefit from the prohibited is also terminated, in accordance with the ruling: "A thing which is permissible by reason of the existence of some excuse thereof, ceases to be permissible with the disappearance of that excuse".[158]

5. An evil cannot be removed by an evil of similar gravity: when both are equal, choosing one in order to remove the other is prohibited. For example, a starving man is not allowed to take food from another man if it means that by depriving him, he too will starve. This concept is in accordance with the juristic norm, "an injury can not be removed by the commission of a similar injury".[159]

Another example is that no one has the right to violate someone else's personal rights in order to satisfy his needs. Selfishness can never be a reason. In fact, if a person takes someone else's food in a situation of necessity, under threat of force or without permission, then the *ḍarar* attached to the victim has to be compensated for. For example, if a hungry person eats bread belonging to another, that person must later pay the value.

This rule is based on the following statement: "Necessity does not invalidate the rights of another".[160]

Examples of istiḥsān based on necessity (ḍarūrah)

There are many examples of *istiḥsān* based on *ḍarūrah* according to the Ḥanafī School of law. Some of them are as follows:

1. A letter is sent by a judge from one place to another in order to provide evidence in support of a court case, since he is unable to be there in person. Under the rule of *ḍarūrah*, the evidence given by letter is as acceptable as evidence given in person in this particular case, since it eases hardship and secures the rights of those involved in, or affected by, the court case. According to *qiyās*, however, for a judge to provide evidence in this way is deemed invalid: *qiyās* does not recognise the personal information given by a judge to a court outside his jurisdiction. However, it is considered as evidence by *ḍarūrah* due to the needs of the people.[161]

2. The cleaning of wells and pools. According to the established ruling of *qiyās* even if wells and pools have been totally emptied, they are still not considered ritually pure. Emptying some of the water does not mean that it cleans all of the water. Even if all of the water is taken out, there is no difference. Fresh spring water from the well, or dropped into the well, will never be clean if the fresh water mixed with the polluted water remains adjacent to the wall of the well or pool and on the ground of the well._However, Ḥanafī jurists have departed from the general established ruling in this case, and have declared that the water will be considered clean by emptying just some of the water. This ruling, despite its opposition to *qiyās*, is accepted by Ḥanafī

jurists based on *istiḥsān* because of necessity and avoidance of difficulties for the people.[162]

3. If a flying or running animal collapses and dies immediately after it has been shot, this animal is edible according to *istiḥsān*. According to *qiyās*, however, it may not be eaten, since there is doubt that it may have died not from the actual shot but from the impact with the ground.

In this case, this kind of game is known as *mutaraddiyah* (dead by headlong fall), as indicated in the Qur'an:

"Forbidden to you (for food) are: *al-maytatah* (the dead animals-cattle beast not slaughtered), blood, the flesh of swine, and the meat of that which has been slaughtered as a sacrifice for others than God, or has been slaughtered for idols etc., or on which God's Name has not been mentioned while slaughtering, and that which has been killed by strangling, or by a violent blow, or by a headlong fall, or by the goring of horns—and that which has been (partly) eaten by a wild animal-unless you are able to slaughter it (before its death)—and that which is sacrificed (slaughtered) on *nuṣub* (stone altars)..." (5:3).

Istiḥsān ignores the doubt concerning the actual cause of death in such cases, since it is almost always impossible to tell.[163]

4. The contract of sale on foodstuffs such as nuts, eggs, fruit, vegetables and so on is valid even when the buyer discovers that some of them are spoilt, provided that the damaged food is little. This is the ruling of *istiḥsān*; the buyer is always at risk of such minor damages, which are unavoidable. However, if most of the food is spoilt, then the contract is null and void. Despite the ruling of *istiḥsān*, the contract is considered invalid by *qiyās*, regardless of the amount of damaged food.[164]

Istiḥsān based on benefit or public good (maṣlaḥah)[165]

As I have shown earlier, *maṣlaḥah* is one of the most controversial sources of Islamic law. It is also a principle that is used to drive rulings based on *istiḥsān*. Some examples are as follows:

1. According to the established ruling in the Ḥanafī School, even if someone has not yet paid the dowry in full, he may establish their home wherever he wishes even if his wife disagrees.[166] However, this ruling has been challenged by many scholars, who believe that it often leads to mental cruelty, with women being forced to live far from their places of birth and families. Therefore, they rule, even if the dowry is paid in full, her husband cannot force her to go anywhere. The new ruling is given in consideration of the need to protect from unforeseen hardships that may arise. This ruling has been chosen as the preferred ruling among all the schools, and is based on the principle of *maṣlaḥah.*[167]

2. According to the established ruling of the Ḥanafī School, a person is free to dispose of his own property as he wills. For example, one may dig a well on one's own land or build whatever one wishes. Such activities cannot be stopped even if they might cause harm to one's neighbours.[168] However, despite this ruling, at some point during the 8th and 9th century,[169] Ḥanafī jurists declared that the rights of personal ownership are not absolute. Therefore, the condition must be that disposal of one's property is allowed so long as it does not harm others.[170] In order to avoid harm and protect the public good a new ruling is established based on the principle of *maṣlaḥah*, which is a major consideration in *istiḥsān.*

While one may dispose of one's personal property as one wishes as far as *qiyās* is concerned, *istiḥsān* changes this by considering what is more beneficial for the majority.

3. According to *qiyās* both contract of *muḍārabah* (a contract of co-partnership) and the contract of lease are nullified when either one of the partners dies. However, some situations are considered as exceptional in order to avoid hardship and secure the greater good. For example, if the joint owner of a piece of agricultural land dies before the harvest has been collected, his partner is not obliged to sell and /or vacate the land at the behest of the dead partner's heirs, despite the general ruling which deems the contract null and void. This *istiḥsān* ruling is given in order to protect people's rights.[171] The same ruling is applicable for the contract of *musāqāt*.[172]

Istiḥsān based on custom ('urf)

From the point of view its validity, custom (*'urf*) can be divided into two types: *'urf, ṣaḥīḥ* (acceptable custom), which is a valid source of law according to the Qur'an and the *Sunnah;* and *'urf fāsid* (reprehensible custom), which is not accepted as a definite source of law.[173]

Custom is further defined as being either *qawlī* (verbal) or *fi'lī* (actual).[174]

'Urf qawlī consists of the agreement of people as to the meaning of words established for functions other than their literal meaning. Consequently, the agreed meaning can be understood by itself without any explanation.[175]

For example, the word "*dirham*" has been used to mean money that is presently used as currency. As such, it points only to this meaning rather than any other.[176]

However, *dirham* in fact literally means "silver coin", a meaning which does not come to mind when it is used on a day-to-day basis.[177] Another example of verbal *'urf* is the word "*walad*", which literally means offspring, whether a son or daughter, but which in popular usage is used for son only. It occurs in the Qur'an: "God commands you as regards your children's (inheritance): to the male, a portion equal to that of two females..." (4:11). An example of actual (*fi'lī*) *'urf* is the "*bay' al-ṭa'āti*" (give-and-take sale) which is normally concluded without utterance of offer and acceptance.

Consequently, jurists have asserted that "the original meaning of the word is departed from with respect to current custom".[178] According to *al-Majallah,* "In the presence of custom, no regard is paid to the literal meaning of a thing".[179] For example, a man takes an oath and says: "If such-and-such happens, I will make sure my clothes press against Ka'ba." According to *qiyās,* however, no action needs to be taken, since there is no such act of worship as 'pressing one's clothes against the Ka'ba. Where *qiyās* focuses on the literal meaning, *istiḥsān* adopts the customary interpretation of the oath. The literal meaning of this oath is not that the person will give his clothes to charity, and indeed *istiḥsān* supports this.[180]

Actual custom (*'urf fi'lī*) consists of commonly recurrent practices that are accepted by the people, such as the ways in which payment is made on houses and shops; the payment of dowry in marriage, where a certain amount is paid at the time of the contract and the rest is paid later; the delivery of purchased commodities at a buyer's house or shop, and so on.[181]

'Urf, regardless of whether it is *qawlī* (verbal) or *fi'lī* (actual), is also divided into two types: *al-'āmm* (general) and *al-khāṣṣ* (particular): *'urf ām* denotes customs which are practiced by all, regardless of time and place; *'urf khāṣṣ* denotes customs which are particular to a certain country, locality or group.[182]

We now turn to examples of situations in which custom may be invoked as a reason to overturn an established legal ruling.

The importance of custom as a consideration in the formulation of law cannot be overestimated. Because of the dynamic nature of human custom, consideration of this principle is crucial.[183]

We have already indicated that custom is a valid source of Islamic law. According to *al-Majallah,* "Custom is an arbitrator: that is to say, custom, whether public or private, may be invoked to justify the giving of judgement".[184] This in turn is derived from the saying of the Prophet (ṣ) "What the Muslims deem to be good is good in the sight of God."[185]

Many issues fall within the remit of custom-based *istiḥsān:* contracts; *waqf* (endowment); public rights; personal rights and so on.

1. Shaybānī has pointed out, under the subject of usury, loans and the borrowing of money, that lending and borrowing bread between neighbours is permitted, based on the principle of *istiḥsān,* since everyday need has made it into a custom. Later, rulings were established by Ḥanafī jurists based on the opinion of Shaybānī. However, strictly speaking, and according to *naṣṣ,* goods exchanged must be of the same kind and of equal value; if not, shortage or surplus may lead to unlawful usury, thus annulling the contract.[186] However, even though the lending and borrowing of bread may not always involve exactly equal exchange, *istiḥsān* allows it on the ground of custom. Custom ignores small differences and only takes into the consideration the number of items involved,[187] thus ensuring that these the transactions remain fair. In the example of the lending and borrowing of bread, a slight discrepancy in the amount exchanged is not enough to warrant a charge of usury.

2. According to most Ḥanafī jurists, the conditions and stipulations inserted into contracts are recognised so long as they are accepted by society in general. This *istiḥsān* ruling is clearly based on custom. In fact, conditions and stipulations which are unacceptable to the majority are deemed invalid. This is in accordance with the general meaning of the *ḥadīth* "The Prophet (ṣ) has forbidden sales with stipulations".[188] For example, to stipulate handing back a house after staying in it for a month, or handing over a field after cultivating it for a year; selling something to someone on the condition that they later sell it back-all of these nullify the contract.[189] However, Ḥanafī jurists permit two exceptions to this Prophetic norm: a- stipulation of the freedom to choose, b- stipulations which are customary.[190]

According to most Ḥanafī scholars, such conditions should be recognised and considered. According to *al-Majallah,* "A matter recognised by custom is regarded as though it were a contractual obligation".[191] For example, according to established rule of *fiqh, waqf* (charitable endowment) is a "lasting" endowment that can only involve immovable property. Therefore, movable property, which is susceptible to damage and loss, is not to be included in *waqf.*[192] However, Shaybānī put aside this general rule and validated the *waqf* of movable goods such as books, in keeping with popular custom. The reason behind this is to encourage people to practice charity and do good works. Here, Shaybānī overrules *qiyās* and chooses *istiḥsān,* based on popular custom.[193]

3. *Bayʿ bi* al-wafā[194] (sale with right of return) was considered invalid before it was recognised by popular custom. Such a sale is considered to be permissible in view of the fact that the purchaser has a right to enjoy the goods he has purchased. It is also in the nature of an avoidable sale in as much as the two parties have the right to cancel it. It is also in the nature of a

pledge, in view of the fact that the purchaser cannot sell the property sold to any third party.[195]

i. This sale had been used commonly in the region of Bukhārā and Balkh as a valid sale because of people's needs since the 6th century. Nasafī (d. 537/1142) explains, saying "This is a kind of sale which people were accustomed to in order to avoid usury; however, in fact, it is a kind of pledge".[196] In this context, nullifying *naṣṣ* (text) and ignoring it is not an issue, since application of custom here is actually in keeping with the purpose of *naṣṣ* (text).[197]

4. According to most Ḥanafī jurists, the right to water (*ḥaqq al-shurb*) may not be sold on its own, independently of the agricultural land which is irrigated by it, owing to the ambiguity over the contract of such a sale. Obtaining ownership of water can occur only by actual possession; it can not be possessed while it is actually in the watercourse. However, some Ḥanafī jurists consider this permissible by way of *istiḥsān*, which is based on the customary approval of such a sale. In fact, the selling of the water on its own is against the general established ruling. Therefore, the new ruling is preferred by way of *istiḥsān* in respect of the common custom, and departs from the rule of *qiyās*.[198]

Conditions of validity of 'urf

Scholars assert that certain conditions must be fulfilled before custom (*'urf*) can be deemed valid.

1. The principle of *'urf* must be relevant and actually applicable; it must also be prevalent. As is indicated in *al-Majallah*, "Effect is only given to custom where it is of regular occurrence or when universally prevailing"[199] and "Effect is

given to what is of common occurrence; not to what happens infrequently".[200] These statements form important maxims of *fiqh*.

2. *'Urf* must be actually be in practice at the time of the case which is referred to it. To rule on the basis of past or future custom is invalid.[201] Ibn Nujaym says "The *'urf* connected to a case must be recent or current; possible future custom is not given any credence."[202]

3. Custom must not contradict evidence which is stronger than itself. If custom opposes a ruling of *naṣṣ*, and cannot be reconciled to it, then it is neither valid nor recognised. Hence, no ruling can be adopted on such kinds of custom.[203]

We now turn to those instances in which custom contradicts *naṣṣ* or other principles. Can such customs still be considered a valid source of law?

In this context, *'urf* may contradict *naṣṣ* in two ways. Firstly, it may contradict a specific *naṣṣ* involving a specific situation and meanings. Secondly, it may contradict the general *naṣṣ* involving general situations and meanings.

Opposition of 'urf to a specific naṣṣ

A specific *naṣṣ* is one which involves specific matters, for example, adultery, gambling, alcohol, usury, and so on. If such acts are customary in a society, the fact that they are *'urf* carries no weight or credence: these are acts which are outlawed by the Sharī'ah, and they are thus non-negotiable. Islam aims to abrogate some customs completely, to accept some of them as they are, or to rehabilitate some of them.[204] For example, regarding a contract which clearly contradicted a *ḥadīth*, Sarakhsī says: "An *'urf* which contradict a *naṣṣ* is not valid".[205]

The question which arises in this context is whether a specific *naṣṣ* can change a custom? Abū Ḥanīfah and Shaybānī preferred to follow a specific *naṣṣ* than custom. Abū Yūsuf, however, tended to prefer the custom.[206]

An example of scholarly disagreement concerned the *ḥadīth* about usury which stipulated that in lending and borrowing, the commodities exchanged had to be the same kind, amount and value: "Gold for gold, silver for silver, wheat for wheat, barley for barley, dates for dates, salt for salt and like for like".[207] Abū Ḥanīfah and Shaybānī were of the opinion that the *ḥadīth* must be followed to the letter. However, Abū Yūsuf points out that custom often dictates other ways of exchange in these circumstances, and that as long as it is acceptable to the people and considered normal, then there is nothing wrong with it. In this case, it is *'urf* and the habitual practice (*'ādat*) of the people that has to be taken into consideration. If the only difference between *'urf* and *naṣṣ* is, as in this example, one of details only, then it cannot be considered as an actual contradiction of the purpose of the *naṣṣ*.[208]

Abū Yūsuf's practice was to focus on the meaning of the text and understand the exact purpose of it by application of *'urf*, not by preferring *'urf* to text, or ignoring the text, or falsifying and confining its limits.[209]

The first type of opposition of *'urf* to *naṣṣ* is not considered valid since it is not in accord with the aims of the Sharī'ah. Therefore, it is not included within the scope of *istiḥsān*. The first thing for *istiḥsān* is that there must be valid evidence. However, Abū Yūsuf's judgement does not amount to *istiḥsān*.

Opposition of 'urf to a general naṣṣ

When a general *naṣṣ* contradicts an *'urf qawli* (verbal), the use of the latter in society is considered. For example, the people of a country may depart from the literal meaning of a word and become accustomed to understanding that word in a different context. For example, in some communities, the word 'food' is understood as referring to maybe no more than one or two foodstuffs, and they may be unaware of the vast range of things that the general word 'food' actually signifies. Thus the *naṣṣ* becomes particularized in accordance with the specific *'urf.* That specific *'urf* is then considered to be an exception to the general meaning of the *naṣṣ*. Jurists are in agreement on this issue. In this case, the general *naṣṣ* is interpreted according to the custom. The general *naṣṣ* is particularized by the custom in that its indication to a particular meaning is approved, based on *istiḥsān* according to Ḥanafis.[210] However, if the metaphorical meaning of a word becomes *'urf*, Ḥanafi jurists disagree as to which is to be preferred, the literal meaning or the metaphorical. According to Abū Ḥanīfah, the actual meaning is the preferable one, while Abū Yūsuf and Shaybānī prefer the metaphorical meaning that has become customary.[211]

For instance if someone vows to walk to the Ka'ba, then he has to fulfil either *ḥajj* or *'umrah*. This is the view point of Abū Yūsuf and Shaybānī. However, nothing is required according to Abū Ḥanifa based on *qiyās*. The reason why nothing is required is that a vow becomes obligatory if there is a customary act of worship available through which that vow may be fulfilled. In this context, there is no obligatory (*wājib*) duty of walking to Ka'ba, and so the vow is nullified. However, Abū Yūsuf and Shaybānī performed *istiḥsān*, claiming that 'walking to the Ka'ba was a customary way of meaning *ḥajj* or *'umrah*. Therefore, they preferred this custom to the actual meaning of the word.[212]

The main reason of the disagreement among Abū Yūsuf, Shaybānī and Abū Ḥanīfah concerns the availability of the one of the conditions of the validation of *'urf*, which is that "*'urf* must be in existence at the time a transaction is concluded". For the custom to be valid, it has to fulfil certain conditions; otherwise, it will be invalid.[213]

In actual custom (*'urf 'amalī*), the main point is to discover the *Shārī's* objectives. 'Alī Ḥaydar Afandī explaining the maxim "Custom is an arbitrator; that is to say, custom, whether public or private, may be invoked to justify the giving of judgement",[214] says "*'urf* (custom) and *ādat* (tradition), whether general (*'āmm*) or specific (*khāṣṣ*), are as a judge who validates the legal ruling".[215] Here it is indicated that *'urf* would take a role in determining legal rulings; however, it must not actually ignore *naṣṣ* or alter it. Where there are two contradictory proofs, the one which is more suitable and adequate to materialize the *Shārī's* purposes is preferred to the other. In fact, the conflict here is not between *'urf* and *naṣṣ*, but rather of two evidences.

The question which arises here is that if *'urf* is a type of specific custom, can it particularize the general *naṣṣ* or not? Most Ḥanafī scholars claim that a specific custom will not particularize the general *naṣṣ*. In order for a specific custom to be a source of law, it has to be in use everywhere.[216] According to *al-Majallah*, "Effect is only given to custom where it is of regular occurrence or when universally prevailing".[217] Nevertheless, al-Nasafī (d. 424/1033), and Ibn Nujaym (d. 970/1562) claim that the general *naṣṣ* maybe particularized by a specific *'urf*.[218]

However, specific *'urf* will not be valid if it contradicts *naṣṣ*.[219] Furthermore, if a custom does not wholly contradict a *naṣṣ* and there is thus a way to reconcile it with a *naṣṣ* or a *shar'ī* evidence, then it is considered as valid, based on one of the principles of *Sunnah Taqrīrī*, *ijmā'* (*ijmā' sukūtī*) or *ḍarurah*, and as was practised in the example of *bay'* al-wafā[220] (sale with right of return) and *istiṣnā'*. Otherwise, it would be rejected.[221]

Istiḥsān based on the opposition of 'urf to qiyās

This kind of *istiḥsān* becomes relevant when people are accustomed to practices that contradict a ruling of *qiyās* or an already established general ruling. Sarakhsī expresses the importance of custom by declaring that to obstruct people in their practice of what is customary is to do them much harm.[222] According to *al-Majallah,* "A matter established by custom is like a matter established by law."[223]

In Ḥanafī works there are many examples of this type of *istiḥsān,* some of which are included here:

1. According to the general established ruling of Abū Ḥanīfah, the endowment of movable property is not allowed. However, Abū Yūsuf allowed endowment of horses and war equipment based on the *athar* (practices) of the Companions. In addition, Shaybānī condoned the endowment of camels, axes, ropes, shovels, saws, cauldrons, clothes, funeral equipment, and the Qur'an—in short anything moveable which it was customary to endow. In this respect, he departed from *qiyās* in favour of custom. Later, many Ḥanafī scholars followed Shaybānī and gave judgements according to his opinion.[224]
2. In the case of *bay'* al-wafā, the practice was prevalent in order to meet people's needs without charging interest.[225] In fact, in Islamic law, pledging a condition in advance in order to benefit from that pledge is considered as a kind of *ribā* (interest) and is therefore not permitted. One interpretation of it is that it is a kind of "valid agreement" which a buyer has the right to benefit from; it is a kind of "nullified agreement" in respect of the buyer's right to nullify; and is a kind of "pledge agreement" in respect of the buyer's inability to sell the commodity. However, later it became a custom because of people's need and is therefore, based on the principle of

istiḥsān.[226] A similar transaction is *bay' al-istighlāl* (sale by sub-letting). According to *al-Majallah,* "A person may make a valid pledge of property borrowed from some third person, provided he has received the permission of that person. This is known as a pledge of a borrowed article".[227] These kinds of transaction have become a customary and are thus permitted by *istiḥsān.*[228]

3. According to Abū Ḥanīfah, selling bees and silkworms is not allowed, because at his time they were not a valuable commodity. Abū Ḥanīfah compared their sale to the sale of reptiles such as snakes and lizards. Abū Yūsuf's opinion is similar to Abū Ḥanīfah, although in the case of silkworms, he says that if they are used to make silk, then it is permitted. Despite Abū Ḥanīfah's opinion, Shaybānī departs from *qiyās* to *istiḥsān,* based on the judgment that the sale of such things had become customary among the people.[229]

Conclusion

Different scholars posit different typologies of *istiḥsān.* On the whole, it is divided into two main types **a**: analogical *istiḥsān*, which consists of a departure from *qiyās jalī* to *qiyās khafī,* and **b**: exceptional *istiḥsān* (*istiḥsān istithnā'ī*) which consists of making an exception to a general rule of existing law, and which is approved when the jurist is convinced that in making such an exceptions, justice might be better served.[230] Besides this main distinction, scholars divided *istiḥsān* into many different types and sub-types, as I have mentioned earlier.[231]

We can see that *istiḥsān* which is based on *naṣṣ*, *ijmā'* and *ḍarūrah* is not extendable to parallel cases when we compare the two main types of *istiḥsān,* namely the analogical and the exceptional. Ḥanafī jurists point out that the *qiyās khafī*, which they called *istiḥsān*, is in reality a kind of *qiyās* (analogy) and therefore its ruling can be extended (*ta'diyah*) to other cases.[232] In order to move a ruling of *qiyās*, the *'illah* must be the same in both cases. This is the ruling of the validated *qiyās*. *Ta'diyah* applying a ruling to other cases is an indispensable factor of *ijtihād*.[233] However, the ruling of *qiyās* is not extendable to similar cases if the applicability is uncertain or unreasonable. Despite this, *istiḥsān* which is based on implicit (*khafī*) analogy is extendable by further analogy to parallel cases.[234]

When we compare the Ḥanafī and Mālikī views of *istiḥsān*, we see that the Ḥanafī *istiḥsān* derives much of its substance largely from necessity (*ḍarūrah*). The Mālikī approach to *istiḥsān*, however, is based on *maṣlaḥah* and the removal of hardship (*raf' al-ḥarāj*). Despite the different methods they used to approach the problem, they eventually arrived at the same results. Their use of *maṣlaḥah* differs mainly in respect of the degree of importance they accord it. Ḥanafīs resorted to *istiḥsān* where there was conflict between obvious (*jalī*) and implicit (*khafī*) *qiyās* which inclined to a stronger evidence and necessity (*ḍarūrah*), while the Mālikīs were inclined to resort to *istiḥsān* where there was conflict between analogy and *maṣlaḥah*.[235]

A contemporary scholar, Kamālī, discusses the division of *istiḥsān* in the context of equity. He highlights the unnecessary classification and complains about the consideration of *istiḥsān* in the context of equity and fairness, which he says were not considered by the scholars. According to him, *istiḥsān* which is based on equity and consideration of fairness has not been given a separate category by either the Ḥanafīs or the Mālikīs. Instances of equitable *istiḥsān* often seem to have been subsumed under consideration of *raf' al-ḥaraj*. Removal of hardship is admittedly the nearest concept to that of equity and fairness; it has a definite Qur'anic identity and seems an eminently suitable basis for *istiḥsān*. Yet it is ironic that neither of these (i.e. equity and *raf' al-ḥaraj*) find a separate entry in the scholastic typology of *istiḥsān*. It seems that the *maṣlaḥah* based *istiḥsān* has a strong base of identity with *raf' al-ḥaraj*, and the *'ulamā'* do tend to almost equate the one with the other. This can also be said of custom (*'urf*) which is recognized as a proof precisely because acting on custom is in the spirit of *raf' al-ḥaraj*. Kamāli concludes that when both *maṣlaḥah* and custom are recognized as separate bases of *istiḥsān*, *raf' al-ḥaraj*, and also equity and fairness (*iḥsān*) could easily be added to the existing varieties of *istiḥsān*".[236]

As Kamālī indicates, equity and fairness are indeed concepts that would seem to be in conformity with *istiḥsān*. After all, linguistically it is derived from *iḥsān* (goodness), and connotes justice (*shar'iyyah*). Therefore, equity and fairness should be considered in a contemporary approach. The basis of *iḥsān* finds a sufficient support in the Qur'an: "Verily, God enjoins *al-'adl* (justice) and *iḥsān* (the doing of good and liberality) and giving (help) to kith and kin..." (16:90). According to Kamālī, the main differences between justice and *iḥsān* may be said to be that justice is the normal requirement which is to be administered under the Sharī'ah. *Iḥsān* on the other hand opens up the scope of justice under positive law to considerations of equity and good conscience, especially in cases where the application of normal rules may not actually secure justice. Then, one should act in the spirit of *iḥsān* and find a method that serves the ideas of Qur'anic justice, even if it entails a certain departure from specific rules.[237]

Notes

1. Ibn al-Humām, "*Taḥrīr*", vol. 4, p. 78; Bazdawī, "*Kashf*", vol. 4, pp. 3, 5-6; Jaṣṣāṣ, "*Al-Fuṣūl*" vol. 4, pp. 234, 243; Ṣadr al-Sharī'ah, "*Tawḍīḥ*", vol. 2, pp. 162-3.
2. Ibid., vol. 2, pp. 161-163.

3. Bazdawī, "*Uṣūl*", vol. 4, p. 3, 5-6. See Anṣārī, "*Fawātiḥ*" vol. 2, pp. 320-1; Sarakhsī, "*Uṣūl*", vol. 2, pp. 200, 202-3.
4. Khallaf, "*Maṣāder*", p. 72,
5. Ibn Nujaym, "*Fatḥ al-Ghaffār*"vol. 3, p. 30.
6. Shāṭibī, "*Al-Muwāfaqāt*", vol. 4, p. 208.
7. Sarakhsī, "*Uṣūl*", vol. 2, p. 200.
8. See Yūsuf, "*The Theory*", p. 111; also see Dönmez, "*Kaynak Kavramı*", p. 132.
9. Sarakhsī, "*Uṣūl*", vol. 2, p. 200.
10. Dönmez, "*Kaynak Kavramı*", p. 132; 'Alī Bakkal, "*İslam Hukukunda Hikmet, İllet ve İctimā'i Vākıa Munasebetlerinin Hukuki Neticeleri*", unpublished PhD dissertation, (Erzurum: 1986), p. 333.
11. Jaṣṣāṣ, "*Fusūl*", vol. 4, p. 233.
12. Khallāf, "*Masāder*", p. 72.
13. Ḥasan, "*Analogical reasoning*", p. 92.
14. Bazdawī, "*Uṣūl*", vol. 4, p. 6; Sarakhsī, "*Uṣūl*", vol. 2, p. 203
15. Sarakhsī, "*Uṣūl*", vol. 2, pp. 202-3, 206; Bazdawī, "*Uṣūl*", vol. 4, pp. 3, 6, 10; Nasafī, "*Kashf*", vol. 2, p. 296; Ṣadr al-Sharī'ah, "*Tawḍīḥ*", vol. 2, pp. 162, 169.
16. 19. Karamastī, "*Al-Wajīz*" p. 185; Bazdawī, "*Uṣūl*", vol. 3, p. 389; Sarakhsī, "*Uṣūl*", vol. 2, pp. 192, 206; Bukhārī, "*Kashf*", vol.3, p. 389; vol. 2, p. 11.
17. Sha'bān, "*İslam Hukuk İlminin Esasları*", p. 168; Khallāf, "*Masāder*", p. 72.
18. Ibn al-Humām, "*Fatḥ al-Qadīr*", vol. 6, p. 215; Khallāf, "*Masāder*", pp. 72-3; Sha'bān "*İslam Hukuk İlminin Esasları*" p. 168.
19. Bayḥāqī, "*Al-Sunan al-Kubrā*", vol. 7, pp. 371, 418; Ibn Ḥajar, "*Fatḥ al-Bārī*", vol. 9, p. 392; Ḥākim, "*Al-Mustadrak*", vol. 2, p. 458; Ibn Abī Shaybah, "*Al-Muṣannaf*", v. 4, p. 199.
20. Jaṣṣāṣ, "*Fuṣūl*", vol. 4, pp. 234-236, Sarakhsī, "*Uṣūl*", vol. 2, p. 202.
21. Sarakhsī, "*Uṣūl*", vol. 2, p. 201; Jaṣṣāṣ, "*Fuṣūl*", vol. 4, p. 238.
22. Jaṣṣāṣ, "*Fuṣūl*" vol. 4, p. 239.
23. Salam: This is an investment as a forward sale contract involving the current payment for assets to be delivered in the future. The goods or assets to be purchased do not need to be in existence or in completed

form at the time of contracting, but must be ascertainable. The Prophet (ṣ) said: "Whoever concludes salam, let him do so over a specified measure, specified weight and specified period of time". See Bukhārī, "*Ṣaḥīḥ*", ḥadīth no: 441, vol. 3, p. 243.

24. Conditions of Salam: 1. It is necessary for the validity of salam that the buyer pays the price in full to the seller at the time of the sale. In the absence of full payment, it will be tantamount to sale of a debt against a debt, which is expressly prohibited by the Holy Prophet (ṣ). Moreover, the basic wisdom for allowing salam is to fulfil the «instant need» of the seller. If it is not paid in full, the basic purpose will not be achieved. 2. Only those goods can be sold through a salam contract in which the quantity and quality can be exactly specified. Precious stones cannot be sold on the basis of salam because each stone differs in quality, size, weight and their exact specification is not possible. 3. Salam cannot be effected on a particular commodity or on a product of a particular field or farm e.g. Supply of wheat of a particular field or the fruit of a particular tree since there is a possibility that the crop will be destroyed before delivery and given such a possibility, the delivery remains uncertain. 4. All details in respect to quality of goods sold must be expressly specified leaving no ambiguity which may lead to a dispute. 5. It is necessary that the quantity of the commodity be agreed upon in absolute terms. It should be measured or weighed in its usual measure only, meaning what is normally weighed cannot be quantified and vice versa. 6. The exact date and place of delivery must be specified in the contract. 7. Salam cannot be effected in respect of things which must be delivered on the spot. 8. The commodity for salam contract should remain in the market right from the day of contract up to the date of delivery. 9. The time of delivery should be at least fifteen days or one month from the date of the agreement. The price in salam is generally lower than the price in a spot sale. The period should be long enough to affect prices. But Ḥanafi fiqh does not specify any minimum period for the validity of salam. It is alright to have an earlier date of delivery if the seller consents to it. 10. Since the price in salam is generally lower than the price in a spot sale, the difference in the two prices may be a valid profit for the Bank. 11. A security in the form of a guarantee, mortgage or hypothecation may be required for a salam in order to ensure that the seller delivers. 12. The seller at the time of delivery delivers commodities and not money to the buyer who would have to establish a special cell for dealing in commodities. See: Meezan Bank: salam: *http://www.meezanbank.com/knowledge-islamic-section-4-5.asp*.

25. Shaybānī, "*Al-Aṣl*", vol. 5, pp. 42-3.

26. Bakkal, "*Neticeleri*", pp. 348-9.
27. Sha'bān, "*İslam Hukuk İlminin Esasları*", p. 265.
28. Sha'bān, ibid., p. 266.
29. This term was translated as specification, particularization, specialization or limitation. George Makdisi used it in the meaning for "limitation". See Makdisi "*Ibn Taymiyyah Authograph Manuscript on Istiḥsān" in the Arabic And Islamic Studies In Honor of Hamilton A. R. Gibb*, (Cambridge: Harward University Press, 1965), p. 446.
30. Atar, "*Fıkıh Uṣulü*", p. 195; Sha'bān, ibid., p. 297.
31. Ibn Taymiyyah, "*Mas'alah*", pp. 457-8.
32. Abū Dāwūd, "*Ṭahārah*", 41.
33. Sha'bān, ibid., p. 299.
34. Shāṭibī, "*Al-Muwāfaqāt*", vol. 4, p. 208.
35. Ismā'īl, "*Uṣūl*", vol. 2, p. 77.
36. Ibn Humam, "*Fatḥ al-Qadīr*", vol. 4, p. 299; Khallāf, "*Masāder*", p. 72; Ismāīl, "*Uṣūl*", vol. 2, p. 79.
37. Abū Dāwud, "*Sunan*", vol. 3, pp. 426-7.
38. Ibn Qudāmah, "*Rawdat*", vol. 10, pp. 288-9
39. Zaydān, "*Al-Wajīz*" p. 232.
40. Ibn Humām, "*Fatḥ al-Qadīr*", vol. 6, p. 201.
41. Molla Jiwān, "*Sharh Nūr al-Anwār*", vol. 6, p. 164.
42. Sarakhsī, "*Al-Mabsūṭ*", vol. 4, pp. 93, 130, vol. 8, p. 140, vol. 9, p. 121, vol. 12, p. 129, vol. 13, p. 99, 137, vol. 26, pp. 127, 190.
43. Sarakhsī, "*Al-Mabsūṭ*", vol. 3, p. 113, vol. 4, p. 168, vol. 10, pp. 126, 127, vol. 11, p. 5, vol. 12, p. 62, vol. 14, p. 123, vol. 15, p. 50, vol. 17, p. 83, vol. 23, p. 124.
44. Sarakhsī, "*Al-Mabsūṭ*", vol. 10, pp. 36, 75, vol. 11, pp. 25, 142, 251, vol. 12, p. 12, 145, vol. 14, p. 133, vol. 15, p. 131, vol. 19, p. 151, vol. 23, p. 124.
45. Abū Yūsuf, "*Al-Kharāj*", p. 189; Sarakhsī, "*Al-Mabsūṭ*", vol. 9, p. 76, vol. 11, pp. 27, 88.
46. Athar literally means the remains of something the plural is āthār and uthūr. See Ibn Manzūr, "*Lisān al-'Arab*", vol. 4, pp. 5-6; Al-Zābidī, "*Tāj al-'Arūs min Jawāhir al-Qāmūs*", vol. 10, pp. 12-14, Fīrīzabādī "*Qāmus al-Muḥīṭ*", pp. 435, 436. In the science of ḥadīth it is used with the same meaning of khabar and tradition (ḥadīth). Athar not only contains

the acta dicta, sayings and taqrīrs of the Prophet (ṣ), but also contains akhbār which is related to the Companions. Some scholars have named their books athar, e.g. as Al-Shaybānī's "*Al Athar*" which contains the narrations from the Prophet (ṣ) and the Companions. Also Tahawī called his book, "*Sharḥ al-Ma'ānī athar*" which contains the same ḥadiths, al-Bayḥākī (d. 458/1066) also called his book "*Ma'rifah al-Sunan wa al-Athar*". See Sahawī, Abū 'Abd Allah Muḥamad,"*Fatḥ al-Mughis bi Sharḥi Alfiyat al-Ḥadīth li al-Irāqiyyah*", edited by 'Alī Ḥusayn 'Alī, (Dār al-Imām al-Ṭabarī, 1992), vol. 1, pp. 123-125; Jalāl al-Dīn 'Abd al-Raḥmān Suyūṭī, "*Tadrīb al-Rāwī fi Sharḥi Taqrīb al-Rāwī*", edited by 'Abd al-Wahhāb 'Abd al-Lāṭīf, (Beirut: Dār al-Iḥyā' al-Sunan al-Nabawiyyah, 1979), vol. 1, pp. 184-5.

47. Sahawī, "*Fatḥ al-Mughīth*", vol. 1, pp. 124-5.

48. Bazdawī, "*Uṣūl*", vol. 4, p. 5, 10, Ṣadr al-Sharī'ah "*Tawdīḥ*", vol. 2, p. 163; Jaṣṣāṣ, "*Fuṣūl*", vol. 4, p. 246,-7; Ḥādimī, "*Majāmi' al-Ḥaqāiq*" , p. 234; Karamastī ,"*Al-Wajīz*", p. 187; Molla Husraw "*Mir'āt al-Uṣūl*", p. 336; Nasafī, "*Kashf*", vol. 2, pp. 290, 296; Ibn Kamāl,"*Taghāyīr al-Tanqīḥ fī al-Uṣūl*", p. 192.

49. Sarakhsī, "*Al-Mabsūṭ*", vol. 26, p. 127; Abū Yūsuf, "*Al-Kharāj*", p. 178.

50. Shāṭibī, "*Al-Muwāfaqāt*", vol. 4, p. 208; Shāṭibī, "*Al-I'tiṣām*", vol. 2, p. 139.

51. The first three types of Istiḥsān have been mentioned in the book "*Al-I'tiṣām*" vol. 2, p. 139, and the last one which is ijmā' (consensus) is mentioned in the book of "*Al-Muwāfaqāt*", vol. 4, p. 208.

52. Khallāf, "*Maṣāder*", p. 75.

53. Ibid.

54. Bazdawī, "*Kashf*",vol. 4, p. 5.

55. Sarakhsī, "*Uṣūl*", vol. 2, p. 202.

56. Mutawātir: literally means continuously recurrent. In the present context, it means a report by an indefinite number of people related in such a way as to preclude the possibility of their agreement to perpetuate a lie. Such a possibility is inconceivable owing to their large number, diversity of residence, and reliability. See Kamālī, "*Principles*", p. 68; Khudarī, "*Uṣūl*", p. 214; Aghnides Nicolas P. "*Muhammedan Theories of Finance*", (New York: Longmans Green & Co. 1916), reprint, (Lahore: Premier Book House, 1957), p: 40.

57. Mashhūr: is defined as a ḥadīth which is originally reported by one, two or more Companions from the Prophet (ṣ) or from another Companion but which has later become well-known and transmitted

by an indefinite number of people. See: Aghnides, "*Muhammedan Theories*", p. 44; Abū Zahrah, "*Uṣūl*", p. 84.

58. Sarakhsī, "*Uṣūl*", v. 1, p. 282; Bazdawī, "*Uṣūl*", vol. 2, pp. 360-369.
59. Sarakhsī, "*Uṣūl*", vol. 1, p. 321; Nasafī, "*Kashf*", vol. 2, p. 14; Bazdawī, "*Uṣūl*", vol. 2, p. 370.
60. Preferring an Isolated tradition (khabar al-wāḥīd), which is narrated by a just and honest narrator, to qiyās (analogy) is also considered a kind of istiḥsān and therefore it is disputable.
61. Zarqā, "*Al-Madkhal*", vol. 1, pp. 85-6.
62. Taftazānī, "*Al-Talwīḥ*" vol. 2, pp. 163-4.
63. Sarakhsī, "*Al-Mabsūṭ*", vol. 9, p. 204.
64. Marghinānī, "*Al-Hidāyah*", vol. 1, p. 127.
65. Yavuz, "*İctihad Felsefesi*", pp. 313-4; Sarakhsī, "*Al-Mabsūṭ*", vol. 5, p. 206.
66. Jaṣṣāṣ, "*Fuṣūl*" vol. 4, p. 116; Sarakhsī, "*Al-Mabsūṭ*", vol. 3, p. 65.
67. Ibn Rushd, "*Bidāyat al Mujtahid*" vol. 1, p. 303.
68. Shawkanī, "*Nayl al-Awṭār*", vol. 4, p. 231.
69. Kāṣānī, "*Badāī' al-Ṣanāī'*", vol. 2, p. 90; Dihlawī, "*Ḥujjat Allah al-Bālighah*", vol. 1, p. 161; Shaibānī, "*Al-Ḥujjah*" vol. 1, p. 392; Haytamī, "*Al-Ḥayāt al-Ḥisān*", p. 104.
70. Sarakhsī, "*Al-Mabsūṭ*" vol. 4, p. 93.
71. Abū Dāwūd, "*Buyū'*", 70.
72. Bukhārī, "*Ṣaḥīḥ*", ḥadīth no: 441, vol. 3, p. 243; Muslim, "*Musāqāt*", 25; Abū Dāwūd "*Buyū'*", 57.
73. Nasafī, "*Kashf*", vol. 2, p. 291; Sarakhsī, "*Uṣūl*", vol. 2, p. 203.
74. Suyūṭī, "*Tadrib al-Rāwī*" vol. 1, pp. 184-18; Saḥawī, "*Fatḥ al-Mughīth*" vol. 1, pp. 123-125.
75. Nasafī, "*Kashf*", vol. 2, p. 177; Ibn Humām, "*Taḥrīr*", v. 3, p. 133; Anṣārī, "*Fawātiḥ al-Raḥamūt*", vol. 2, p. 186.
76. Abū Yūsuf, "*Al-Kharāj*", p. 178; Ḥassan, "*The Early*" p. 146.
77. Jaṣṣāṣ, "*Fuṣūl*", vol. 3, p. 361.
78. Mālik, "*Muwaṭṭā'*", vol. 2, p. 871; Bayḥāqī, "*Sunan*", vol. 8, pp. 40-41; Ibn Abī Shaybah, "*Al-Musannaf*", vol. 5, p. 410, 429; Sarakhsī, "*Al-Mabsūṭ*", vol. 26, p. 127; Zaylāī, "*Nasb al-Rā'yah*" v. 4, p. 353.

79. For more about ijmā‘ see in the Introductory Chapter.
80. Ṣadr al-Sharī‘ah, "*Al-Tawḍīḥ*", vol. 2, p. 41; Bukhārī, "*Kashf*", vol. 2, p. 227; Āmidī, "*Iḥkām*", vol. 1, p. 196; Ghazālī, "*Mustaṣfā*", vol. 1, p. 110; Qarafī, "*Sharḥ*", p. 141.
81. Istiṣnā‘: This is the giving of an order to a labourer or artisan to make a definite article with agreement to pay a definite price for that article when made. See Ṣāleḥ A. Nabīl, "*Unlawful gain and legitimate profit in Islamic law*", (Cambridge: University Press, 1986), p. 61.
82. Abū Dāwūd, "*Buyū‘*", 70; Taḥawī, "*Sharḥ*" vol. 4, pp. 38, 40.
83. Nasafī, "*Kashf*", vol. 2, p. 292; Ibn Malak, "*Sharḥ*", p. 813.
84. Sarakhsī, "*Uṣūl*", vol. 2, p. 203.
85. Shāṭibī, "*I‘tiṣām*", vol. 2, p. 319; Āmidī, "*Iḥkām*", vol. 1, p. 214; Ibn Ḥanbal, "*Al-Musnad*", vol. 1, p. 379; Ḥākim, "*Mustadrak*", vol. 3, p. 83; Tabarānī "*Al-Mū‘jam*", vol. 4, p. 58.
86. Ibn Mājah, "*Sunan*", in abwāb al-fitan, 8; Ḥakim, "*Mustadrak*" vol. 1, pp. 200-1.
87. Bukhārī, "*Zakāt*", 1; Muslim, "*Īmān*", 8.
88. Sarakhsī, "*Al-Mabsūṭ*", vol. 5, p. 49.
89. For more about tacit consensus, see the Introduction Chapter.
90. Iḥram: the ritual garment worn for ḥajj.
91. Sarakhsī, "*Al-Mabsūṭ*", vol. 4, p. 79.
92. Shāṭibī, "*Al-Muwāfaqāt*", vol. 4, p. 208; Shāṭibī, "*Al-I‘tiṣām*", vol. 2, p. 139.
93. Fīrūzabādī, "*Qāmūs*", p. 550.
94. Ibn Manzūr, "*Lisān*", vol. 4, p. 484.
95. See also Qur'an, 2:173; 16:115; 5:3.
96. Jaṣṣāṣ, "*Aḥkām*", vol. 1, pp. 156,159.
97. Ikrāh: al-ikrāh means forcing someone to do or say something against his will. See: Nyazee, "*Theories of Islamic Law*" p. 100. The coerced person is called "*mukrah*". Its opposite is al-Ikhtiyār which means choice, free wills. The juristic scholars have defined it as follows: "Forcing somebody to something which he had never agreed to do, and never will desire to do while he had free choice." See Taftazānī, "*Talwīh*", vol. 2, p. 196; also see in "*Kashf al-Asrār*": "the person threatening is capable of that thing which he threatens: a threat which the coerced person is really frightened of." See vol. 3, p. 1503.

If this coercion accompanies threats to kill or destroy some parts of the body, then it is called "*ikrāh muljī*". Tortures by robbers or oppressors would constitute "*ikrāh muljī*". At such instances, it becomes necessary to carry out their commands. Coercion through jailing or beating is called light coercion. Anyone who is faced with light coercion is not permitted to bow to the oppressor's commands. Thus ikrāh is divided in to two types a: *ikrāh muljī*: someone threats to kill or destroy some parts of the body or deliver a strong blow, b: ikrāh ghairi muljī: someone makes a threat lower than that, for example jailing or beating. There are some conditions: 1- The person who threatens must be capable of carrying out the threat and must be serious in his in threat. 2- The threatened person has overpowering assumption to go ahead with the action. 3- Coercion must involve the threat to kill or destroy some parts of the body. 4- The coercion must be a serious hazard. 5- It must be directed to the five essential values of human life, which are religion, life, intellect, lineage, and property. 6- ikrah must be unjust, otherwise it is not considered as an ikrāh. See Saymen, "*Borçlar Hukuku*", vol. 1, p. 276; Bukhāri, "*Kashf*", vol. 4, p. 1502; Ibn al-Qudāmah "*Al-Mughnī*", vol. 7, p. 120; Shīrāzī, "*Al-Muhazzab*" vol. 2, p. 83.

98. Bukhārī, "*Kashf*" vol. 4, p. 398.

99. Bukhārī, "*Kashf*" vol. 4, p. 398

100. Saraksī, "*Al-Mabsūṭ*", vol. 24, pp. 46, 48, 49-50.

101. Al-Majallah al-Aḥkām al-Adliyyah (the Ottoman courts manual (Ḥanafī): clause: 21; Ibn Nujām, "*Al-Ashbāh*", p. 85.

102. Anṣārī, "*Fawātiḥ*", vol. 2, p. 262.

103. 'Alī Ḥaydar, "*Sharḥ al-Qawāid*", p. 76.

104. Shāṭibī, "*Al-Muwāfaqāt*", vol. 1, p. 476.

105. Ibn Mubārak, "*Nazariyyāt al-Ḍarūrah*" p. 28.

106. Anṣārī, "*Fawātiḥ*", vol. 2, p. 262.

107. Aḥmad Zarkā (d. 1938), "*Sharḥ Qawāid al-Fiqhīyyah*", (Beirut: 1983), p. 155.

108. Suyūṭī, "*Al-Ashbāh*", vol. 1, p. 191; Zarkā, "*Sharḥ Qawāid*" pp. 155-158; Ibn Humayd, pp. 175-182, Ibn Nujāym, "*Al-Ashbāh*" pp. 91-2.

109. Al-Majallah al-Aḥkām: clause: 32.

110. Sarakhsī, "*Al-Mabsūṭ*", vol. 11, p. 141, vol. 12, pp. 62, 139, vol. 14, p. 133, vol. 23, pp. 45-47.

111. Al-Majallah: clause: 21.

112. Suyūṭī, "*Al-Ashbāh*", vol. 1, p. 165.

113. Ibn Mājah, "*Sunan*", ḥadīth no. 2340, vol. 2, p. 784.

114. Returning the goods is only for the reason of avoiding harm (ḍarar) for the customer.

115. The goal of freedom of choice is to avoid harm and to protect people's honour and properties, and to prevent oppression and cheating. The freedom of choice is based on the Prophet's (ṣ) saying, "The buyer and seller are on option till they do not become separate till they choose". See Fazl al-Karīm "*Mishkāt al-Maṣābiḥ*", (Karachi: Dār al-Isḥāt, 1994), vol. 2, p. 272.

116. See Qur'an: 2:179: "And there is (a saving of) life for you in (Al-Qaṣāṣ) the law of equality in punishment, o men of understanding, that you may become Al-Muttaqūn (the pious)."

117. Suyūṭī, "*Al-Ashbāh*", vol. 1, p. 168.

118. Ibn Manzūr, "*Lisān*", vol. 2, pp. 233-235; Fīrūzabādī, "*Al-Qāmūs*", pp. 234-235; Zabīdī, "*Tājj*" vol. 5, pp. 473-476.

119. Ibn Humayd "*Raf' al-Ḥarāj*", p. 47

120. Ibid., p. 48.

121. For more examples see: Sarakhsī, "*Al-Mabsūṭ*", vol. 11, pp. 25, 159, 251; vol. 25, pp. 131, 160

122. Bāhusayn, "*Raf' al-Ḥarāj*", p. 6.

123. See also Qur'an: 4:28; 5:67; 30:30.

124. See also Qur'an: 2:286, 5:6; 7:42; 22:78; 24:61; 33:37.

125. Ibn Ḥanbal, "*Al-Musnad*", ḥadīth no. 15942, vol. 3, p. 582.

126. Suyūṭī, "*Al-Ashbāh*", p. 157; Zarka, "*Sharḥ al-Qawāid*", p. 111; Al-Majallah: clause: 18.

127. 'Alī Ḥaydar, "*Sharḥ al-Qawāid*", p. 72.

128. Zarkā, "*Sharḥ al-Qawāid*", p. 111; 'Alī Ḥaydar, "*Sharḥ al-Qawāid*", p. 72; Al-Majallah: clause: 24.

129. See Al-Majallah: clause 17.

130. Ibn Manzūr, "*Lisān*", vol. 10, pp. 181-184; Fīrūzabādī, "*Al-Qāmūs*", p. 1159; Zābidī, "*Tājj*", vol. 25, pp. 511-2.

131. Al-Majallah: clause: 17.

132. Alī Ḥaydar, "*Durar al-Ḥukkām*", p. 70.

133. See Qur'an: 22:78.

134. Ibn Ḥanbal, "*Al-Musnad*", ḥadīth no. 15942, vol. 3, p. 582; and the similar meanings see ibid., ḥadīth no. 22354, vol. 5, p. 314; ibid., ḥadīth no 24908, vol. 6, p. 130; Tabarānī, "*Al-Awsaṭ*", ḥadīth no. 1006, vol. 1, p. 300-1,; Bukhārī, "*Al-Wuḍū*", ḥadīth no. 220, vol. 1, p. 386; Abū Dāwūd, "*Al-Tahārah*", ḥadīth no. 380, vol. 1, p. 101; ibid, "*Al'Ilm*", ḥadīth. 69, vol. 1, p. 196; Muslim, "*Al-Jihād*", vol. 3, p. 1359.

135. Suyūṭī, "*Al-Ashbāh*", vol. 1, pp. 158-162; Ibn Nujaym, "*Al-Ashbāh*", pp. 75-78; for more on this see. Aḥmad Zarkā (d. 1938), "*Sharḥ al-Qawāid*", pp. 105-109.

136. Shāṭībī, "*Al-Muwāfaqāt*", in Turkish translation, "*İslāmi İlimler Metodolojisi*", by Mehmet Erdoğan, (İstanbul: iz yayıncılık, 1999), vol. 1, p. 336.

137. Suyūṭī, "*Al-Ashbāh*", vol. 1, p. 162; Ibn Nujaym, "*Al-Ashbāh*", p. 82; Zarkā, "*Sharḥ al-Qawāid*", p. 105; Jum'a "*Raf' al-Ḥarāj*", pp. 35-36.

138. Tayammum: to wash with clean sand or earth where water is unavailable.

139. Suyūṭī, "*Al-Ashbāh*", vol. 1, p. 162.

140. Ibn Nujāym, "*Al-Ashbāh*", pp. 82-3.

141. Zuhaylī, "*Nazariyyāt*", p. 202, for more on this see Ibn Mubārak, "*Nazariyyāt al-Ḍarūrah*", pp. 51-59; Ibn Humayd, "*Raf' al-Ḥarāj*", pp. 33-41.

142. Zuhaylī, "*Ḍarūrah*", p. 69; Ibn Mubārak, "*Ḍarūrah*" p. 312.

143. Al-Majallah: clause: 74.

144. Zuhaylī, ibid., p. 70; Ibn Mubārak, ibid., p. 305.

145. Ibn Mubārak, ibid., p. 319; Bāhusayn, "*Raf' al-Ḥarāj*", p. 602.

146. Al-Majallah: clause: 21.

147. Ibid., pp. 87-90.

148. Ibid., p. 90.

149. Zarkā, "*Çağdaş Yaklaşımla İslam Hukuku*", trans. Servet Armağan, (İstanbul: Timaş, 1993), vol. 2, p. 689.

150. Haskafī, "*Al-Durar*", clause: Ikrāh, (Beirut: 1979), vol. 5, p. 85.

151. Al-Majallah: clause: 26 for more on this see Zarkā, ibid., vol. 2, pp. 681-683.

152. Al-Majallah: clause: 27.

153. Ibid., 28.

154. Ibid., 29.

155. Ibid., 30.

156. Zuhaylī, "*Ḍarūrah*", p. 71, Ibn Mubārak, "*Ḍarūrah*", p. 336; Bāhusayn, "*Ḍarūrah*", pp. 602-3.

157. Suyūṭī, "*Al-Ashbāh*", vol. 1, p. 170; Al-Majallah: clause: 22.

158. Ibid., 23.

159. Suyūṭī, ibid., vol. 1, p. 178; Al-Majallah: clause: 25.

160. Al-Majallah: clause: 33; Ḥādimī, "*Majāmi' al-Ḥaqāiq*", p. 312.

161. Ibn al-Humām, "*Fatḥ al-Qadīr*", vol. 7, pp. 461-2; Ibn Abidīn, "*Radd al-Mukhtār*", vol. 5, p. 499.

162. Sarakhsī, "*Uṣūl*", vol. 2, p. 203; Bukhārī, "*Kashf al-Asrār*", vol. 4, p. 6.

163. Sarakhsī, "*Al-Mabsūṭ*", vol. 11, p. 251; Marghinānī, "*Al-Hidāyah*", vol. 4, p. 122.

164. Ibn Humām, "*Fatḥ al-Qadīr*", vol. 6, pp. 372-3.

165. For more on maṣlaḥah see Ramaḍan al-Būtī, "*Dawābiṭ*"; Muṣtafa Zayd, "*Al-Maṣlaḥah*"; Ḥusayn Ḥāmid Ḥasan, "*Nazariyyāt al-Maṣlaḥah*"; Şener, "*İslam Hukukunun Kaynaklarından Kıyas, İstiḥsān ve İstiṣlāḥ*", pp. 137-156; Zarkā, "*Al-Istiṣlāḥ wa al-Maṣāliḥ al-Mursalah*"; Sa'd Muḥammad al-Sanawī, "*Madai' Ḥājāt li al-Aḥdi bi Nazariyyāt al-Maṣlaḥah al-Mursalah fī al-Fiqh al-Islāmī*", (Cairo: 1981); Ferhat Koca, "İslam Hukukunda Maṣlaḥah Mursalah wa Najm al-Dīn al-Ṭūfī'nin bu konudaki görüşlerinin değerlendirilmesi", *ILAM araştırma dergisi*, vol. 1, no. 1 (January-June 1996), pp. 93-116; Jamāl al-Dīn 'Abd al-Raḥmān, "*Al-Maṣlaḥah al-Mursalah wa makānātuhā fī al-Tashri'*", (Cairo: Dār al-Kitāb al-Jāmi', 1983).

166. Marghinānī, "*Al-Hidāyah*", vol. 4, pp. 211-2.

167. Ibn 'Abidīn, "*Radd al-Mukhtār*", vol. 3, pp. 146-7; Ibn Humām, "*Fatḥ al-Qadīr*", vol. 3, p. 373.

168. Marghinānī, "*Al-Hidāyah*", vol. 3, p. 109; Sarakhsī, "*Al-Mabsūṭ*", vol. 15, p. 21; Kāsānī, "*Badāi al-Sanāi*" vol. 6, p. 264, vol. 7, pp. 28-9.

169. Saffet Köse, "*İslam Hukukunda Hakkın Kötüye Kullanılması*", (İstanbul: 1997), p. 199.

170. Ibn Humām, "*Fatḥ al-Qadīr*", vol. 7, pp. 326-7; Zaylāī, "*Ta'yīn al-Ḥaqāiq*" vol. 4, pp. 195-6; Haskafī, "*Durar al-Mukhtār*", vol. 5, pp. 443-448.

171. Sarakhsī, "*Al-Mabsūṭ*", vol. 23, p. 45.

172. Musāqāt: This is a lease contract for palm gardens in which one partner provides the land and seed and the other the oxen and labour.

173. Khallāf, "*Maṣāder*", p. 146; Ibn 'Abidīn, "*Nashr al-'Urf*", vol. 2, p. 116.

174. Abū Sunnah, "*Al-'Urf wa al-'Ādah*", p. 18; Zarkā, "*Al-Madkhal*", vol. 2, p. 845; 'Alī Ḥaydar, "*Sharḥ al-Qawāid al-Kulliyyah*", p. 95; İzmirli, "*'Ilmi Khilāf*", p. 110.

175. Zarkā, ibid., vol. 2, p. 845.

176. Sarakhsī, "*Uṣūl*", vol. 1, p. 190.

177. Karaman, "Ādāt", *Türkiye Diyanet Vakfı İslam Ansiklopedisi (DIA)*, vol. 1, p. 370.

178. Sarakhsī, "*Uṣūl*", vol. 1, p. 190; Nasafī, "*Kashf*", vol. 1, p. 267; Ibn Nujāym, "*Al-Ashbāh*", p. 93.

179. Al-Majallah clause: 40.

180. Bukhari, "*Kashf*", vol. 2, p. 97.

181. Zarkā, "*Al-Madkhal*", vol. 2, pp. 846-7.

182. Abu Sunnah, ibid., p. 19; 'Alī Ḥaydar, "*Sharḥ al-Qawāid*" pp. 93-4; Ibn 'Abidīn "*Nashr al-'Urf*", vol. 2, pp. 116, 132; İzmirli "*Ilmi Khilāf*", p. 110.

183. Zarkā, "*Al-Madkhal*", vol. 2, p. 850; Karaman, "Adet", *Türkiye Diyanet Vakfı İslam Ansiklopedisi*, vol. 1, pp. 369-372.

184. Al-Majallah clause: 36.

185. Shāṭibī, "*I'tiṣām*", vol. 2, p. 319; Suyūṭī, "*Al-Ashbah*", vol. 1, p. 193; Āmidī, "*Iḥkām*", vol. 1, p. 214.

186. Ibn Humām, "*Fatḥ al-Qadīr*", vol. 7, p. 37; Ibn 'Abidīn, "*Radd al-Mukhtār*", vol. 5, p. 185.

187. Ibn 'Abidīn, "*Radd al-Mukhtār*", vol. 5, p. 185.

188. Zaylāī, "*Naṣb al-Rā'ya*", vol. 4, pp. 17-18; Tirmīzī, "*Buyū'*", 19.

189. Zarkā, "*Al-Madkhal*", vol. 2, pp. 905-6.

190. Zarkā, "*Al-Madkhal*", vol. 2, p. 906; Al-Majallah clause: 186: (If a contract of a sale is concluded with an essential condition attached, both sale and condition are valid), 188: (In the case of a sale concluded subject to a condition sanctioned by custom established and recognised is a particular locality, both sale and condition are valid.), 300: (The vendor, or the purchaser, or both, may insert a condition in the contract of sale giving them an option, within a fixed period, to cancel the sale or to ratify it by carrying out the term thereof).

191. Al-Majallah clause: 43.

192. Zaydān, "*İslam Hukukuna Giriş*", trans 'Alī Şafak, (İstanbul: Kayıhan Yayınları, 1985), p. 305.

193. Sa'bān, "*İslam Hukuk İlminin Esasları*", p. 170; Kamālī, "*Istiḥsān*", pp. 55-6.

194. A sale subject to a right of redemption is a sale in which one person sells property to another for a certain sum of money, subject to the right of redeeming such property, upon the price thereof being returned.

195. Karaman, "*Anahatlarıyla İslam Hukuku*", vol. 3, p. 271; Al-Majallah clause: 118.

196. Ibn 'Abidīn,"*Radd al-Mukhtār*", vol. 5, p. 276.

197. Ibn 'Abidīn, "*Nashr al-'Urf*", vol. 2, p. 121; Zarkā, "*Al-Madkhal*", vol. 2, pp. 907-8.

198. Sa'bān, "*İslam Hukuk İlminin Esasları*", p. 171

199. Al-Majallah, clause: 41.

200. Ibid., 42.

201. Abū Sunnah, "*Al-'Urf*", p. 65; İzmirlī, "*'Ilmi Khilāf*", p. 116.

202. Ibn Nujāym, "*Al-Ashbah*", p. 101.

203. Abū Sunnah, "*Al-'Urf*", pp. 61-64; Khallāf, "*Maṣāder*", pp. 146-7; Karaman, "Adet", vol. 1, p. 370.

204. Ibn 'Abidīn, "*Nashr al-'Urf*", vol. 2, p. 116; Karaman, "Adet" *Türkiye Diyanet Vakfı İslam Ansiklopedisi*, vol. 1, pp. 369-372.

205. Sarakhsī, "*Al-Mabsūṭ*", vol. 12, p. 196.

206. Abū Sunnah, "*Al-'Urf*", pp. 62-3; Ibn 'Abidīn, "*Nashr al-'Urf*", vol. 2, p. 118; Karaman, "Ādet", *Türkiye Diyanet Vakfı İslam Ansiklopedisi*, vol. 1, p. 370.

207. Dāwud, "*Buyū'*", 12; Bukhārī, "*Buyū'*", 74, 76, 77, 78; Muslim, "*Musaqāt*", 79, 82.

208. Ibn Humām, "*Fatḥ al-Qadīr*", vol. 7, p. 15; Sarakhsī, "*Al-Mabsūṭ*", vol. 12, p. 142; 'Abidīn, "*Nashr al-'Urf*", vol. 2, p. 118; Karaman, "Ādet" *Türkiye Diyanet Vakfı İslam Ansiklopedisi*, vol. 1, p. 371

209. Koca, "*Takhṣīṣ*", p. 256.

210. Sarakhsī, "*Uṣūl*", vol. 1, p. 190; Nasafī, "*Kashf*", vol. 1, p. 267; Bazdawī, "*Uṣūl*", vol. 2, p. 95; Ibn 'Abd al-Shakūr, "*Musallamat al-Subūt*", vol. 1,

p. 345; Suyūṭī, "*Al-Ashbāh*", p. 66; Abū Sunnah, "*Al-'Urfu wa al-Ādah*", pp. 122-3; Koca, "*Takhṣīṣ*", p. 257.

211. Ibn Humām, "*Taḥrīr*" v. 1, p. 317, vol. 2, p. 57; Molla Husraw, "*Al-Mir'āt*", vol. 1, pp. 445, 448; Nasafī, "*Kashf*", vol. 1, pp. 256-7, 260-262, 267-271

212. Sarakhsī, "*Uṣūl*", vol. 1, p. 191; Bukhārī, "*Kashf*", vol. 2, p. 97; Bazdawī, "*Uṣūl*", vol. 2, p. 97.

213. Bukharī, "*Kashf*", vol. 2, pp. 97-8.

214. Al-Majallah clause: 36.

215. 'Alī Ḥaydar, "*Sharḥ al-Qawāid*", p. 93.

216. Ibn Nujaym, "*Al-Ashbāh*", pp. 94-5; Abū Sunnah, "*Al-'Urf*", p. 58; 'Al Ḥaydar, "*Sharḥ al-Qawāid*", pp. 105-6; Zarkā, "*Sharḥ al-Qawāid*", p. 179.

217. Al-Majallah clause: 41.

218. Ibn Nujaym, "*Al-Ashbāh*", p. 103; Ibn 'Abidīn, "*Nashr al-'Urf*", vol. 2, pp. 116-7; Abū Sunnah "*Al-'Urf*", p. 58; 'Alī Ḥaydar, "*Sharḥ al-Qawāid*", p. 95; Zarkā, "*Sharḥ al-Qawāid*", p. 166.

219. Ibn 'Abidīn, "*Nashr al-'Urf*", vol. 2, p. 132; Abū Sunnah, "*Al-'Urf*", p. 60.

220. Karaman, "*İslam Hukuku*", vol. 3, pp. 270-1; Abū Sunnah, "*Al-'Urf*", pp. 96-98, 100-1.

221. Ibid., p. 95.

222. Sarakhsī, "*Al-Mabsūṭ*", vol. 11, p. 159, vol. 13, p. 14.

223. Al-Majallah clause: 45.

224. Ibn 'Abidīn, "*Radd al-Mukhtār*", vol. 4, pp. 363, 365; Ibn al-Humām, "*Fatḥ al-Qadīr*", vol. 6, pp. 216, 218.

225. Ibn Humām, "*Fatḥ al-Qadīr*", vol. 6, p. 291.

226. Ibn 'Abidīn, "*Radd al-Mukhtār*", vol. 4, pp. 363, 365; Bilmen, "*Iṣṭilāḥāti Fiqhiyyah Kamusu*", vol. 6, pp. 126-129; Abū Sunnah, "*Al-'Urf*", pp. 167-8; Karaman, "İslām *Hukuku*", v. 2, pp. 328-331; al-Majallah: clause: 118.

227. Al-Majallah: clause: 726.

228. Ibn 'Abidīn "*Radd al-Mukhtār*", v. 5, p. 279; Karaman, "*İslām Hukuku*", v. 2, p. 331.

229. Ibn 'Abidīn, ibid., vol. 5, p. 68; Ibn al-Humām, "*Fatḥ al-Qadīr*", vol. 4, pp. 419-421; Abū Sunnah, "*Al-'Urf*", p. 103.

230. Ibn al-Humām, "*Taḥrīr*", vol. 4, p. 78; Bazdawī, "*Kashf*" vol. 4, pp. 3, 5-6; Jaṣṣāṣ, "*Al-Fuṣūl*" vol. 4, pp. 234, 243; Ṣadr al-Sharī'ah, "*Tawḍīḥ*", vol. 2, pp. 162-3.

231. See at the beginning of the Chapter Three.

232. Sarakhsī, "*Uṣūl*", vol. 2, pp. 202-3, 206; Bazdawī, "*Uṣūl*", vol. 4, pp. 3, 6, 10; Nasafī, "*Kashf*", vol. 2, p. 296; Ṣadr al-Sharī'ah, "*Tawḍīḥ*", vol. 2, pp. 162, 169.

233. Karamastī, "*Al-Wajīz*" p. 185; Bazdawī, "*Uṣūl*", vol. 3, p. 389; Sarakhsī, "*Uṣūl*", vol. 2, pp. 192, 206; Bukhārī, "*Kashf*", vol. 3, p. 389; vol. 2, p. 11.

234. For example, see Chapter Three under the title of the departure from qiyās jalī to qiyās khafī.

235. Mikadī, "*Baḥth fi al-istiḥsān*", p. 315.

236. Kamālī, "*Istiḥsān*", p. 65.

237. Kamālī, ibid., p. 66.

Conclusion

Deducing rulings is an important element for the development of Islamic law. The fundamental sources of Islamic law are the Qur'an, the *Sunnah, ijmā'* (consensus), and *qiyās* (analogy) which are unanimously accepted by the majority of jurists. There are also other controversial principles that are activated when the fundamental principles are silent and unable to help the law for its continuity.

The *ḥadīth* of Mu'ādh ibn Jabal is very good example of the fact that Muslims believe that Islamic Law is able to find answers for human problems. For this reason, jurists must know the main requirements for legislation. The knowledge of jurisprudence was formulated as *uṣūl al-fiqh* (the principle of jurisprudence) and the meaning of *uṣūl al-fiqh* combines the understanding of the meaning of *uṣūl* and *fiqh* individually.

The term *uṣūl* is the plural of *aṣl.* One of the uses of *a-ṣ-l* is the meaning of *dalīl.* In Islamic law, the word *dalīl* is used in two ways: *dalīl tafṣīl* is like an individual verse of the Qur'an or an individual *Sunnah* in a *ḥadīth.* We may refer to it as "specific evidence", though it is sometimes translated as "detailed proof".

And the *dalīl ijmālī* has nothing to do with direct, absolute order and prohibition. However, it produces general rulings as *wujūb* (necessity), *taḥrīm* (prohibition) and so on.

Dalīl (proof) is distinguished from *amārah* (indication), which literally means a sign or an allusion. *Dalīl* could only relate to evidence which leads to a definitive ruling or to positive knowledge (*'ilm*). *Amārah* on the other hand is reserved for evidence or indication that only leads to a *ẓannī* (speculative) ruling. In this way, the term *dalīl* could only be concerned with the definitive proofs, namely the Qur'an, the *Sunnah,* and *ijmā',* while the remaining proof which contains a measure of speculation, such as *qiyās, istiḥsān, istiṣḥāb, maṣāleḥ mursalah,* and so on, could fall under the category of *amārah* (signs or allusions, probable evidence). However, most jurists consider both *dalīl* and *amārah,* whether *qaṭ'ī* (definitive) or *ẓannī* (speculative), as a *dalīl* (proof). The term *aṣl* is actually *dalīl,* which is a proof or an evidence of Islamic Law.

The term *fiqh* is synonymous with *al-fahm* (understanding) in the linguistic sense. It is used to denote the exercise of intelligence, as in the case of the Successors of the Companions of the Prophet (ṣ), most of whom were *fuqahā'* (jurists) who gave legal judgments using their own reason and intelligence; in that respect the term *fiqh* is actually used for the knowledge of the law.

The procedure of giving judgments among the Companions was that they used to refer first to the Qur'an whenever a claimant-defendant asked them for guidance. If the Companions were unable to find the result in the Qur'an, they would then seek a judgment in the *Sunnah.* Failing to discover the answer within these sources, they would then consult the righteous men of the community who would convene to discuss the matter and arrive at a solution. If they arrived at an opinion which was unanimously accepted, the consensus was that they should judge accordingly.

Despite the controversy among the scholars, it has been shown that the use of *ijtihād* by *ra'y* was practiced from the time of the Prophet (ṣ); this is evident from several narrations such as the *ḥadīth* of Mu'adh Ibn Jabal or the incident when the Prophet (ṣ) saw the people of Madīnah fertilizing palm trees.

Between *ijtihād* and *ra'y* there is a very close relationship. However, as we have seen, *ijtihād* is more comprehensive than *ra'y*. At the time of the Companions and the Successors, the constituent parts of *ra'y* were clear and extensive, as opposed to the *naṣṣ*, which is not obviously clarified and defined. Following that period, some jurists continued to use *ra'y* in the meaning of *ijtihād* in a wider range. At the same time, the majority of jurists confined the use of inference to issues where there were no *naṣṣ* (text) to reach a right and just *ḥukm* (ruling).

Performing *ijtihād* is seen as a religious duty. The Qur'an and the *Sunnah* of the Prophet (ṣ) encourage Muslims to avoid disagreements amongst themselves by using *ijtihād;* it is said that whenever a judge exercises *ijtihād* and gives a right judgment, he will have two rewards, but if he errs in his judgment, he will still have earned one reward. Therefore, *ijtihād* becomes a very demanding requirement in modern day life, and sometimes performing it will be an individual duty (*farḍ 'ayn*) and sometimes a collective duty (*farḍ kifāyah*) for Muslims. Eventually, if the requirement of *ijtihād* is ignored then the whole Muslim community will be considered sinful.

There are some conditions which are aimed to ensure the ability of a person to perform *ijtihād*. The earliest complete accounts of the qualifications of a *mujtahid* were given by scholars such as Abū al-Ḥusayn al-Baṣrī (d. 436/1044), Shīrāzī (d. 467/1083), Ghazālī (d. 505/1111), Āmidī (d. 632/1234), Ibn al-Subkī (d. 771/1370) and Shāṭibī (d. 790/1388). They and many others prepared extensive lists of the abilities jurists must possess to enable them to perform *ijtihād*. Some increased and others decreased the conditions. An outstanding scholar, Shāṭibī, ignored these lists and reduced the conditions of *ijtihād* to one comprehensive point: the precise comprehension of the *maqāṣid* and in the light of this comprehension the ability to deduce rules from the sources.

Regarding the door of *ijtihād*, besides the early and contemporary Muslim scholars, some recent western scholars, in particular Wael Hallaq, and W. Montgomery Watt, have indicated that the gate of *ijtihād* is still open and the term "The closing of the gate of *ijtihād*"is a myth. In reality, the gate of *ijtihād* was never completely closed, as properly qualified scholars must have the right to perform *ijtihād* continuously. *Ijtihād* is not confined to the four schools of law and can be performed by all capable scholars. Consequently, the gate of *ijtihād*, in my personal opinion, is still and must remain open.

Iijtihād has been practiced largely in terms of *istiḥsān*. Sometimes when an issue is not within the range of a *naṣṣ*, *qiyās* is then used to judge. Here we come across two different possibilities: apparent clear analogy and implicit analogy. If the *mujtahid* finds that the second one is stronger (*khafī qiyās*) the judgment given accordingly is called *istiḥsān*. Through *istiḥsān* some issues within the range of common *naṣṣ*, and criteria such as difficulty, complexity, necessity, and need are removed because of their specific nature and a new judgement is given to this special situation to implement *maṣlaḥah*.

As such it is the Lawgiver (i.e. God) who considers the special situations and circumstances with specific conditions, and who abolishes the difficulty, complexity and harm. This provides an ideal guide for the *mujtahid*. On this issue Muṣṭafā Zarqā says that the Qur'an and the *Sunnah* are both *istiḥsān*, which is the creation of the *Shāri'*. The concept of *istiḥsān* is to guide the *mujtahid* when applying the *naṣṣ* of the *Shāri‘* to issues everyday of life. The *mujtahid* performing *istiḥsān* is inspired by the method that the *Shāri‘* applies and in this way, the *mujtahid* implements the *Shāri‘*'s purpose and intentions. We have mentioned some examples in regards to this issue throughout the chapter.

No technical definitions of *istiḥsān* have reached us from the early Islamic period, simply because there was no reason for *istiḥsān* to be defined. Abū Ḥanīfah and other early Ḥanafī jurists such as Abū Yūsuf (d. 182) and Shaybānī (d. 189) have directly given rulings using the concept of *istiḥsān* without giving any specific definitions or explanations. It is said that their judgments were based on the fundamental principles of securing ease and avoiding hardship, in line with the Qur'an: "The best of your religion is that which brings ease" and "God intends facility and ease for you, He does not intend to put you to hardship" (2:185).

The fact that the Ḥanafīs were attacked by the Shāfi‘ī jurists, and especially by Shāfi‘ī himself, shows that the Shāfi‘ī schools did not recognize *istiḥsān* as a basis of Islamic law. They dismissed it as "Arbitrary law-making in religion". Indeed, Shāfi‘ī jurists did not understand what Ḥanafīs meant by *istiḥsān*. Ḥanafī jurists spent much time defending their position and trying to show that *istiḥsān* was a valid source of law, and not merely an ad hoc method. However, among the jurists there was no consensus as to the precise meaning and definition of *istiḥsān*. Yet in spite of all the different definitions, the meanings are very close. In fact all the definitions may be derived from that of Karkhī which is arguably more comprehensive than the others as we discussed earlier.

It is quite difficult to determine the applications of *istiḥsān* in the very early period. However, 'Umar's decisions provided the means by which researchers have been able to gain some indication of how to implement *istiḥsān* in legal matters. Early *istiḥsān*, then, involved making a decision which was a complete departure from an established rule for the sake of equity and public interest. I have not been able to discover any authentic source that leads me to believe that the concept of *istiḥsān* was used prior to the time of 'Umar ibn 'Abd al-'Azīz.

When Iyās b. Muā'wiyah's use of the term *istiḥsān* is compared to Abū Ḥanīfah's, much similarity can be seen. For them, the main purpose of applying *istiḥsān* was to avoid the possibility of causing harm to the public interest. The reason for their emphasis on *istiḥsān* was their desire to avoid the negative results that often occurred when *qiyās* was applied incorrectly. However, *istiḥsān* owes its existence to *qiyās*, and would not have superseded it had *qiyās* not proved to be ineffective in some cases.

The investigation that I made throughout the research, and the opinions given by scholars such as Ibn Ḥazm, Schacht (d. 1969), Goldziher (d. 1921) and so on, show that the first usage of *istiḥsān* in its technical sense did not occur before Iyās bin Muā'wiyah (d. 122/740).

The concept of *istiḥsān* is recognized by the Ḥanafī, Mālikī, Ḥanbalī and Zaydī schools. Ḥanafī scholars are adamant that *istiḥsān* is a source of law and not in any way a form of ruling made according to personal desire. For the Ḥanafī school *istiḥsān* means acting according to one of the two forms of *qiyās*. *Istiḥsān* may also be acted upon based on *athar* (*ḥadīth*), *ijmā'* or necessity. However, despite the fact that *'ulamā'* from these different schools recognized the validity of *istiḥsān* as a principle they often disagreed over the meaning of the term. The supporters of the validity of *istiḥsān* resort to proof from the Qur'an, *Sunnah*, and *ijmā'*. According to Ḥanafī scholars, to perform *istiḥsān* is to comply with Qur'anic verses which command man to follow what is best, good and beautiful.

The first figure to reject *istiḥsān* was Imām Shāfi'ī with his famous statement: "*Man istaḥsana faqad sharra'a*" (whoever approves of juristic preference is making himself the Lawmaker). According to Shāf'i'ī, nobody is ordered to rule according to *ḥaqq* (truth) unless he knows what *ḥaqq* is and *ḥaqq* cannot become known unless it is from God either as *naṣṣ* or by indication, as God made *ḥaqq* in his Book and in the *Sunnah* of his prophet. Among those who agreed with him on this issue were: Isnawī (d. 772/1370); Bishr b. Ghiyās (d. 218/833); Shīrāzī (d. 476/1083); Ghazālī (d. 505/1111); Dāwūd al-Ẓāhirī (d. 270/884); Ibn Ḥazm; and the Imāmi Shī'ah.

In reality, everybody, including those who recognize *istiḥsān*, reject *istiḥsān* that is based on personal desire. Shāfi'ī said, with regards to the case of the thinkers and the literate, that if they were allowed to rule by *istiḥsān* it would be in contradiction to the use of *istiḥsān*, as those who recognize *istiḥsān* understand that its meaning is the departure from *qiyās* to a stronger *dalīl*. The situations are such that the *dalīl* can only be expected from a *mujtahīd* who is competent in the Sharī'ah rulings and the *dalīl*, while it is unacceptable from thinkers and the literate who are not qualified.

Owing to the lack of written material, Abū Ḥanīfah has often been accused of judging cases without depending on any textual evidence, and this is the main source of conflict amongst the jurists. However, it is not entirely true to say that there is no trace of any reports regarding Abū Ḥanīfah's techniques; in fact he left writings giving indications as to his methods of performing *ijtihād* and his use of the principle of *istiḥsān*. He declared that he used to read God's book to obtain guidance. If he was unable to find any guidance in the Qur'an then he would resort to the *Sunnah* of the Prophet (ṣ) and the true reports (*ḥadīth*) which had transmitted from generation to generation by trustworthy narrators. If neither the Qur'an nor the *Sunnah* yielded any guidance, he would then refer to the opinions of the Companions. Consequently, when he made his personal decision he would not ask others' opinions. However, if a matter had been considered by the likes of Ibrāhīm al-Nakhā'ī (d. 96), Shā'bī (d. 103), *Ḥasan* (d. 110), Muḥammad b. Sīrīn (d. 110), Sa'īd b. al-Musayyab (d. 94) *et al,* he would also act on their *ijtihād.*

Moreover, in the writings of his disciples, Abū Yūsuf (d. 182) and Shaibānī (d. 189), the use of the concept of *istiḥsān* by Abū Ḥanīfah and the early Ḥanafis is explained. The examples of the practice of *istiḥsān* in the writings of Abū Yūsuf (d. 182) and Shaibānī (d. 189) reveal that the use of the concept could mean the following: leaving *qiyās* due to the precedents of the Companions; leaving *qiyās* owing to the consensus (*ijmā'*); leaving *qiyās* in favour of *sadd al-dharā'ī'* (blocking the means); leaving *qiyās* due to authentic Tradition (*ḥadīth ṣaḥīḥ*). Abū Ḥanīfah and his disciples were highly respectful of the Traditions, and used them in their *ijtihād;* even if it was a *ḥadīth ḍaif* (weak tradition) they would prefer it over *qiyās.*

Division of *istiḥsān* among the scholars differs from one jurist to another: mainly it is considered as being of two types **a:** analogical *istiḥsān*, which consists of a departure from *qiyās jalī* to *qiyās khafī* and **b:** exceptional *istiḥsān* (*istiḥsān istithnā'ī*) which consists of making an exception to a general rule of the existing law. Ṣadr al-Sharī'ah (d. 747/1346) also divides it into several types such as *ijmā'*, *ḍarūrah* (necessity), *athar.* These are actually established against explicit analogy. He considers the implicit (*khafī*) analogy is *istiḥsān.* However, despite the fact that implicit analogy is *istiḥsān,* it is more comprehensive than implicit analogy. We can conclude that while every implicit analogy can be called *istiḥsān,* not every case of *istiḥsān* can be called implicit (*khafī*) analogy. Another jurist, Bazdawī, also indicates that *istiḥsān* is an implicit analogy. In fact *istiḥsān* is not merely an implicit analogy. In general, the Ḥanafīs considered *istiḥsān* as four types as follows: *istiḥsān* based on *naṣṣ* (*athar*); on *ijmā‘* (consensus); on *ḍarūrah* (necessity) and on *qiyās khafī* (implicit analogy).

The Mālikīs divide *istiḥsān* into four types: *istiḥsān* based on *‘urf;* on *maṣlaḥah;* on *ijmā‘;* and on *qiyās.* Even though there are different opinions over the divisions of *istiḥsān*, some common issues with regard to the types of *istiḥsān* are generally agreed upon, namely the first type of *istiḥsān*—the departure from *jalī* to *khafi-* which is agreed upon by all the scholars.

Ḥanafīs considered that *qiyās khafī* was *istiḥsān.* The *‘illah* (effective cause) of *qiyās khafī* can not be discovered easily. However in *qiyās jalī* the *‘illah* (effective cause) appears at first glance without careful consideration being given to it. In other words, *qiyās khafī* is preferred over *qiyās jalī* if they are opposed to each other, on account of the effective cause (*‘illah*) which is stronger in *khafī.*

So many efforts were made by outstanding scholars throughout the history of Islamic juridical life to develop it in order to allow *maṣlaḥah* to prevail and to prevent evil. Abū Ḥanīfah was one of them. He made *istiḥsān* and *qiyās* essential to *uṣūl al-fiqh*, allowing society the freedom and flexibility with which to function and progress healthily, in line with the objectives of the *shari‘ah.*

Najm al-Dīn al-Ṭūfī (d. 719/1316) took the concept of *maṣlaḥah* to the furthest extent ever known. He emphasized the importance of the concept and considered it suitable for applications in all areas of social life and human relations, apart from *ibādāt* (worshiping) and those general principles of law already determined and deemed inviolate. The general principles of religion are binding and fixed for mankind until the day of judgment; particular principles, however, are subject to public interest (*maṣlaḥah*) and the public changes as circumstances change. The Qur'an promotes reforms and new solutions by saying that if man does not know, he should go and ask someone who does. As the verse indicates, "So ask the people of the reminder" (21:7). Therefore understanding the purposes of the Sharīʻah is an indispensable qualification for a *mujtahid* in order to perform *ijtihād* and realize the role of the concept of *istiḥsān*, as Imām Mālik regards it a purpose-centred method of interpretation, adding that *istiḥsān* represents nine-tenth of human knowledge. Consequently, contemporary scholars should work on the principle of *istiḥsān*, and develop it in the framework of contemporary issues under the light of the fundamental principle of Islamic law.

Bibliography

'Abd al-Ḥāfiẓ, Madīḥah 'Alī, *Al-Istiḥsān wa Atharuh fī-Bināi al-Fiqh al-Islāmī*, unpublished Ph.D dissertation, Faculty of Arabic and Islamic Studies, University of Al-Azhar, Egypt, 1984.

'Abd al-Karīm Soroush, "*Maksimum ve Mimimum Dīn*", tr. Yasin Demirkan, *Fecre Doğru Magazin*, 4/37-38-39, November, December 1999, January 1999, *Kıyan Magazin*, March-April 1998, vol. 8, no. 41.

'Abd al-Qādīr, 'Alī Ḥassan, *Naẓariyāt al-'Āmmah fī Tārikh al-Fiqh al-Islāmī*, Dār al-Kutub al-Ḥādīsah, Cairo, 1965.

'Abd al-Razzāq, Abū Bakr, 'Abd al-Raḥmān b. Humām (d. 211/826), *Muṣannaf*, ed. Ḥabīb al-Raḥmān al-Aẓamī, Beirut, 1403.

'Abd Ḥatamī, Ramaḍan Muḥammad, *Al-Maṣaliḥ al-Mursalah wa Atharuhā fī al-Fiqh al-Islāmī*, unpublished Ph.D dissertation, Faculty of Sharī'ah and Qānūn, University of Al-Azhar, Cairo, 1984.

Abū Dāwūd Sulaymān bin al-Ash'ās (d. 275/888), *Sunan*, tr. Aḥmad Ḥasan, Muḥammad Ashraf, Lahore, 1984.

— *Sunan*, Istanbul, 1981.

Abū Dunyā Fāruq Aḥmad Ḥusayn, *Mabāḥis al-Qiyās min Kitāb Nafāis al-Uṣūl fī Sharḥ al-Maḥsūl*, unpublished Ph.D dissertation, Faculty of Arabic and Islamic Studies, University of Al-Azhar, Egypt, 1988.

Abū ʻIyad Ḥasan Muḥammad Salīm, *Al-Imām al-Shāfiʻī wa Atharuh fī Uṣūl al-Fiqh*, unpublished Ph.D dissertation, Faculty of Sharīʻah and Qānūn University of Al-Azhar, Egypt, 1976.

Abū Jayb Saʻdī, *Al-Qāmūs al-Fiqh Lughatan wa-Iṣṭilāḥan* (63), Dār al-Fiqr, Syria, 1988.

Abū Rīsh Mūsā ʻĀyish Ṣabīḥ, *Qāʻidah al-Taḥsīn wa al-Taqbīḥ wa Atharuhā fī Uṣūl al-Fiqh*, unpublished Ph.D dissertation, Faculty of Sharīʻah and Qānūn, University of Al-Azhar, Egypt, 1987.

Abū Sulaymān, ʻAbd al-Raḥmān Ibrāhīm, *Al-Fiqh al-Uṣūl*, Dār al-Shurūq, Jeddah.

Abū Sunnah, Aḥmad Fahmī, *Al-ʻUrf wa al-ʻAdah fi-Ra'y al-Fuqahā*, Cairo, 1947.

— *Ḥuqm al-ʻIlāj bi-Naql Ḍammi al-Insān*, in *Majallat al-Majmāʻ al-Fiqh*, no. 1, 1987.

Abū Yāʻlā Muḥammad bin al-Ḥusayn bin Muḥammad bin Aḥmad bin al-Farrā' Ḥanbalī (d. 458/1065), *Al-ʻUddah fī Uṣūl al-Fiqh*, ed. Aḥmad Sayr al-Mubārak, Muassasah al-Risālah, Beirut, 1400/1980.

Abū Yūsuf, Yāqūp Ibrāhīm (d. 182), *Kitāb al-Kharāj*, Dār al-Maʻrifah, Beirut, 1970.

— *Kitāb al-Āthār*, with a commentary by the editor Shaykh Abū al-Wafā, Cairo, 1355.

Abū Zahrah, Muḥammad (d. 1395/1974), *Taʻlīq ʻalā Mawḍū' al-Istiḥsān wal-Maṣaliḥ al-Mursalah*, p.361-366, in *Al-Majlis al-ʻAlā li-Ri'āyat al-Funūn*, Usbūʻ al-Fiqh al-Islāmī, Damascus, 1380/1960.

— *Abū Ḥanīfah*, tr. by Osman Keskioğlu, 3rd ed., Ankara, Diyanet Yayınları, 1999.

— *Al-Imām al-Ṣādiq Ḥayātuhū wa ʻAṣruhū Ārāuhū wa Fiqhuhū*, Cairo.

— *Al-Imām Zayd Ḥayātuhū wa ʻAṣruhū Ārāuhū wa Fiqhuhū*, Dār al-Nadwat al-Jadīydah, Beirut.

— *Tarīkh Mazāhib al-Islāmiyyah*, Dār al-Fiqr al-ʻArabi, Beirut.

— *Uṣūl al-Fiqh*, Dār al-Fikr al-ʻArabī, Cairo, 1958.

Afghanī, Muḥammad ʻAbd al-Bāqī, *Kitāb Rawdat Ithbāt al-Istiḥsān fī Madhhab Abū Ḥanīfah al-Nuʻmān*, Damascus, 1897.

Aghnides, Nicolas P, *Muḥammadan Theories of Finance*, New York, Longmans Green & Co., 1916, reprint by Premier Book House, Lahore, 1957.

Aḥmad Zarqā (d. 1938), *Sharḥ Qawāi'd al-Fiqhiyyah*, Beirut, 1983.

Aḥmad 'Azīz, *Hindistanda Kültür Çalışmaları*, tr. Latif Boyacı, İstanbul, 1995.

Aktan, Hamza, *Ticaret Hukukunun Yeni Bazı Problemleri Üzerine İslam Hukuku Açısından Bir Değerlendirme*, I. Uluslararası İslam Ticaret Hukukunun Günümüzdeki Meseleleri Kongresi, Konya.

Ālim, Yūsuf Ḥāmid, *Al-Maqāṣid al-'Āmmah*, International Islamic Publishing House, Riyadh, 1994.

'Alī al-Tījānī Abū Bakr, *Uṣūl wa Qawā'id Fiqh Ibrāhīm al-Nakhāī*, unpublished Ph.D dissertation, Faculty of Sharī'ah and Qānūn, University of Al-Azhar, Egypt, 1988-1989.

'Alī Ḥaydar Afandi (d. 1936), *Durar al-Ḥukkām Sharḥ Majallat al-Aḥkām, Sharḥ al-Qawāid al-Kulliyyah*, Istanbul, 1330.

— *Uṣūli Fıqıh Dersleri*, Üçdal Neşriyat, İstanbul, 1966.

'Alī Himmet Berk, *Hukuk Mantığı ve Tefsir*, Ankara, 1948.

'Allāl Fāsī, *Maqāṣid al-Sharī'ah al-Islāmīyah wa-Maqārimuhā*, Matba'ah al-Risālah, Al-Maghrib, 1979.

'Alwānī, Ṭāhā Jābir, *The Ethics of Disagreement in Islam*, the International Institute of Islamic Thought, VA, USA, 1993.

— "*Taqlīd and Ijtihād*", *American Journal of Islamic Social Sciences*, vol. 8, no.1, 1991.

Āmidī, 'Alī bin Abī 'Alī Muḥammad bin Sālim al-Thaglabī, Sayf al-Dīn al-Āmidī (d. 631/1233), "*Al-Iḥkām fī Uṣūl al-Aḥkām*", ed. 'Abd al-Razzāq 'Afīfī, 2nd ed., Maktabah al-Islāmī, Beirut, 1402/1982.

Amīn, Aḥmad (d. 1954), *Duhāl Islām*, Dār al-Kutub al-'Ilmiyyah, Beirut.

— *Fajr al-Islām*, Beirut, 1969.

Amīnī, Mohd Taqī, *Time Changes and Islamic Law*, tr. Gulam Aḥmad Khan, Idārahi Adabiyati, Delhi, 1988.

Amīr Pādishah, Muḥammad Amīn al-Ḥanafī (d. 987/1579), *Taysīr al-Taḥrīr 'alā Kitāb al-Taḥrīr fi-Uṣūl al-Fiqh*, Beirut.

Anderson, J.N.D, *Islamic Law in the Modern World*, Stevens and Sons Ltd., London, 1959.

— *Law Reform in the Muslim World*, University Printing House, Cambridge, 1976.

Anees Ibrāhīm, *Al-Mu'jam Al-Wasīṭ*, Dār al-Ma'ārif, Cairo, 1973.

Anṣārī, Abū Yaḥyā Zakariyyah Shaykh al-Islām al-Shāfi'ī, *Ghāyāt al-Wuṣūl Sharḥ lub al-Uṣūl*, Muṣṭafā Bāb al-Ḥalabī wa-Awlāduh, 1360/1941, Cairo.

"Apaydın, Yunus", *Diyanet İslam Ansiklopedisi* (*DIA*), xx, p. 291-292.

Aras M. Özgü, *Ebu Hanife'nin Hocası Ḥammād ve Fıkhi Görüşleri*, Beyan, Istanbul, 1996.

— "Ḥammad b. Ebu Süleyman", *DIA*, Ankara.

Artuk Ibrāhīm, "Adli Altın", *DIA*, vol. 1, p. 389.

— "Cihadiyye", *DIA*, vol. 7, p. 534.

Ash'arī, Abū al-Ḥasan 'Alī ibn Ismā'īl, *Risālat Istiḥsān al-Khawd fi 'Ilm al-Kalām*, Matba'ah Majlis Dāirat al-Ma'ārif al-Nizāmiyah, Haydarabad, 1991.

Atar Fahreddin, *Fıkıh Uṣūlü*, MUIFY, İstanbul, 1996.

Aṭṭār, Ḥasan bin Muḥammad bin Maḥmūd (d. 1250/1835), *Ḥāshiyah 'alā Sharḥ Jalāl al-Maḥallī 'alā Jam'u al-Jawāmi'*, Maṭba'ah 'Ilmiyyah, Egypt, 1316 H.

Āyāt Allāh Ṣāliḥi Najafabādī, *Velayeti Fakih; Hükümeti Salihan*, Muassaseai Hudamāti Farhangi Resa, 1984.

A'zamī M. Muṣṭafā, *Al-Mustashriq Schacht wa al-Sunnah al-Nabawiyyah*, Riyadh, 1985.

Azharī, Abū Manṣūr Muḥammad b. Aḥmad (d. 370/980), *Tahdhib Al-Lughah*, al-Dār al-Misriyyah, Cairo, 1966.

Ba' Bakr Ḥalīfah, *Takhṣīṣ al-Nuṣūṣ bi al-Adillat al-Ijtihādiyyah 'Inda al-Uṣūliyyah*, Maktabat Wahbah, Cairo.

Badrān, Abū al-'Aynāyn Badrān, *Uṣūl al-Fiqh al-Islāmi*, Muassasah Shabāb al-Jāmi'ah, Alaxandria, 1404/1984.

Baghdādī, Abū Bakr Aḥmad b. 'Alī, *Tārikh*, vol. xiii, Dār al-Kutub al-'Arabī, Beirut.

Bāhit, Muḥammad b. Ḥusayn, *Sullam al-Wuṣūl Sharḥ Nihāyat al-Sūl*, Beirut.

Bahiy Muḥammad, *Al-Islām fī Ḥalli Mashākil al-Mujtama'āt al-Islāmiyyah al-Muāsirah*, 13, Cairo, 1981.

Bāhusayn, Ya'qūb 'Abd al-Wahhāb, *Raf' al-Ḥarāj fī al-Sharī'ah al-Islāmiah*, Lajnat al-Waṭaniyyah, Iraq.

Baydhāwī, Naṣr al-Dīn 'Abd Allāh bin 'Umar bin Muḥammad bin 'Alī Al-Shīrāzī (d. 685/1286), *Al-Ibhāj fī Sharḥ Al-Minhāj 'alā' Minhāj al-Wuṣūl ilā 'Ilm al-Uṣūl*, Beirut.

Bājī, Abū Walīd Sulaymān (d. 474/1081), *Iḥkām al-Fuṣūl fī Aḥkām al-Uṣūl*, 2nd ed., ed. 'Abd al-Majīd Turkī, Beirut, 1995.

— *Al-Muntaqā Sharḥ al-Muwaṭṭa Al-Imām Mālik*, Cairo, 1332, Dār al-Fikr al-'Arabī.

Baktri, Muṣṭafā, *İslam Hukukunda Zaruret*, Ankara, 1986.

Baljon, J M S, *Religion and Thought of Shah Wali Allah Dihlawī*, Leiden E. J. Brill, Netherlands, 1986.

Baltaci, Muḥammad, *Manāhij at-Tashrī' al-Islāmī fī al-Qarn al-Thānī al-Hijrī*, Riyadh, 1977.

Bannānī, 'Abd al-Raḥmān bin Jād Allāh al-Bannānī, al-Maghribī (d. 1198/1784), *Ḥāshiyah 'alā Sharḥ Jalāl al-Dīn al-Maḥallī 'alā Jam' al-Jawāmī' li Ibn Subkī*, Muṣṭafa Bābī al-Ḥalabī, Cairo 1937.

Baqqāl, 'Alī, *Islām Ḥukukunda Hikmet, İllet ve İctimāī' Vākia Munasebetlerinin Hukuki Neticeleri*, unpublished Ph.D dissertation, Erzurum, 1986.

Bardakoğlu, Alī, "*Tabii Hukuk Düşüncesi Açısından İslam Hukukçularının Istiḥsān ve Istiṣlāḥ Görüşü*", *EUIF Magazine*, p. 111-138, no. 3, Kayseri, 1986.

Barr, Muḥammad 'Alī, *Ṭifl al-Unbūb wa al-Talḥiq al-Ṣināī'*, Jeddah, 1986.

Bashīr Idrīs Jum'ah, *Al-Ra'y wa Asaruhū fī Fiqh al-Islāmī*, Cairo.

Baṣrī Abī al-Ḥusayn Muḥammad b. 'Alī b. al-Ṭayyib al-Basrī al-Mu'razilī (d. 436/1044), *Al-Mu'tamad fī 'Uṣūl al-Fiqh*, ed. Shaykh Khalīl al-Mays, Beirut, 1983.

Bayhaqī Aḥmad b. Ḥusayn (d. 458/1065), *Al-Sunan al-Kubrā*, ed. Muḥammad 'Abd al-Qadīr 'Aṭā, Makkah, 1994.

Bazdawī, 'Alī bin Muḥammad bin 'Abd al-Karīm Abū al-Ḥasan Fakhr al-Islām al-Bazdawī al-Ḥanafī (d. 482/1089), *Uṣūl al-Bazdawī on the*

Margin of 'Abd al-'Azīz al-Bukhārī Khashf al-Asrār, Istanbul, 1308 H, Dār al-Kitāb al-'Arabī, Beirut, 1394/1974.

Bedir Murteza, "Fıkıh to Law: Secularization Through Curriculum", pp. 378-401, *Islamic Law and Society*, (11,3), Leiden, 2004.

Bilmen, Ömer Nasūhi (d. 1972), *Ḥukuku Islāmiyya ve Iṣṭilaḥāti Fiqhiyya Kamusu*, vol. 6, pp. 126-129, Bilmen Yayınevi, İstanbul.

Birisik 'Abd al-Ḥamīd, *Hint Alt Kıtasında Düşünce ve Tefsir Ekolleri*, İnsan, İstanbul, 2001.

Bugha, Muṣṭafā Adīb, *Atharu al-Adillah al-Mukhtalaf fīyhā fī al-Islām*, Ph.D dissertation, University of Al-Azhar, Dār al-Qalam, Dimishq, 1993.

Bukhārī, 'Abd al-'Azīz bin Aḥmad bin Muḥammad, 'Alā al-Dīn al- (d. 730/1329), *Sharḥ Kashf al-Asrār 'alā Uṣūl al-Bazdawī*, Dār al-Kutūb al-'Arabī, Beirut, 1394.

— *Kashf al-Asrār 'alā Uṣūl al-Bazdawī*, Istanbul, 1307 H.

Bukhārī, Abū 'Abd Allāh Muḥammad b. Ismā'īl (d. 256/69), *Al-Jāmī' al-Ṣaḥīh*", Istanbul, 1981.

Būtī, Ramaḍān, *Dawābiṭ al-Maṣlaḥah fī al-Sharī'ah al-Islāmiyyah*, Muassasah al-Risālah, 1982.

— *Dawābiṭ al-Maṣlaḥah fī al-Sharī'ah al-Islāmiyyah*, Beirut, 1986.

Celal Nuri, İleri, "*La Yunkeru Tagayyur al-Aḥkām*", *İjtihād* magazine, no. 67, Istanbul, 1329/1913.

Celalizade Celal, *Bediuzzaman ve Muḥammed Ikbal'in Fikirlerinin Mukayesesi*, 3, uluslararası Bediuzzaman Said Nursi Sempozyumu. İslam Düşüncesinin 20. Asırda yeniden yapılandırılması ve Bediuzzaman Sai'd Nursi, 24-26 Eylül 1995 Istanbul.

Cevdet Paşa Aḥmet, *Tazākir*, Tatimmah, Cavid Baysun, TTK basımevi, Ankara, 1986

Chehata Chafik, "*L'èquitè en Tant que Source du Droit Ḥanafite*", 23, *Studia Islamica*, 7-8, 1965.

Chejne A.G., *Ibn Ḥazm*, Kazi Publications., Chicago, 1982.

Coulson, Noel J., *Conflicts and Tensions in Islamic Jurisprudence*, The University of Chicago Press, Chicago, 1969.

— *Succession in the Muslim Family*, Cambridge University Press, London 1971.

Çağıl, Orhan Münir, "*Ḥukuk Felsefesinde Ṭabii Ḥukuk*", IUHF, Tahir Taner'e armağan, Istanbul, 1956.

— *Hukuk ve Hukuk Ilmine Giriş*, Istanbul, 1971.

Çeker Orhan, "*Iftā ve Bir Fetva Defteri Örneği*", Damla offset, Konya, 2000.

— "Fıkıh Dersleri", 1, Konya, 1991.

Dabbūsī, Abu Zayd 'Abd Allah, 'Ubayd Allah b. 'Umar bin 'Iysā (d. 430/1039), *Taqwīm al-Adillah al-Shar', al-Asrār fī al-Uṣūl wa al-Furū'* (original paper), Suleymaniye, Laleli 690.

— *Kitāb Ta'sīs al-Naẓar*, ed. Muṣṭafa Muḥammad al-Qubbānī, Beirut.

Dārimī 'Abd Allāh b. Bahram (d. 255/868), *Al-Sunan*, Beirut, 1994.

Dasūqī Muḥammad, *Al-Ijtihād wa al-Taqlīd fī al-Sharī'ah al-Islāmiyah*, Dār al-Saqāfah, Doha.

— *Al-Imām Muḥammad bin Ḥasan al-Shaybānī*, Qatar, 1987.

Davutoğlu Aḥmet, *Civilizational Transformation and the Muslim World*, Mahir Publications, Kuala Lumpur, 1994.

Dihlawī, Shaḥ Walī Allah (d. 1176/1776), *Fuyūd al-Ḥaramayn: Mushāhadāt wa Ma'ārif* (Urdu), tr. Muḥammad Surur, Karachi, Dār al-Ishātat, 1414 H.

— *Ḥujjah Allāh al-Bāligha*", tr. Mehmet Erdoğan, İz yayınları, Istanbul, 1994.

— *Ḥujjah Allāh al-Bāligha*, I, 130, Delhi, 1954.

— *Iqd al-Jid fī Aḥkam al-Ijtihād wa al-Taqlīd, 'alā al-Madhāhib al-'Arba'ah*, Cairo, 1327-1909.

— *Iqd al-Jid (Ictihad, Taklid ve Telfik Üzerine Dört Risale)*, tr. Hayreddin Karaman, Istanbul, 2000.

— *Tafhīmati Ilāhiyyah*, Dabhel, 1936.

— *Iqd al-Jid fī Bayān Aḥkām al-Ijtihād wa al-Taqlīd*, Karachi, 1959/60.

Dīrīnī Muḥammad Fatḥī, *Al-Manāhij al-Uṣūlīyyah fi al-Ijtihād bi al-Ra'y fi al-Tashrī' al-Islāmī*, Al-Risālah, Beirut, 1418/1997.

Doi, 'Abd al-Raḥmān I, *Sharī'ah the Islamic Law*, Ṭā Hā Publishers, London, 1997.

Döndüren Hamdi, *Delilleriyle İslam Ḥukuku*, Istanbul, 1983.

Dönmez, İbrahim Kafi, *Islām Ḥukuk'unda Kaynak Kavramı*, unpublished Ph.D dissertation, Istanbul, 1981.

— *Islām Ḥukukunda Müctehidin Naslar Karşısındaki Durumu*, MUIFD, Istanbul, 1986.

Dutton, Yasin, *The Origins of Islamic Law: The Qur'an, the Muwatta' and Madinan 'Amal*, Curzon Press, Richmond, 2002.

E.W. Lane, *Arabic English Lexicon*, London, 1863.

Elias A. Elias, *Elias Modern Dictionary*, 5th ed., Cairo, 1950.

Erdoğan Mehmet, *Islām Ḥukukunda Aḥkāmın Değişmesi*, MUIFV Yayınları, İstanbul, 1994.

Esposito John L., *Women in Muslim Family Law*, Syracuse University Press, 1982.

Fadl Allah, M. Ḥusain, *Islāmi Söylem ve Gelecek*, Pınar, Istanbul, 2000.

Fakhrī Mājid, *Islām Felsefesi Tārihi*, tr. Kasım Turhan, Istanbul, 1992.

Farrūr, Muḥammad, 'Abd al-Laṭīf, *Naẓariyat al-Istiḥsān fī al-Tashrī' al-Islāmī wa Silatuhā bi al-Maṣlahat al-Mursalah*, Dār Dimishq, Shām 1987.

Fārukī, Kamāl A., *Islamic Jurisprudence*, Pakistan Publishing House, Karachi, 1962.

Fazl al-Karīm, *Mishkāt al-Maṣabiḥ*, Dār al-Isḥaat, Karachi, 1994.

Fidan, Yusuf, *Islam'da Yabancılar ve Azınlıklar Hukuku*, Ensar Yayıncılık, Konya, October, 2005.

Fīruzabādī, Muḥammad ibn Ya'qūb al-Fīruzabādī al-Shīrāzī (d. 817/1414), *Al-Qāmūs al-Muḥīt*, Muassasat al-Risālah, Beirut, 1986.

Fowler, H.W., *The Concise Oxford Dictionary*, Oxford, 1995.

Ghannūshī, Rāshid, *Islāmi Yöneliş*, Bir, Istanbul, 1987.

Ghazālī, Abu Ḥāmid Muḥammad ibn Muḥammad (d. 505/1111), *Al-Mankhūl min Ta'līqāt al-Uṣūl*, al-Ṭab'ah al-Thāniyah, Dār al-Fikr al-'Arabi, Damascus.

— *Al-Mustaṣfā' min 'Ilm al-Uṣūl*, Al-Maktabah al-Tijāriyyah, Cairo 1356/1937.

Göksoy, Ismā'īl Hakkı, *Fulaniler* maddesi, TDV İslam Ansiklopedisi, Istanbul, 1996.

Goldziher, Ignaz (d. 1921), *Introduction to Islamic Theology and Law*, Princeton University Press, Princeton, 1981.

— *The Zahiris, the Doctrine and their History*, E.J. Brill, Leiden, 1971.

Hackali ʿAbd Raḥmān, "*Islām Ḥukuk Tarihinde Maṣlaḥat Tanımları ve Bunların Analizi*", *İslami Araştırmalar Magazine*, vol. 13, no. 1, 2000.

Ḥādimī, Abū Saīʿd Muḥammad (d. 1168/1755), *Manāfiʾ al-Daqāyiq fī Sharḥi Majāmiʾ al-Ḥaqāyiq fī Uṣūl al-Fiqh*, Istanbul, 1915.

Ḥādimī, Nūr al-Dīn M., *Al-Ijtihād al-Maqāṣidi Hujjiyyātuh Dawābituh Majālātuh*, Katar, 1998.

Ḥajawī, Muḥammad b. Ḥassan, *Al-Fiqh al-Sāmī fī Tārihk al-Fiqh al-Islāmī*, vol. I, p. 94, Dār al-Turās, Cairo, 1396 H.

Ḥakīm, Muḥammad b. ʿAbd Allāh (d. 405/1015), *Al-Mustadraq ʿalā al-Ṣaḥīḥayn*, ed. Muṣṭafā ʿAbd al-Qadīr ʿAṭā, Beirut, 1990.

Ḥakīm, Muḥammad Taqī, *Al-Uṣūl al-Āmmah li al-Fiqh al-Muqāran*, Beirut, 1963.

Hallaq Wael B, "Consideration on the Function and Character of Sunni Legal Theory", *Journal of the American Oriental Society*, p. 683, 104. 4, 1984.

— *The Gate of Ijtihād: A Study in Islamic Legal History*, Ph.D dissertation, University of Washington.

— "Was the Gate of Ijtihād Closed", *International Journal of Middle Eastern Studies*, 16, 1, 1984.

— *A History of Islamic Legal Theories*, Cambridge University Press.

— *The Origins and Evolution of Islamic Law*, Cambridge University Press, 2005.

Ḥamawī, ʿUsāmah, *Naẓariyyāt al-Istiḥsān*, MA dissertation at the Faculty of Sharīʿah at the Dimishq University, Dār al-Khayr, Beirut, 1992.

Ḥamīd Allāh, Muḥammad, "*Al-Ijtihād fī ʿAṣr al-Ṣaḥābah*", vol. 3, issue 4, p. 23, *Majallat al-Kulliyāt al-Dirāsāt al-Islāmiyyat wa al-ʿArabiyyah*, 1984.

— *İslām Peygamberi*, Istanbul 1980.

Hans Wehr, *A Dictionary of Modern Written Arabic*, ed. J. Milton Cowan, 4th ed., Germany, 1979.

Hārithī, Muḥammad Qāsim 'Abduh, *Makānāt al-Imām Abū Ḥanīfah bayn al-Muḥaddithiyn*, Ph.D dissertations, at University of Islamic Studies, Pakistan.

Hart H.L.A.(Herbert Lionel Adolphus), *The Concept of Law*, Oxford, 1961.

Ḥasan Ḥanafī, *Otoriteryenligin Epistomolojik, Ontolojik, Ahlaki, Siyasi ve Tarihi Kokleri*, tr. İlhami Güler, İslamiyat Dergisi, Ankara, 1999, vol. 2, no. 2, April-June 1999.

Ḥasan Turābī, *Islāmi Düşüncenin İhyası*, tr. Sefer Turan, Adem Yerinde, Ekin, Istanbul, 1997.

Ḥasan, Aḥmad, *The Early Development of Islamic Jurisprudence*, Islamic Research Institute, International Islamic University, Islamabad, 1994.

— *The Doctrine of Ijma' in Islam*, Islamic Research Institute, Islamabad, 1992.

— *Analogical Reasoning in Islamic Jurisprudence*, Islamic Research Institute, Islamabad, 1986.

— "The Principle of Istiḥsān in Islamic Jurisprudence", *Islamic Studies*, 16, 1967.

Haskafi, 'Alā al-Dīn Muḥammad b. 'Alī (1088/1677), *Al-Durar al-Mukhtār Sharḥu Tanwīyr al-Absar*, Beirut, 1979.

Ḥaṭīb, Abū Bakr Aḥmad bin 'Alī al-Baghdādī (d. 463/1071), *Al-Faqīh wa al-Mutafaqqih*, Makkah, 1975.

Hatipoğlu, Mehmet Sai'd, "*Hz. 'Ai'şe'nin Ḥadis Tenkitçiligi*", *AUIFD*, XIX, pp. 59-74, 1973.

— "*Islām'ın Aktüel Değeri Üzerine*", 12, *İslami Araştırmalar*, no. 1, Ankara, 1986.

Hawarizmī, Abū Muayyad Muḥammad b. Maḥmūd (d. 665/1267), *Jāmi' Masānīd al-Imām*, Dār al-Kutub al-Ilmiyyah, Beirut.

Ḥaydarī, 'Alī Taqiy, *Uṣūl al-Istinbāṭ*, Maṭba'ah al-Rābiṭah, Baghdad, 1959.

Haythamī, Shihāb al-Dīn Aḥmad b. Ḥajar (d. 973/1565), *Al-Ḥayat al-Ḥisān Manāqib al-Imām 'Aẓam Abū Ḥanifah an-Nu'mān*, ed. Khalīl al-Mays, Dār al-Kutub al-Ilmiyyah, Beirut, 1983.

Hiskett, Mervyn, *The Sword of Truth: The Life and Times of the Shehu Usuman Dan Fodio*, New York, 1973.

Ḥusayn Ḥāmid *Ḥasan, Naẓariyyāt al-Maṣlaḥah fī al-Fiqh al-Islāmī,* Maṭba'ah al-Mutanabbī, Cairo, 1981.

Ḥusayni, Ḥāshim Maghrūf, *Mabādī al-'Āmmah li al-Fiqh al-Jaghfarī,* Dār al-Nashr li al-Jam'iyyin Maktabah al-Naḥḍah, Baghdad.

Ibn 'Abd al-Shakūr, Muḥib Allāh al-Baḥarī al-Hindī (d. 1119/1707), *Musallam al-Thubūt ma'a Fawātiḥ al-Rahamūt fī 'Uṣūl al-Fiqh,* Cairo 1906.

Ibn 'Abd al-Bār, Abū 'Umar Yūsuf (d. 463/1071), *Jāmī' Bayān al-'Ilm,* ed. Muḥammad 'Abd al-Qadīr 'Aṭā, Muassasah al-Kutub al-Saqafiyyah, Beirut, 1997.

Ibn 'Abd al-Salām, 'Izz al-Dīn 'Abd al-'Azīz (d. 660/1262), *Qawāid al-Aḥkām fī Maṣāliḥ al-An'ām,* Cairo.

Ibn Abī Shaybah, Abū Bakr 'Abd Allāh b. Muḥammad (d. 235/849), *Al-Musannaf fi al-Aḥādīth wal Āṣār,* ed. Kamāl Yūsuf al-Hut, Riyadh, 1409.

Ibn 'Ābidīn, Muḥammad Amīn (d. 1252/1836), *Nashr al-'Urf fī bināi Ba'ḍ al-Aḥkām 'ala al-'Urf,* Beirut.

— *Radd al-Mukhṭār 'alā al-Durar al-Mukhṭār,* Beirut, 1979.

— *Ḥāshiyat al-Nasamāt al-Ashār,* Muṣṭafa Bābī al-Ḥalabī, Cairo.

Ibn Amīr al-Ḥajj Muḥammad bin Muḥammad Shams ad-Dīn (d. 879), *Al-Taqrīr wa al-Takhbīr 'alā Taḥrīr al-Kamāl* ibn al-Humām *fī 'Ilm al-Uṣūl*", Matbaah al-Amīriyyah, Bulāq, 1316.

Ibn 'Āshūr, Muḥammad Ṭāhir (d. 1973), "*Maqāṣid al-Sharī'ah al-Islāmīyyah*" (*İslam Hukuk Felsefesi, Gaye Problemi*), Rağbet, translated by Vecdi Akyüz, Mehmet Erdoğan, İstanbul, 1999.

— "*Ālam al-Fikr al-Islāmī fī Tarīkh al-Maghrib al-'Arabi*", Tunus.

— "*Maqāṣid al-Sharī'ah al-Islāmīyyah*", Tunus, 1366.

Ibn Athīr, *Imām* Majd al-Dīn, "*Jāmi' al-Uṣūl fī Aḥādith al-Rasūl*", Maktabat al-Ḥalwānī, Beirut.

Ibn Badrān 'Abd al-Qādir b. Aḥmad, "*Sharḥ Roudat al-Nazāir wa Jannat al-Manāzer li Ibn Qudāmah al-Maqdisi*", Salafī Printing Press, Cairo, 1342.

Ibn Fāris, Aḥmad (d. 395/1004), "*Mu'ājam Maqāyīs al-Lughah*", Dār Iḥyā' al-Turāth al-'Arabi, Beirut.

Ibn Ḥajar al-Asqalānī, Aḥmad b. 'Alī (d. 973/1565), *Fatḥ al-Bārī*, edited by Muḥib al-Dīn al-Ḥatīb, Cairo, 1408.

Ibn Ḥājib, 'Uthmān b. 'Amr b. Abū Bakr b. Yūnus Abū 'Amr Jamāl al-Dīn (d. 646/1249), "*Mukhtaṣar Muntaha' al-Sūl wa al-'Āmāl*", Constantinople, al-Maktabah al-Islāmiyyah, 1310.

Ibn Ḥallikān, Abu al-'Abbās Shams al-Dīn Aḥmad b. Muḥammad (d. 681/1282), "*Walāyat al-'A'yān wa Anbāu Abnā' al-Zamān*", ed. Muḥammad Muḥy al-Dīn 'Abd al-Ḥamīd, al-Saādah, Cairo, 1950.

Ibn Ḥanbal, Aḥmad Ibn Muḥammad, 'Abd Allāh al-Dhuhlā al-Shaybānī al-Marwāzī al-Baghdādī (d. 241/855), *Al-Musnad*, Beirut, 1985.

Ibn Ḥazm Abū Muḥammad 'Alī al-Andalūsī al-Ẓāhirī (d. 456/1064), *Mulakhkhasi ibṭāl al-Qiyās wa al-Ra'y wa al-Istiḥsān wa al-Taqlīd wa al-Ta'līl*, ed. Sa'īd al-Afghānī Maṭba'atu Jāmi'ah Dimishq, 1960.

— *Al-Iḥkām fī Uṣūl al-Aḥkām*, Dār al-Kutub al-'Ilmiyyah, Beirut.

— *Al-Nubadh fī Uṣūl al-Fiqh*", ed. Muḥammad Zāhid al-Ḥasan al-Kawtharī, Maṭba'ah al-Anwār, Cairo, 1940.

Ibn Hishām, 'Abd al-Malik, (d. 218/833), *Al Ṣīrah al-Nabawiyyah*", ii, ed. Muṣṭafā as-Saqā, Ibrāhīm al-Abyārī, 'Abd al-Ḥāfiẓ Shalabī, Dār al-Khayr, Beirut 1992.

Ibn Humām, Kamāl al-Dīn, Muḥammad bin 'Abd al-Waḥīd bin 'Abd al-Ḥamīd bin Mas'ūd al-Ḥanafī (d. 861/1457), *Fatḥ al-Qadīr*, Maṭba'ah al-Amīriyyah Bulāq, Cairo, 1316.

— *Al-Taysīr Sharḥ Al-Tahrīr fī 'Uṣūl al-Fiqh*, al-Amīriyyah Bulāq Cairo, 1317.

— *Sharḥ Fatḥ al-Qadīr*, Dār al-Fiqr, Beirut.

Ibn Humayd Ṣāliḥ b. 'Abd Allāh, *Raf' al-Ḥarāj fī al-Sharī'ah al-Islāmiyyah Ḍawābiṭuh Taṭbiyqātuh*, Makkah, 1403.

Ibn Kamāl, Shams al-Dīn Aḥmad b. Sulaymān (d. 904/1534), *Taghyīr al-Tanqīḥ fī al-Uṣūl*, Istanbul, 1308.

Ibn Khaldūn 'Abd al-Raḥmān bin Muḥammad (d. 808/1405), *Muqaddimah*, ed. 'Alī, Abd al-Wāḥīd Wāfī, Naḥḍat al-Miṣr, Cairo.

Ibn Mājah Abū 'Abd Allāh Muḥammad (d. 273/886), *Sunan*, Istanbul, 1981.

Ibn Malak 'Izz al-Dīn 'Abd al-Laṭīf (d. 801/1398), *Sharḥ Matn al-Manār*, Istanbul, 1315.

Ibn Manẓūr, Jamāl al-Dīn Muḥammad ibn Mukarram al-Anṣārī (d. 711/1311), *Lisān Al-'Arab*, Ṭaba'ah Bulāq, Manṣūrah, Cairo.

Ibn Mubārak, Jamīl Muḥammad, *Naẓariyyāt al-Ḍarūrah al-Shar'iyyah, Ḥudūduhā wa Ḍawābiṭuhā*, Dār al-Wafā, Manṣūrah Egypt, 1988.

Ibn Muqaffā (d. 137/756), *Risālah fī al-Ṣaḥābah*, ed. Muḥammad Kurd 'Alī, 4th ed., Rasāil al-Bulagh, Cairo, 1954.

Ibn Nadīm Abū al-Farāj Muḥammad b. Isḥāq (d. 438/1047), *Al-Fihrist*, Beirut, 1965.

Ibn Nujāym, Zayn al-'Ābidīn b. Ibrāhīm al-Shāhir (d. 970/1562), *Fatḥ al-Ghaffār al-Maghrūf bi-Mishqāt al-Anwār fī Uṣūl al-Fiqh*, Maṭba'ah Muṣṭafā Ḥalabī, Cairo, 1936.

— *Al-Ashbāh wa al-Naẓāir*, Dār al-Kutub al-'Ilmiyyah, Beirut, 1985.

Ibn Qayyim Muḥammad b. Abū Bakr b. Ayyūb b. Sa'd Shams al-Dīn al-Jawziyyah Dimishqī (d. 751/1350), *Al-Ṭuruq al-Ḥukumiyyah fī al-Siyāsah al-Shar'iyyah*, Egypt, 1317.

— *Ighāsat al-Lahfān min Masāyidi al-Shaiṭān*, ed. Majdī Fathī al-Sayyīd, Cairo, 1310.

— *I'lām al-Muwaqqi'īn min Rabb al-'Ālamīn*, ed. 'Abd al-Raḥmān al-Wakīl, Cairo.

Ibn Qudāmah, Abū Muḥammad Muwaffiq al-Dīn, 'Abd Allāh bin Aḥmad bin Muḥammad bin Qudāmah, Al-Maqdisī (d. 620/1223), *Rawḍah al-Nāẓāir wa Jannah al-Manāẓir*, Maṭba'ah al-Salafiyyah Cairo, 1342.

— *Al-Mughnī, al-Nūr al-Islāmiyyah*, Cairo.

Ibn Rushd, Abū Walīd Muḥammad b. Aḥmad b. Muḥammad, al-Qurtubī al-Mālikī (d. 520/1126), *Bidāyat al-Mujtahid wa Nihāyat al-Muqtaṣid*, Dār al-Ma'rifah, Beirut.

Ibn Sa'd Muḥammad (d. 230/844), *Al-Ṭabaqāṭ al-Kubrā*, Beirut, 1957.

Ibn Taymiyyah, Taqī al-Dīn Abū al-Abbās Aḥmad b. 'Abd al-Ḥalīm (d. 728/1328), *Mas'alat al-Istiḥsān*, ed. G. Makdisi, *Ibn Taimiya's Autograph Manuscript on Istiḥsān: Materials for Study of Islamic Legal Thought*, , in *Arabic and Islamic Studies in Honour of H.A.R. Gibb*, Harvard University Press, Cambridge, 1965.

— *Al-Musawwadah fī Uṣūl al-Fiqh*, Al-Maṭba'ah al-Madani, Cairo, 1964.

— *Al-Fatāwā al-Kubrā*, 19/ 200-201, Dār al-Kutub al-'Ilmiyyah.

— *Al-Musawwadah fī Uṣūl al-Fiqh*, ed. Muḥammad Muḥy al-Dīn 'Abd al-Ḥamīd, Dār al-Kitāb al-'Arabī, Beirut.

Ijī, 'Aḍuḍ al-Dīn 'Abd al-Raḥmān bin Aḥmad bin 'Abd al-Ghaffār, Abū al-Faḍl (d. 756/1355), *Sharḥ Mukhtaṣar al-Muntaha al-Uṣūlī*, Cairo, 1310.

İkbal Cavid, *Uluslararası Muhammed İkbal Sempozyumu Bildirileri, Muḥammed İkbal Kitabı*, IBBKDY, Istanbul, 1997.

İkbal Muḥammad, *İslamda Dini Düşüncenin Yeniden Doğuşu*, tr. Dr. N. Aḥmad Asrar, Birleşik, Istanbul.

Imām Māturīdī Abū Manṣūr Muḥammad b. Muḥammad (d. 333/944), *Ta'wilāt al-Ahl al-Sunnah* (*Ta'wilat al-Qur'ān*), Fatḥ Allah Hulfayf, Rashid Ef. Library no: 2159, Kayseri.

Isnawī, Jamāl al-Dīn 'Abd al-Raḥīm al-Ḥusayn Shāfi'ī (d. 772/1370), *Sullam al-Wusūl li-Sharḥ Nihāyat al-Sūl*, Maṭba'ah al-Salafiyyah, 1345.

— *Nihāyat al-Sūl fī Sharḥ al-Minhāj al-Uṣūl*, Beirut 1982.

İşcan Zeki, *Muḥammed 'Abduh'un Dini ve Siyasi Görüşleri*, Dergah, Istanbul, 1998.

Ismā'īl, Muḥammad Sha'bān, *Uṣūl al-Fiqh Tārikhuhu wa-Rijāluh*, Dār *al-Salām*, 2nd edition, Makkah al-Mukarramah, 1419/1998.

— *Al-Istiḥsān bayn al-Naẓariyyah wa al-Tatbīq*, Dār al-Saqāfah, Doha, Qatar, 1992.

— *Uṣūl al-Fiqh al-Muyassar*, Dār al-Kitāb al-Jāmī', Tawfīqīyyah, Cairo, 1994.

Isma'il b. Muḥammad al-'Ajlūni, *Kashf al-Khafa'*, Cairo, n.d.

'Iwaḍ, Al-Sayyid Ṣāliḥ, "*Al-Istiḥsān 'inda 'Ulamā' Uṣūl*", *Majallat al-Kulliyāt al-Sharī'ah wa al-Qānūn*, p. 6-100, no. 5, Cairo 1990.

'Īsāwī an-Najdā Aḥmad Muḥammad, *Dirāsah wa Taḥqīq Kitāb al-Adillah al-Mukhtalaf fīhā li-Imām Badr al-Dīn al-Zarkashī*, unpublished Ph.D dissertation, Faculty of Sharī'ah and Qānūn, University of al-Azhar, Cairo, 1988.

İzmiri, Sulaymān Muḥammad b.Wali (d. 1102 AH), *Mir'at al-Uṣūl fī Sharḥ al- Mirqāt al-Wuṣūl*, İstanbul, 1309.

İzmirlī, Ismā'īl Hakkī (d. 1946), *Sebīl al-Re;ād*, nu. 297, p. 190-195, nu. 293, p. 129-132.

— *'Ilmi Khilāf'*, Istanbul, 1330.

Jāḥiẓ, Abū Uthmān 'Amr b. Baḥr (d. 255/869), *Al-Bayān wa al-Tabyīn*, Beirut, 1967.

Jamāl al-Dīn 'Abd al-Raḥmān, *Al-Maṣlaḥah al-Mursalah wa Makānātuhā fī al-Tashrī'*, Dār al-Kitāb al-Jāmī', Cairo, 1983.

Jār Allāh Mūsā, Bilgiyaf (d. 1874/1949), *Kitāb al-Sunnah*, translated by Mehmet Görmez, Ankara Okulu, Ankara, 1988.

Jaṣṣāṣ Abū Bakr Aḥmad b. 'Alī al-Rāzī (d. 370/981), *Al-Fuṣūl fi al-Uṣūl*, ed. Ājil Jasīm an-Nashmī, Wazarāt al-Awkāf wa al-Shu'ūn al-Islāmiyyah, Kuwait, 1988.

— *Aḥkām al-*Qur'an, edited by Muḥammad al-Sādiq Kamḥāwī, Dār al-Musḥāf, Cairo.

John Cooper, Ronald L. Nettler and Muḥammad Maḥmūd, *Islām and Modernity - Muslim Intellectuals Respond*, I.B.Tauris, London, 1998.

Joseph Catafago, *English and Arabic Dictionary*, London, 1958.

Jowharī, al-Shaykh Abū Naṣr Ismā'īl bin Ḥammād (d. 398), *Tāj al-Lughah and Ṣiḥaḥ al-Arabiyyah*, Part 5, 2099, Cairo, 1382.

Jum'ah 'Adnān Muḥammad, *Al-Istiṣḥāb fī al-Sharī'ah al-Islāmiyyah*, unpublished Ph.D dissertation, Faculty of Sharī'ah and Qānūn, University of al-Azhar, Cairo,1989

— *Raf' al-Ḥaraj fī Sharī'ah al-Islāmiyyah*, Damascus, 1993.

Juwaynī Abu al-Ma'ālī 'Abd al-Malik b. 'Abd Allāh (d. 478/1085), *Al-Talkhīṣ fī Uṣūl al-Fiqh*, ed. 'Abd Allāh b. Jawlim, al-Nibālī Shabbi Aḥmad al-'Umarī, Beirut, 1996.

— *Al-Burḥan fī Uṣūl al-Fiqh*, Cairo, 1400.

Kal'ajī, Muḥammad Rawas Ḥāmid Ṣādiq Kanibī, *Mū'jam al-Lughah al-Fuqahā*, Dār al-Nafāis, Beirut, 1988.

Kamālī, Muḥammad Hāshim, *Istiḥsān Juristic Preference and its Application to Contemporary Issues*, Islamic Development Bank, IRTI, Jeddah, Saudi Arabia, 1997.

— *Principles of Islamic Jurisprudence*, Islamic Text Society, Cambridge. 1997.

Kapani Munci, *İnsan Haklarının Uluslararası Boyutları*, İstanbul, 1987.

Kara İsmail, *Türkiye'de İslamcılık Düşncesi*, Risale, İstanbul, 1986.

Karaman Ḥayreddin, "*Modernist Proje ve İctihad, Yaman Aḥmed*" in *Makasıd ve İctihad, İslam Hukuk Felsefesi Araştırmaları*, Hüner, Konya, 2002.

— *Mukayeseli İslām Ḥukuku*, Nesil yayınları, İstanbul, 1991.

— "Adet", *DIA*, vol. 1, p. 369-372.

— *Gerçek İslam'da Birlik Afgani, Abduh, Reşit Riza*, Nesil, İstanbul.

— *Günün Meseleleri*, 1/197, Gerçek Hayat, İz Yayıncılık, İstanbul, 2003.

— *İslām Ḥukuk Tarihi*, İz Yayıncılık, İstanbul, 1999.

— *Günlük Yaşantımızda Helaller ve Haramalar*, İstanbul, 1982.

— *İslām Ḥukukunda İctihad*, MUIFV, İstanbul, 1996.

— *Yeni gelişmeler karşısında İslam Ḥukuk'u*, İz yayıncılık İstanbul, 1998.

Karamasti, Yūsuf b. Ḥusayn (d. 906/1500), *Al-Wajīz fī Uṣūl al-Fiqh*, ed. al-Sayyid 'Abd al-Laṭīf Kassāb, Dār al-Hady, Cairo, 1984.

Kasānī, Abū Bakr 'Alā al-Dīn b. Mas'ūd (d. 587/1191), *Badāi' al-Sanāi' fī Tartīb al-Sharā'*, Dār al-Kutub al-'Arabī, Beirut, 1982.

Kashanī, Mullah Muḥsīn Fayd, *Tafsīr al-Ṣāfī*, Tehran, 1269.

Kassim Ḥussain, "Sarakhsi's Doctrine of Juristic Preference (Istiḥsān) as a Methodological Approach Toward Worldly Affairs (*Aḥkām al-Dunyā*)", 5, *The American Journal of Islamic Social Sciences*, 181-205, 1988.

Kassab, al-Sayyid 'Abd al-Laṭīf, *Adwā' Ḥawl Qadiyyah al-Ijtihād fī al-Sharī'ah al-Islāmiyah*, Dār al-Tawfīq, Cairo, 1404/1984.

Kātip Chalabi, *Balance of Truth*, tr. from Turkish by G. L. Lewis, London, 1957.

Kawtharī, Muḥammad Zāhid (d. 1952), *Fiqh Ahli Iraq wa Ḥadīthuhum*, ed. 'Abd al-Fattāh 'Abū Ghuddah, Beirut.

— *Maqālāt*, Cairo, 1388.

Kerr, H. Malcolm, *Islamic Reform, the Political and Legal Theories of Muḥammad 'Abduh and Rashīd Riḍā*, University of California Press, USA, 1966.

Keskioğlu Osman, *Fıkıh Tarihi ve İslām Ḥukuku*, Ankara, 1969.

Khadduri, Majid and Liebesny, J. Herbert, *Law in the Middle East*, the Middle East Institute, Washington, 1955.

Khadimi, Noraddin b. Mukhtār, "*Al-Ijtihād al-Maqāṣidi*", *Kitāb al-Ummah Magazine*, Qatar, no. 66, vol. 2, 1419.

Khallāf, 'Abd al-Wahhāb (d. 1376/1956), *Al-Ijtihād bi al-Ra'y, al-Qiyās, al-Istiḥsān, al-Istiṣlāḥ, al-Istiṣḥāb*, Dār al-Kutub al-'Arabī, Cairo, 1950.

— *Hulāsatu Tārīhi al-Tashrī al-Islāmī*, al-Maktabah al-Islāmīyyah, Istanbul 1984.

— *Maṣāder al-Tashrī al-Islāmī fī mā lā Naṣṣah fīhī*, Dār al-Qalam, Kuwait, 1993.

— *'Ilm Uṣūl al-Fiqh*, 12th ed., Dār al-Qalam, Kuwait, 1398/1978.

Khatib Abū Bakr Aḥmad b. 'Alī al-Baghdādī (d. 463/1071), *Al-Faqīh wa al-Mutafaqqih*, Makkah, 1975.

— *Tārikhi Baghdad*, Beirut.

Khayyāt, 'Abd al-'Azīz, *Naẓariyyāt al-'Urf*, Maktabah al-Aqṣā, Amman, 1997.

Khuḍarī, Muḥammad (d. 1927), *Tārīkh Tashrī' al-Islāmī*, tr. into Turkish Ḥaydar Ḥatipoğlu, Kahraman yayınları, İstanbul, 1974.

— *Tārīkh Tashrī' al-Islāmi*, Dār al-Kutub al-'Ilmiyyah, Beirut, 1985

— *Uṣūl al-Fıqh*, 7th ed., Dār al-Fikr, Cairo, 1401/1981.

Kılıç, Muharrem, "The Two Methods of Tackling Methodological Formalism in the Comparative Legal History: *Istiḥsān* and Equity", *Journal of Islamic Law Studies*, p. 147-165, no.1, 2003, Konya/Turkey.

Koca Ferhat, "*İslam Hukukunda Maslahat'ı Mursalah ve Necmeddin el-Ṭūfī'nin bu Konudaki Görüşlerinin Değerlendirilmesi*", *ILAM Research Magazine*, vol. 1, no.1 (January- June), pp. 93-122, İstanbul, 1996.

— *İslām Ḥukuk Metodolojisinde Takhṣīṣ*, Ph.D dissertation, Istanbul, 1993.

Köksal Muṣṭafa Āsım, *İslām Tārikhi*, Şamil Yayınevi, Sultanahmet Istanbul, 1987.

Köprülü, M. Fuad, *İslam ve Türk Ḥukuk Tārihi Araştırmaları Vakfi Muessesesi*, İstanbul, 1983.

Köse, Saffet, *Islam Hukukunda Hakkın Kötüye Kullanılması*, Istanbul, 1997.

Kurzman Charles, *Liberal Islam: A Sourcebook*, Oxford University press, 1998.

Laknawī, 'Abd al-'Alī Muḥammad bin Nizām al-Dīn Ansārī, Baḥr al-'Ulūm, Abū al-'Abbās, Ḥanafī (d. 1180/1767), *Fawātiḥ al-Raḥamūt Sharḥ Musallam al-Subūt fī Uṣūl al-Fiqh*, Matba'ah al-Amīriyyah, Bulāq, Cairo 1906, Dār al-Ma'rifah, Beirut.

Madhkūr, Muḥammas Sallām, *Al-Ijtihād fī al-Tashrī' al-Islāmī*, Dār al-Nahdat al-'Arabiyyah, Cairo, 1984.

Maḥillāwī, Muḥammad 'Abd al-Raḥmān 'Aid, Al-Ḥanafī al-Qāḍī bil-Maḥkamah al-'Ulyā' al-Shar'iyyah, *Tashīl al-Wuṣūl ilā 'Ilm al-Uṣūl*, Bāb Al-Ḥalabī Publishers, Rabī' al-Awwal, 1341H, Cairo.

The Ottoman courts manual *Majallah al-Aḥkām*, promulgated by the Royal Iradah, 26 Sha'ban, 1293.

Majallat al-Majmā' al-Fiqh al-Islāmī, *Qarārāt wa al-Tawṣiyyāt*, 9, Kuwait, 1988.

Makhlūf, Muḥammad Ḥasanayn al-Adawīy al-Mālikī, *Bulūgh al-Sūl fī Madkhal 'Ilm al-Uṣūl*, Bābi Al-Ḥalabī, second Edition, 1386 H, 1966.

Makkī, Muwaffaq b. Aḥmad (d. 568/1172), *Manāqib al-Abu Ḥanīfah*, Beirut, 1981.

Mālik b. Anas (d. 179/795), *Al-Muwaṭṭā'*, Cairo, 1951.

Mallat Chibli, *The Renewal of Islamic Law*, Cambridge University Press, 1993.

Makdisi George, "Legal Logic and Equity in Islamic Law", 33, *American Journal of Comparative Law*, 63-92, 1985.

— Ibn Taymiyyah's Autograph Manuscript on *Istiḥsān*: Materials for Study of Islamic Legal Thought, pp. 446-479 in *Arabic and Islamic Studies in Honour of H.A.R. Gibb*, Cambridge: Harvard University Press, 1965.

Marghinānī, Burhān al-Dīn 'Alī b. Abī Bakr al-Ḥanafī (d. 593), *Al-Hidayah Sharḥ Bidāyat al-Mubtadī*, Istanbul, 1327.

Mar'ī Ḥasan Aḥmad, "*Al-Istiḥsān 'inda al-Aimmat al-'Arba'ah wa Taṭbīqāt al-Fiqhiyyah*", *Majallat Kulliyyāt al-Dirāsāt al-Islāmiyyah wa al-'Arabiyyah*, pp. 9-46, no. 15, 1998/1418.

Martin Elizabeth A., "*A Dictionary of Law*", Oxford University Press, 2003, UK.

Mas'ūd Afandi, "*Mir'āti Majallah*", Istanbul, 1299.

Masood M. Khālid, *Islamic Legal Philosophy*, International Islamic Publishers Delhi, 1989.

— *Islām Ḥukuk Teorisi*, translated by Muḥarrem Kılıç, İstanbul, 1977.

Matlūb, Maḥmūd, *Abū Yūsuf*, University of Baghdad, Iraq, 1972.

Mawdūdī, Abū al-'Alā (d. 1979), *Towards Understanding of Islām*, tr. Khurshid Aḥmad, Islamic Publications Ltd., Lahore, 1960.

— *Islām Düşüncesi Tarihi*, ed. M. M. Sharif.

— *Islamic Law and Constitution*, tr. Khurshid Aḥmad, Islamic Publications Ltd., Lahore, 1960.

Māwardī, 'Alī b. Muḥammad b. Ḥabīb Abu al-Ḥasan al-Māwardī al-Baṣrī al-Shāfi'ī (d. 450/1058), *Adab al-Qāḍī*, ed. Muḥyi Hilāl al-Sarhan, Matba'at al-Irshad, Baghdad 1971.

Meezan Bank: *http://www.meezanbank.com/knowledge-islamic-section-4-5.asp.*

Mehmet Aydın, *Elmalılı'da Teceddüd Fikri*, İslam Felsefesi Yazıları, Ufuk, İstanbul, 2000.

Mik'ah, Abū Bakr Ismā'īl, *Al-Ra'y wa Atharuh fī Madrasat al-Madīnah*, Muassasat al-Risālah, Beirut, 1985

Mikadī, Maḥmūd 'Abd al-Qādir, *Bahth fī al-Istiḥsān*", pp. 297-343, in *Al-Majlis al-'Alā li-Ri'āyat al-Funūn wa al-Adab wa al-'Ulūm al-Ijtimā'iyyah*, Usbū' al-Fiqh al-Islāmī, Damascus, 1380/1960.

Molla Jiwān, Aḥmad b. Abī Sa'īd b. 'Ubayd Allāh al-Ḥanafī (d. 1130/1718), *Sharḥ Nur al-Anwār 'alā al-Manār*, 1st edition, Matba'ah al-Amīriyyah, Bulaq, Cairo.

Mullah Ḥusraw, Muḥammad bin Firāmūz (885/1480), *Mir'āt al-Uṣūl Sharḥ Mirkāt al-Wuṣūl*, Matba'ah al-Amīrah, Istanbul, 1309.

Mu'tamar al-Awwal li Majmā' al-Buḥūs al-Islāmiyyah, pp. 393-395, Al-Azhar University, Cairo, 1964.

Muḥammad 'Abid al-Jābirī, *Takwīn al-'Aql al-'Arabī* (*'Arap Aklının oluşumu*), tr. İbrahim Akbaba, İz, İstanbul, 1997.

Muqrī, al-'Ālim Aḥmad b. Muḥammad b. 'Alī al-Fayyūmī (d. 770), "*Missbāḥ al-Munīr fī Gharīb al-Sharkh al-Kabīr li al-Rāf'* ", ed. 'Abd al-'Aẓīm al-Shannāwī, Dār al-Maārif, Cairo.

Mūsā, Muḥammad Yūsuf, *Tārikh al-Fiqh al-Islām*, Maktabat al-Sundus, Kuwait.

Muslaḥ al-Dīn, Muḥammad, *Islamic Jurisprudence and the Rule of Necessity and Need*, Abu al-Qāsim Bookstore, Jeddah, 1410.

— *Philosophy of Islamic Law and the Orientalists*, Markazi Maktabah Islāmī, Delhi, June 1985.

Muslim, Abū al-Ḥusayn Muslim bin Ḥajjāj (d. 261/874), *Al-Jāmi' al-Ṣaḥīḥ*, Istanbul, 1981.

Muṣṭafā Zayd, *Al-Maṣlaḥah fī al-Tashrī' al-Islāmī wa Najm al-Dīn al-Ṭūfī*, Dār al-Fikr al-'Arabi, Cairo.

Mutahhari, Murtaza, *Jurisprudence and its Principles*, tr. Moḥammed Salmān Tawḥīd, New York, 1982.

Nadwī, 'Alī Aḥmad, *Al-Qawā'id al-Fiqhiyyah*, Dār al-Qalam, Dimishq, 1994.

Nāim 'Abd Allāh Aḥmad, *Toward an Islamic Reformation*, Syracuse University Press, New York, 1990.

Nasafī, 'Abd Allāh bin Aḥmad bin Maḥmūd, Ḥāfiz al-Din Abu al-Baraqāt Al-Ḥanafī (d. 710/1310), *Kashf al-Asrār fī Sharḥ al-Muṣannaf 'alā al-Manār fī al-Uṣūl*, 2 vols, al-Maṭba'ah al-Kubrā al-Amīrīyyah, Cairo, 1316.

— *Madārik al-Tanzīl wa Ḥaqāiku al-Ta'wīl*, Beirut.

Nashmī 'Ajil Jasīm, "*Al-Istiḥsān; Ḥaqīqatuhu wa Mazāhib al-Uṣūliyyin fih*", *Majallat al-Sharī'ati wa al-Dirāsāt al-Islāmiyyah*, pp. 107-136, no. 1, Kuwait, April 1984/1404.

Nashshār, 'Alī Sāmī, *Islamda Felsefi Düşüncenin Doğuşu*, tr. Osman Tunç, Istanbul, 1999.

— *Nash'at al-Fikr al-Falsafī*, Dār al-Maārif, Cairo, 1977

Nasr, Seyyed Hossein, *Ideals and Realities of Islam*, George Allen Unwin Ltd, London, 1966.

Nu'mani, Shibli, *Life of Umar the Great: the Second Caliph of Islām*, vol.2, tr. Muḥammad Saleem, Ashraf Press, Lahore, 1962.

Nursi, Said Badi' al-Zamān, *Risalai Nur Külliyyatından Sözler*, Yeni Asya Neşriyat, İstanbul, 1998.

Nyazee, Imran Aḥsan Khan, *Theories of Islamic Law*, Delhi, 1996.

Öğüt, Salim, "Ebu Yusuf", p.263, X, *DIA*.

Önder, Muḥarrem, *Ḥanefi Mezhebinde Istiḥsān Anlayışı ve Uygulaması*, Unpublished Ph.D dissertation, University of Selçuk, Konya, 2000.

Özcan, Ḥanifi, *Maturidi'de Dini. Çoğulculuk*, İstanbul, 1995.

Özen Şükrü, *Istiḥsān and Maṣlaḥat Concepts in Second Century after the Hegira*, Marife, pp. 31-57 year, 3, no. 1, Spring 2003, Konya, Turkey.

Özköse Kadir, *Muḥammed Sanusi Hayatı, Eserleri, Hareketi*, İnsan yayınları, İstanbul, 2000.

Qaradāwī, Yūsuf, *İslam Ḥukuku Evrensellik Süreklilik*, tr. Yusuf Işıcık, Aḥmet Yaman, Marifet Yayınları, İstanbul, Ekim, 1999.

— *Al-Khaṣāiṣ al-Āmmah li al-Islām*, Beirut, 1985.

— *Al-Ijtihād fi Sharī'ah al-Islāmiah*, Kuwait, 1989.

— "*Al-Halāl wa al-Ḥarām fī al-Islām*", Cairo, 1976.

Qarafī, Aḥmad bin Idrīs bin 'Abd al-Raḥmān, Abū 'Abbās Sha'b al-Dīn al-Sanhājī Al-Mālikī (d. 684/1285), *Sharḥ Tanqīḥ al-Fuṣūl fī Ikhtisār al-Mahṣūl fī al-'Uṣūl*, ed. Ṭāhā 'Abd al-Raūf Sa'd, Maktabah al-Azharīyyah, Cairo.

— *Kitāb Anwār al-Burūq fī Anwār al-Furūq*, Dār al Mā'rifah, Beirut.

Qurashi, Galib 'Abd al-Kāfi, *Awwaliyyat al-Fārūq al-Siyāsīyyah*, Dār al-Wafā, Manṣūrah, Egypt, 1990.

Qurtubī, Abū 'Abd Allah Muḥammad b. Aḥmad (d. 760/1359), *Al-Jāmī' li Aḥkām al-Qur'an*, Dār al-Iḥyā al-Turās al-'Arabī, Beirut, 1967.

Qutb, Sayyid (d. 1967), *Islām Toplumuna Doğru*, tr. Aḥmed Pakalin, İslamoğlu, İstanbul, 1988.

Rabī'ah, 'Abd al-'Azīz ibn 'Abd al-Raḥmān, *Adillat al-Tashri' al-Mukhtalaf fī al-Ihtijāj bi-hā: al-Qiyās, al-Istiḥsān, al-Istiṣlāḥ, al-Istiṣḥāb*, Riyadh, 1981.

Rāghib Iṣfahānī, Abū Qāṣim Ḥusayin (d. 502/1108), *Mufradāt fī Gharīb* Qur'an, ed. Muḥammad Ḥusayn Kaylānī, Dārul Ma'rifah, Beirut.

Rahawī Yahya b. Mūsā al-Mālikī (d. 774/1372), *Hashiyat al-Rahawi 'alal Manār,* Istanbul, 1315.

Raḥman, Fazlur, "Revival and Reform in Islām", *Cambridge History of Islam*, D.M. Halt, C.B, Cambridge Uni. Press, Cambridge 1970.

— *İslam ve Çağdaşlık,* tr. Alparslan Açıkgenç, Okulu Yayınları, Ankara, 2002.

— "Islam and Political Action: Politics in the Service of Religion", *Cities of Gods*, ed. N. Biggar, J.S. Scott.

— *Islamic Methodology in History*, Lahore, 1965.

— *Islām*, London, 1966. and *Islām*, tr. Mehmet Dağ, Mehmet Aydın, Ankara Okulu, 2000.

— "Islamic Modernism: Its Scope, Method and Alternatives", *IJMES*, 1, 1970, pp. 317-333.

— "Law and Ethics in Islam", *Ethics in Islam*, ed. R. Hovannisian, Undena Publications, California, 1985.

— *Revival and Reform in Islām*, ed. Ebrahim Moosa, Oneworld Publications, Oxford, 2000.

— *Makaleler I*, tr. Adil Çiftçi, Ankara Okulu, 2000.

— *Makaleler II*, tr. Adil Çiftçi, Ankara Okulu, 1999.

— *Makaleler III*, tr. Adil Çiftçi, Ankara Okulu, 2002.

— *Makaleler IV*, tr. Adil Çiftçi, Ankara Okulu, 2003.

— *Islam and Modernity*, University of Chicago, 1982.

Raysūnī Aḥmad, "*An-Naṣ wa al-Maṣlaḥah bayn al-Taṭbīq wa al-Taāruḍ*", *Islāmīyyāt al-Ma'rifah*, vol. IV, no. 13, Summer, IIIT, Herndon, 1419/1998.

— *Nazariyyāt al-Maqāṣid 'inda al-Imām al-Shāṭibī*, p. 353, IIIT, Maryland, 1995.

Rāzī Fakhr al-Dīn Muḥammad b. 'Umar al-Ḥusayn (d. 606/1210), *Al-Maḥṣūl fī 'Ilm al-Uṣūl al-Fiqh*, Beirut, 1988.

Mafātīḥ al-Ghayb: Al-Mushtahar bi-al-Tafsīr al-Kabīr, al-Matba'ah al-Āmirah al-Sharafiyyah, Cairo, 1324-1327.

Rāzī, Muḥammad b. Abī Bakr (d. 660), *Mukhtār al-Ṣiḥaḥ*, Dār al-Ma'rifah, Beirut.

Riḍā, Rāshīd, *Al-Manār*, vol. 9, no. 10, Cairo, 1909.

Sa'dī 'Abd al-Ḥakīm 'Abd al-Raḥmān As'ad, *Mabāḥith al-'Illah fī al-Qiyās 'inda al-Uṣūliyyīn*, unpublished Ph.D dissertation, Faculty of Sharī'ah and Qānūn, Al-Azhar University, Egypt,1985.

Ṣadr al-Sharī'ah, 'Ubayd Allāh Ibn Mas'ūd bin Tāj Al-Sharī'ah al-Ḥanafī (d. 747/1346), *Al-Tawdīḥ fī Ḥall Jawāmid al-Tanqīḥ*, Matba'ah Muḥammad 'Alī Ṣabīh, Cairo.

— *Al-Tawdīḥ fī Ḥall Jawāmid al-Tanqīḥ*, Karachi, 1979.

Sahawī Abū 'Abd Allāh Muḥammad (d. 902/1497), *Fath al-Mughith bi Sharḥ Alfiyati al-Ḥadīth li al-'Iraqiyyah*, ed. 'Alī Ḥusayn 'Alī, Dār al-Imām al-Tabari, 1992.

Saḥnūn b. 'Abd al-Salām (d. 240/854), *Al-Mudawwanah al-Kubrā*, a collections and opinions and traditions of Mālik Ibn Qāsim (d. 191), Ibn Wahb (d. 197) and others, 16 vols, Cairo, 1323-24.

Saleh A. Nabil, *Unlawful Gain and Legitimate Profit in Islamic Law*, Cambridge University Press, 1986.

Sālim Rustem Baz, *Sharḥ al-Majallah*, Beirut, 1986.

Samarrāī Ḥasib, *Dini Modernizmin Üç Şovalyesi*, tr. Alī Nar, Sezai Özel, Bedir Publication, Istanbul, 1998.

Ṣana'ānī Muḥammad b. Ismā'īl Amīr (d. 1182 H), *Uṣūl al-Fiqh al-Musammā Ijābat al-Sāil Sharḥ Baghyat al-Āmil*, ed. Ḥusayn b. Aḥmad al-Siyāghī, Muassasah al-Risālah, Beirut, 1988.

Sanawī, Sa'd Muḥammad, *Madai' Ḥājāti li al-'Aḥdi bi Nazariyyāt al-Maṣlaḥati al-Mursalah fī al-Fiqh al-Islāmī*, Cairo, 1981.

Sarakhsī, Muḥammad bin Aḥmad bin Sahl Abū Bakr Shams al-Aimmah al-Ḥanafī (d. 483/1090), *Al-Uṣūl*, ed. Abū al-Wafā al-Afghānī, Dār al-Fiqr , Beirut, 1991.

— *Kitāb al-Mabsūṭ*, Beirut. 2nd ed.

Sawa Pasha, *Islām Ḥukuku Nazariyatı*, tr. Baha Arıkan, Ankara, 1965.

Sayis 'Alī, Muḥammad 'Abd al-Laṭīf al-Subkī, Muḥammad Yūsuf al-Barbarī, *Tārīkh al-Tashrī al-Islāmī*, Cairo, 1939.

Saymari Ḥusayn b. 'Alī (d. 436/1045), *Akhbāru Abū Ḥanifah wa Aṣḥābuh*, Beirut, 1985.

Saymen, F. Hakki/Elbir, H. Kemal, *Türk Borçlar Hukuku, Umumi Hükümler*, Istanbul, 1958.

Sayyid Bay, *Uṣūl al-Fiqh Madkhal*, Istanbul, 1917.

Schacht, Joseph, *An Introduction to Islamic Law*, Oxford at the Clarendom Press, 1964.

— *Islām Ḥukukuna Giriş*, tr. Mehmet Dağ, Abdulkadir Şener, AÜİFY, Ankara, 1977.

— *The Origins of Muḥammadan Jurisprudence*, Oxford University Press, London, 1950.

Şener Abdulkadir, *Islām Ḥukukunun Kaynaklarından Qiyās, Istiḥsān ve Istiṣlāḥ*, Ankara, 1974.

Sha'bān Zaki al-Dīn, *Islām Ḥukuk Ilminin Esaslari*, tr. İbrahim Kafi Dönmez, Ankara, 1990.

— *Uṣūl al-Fiqh al-Islāmī*, University Book House, Cairo, 1964-65.

Shāfi'ī, Imām Abī 'Abd Allah Muḥammad bin Idrīs (d. 204/819), *Islamic Jurisprudence Shafi'ī's Risala*, by Majid Khadduri, Johns Hopkins Press, Baltimore, 1961.

— *Jimā' al-'Ilm*, ed. Muḥammad Aḥmad Abd al-'Aziz, Dār al-Kutub al-'Ilmiyyah, Beirut.

— *Al-Risālah*, ed. M. Sayyīd Kīlāni, 2nd ed., Musṭafā al-Bābi al-Ḥalabī, Cairo, 1983.

Sha'bān M. Ismā'il, *Uṣūl al-Fiqh al-Muyassar*, Dār al-Kutub al-Jāmi'ī, Cairo. 1415/1994.

Shahristānī, Abu al-Fatḥ Muḥammad b. 'Abd al-Karīm b. Abū Bakr (d. 548/1153), *Al-Milal wa al-Niḥal*, 1/348, ed. Muḥammad Sayyid Kaylānī, Cairo, 1976.

Shalabī, Muḥammad Muṣṭafā, *Ta'līl al-Aḥkām 'Arḍ wa Taḥlīl li-Ṭarīqat al-Ta'līl wa Taṭawwurātihā fi 'Uṣūr al-Ijtihād wa al-Taqlīd*, Egypt, 1947.

— *Uṣūl al-Fiqh al-Islāmī*, p. 304, Beirut, 1986.

— *Al-Madkhal fi al-Tā'rīf al-Fiqh al-Islāmī*, Dār an-Nahḍat al-'Arabiyyah, Beirut, 1985.

Shalabi, Ṣalaḥ al-Din 'Abd al-'Aziz, "*Al-Istiḥsān fi al-Fiqh al-Islāmī wa Maṣdariyyatuhu al-Tashrī'iyyah*", Cairo, 1989.

Shaleh, Aḥmad Syukri, *Ibn Taymiyya's Concept of Istiḥsān: An Understanding of Legal Reasoning in Islamic Jurisprudence*, University of Montreal Ann Arbor (Michigan), 1995.

Shaltūt, Maḥmūd, *Al-Islām 'Aqīdah wa Sharī'ah*, Maktabi Dār al-Qalam, Kuwait, 1966.

Sharbasī, Aḥmad, *Yas'alūnaka fī al-Dīni wa al-Ḥayāt*, Beirut, 1981.

Sharī'ati, 'Alī (d. 1977), *Yarının Tarihine Bakiş*, tr. Orhan Pekin, Ejder, Said Okumuş, Birleşik, İstanbul, 1998.

— *Öze Dönüş*, tr. Kerim Güney, Kitabevi, İstanbul, 1999.

— *Ne Yapmalı*, tr. Muḥammad Hizb Allah, Birleşik, İstanbul, 1995.

Sharif M. M. 'Abd al-Ḥamīd, *İslām Düşüncesi Tarihi*, İstanbul, 1992.

Shāshī Isḥāq bin Ibrāhīm 'Abū Ya'qūp al-Khorasānī al-Shāshī (d. 325/937), *Uṣūl Al-Shāshī with 'Umdat Al-Ḥawāshī*, Delhi, 1303 H.

Shāṭibī, Abū Ishāq Ibrāhīm bin Mūsā Al-Ghirnāṭī (d. 790/1388), *Al-Muwāfaqāt fī Uṣūl al-Sharī'ah*" (*İslami ilimler metodolojisi)*, tr. into Turkish Mehmet Erdoğan, İz yayıncılık, İstanbul, 1999.

— *Al-I'tisām*, Beirut.

— *Al-Muwāfaqāt fi-Uṣūl al-Sharī'ah*, ed. 'Abd Allāh Dirāz, Dār al-Ma'rifah, Beirut, 1997.

Shaw, Bernard, *The Muslim Review*, March 1933.

Shawkānī, Abū 'Alī Badr al-Dīn Muḥammad bin 'Alī (d. 1250/1834), *Nayl al-Awtār Sharḥ Muntaqā al-Akhbār min Aḥādīth Sayyid al-Akhbār*, Matba'ah Muṣṭafā Bābi al-Ḥalabī, Cairo.

— *Irshād al-Fuḥūl ilā Taḥqīq al-Ḥaq min 'Ilm al-Uṣūl*, Cairo, 1937.

— *Al-Qawl al-Mufīd fī Adillah al-Ijtihād wa al-Taqlīd*, Kuwait, 1400/1980.

Shaybānī, Muḥammad b. Ḥasan (d. 189/805), *Al-Jāmī' al-Ṣaghīr*, ed. 'Abd al-Ḥayy al-Laknawī, cited by Z. Isḥāq, Anṣārī, *The Early Development of Islamic Fiqh in Kufah*, Unpublished Ph.D dissertation, McGill University, Montreal.

— *Al-Hujjah 'alā Ahl al-Madīnah,* Al-Kailāni Mahdī Ḥasan, 'Ālam al-Kutub, Beirut.

— *Kitab* al-*Āthār*, Lahore, 1329.

— *Al-Aṣl*, ed. Abū al-Wafā al-Afghānī, Beirut, 1990.

— *Al-Jāmi‘ al-Kabīr*, ed. Abū al-Wafā al-Afghānī, Dār al-Iḥyā al-Turāth al-‘Arabī, Beirut, 1399.

— *Al-Siyar al-Kabīr*, ed. Salāḥ al-Dīn al-Munajjid, Matābi‘ Sharikāt al-I‘lānāt al-Sharqiyyah, 1971.

Shīrāzī, Abū Isḥāq Ibrāhīm b. ‘Alī b. Yūsuf al-Fayrūzabādī (d. 476/1083), *Sharḥ al-Luma*, ed. ‘Abd al-Majīd Turkī, Beirut.

— *Al-Tabaṣṣurah fī Uṣūl al-Fiqh*, ed. Muḥammad Ḥusain Hītū, Dār al-Fiqr, n.d.

Smith, ‘Abd Allāh, "The Islamic Revolutions of the 19th Century", *Journal of the Historical Society of Nigeria*, II, 1961, p. 176.

Sobhānī, Āyatollah Ja‘fār, *Doctrines of Shi‘ī Islām*, tr. Reza Shah Kazemi, The Institute of Ismaili Studies, London, 2001.

Sonn, Tamara, "Fazlur Raḥman's Islamic Methodology", *The Muslim World*, 1991.

Subkī, ‘Abd al-Wahhab bin ‘Alī b. ‘Abd al-Kāfī Tāj al-Dīn Abū Naṣr (d. 771/1370), *Al-Ibhāj fī Sharḥ al-Minhāj*, ed. Sha‘bān Muḥammad Ismā‘īl, Maktabat al-Kulliyyāt al-Azhariyyah, Cairo, 1981.

— *Jam‘ al-Jawāmi‘ fī Uṣūl al-Fiqh*, with commentary by al-Maḥallī and al-Bannanī, Cairo, 1297.

— *Ṭabaqāt al-Shāfī‘yyah al-Kubrā’*, A. Muḥammad al-Ḥulw, M. Muḥammad al-Tannāḥī, Matba‘ah ‘Isā al-Bābi al-Ḥalabī, Cairo, 1964.

— *Sharḥ al-Jalāl al-Maḥallī ‘alā’ Jam‘ al-Jawāmi‘*, Maktabah al-Tijāriyyah, Cairo.

Suyūṭī, Jalāl al-Dīn ‘Abd al-Raḥmān bin Abī Bakr bin Muḥammad bin Sābiq al-Dīn al-Khudayrī al-Suyūṭī (d. 911/1505), *Al-Ashbāh wa al-Naẓā’ir*, ed. Muḥammad Ḥusayn Muḥammad H. Ismā‘īl, Dār al-Kutub al-‘Ilmiyyah, Beirut, 1422/2001.

— *Muftāh al-Jannah fī al-Ihtijāj bi al-Sunnah*, Beirut, 1987.

— *Tadrīb al-Rāwī fī Sharḥ Taqrīb al-Rāwī*, ed. ‘Abd al-Wahhāb ‘Abd al-Laṭīf, Dār al-Ihyā’ al-Sunnah al-Nabawiyyah, Beirut, 1979.

Ṭabarānī, Sulaymān b. Aḥmad (d. 360/971), *Al-Mū‘jam al-Saghīr wa al-Mū‘jam al-Awsāt*, M. Shakūr Maḥmūd al Ḥajj Amīr, Beirut, 1985.

Ṭabarī, Abū Ja’far Muḥammad b. Jarīr (d. 310/922), *Jāmi‘ al-Bayān al-Ta’wīl al-Qur’an*, Bulāq, 1329.

Ṭabātabā'ī, 'Allāmah Sayyīd Muḥammad Ḥusayn, *Shi'īte Islām*, tr. Seyyed Hossein Nasr, Ṣadr Publishing House, 1974.

Tabrīzī, Muḥammad b. 'Abd Allāh al-Khatīb, *Mishkāt al-Masābih*, ed. Muḥammad al-Dīn al-Albānī, 2nd ed., Al-Maktaba al-Islāmī, Beirut, 1399/1979.

Taftazānī, Mas'ūd bin 'Umar bin 'Abd Allāh Sa'd al-Dīn al-Shāfi'ī (d. 793/1390), *Al-Talwīḥ 'alā al-Tawḍīḥ*, on the margin of 'Ubayd Allāh bin Mas'ūd Ṣadr al-Sharī'ah", 'Īsā al-Bābi al-Ḥalabī, Cairo, 1327/1957.

— Hāshiyah 'alā Sharḥ al-Qāḍī Aḍūd al-Dīn, Bulāq, 1317.

Tahawī, Abū Ja'far Aḥmad b. Muḥammad (d. 321/933), *Sharḥ Ma'ānī al-Athar*, Muḥammad Zuhrī al-Najjār and M. Sayyid Jād al-Ḥaq, Beirut, 1399.

— *Al-Mukhtasar*, ed. Abū al-Wafā al-Afghānī, Dār al-Iḥyā al-'Ulūm, Beirut, 1986.

Tarık Özbilgen, *Tabii Ḥukuk Düşüncesinden Sosyolojik Ḥukuk Görüşüne*, IUHF Mecmuası, CXXX, İstanbul, 1964.

Tilmisānī, Muḥammad bin Aḥmad bin 'Alī al-Idrīsi, al-Sharif al-Mālikī (d. 771/1370), *Miftāḥ al-Wuṣūl Ilā Binā' al-Furū' 'alā al-Uṣūl*, Jāmi'ah Al-Azhar, Kullīyah al-Sharī'ah, reg.no: 72, Cairo.

Ṭūfī Najm al-Dīn Sulaymān bin Abu al-Qawey bin 'Abd al-Karīm Abū al-'Abbās Ḥanbalī (d. 716/1316), *Sharḥ'u Mukhtasar al-Rawḍah*, ed. 'Abd Allāh b. 'Abd al-Muḥsin al-Turkī, Muassasah al-Risālah, 1409.

— *Risālah fī al-Maṣlaḥah al-Mursalah*, Beirut, 1324/1906.

— *Al-Ta'yīn fī Sharḥ al-'Arba'īn*, ed. Aḥmad H. Muḥammad Osman, Beirut, 1988.

Turkī, 'Abd Allāh b. 'Abd al-Muḥsin, *Uṣūl Mathhab al-Imām Aḥmad Ibn Ḥanbal-Dirāsah Uṣūliyyah Muqārinah* (*Uṣūl Comparative Studies*), p. 515, 'Ain Shams University Press, Cairo, 1394/1974.

Turner, Colin P., *Muceddidlik ve Bediuzzaman, Bediuzzaman ve Tecdit*, Gelenek Publication, Istanbul, 2002.

Tyan Emile, *Methodologie et Sources du Droit en Islam Istiḥsān, Istiṣlāḥ, Siyāsa Shar'iyya*" 79-95, 10, *Studia Islamica*, 1959.

'Ubādah, Muḥammad Anīs, *Tārīkh al-Fiqh al-Islāmi*, Cairo, 1980.

'Umarī, Nadiyah Sharīf, *Ijtihād al-Rasūl*, Beirut, 1987.

Uyanık Mevlüt, *Kur'an'ın Tarihsel ve Evrensel Okunuşu*, tr. Kaşif Hamid Okur, Ankara, 1997.

Uzunpostalcı Muştafa, *Ebu Hanife, Hayatı ve İslam Fıkhındaki Yeri*, Institute of Social Science at University of Selçuk, 1986.

— "Ebu Hanife", *DIA*, X, 136.

Wāfī, 'Alī 'Abd al-Wāḥid, *Ḥuquq al-Insān fi al-Islām*, Cairo, 1979.

Watt, Montgomery W., "The Closing of the Door of Ijtihād" in *Oriehtakia Hispanica*, Sive Studia F M Pareja Octogenaria Dictata Edenda Curavit J M Barral, Leiden, 1974.

— *Islamic Fundamentalism and Modernity*, Routledge, London, 1988.

Wollf, E. and Schneider, *Rechtsphilosophie*, 8th ed, Stuttgart, 1973.

Yaman Aḥmet, *Fıkıh Kaideleri ya da Islām Ḥukuk'unun Genel Ilkeleri* (Aḥmed Ziya Afandi, *Islām Ḥukuk'unun Genel İlkeleri Qawāid al-Kulliyyah Sharḥi*), İstanbul, 1996.

— *Islām Ḥukuk'unun Oluşum Süreci ve Sonrasında Siyaset Ḥukuk İlişkisi*, İstanbul, 1999.

— *Maqāṣid ve İjtihād, İslām Hukuk Felsefesi Araştırmaları*, Hüner, Konya, 2002.

Yavuz Abadan, *Ḥukuk Felsefesi Dersleri*, AUHF Yayını, Ankara, 1954.

Yavuz, Yunus Vehbi, "Ḥanefi Müctehidlerinde İstiḥsān Metodu", *Faculty of Divinity Magazine*, issue 1, vol. 1, Uludağ University, 1986.

— *Ḥanafi Mezhebinde İjtihād Felsefesi*, İşaret Publisher, İstanbul, 1993.

Yusuf Ridwan Aremu, *The Theory of Istiḥsān (Juristic Preference) in Islamic Law*, Unpublished Ph.D Dissertation, McGill University, Montreal, 1993.

Zabīdī al-Sayyid Muḥammad Murtadā al-Ḥanafī (1732/1791), "*Tāj al-'Arūs" from Jawāhir al-Qāmūs*, vol. 9, p. 175, Dār al-Libya, Binghāzī, 1386/1966.

Zamakhsharī, Jār Allāh Maḥmud bin 'Umar (d. 538/1144), *Al-Kashshāf 'al-Ḥaqā'iq Ghawāmiḍ al-Ṭanzī' wa 'Uyūn al-Aqāwīl fī Wujūh al-Ta'wīl*, Dār al-Kitāb al-'Arabī, Beirut,1366.

Zanjānī, Maḥmūd bin Aḥmad bin Maḥmūd Abū al-Manāqib Sha'b al-Dīn, min al-Shāfi'ī (d. 656/1258), *Takhrīj al-Furū' 'alā al-Uṣūl*, ed. Muḥammad Adīb Ṣalīḥ Muassasah al-Risālah, Dimishq, 1962.

Zarkashī Muḥammad bin Bahādir bin 'Abd Allah al-Zarkashī Abū 'Abd Allāh Badr al-Dīn (d. 794/1392), *Al-Bahr al-Muhīt fī 'Uṣūl al-Fiqh*, Al-Ashqar, 'Umar Sulaymān, Dāl al-Safwah, Kuwait, 1992.

Zarqā, Muṣṭafa Aḥmad, *Al-Istiṣlāḥ wa al-Maṣāliḥ al-Mursalah fi al-Sharī'ah al-Islāmiyyah*, Dār al-Qalam, Damascus, 1988.

— *Al-Madkhal al-Fiqh al-'Ām*, Damascus, 1968.

— "*Tark al-Aḥyāi bi Ā'zāil Amwāt*", *Ḥaḍarāt al-Islām*, Rabī' al-Awwāl 1385.

— *Çağdaş Yaklaşımla İslām Ḥukuku*, tr. Servet Armağan, Timaş, İstanbul, 1993.

Zaydān 'Abd al-Karīm, *İslām Ḥukukuna Giriş*, tr. Alī Şafak, Kayıhan Yayınları, İstanbul, 1985.

— *Fıkıh Uṣūlü*, tr. Into Turkish by Ruhi Özcan, İstanbul, 1993.

— *Al-Wajīz fī Uşūl al-Fiqh*, Makṭabah al-Quds, Baghdād, 1976.

— *Al-Madkhal li-Dirāsāt* al-*Shari'ah al-Islāmiyyah*, Muassasat al-Risālah, Beirut, 1986.

Zaylāi, Fakhr al-Dīn 'Uthmān b. 'Alī (d. 740/1342), *Ta'yīn al-Ḥaqāiq Sharḥ Kanzi al-Daqāiq*, Dār al-Kutub al-'Ilmiyyah, Bulaq, 1313.

Zaylāī, Jamāl al-Dīn Yūsuf b. 'Abd Allāh (d. 762/1360), *Nasb al-Rā'yah fī Tashrī' Aḥādīs al-Hidāyah*, IV, p. 64, ed. Muḥammad Yūsuf al-Bannūri, Egypt, 1357.

Zuhaylī, Wahbah, *Uṣūl al-Fiqh al-Islāmi*, Dār al-Fikr al-Muāsir, Beirut, 1406/1986

— *Al-Fiqh al-Islāmī wa Adillatuh*, Damascus, 1985.

Zuhayr, Muḥammad Abū al-Nūr, *Mudhakkarāt fī al-Uṣūl al-Fiqh*, Dār al-Ta'līf, Kullīyyāt al-Sharī'ah, University of Al-Azhar.

Index

A

'Abd al-'Azīz al-Bukhārī, xxxiii, xxxiv, 89, 128
'Abd al-'Azīz al-Ḥulwānī, 139
'Abd Allah b. al-Muqaffā', 98
'Abd Allah b. Mubārak, 95
'Abd Allah Dirāz, 151, 157
Abd al-Raḥmān b. Hujairah, 125
'Abd al-Raḥmān ibn Awf, 121, 259
'Abd al-Wahhāb Khallāf, 61, 134
Abū al-Barakāt al-Nasafī, 140
Abū al-Ḥasan al-Karkhī, 78, 133
Abū al-Ḥusayn al-Baṣrī, 72, 170, 300
Abū al-Khaṭṭāb, 159, 160, 162
Abū al-Walīd Al-Bājī, 155
Abū Bakr al-Jaṣṣāṣ, xxxiii, 24
Abū Ḥanīfah, xxx, xxxii, 6, 44, 57, 96-98, 114, 124-129, 147, 148, 150, 159, 167, 168, 172, 173, 183, 184, 186-201, 205, 211, 254, 255, 258, 277, 278, 280, 281, 302-306
Abū Isḥāq Ibrāhīm al-Shīrāzī, 95
Abū Mūsā al-Ash'arī, 89, 90
Abū Sa'īd Aḥmad b. al-Birdāī, 191
Abū Yā'lā, 158
Abū Yūsuf, xxxiv, 114, 127, 166, 186, 187, 190, 192, 194, 196-203, 211, 250, 258, 277, 278, 280, 281, 302, 305
Abū Zahrah, 133, 188, 189
Abū Zayd al-Dabbūsī, xxxiii, 97
adhān, ix, 86, 214, 215
adillah, ix, xxxiii, 5, 8, 12, 13, 131, 149, 161
'adl, ix, 283
Aḍuḍ al-Dīn al-Ijī, 152
af'āl, ix, 18
aḥkām al-dīn, ix, 171
aḥkām al-mu'āmalāt, ix
aḥkām 'amaliyyah, ix

aḥkām ʻaqliyyah, ix, 10
aḥkām ḥissiyyah, ix, 10
aḥkām khuluqīyyah, ix
aḥkām lughawiyyah, ix, 10
aḥkām sharʻiyyah, ix, 7
aḥkām waḍʻīyyah, ix, 10
ahl al-bayt, ix, 186
ahl al-bidʻah, ix, 171, 173
ahl al-farā'iḍ, x, 118
ahl al-ḥadīth, x, 101
ahl al-iṣābah, ix, 118
ahl al-kahf, x, 143
ahl al-ra'y, x, 101
ahwan al-sharr, x, 266
Āʻishah, 190
al-aḥsan, x, 177
al-anṣāb, x, 24
Al-Baṣrī, 167, 168, 210
Al-Hulwanī, 160
ʻAlī Ḥaydar Afandī, 141, 279
ʻAlī ibn Abī Tālib, 123
Al-Isnawī, 88
Al-Izmīrī, 137
Al-Jaṣṣāṣ, 136
Al-Majallah, xiv, 32, 272-275, 279
Alqamah bin Qays, 124
amārah, x, 5, 167, 168, 299
Āmidī, xxxiv, 8, 12, 20, 23, 25, 68, 72, 149, 150, 151, 157, 170, 208, 210, 213, 300
ʻāmm, x, 39, 185, 272, 279
ʻAmr Ibn al-ʻĀṣ, 70
Anṣārī, 84, 260
ʻaql, x, 27, 28, 58, 62, 144, 147, 149, 150, 171, 172, 175, 177, 212, 216
ʻaqlī, x, xii, 12, 21, 69, 180
arkān, x, 24, 25
ʻaṣabah, x, 91, 92
asās, x, 3
asḥābi furūḍ, x, 91
aṣl, x, xix, 3-5, 23-28, 134, 135, 137, 179, 214, 243, 244, 298, 299
awṣāf, xix
Aws ibn al-Sāmit, 143
āyāh, x, 19, 145
Azharī, 16
ʻazīmah, x
azlām, x, 24

B

Baiḍāwī, 17
Baqillānī, 23, 76
bāṭil, x, xvii, 62, 167, 180, 181, 183
bayʻ al-ṭaʻāṭī, x, 39
Bayt al-Māl, x, 120
Bazdawī, xxxiii, xxxiv, 21, 22, 115, 128, 137, 138, 208, 238, 305
bidʻah, ix, x, 16, 149, 171-174
Bilāl, 121, 214
Bishr b. Ghiyās b. Abī Karīmah ʻAbd al-Raḥmān al-Marīsī, 166
burhān, x, 11
Busr bin Artāī, 82

D

Dabbūsī, xxxiii, 97, 257
dafʻ al-fasād, x, 37

dalā'il, x, 17, 129
ḍalāl, x, 166, 209
ḍalālah, x, 19, 131
dalīl 'ām, x, 78, 133
dalīl ijmālī, xi, 4, 5, 299
dalīl qaṭ'ī:, xi
dalīl tafṣīlī, xi, 3, 4
ḍarar, xi, xxii, 259-262, 267
ḍarūrah, xi, xxii, xxxiii, 78, 79, 133, 141, 210, 211, 238, 239, 250, 251, 259, 260, 261, 262, 265, 266, 267, 268, 281, 282, 305, 306
ḍarūriyyāt, xi, 37
Dasūqī, 70
Dāwūd al-Isfaḥānī, 27
Dāwūd al-Zāhirī, xxxi, 180
Dawūd Ibn 'Ali, 164
dharā'i', xi, xvii, xxi, 12, 40, 42
dharī'ah, xi, 40
Dihlawī, 28, 29, 74
dirhams, xi, 85

E

Egypt, xxiv, xxv, xxxv, 88

F

fahm, xi, 6, 89, 299
Fakhr al-Dīn al-Rāzī, 19
faqīh, xi, xii, 13, 69, 97
far', xi, 23, 24, 25, 26, 27, 28
farḍ 'ayn, xi, 300
farḍ kifāyah, xi, 64, 74, 300
fasād, x, xi, 33, 37
Fatḥī Dīrīnī, 61
fatwā, xi, xv, 43, 63, 65, 96, 97, 142, 144, 149, 184, 203, 204
fawāḥish, xi, 143
Fazlur Raḥmān, 69
fi'lī, xi, 10, 271, 272
fiqh, xi, xxxiii, xxxiv, 3, 5-8, 13-15, 17, 18, 45, 70, 72, 88, 95-97, 124, 141, 153-155, 159, 169, 185, 187, 196, 213, 260, 262, 274, 276, 298, 299, 306
Fīrūzabādī, xxxiv, 259
fuqahā', xi, 6, 9, 299

G

ghanīmah, xi, 202
Ghazālī, xxxi, xxxiv, xxxv, 20-22, 34-37, 60, 68, 71, 72, 76, 133, 135, 136, 147-149, 150-152, 177, 180, 192, 208, 210, 212, 213, 300, 304
ghusl, xi, 86

H

Ḥabāb b. Mundhīr, 82
ḥadīth mashhūr, xi, 239
ḥadīth mutawātir, xi, 239
ḥadīth ṣaḥīḥ, xi, 192, 193, 210, 305
Ḥājiyyāt, xi, 35
ḥajj, xi, xii, 9, 15, 21, 88, 144, 195, 215, 264, 278
Ḥakīm b. Ḥizām, 255
Ḥammad bin Sulaymān al-Ash'arī, 124
ḥaqīqī, xi, 3

ḥaqq al-irtifāq, xii, 241
ḥaqq al-masīl, xii, 241
ḥaqq al-murūr, xii, 241
ḥaqq al-shurb, xii, 241, 275
ḥarām, xii, 9, 10, 35, 63, 122, 146, 180, 181
Hart, 9
ḥasan, xii, 149, 214
Ḥasan al-Baṣrī, 27, 30, 95
hawā', xii, 162, 166, 182, 209
ḥimār, xii, 92, 118
ḥimāriyyah, xii, 91
ḥissī, xii, 21
ḥujjah, xii, 16, 45, 130, 178, 216
ḥukm shar'ī, xii, 5, 8, 9, 45
ḥukm taklīfī, xii, 9
ḥukm waḍ'ī, xii, 9

I

Ibn 'Abbās, 6, 97, 116
Ibn Abī Laylā, 97, 98
Ibn al-Abyārī, 156
Ibn al-'Arabī, 155, 156, 173
Ibn al-Ḥājib, 35
Ibn al-Muqaffa', 126
Ibn al-Qayyīm, xxxiv, 40, 41, 58, 62
Ibn al-Subkī, 73, 151, 157, 300
Ibn Amīr al-Ḥajj, xxxiii, 128
Ibn 'Āshūr, xxxv, 34
Ibn Ḥanbal, 17, 249
Ibn Ḥazm, xxxi, xxxiv, 28, 59, 69, 75, 127, 164-166, 178, 180, 183, 186, 193, 209, 210, 303, 304
Ibn Humām, 115, 140, 208
Ibn Khaldūn, xxxiv, 59
Ibn Mas'ūd, 116, 123, 190, 191
Ibn Nujaym, 238, 276, 279
Ibn Qudāmah Al-Maqdisī, 135
Ibn Rushd, 134, 156, 209
Ibn Ṣiddīq, 66
Ibn 'Umar, 190, 191, 258
Ibrāhīm, 44, 95, 157, 187, 305
Ibrāhim al-Nakhā'ī, 116, 124
ibṭāl al-istiḥsān, xii
iḥram, xii, 9, 258, 259
iḥtiyājāt, xii, 250
ijārah, xii, 178, 241, 242
i'jāz, xii, 15
ijmā' ṣarīḥ, xii, 20
ijmā' sukūtī, xii, 20, 21, 256, 258, 279
ijtihād, xii, xxii-xxx, xxxiii, xxxiv, 11, 13, 43, 57-78, 81, 86-89, 93-99, 121, 139, 145, 146, 150, 181-183, 185, 187, 188, 193, 197, 198, 204, 211, 213, 240, 282, 300, 301, 304, 305, 307
ikrāh, xiii
ilhām, xiii, 11
'illah, xiii, xviii, 3, 23-26, 28, 131, 132, 137, 156, 160, 163, 168, 172, 173, 189, 200, 211, 240, 241, 245, 247, 248, 282, 306
'ilm, xiii, 5, 6, 14, 15, 58, 144, 215, 299
imām, xiii, 74, 75, 88, 90, 159, 179, 216
Imām Aḥmad, 43, 158, 159, 161
Imām al-Rāzī, 10

Imām al-Shāṭibī, 12
Imām Mālik, 37, 43, 85, 127, 152, 153, 154, 307
Imām Shāfi'ī, xxxi, 44, 141, 186
intifā', xiii, 241, 242
'iqāb, xiii, 17
iqtiḍā', xviii, 8
iṣābah, ix, xiii, 58, 118
Ishāq bin Khuwaydh Mindād, 155
ish'ār, xiii, 195
ishārah, xiii, 11
iṣmah, xiii
Isnawī, xxxi, xxxiv, 25, 69, 88, 149-151, 180, 210, 213, 304
istaḥsana, xiii, xxxi, 118, 169, 179,
istidlāl, xiii, 12, 157, 172
istiḥsān istithnā'ī, xiii, 238, 281, 305
iṣṭilāḥī, xiii, 114
istiqrā' nāqiṣ, xiii
istiqrā' tāmm, xiii
istiṣḥāb, xiii, xxi, xxviii, 7, 12, 30, 31, 32
istiṣlāḥ, xiii, xxviii, xxxiii, 33
istiṣwāb, xiii, 126
istithnā, xiii, 238, 281, 305
'itāb, xiii, 17
i'tibār, xiii, 61
i'tiqād, xiii, 58
Iyas bin Mu'āwiyah, 127

J

jadhr, xiii
jahd, xiii, 68
jalb al-ṣalāḥ, xiii, 37
Jaṣṣāṣ, xxxii-xxxiv, 24, 89, 115, 136, 137, 204
jināyah, xiii, 36
juhd, xiv, 68
junub, xiv, 86
Juwaynī, 65, 150, 212
juz'ī, xiv, 35

K

kaffārah, xiv, 214, 255
Kamāl Ibn al-Humām, xii, 69
kamāliyyāt, xiv, 36
khabar wāḥid, xiv, 158, 161, 239, 252
Khair b. Nu'aym, 125
khalwah, xiv, 122
khamr, xiv, 4, 25, 26, 27
kharāj, xiv, 199
khāṣṣ, xiv, 246, 247, 272, 279
khayr, xiv, 38
Khudarī, 96, 116
kufr, xiv, 266
kullī, xi, xiv, 4, 5, 35

L

lughawī, xiv, 21, 212

M

maḍarrāt, xiv, 34
madīnah, xiv, 207
mafqūd, xiv, 32
mafsadah, xiv, 29, 34, 37, 154, 156
Maḥillāwī, 131, 215

makrūh karāḥat al-taḥrīm, xiv, 10
makrūh karāḥat al-tanzīh, xiv, 10
mandūb, xiv, 9, 10, 17, 18, 175
manfa'ah, xiv, 34
māni', xiv, 9, 10
mansūkh, xv, 155
maqāṣid al-'āmmah, xiv, 29
Marwān Ibn al-Ḥakam, 122, 123
maṣdar, xiv, 3
mashaqqah, xiv, xxii, 251, 261, 264
Mashhūr, xiv
maṣlaḥah mursalah, xv, xxi, 12, 34, 36, 151, 157
maytatah, xv, 247, 248, 269
Mihrān bin Maymūn, 2
minārāh, xv, 5
miqyās, xv, 23
Mu'ādh Ibn-Jabal, 67
muallafah al-qulūb, xv, 100
mu'āmalāt, ix, xv, 15, 37
Mu'āwiyah ibn Abī Sufyān, 122
mubāḥ, xv, 9, 10
muḍārabah, xv, 206, 271
muḍārib, xv
muftī, xv, 31, 97, 142, 145, 203
Muḥammad al-Dasūqī, 70
Muḥammad bin Ḥasan al-Ḥajawī, 87
Muḥammad b. Shirīn, 187
Muḥammad ibn Maslamah, 119
Muḥammad Khudari, 88
Muḥammad Tahir b. 'Āshūr, 70
mujtahid, xv, 7, 8, 22, 33, 43, 64, 71, 72, 79, 80, 87, 94, 134, 149, 152, 153, 156, 159, 166, 169, 173, 178, 185, 240, 300, 301, 302, 307
mukallaf, xv, 8, 9, 10, 15, 36
mukhaṣṣaṣ, xv, 160, 247
mukhaṣṣiṣ, xv, 247
munkar, xv, 38
muqallid, xv, 13, 94
muqayyad, xv, 12, 71, 155
mursal, xv, 157
murshid, xv, 11
musāqah, xv
mushtarik, xvi, 91
Muṣṭafā Zarqā', 80
mustaqil, xvi, 12
mut'ah, xvi, 240
mutaraddiyah, xvi, 269
mutawātir, xi, xvi, 239, 252
muṭlaq, xvi, 71
Muwaffaq b. Aḥmad al-Makkī, 125
muzāra'ah, xvi, 201, 202, 206

N

nabīdh, xvi, 4, 25, 26, 27
nāfilah, xvi, 18, 194
Nahrawānī, 27
naqlī, xii, xvi, 12, 27, 69, 180
naqṣ, xvi, 264
nasab, xvi, 3
naskh, xvi, 70, 136, 163
naṣṣ, xvi, xxviii, 25, 28, 36, 39, 59, 61, 62, 64-66, 70, 71, 78-84, 88, 89, 91-93, 95-97, 99, 131, 133, 136, 140, 141, 159, 168,

181, 197, 200, 205, 210, 211, 214, 238, 239, 245, 246, 248, 250-255, 273, 275-279, 281, 300-302, 304, 306
naẓarī, xvi, 10
Naẓẓām, 28
nikāḥ, xvi, 192, 201, 206, 258

Q

qadhf, xvi, 80, 81
qāḍī, xvi, 87, 89, 214
Qaffal, 27
qā'idah fiqhiyyah, xvi, 78, 133
qal'ah, xvi, 207
qalbī, xvi, 10
Qaradāwī, 64
Qarafī, xxxiv, 35, 41, 64, 69, 155
Qāshānī, 27
qaṭ'ī, xi, xii, xvi, 5, 8, 12, 45, 69, 299
qatl, xvi, 266
qawāi'd fiqhiyyah, xvi, 4
qawā'id kullīyyah, xvi
qawā'id pl. *qā'idah*, xvi
qawl, xvii, xxi, 12, 42, 188, 190, 191, 197, 198, 201, 210
qawlī, xvii, 10, 38, 39, 271, 272
qiṣāṣ, al-, xvii
qiyās, xi, xvii, xxi, xxviii, xxx, xxxi-xxxiii, 1, 5, 7, 10, 12, 13, 22-31, 43, 44, 58, 59, 60-63, 65, 69, 72, 77-79, 88, 89, 95-99, 101, 102, 119, 124, 125-131, 133, 134, 136-142, 144-146, 148, 150-152, 154-163, 165-168, 170-173, 181, 182, 185-213, 237-245, 247-258, 268-272, 274, 275, 278, 280-282, 298, 299, 301,
Qurtūbī, 153, 154

R

rabb al-māl, xv
Rabī'a b. Abī 'Abd al-Raḥmān, 84
raf' al-ḥaraj, xvii, xxii, 209, 250, 251, 260, 263, 282, 283
Raḥawī's, 140
rājiḥ, xvii, 70
ra's al-māl, xv
ra'y bāṭil, xvii, 62
ra'y mashkūk, xvii, 62, 63
ra'y saḥīḥ, xvii, 62
riwāyah, xvii, 127, 190
rujḥān, xvii, 5
rukhaṣ, xvii, 35
rukn, xvii, 22
ru'yah, xvii, 58

S

sabab, xvii, 9, 10
Sa'd bin Mu'adh, 83
Sa'd bin 'Ubādah, 83
sadd al-dharā'i', xvii, xxi, 12, 40, 42
Sadr al-Sharī'ah, 138
Ṣadr al-Sharī'ah, xxxiii, 23, 238, 305
ṣaḥābah, xvii, 42, 58, 188, 197, 210
ṣaḥābī, xvii, xxi, 29, 42, 43, 190, 191, 198, 210
Sa'īd b. al-Musayyab, 83, 187, 305

salam, xvii, 78, 81, 82, 137, 138, 140, 204, 206, 245, 255, 261
salām, xvii, 204, 205
ṣalāt, xvii, 4, 9
Sālim b. ʿAbd Allāh, 85
sanad, xvii, 238, 250, 251
Sarakhsī, xxxii, xxxiii, xxxiv, 21, 61, 97, 115, 129, 136-140, 147, 176, 191, 198, 204, 208, 214, 239, 257, 258, 261, 276, 280
Schacht, xxxiv, 98, 127, 198, 303
Shāʿbī, 96, 187, 305
shahādāh al-zur, xvii, 37
shāhid, xviii, 11
Shahristānī, 66
shahwah, xviii, 166, 209
Shams al-Dīn Abū Ḥusayn al-Abyārī, 156
shārʿ, xviii
sharʿ man qablanā, xviii, xxi, 12
sharṭ, xviii, 9, 10
Shāṭibī, xxxv, 12, 33, 34, 35, 36, 37, 40, 41, 73, 149, 150, 151, 155, 156, 157, 171, 172, 173, 215, 251, 264, 300, 301
Shawkānī, xxxiv, 26, 28, 31, 61, 76, 151, 153, 154, 170
Shaybānī, xxxii, xxxiv, 84, 114, 127, 138, 186, 189, 196, 197, 199, 203, 204, 205, 206, 207, 211, 273, 274, 277, 278, 280, 281, 302
Shaykh ʿAbd Allah Dirāz, 151
Shīrāzī, xxxi, 72, 95, 133, 135, 146, 147, 180, 208, 212, 300, 304
shufʿah, xviii, 214, 262
shūrah, xviii, 94
Shurayḥ, 67, 119, 123, 124
Shurayḥ b. al-Ḥarith, 123
shurūṭ, xviii
Subkī, 27, 73, 151, 157, 213, 300
sudan, xviii, 142, 145
Sulaymān b. Yasār, 85
Ṣuyūtī, 73

T

taʿabbudī, xviii, 71
tadbīr, xviii, 58
taʿdiyah, xviii, 241, 282
tafsīr, xviii, 17
Taftazānī, 151, 157, 170, 213
taḥrīf, xviii, 29
taḥrīm, xiv, xviii, 4, 8, 10, 28, 146, 299
taḥsīniyyāt, xviii, 36
takhṣīṣ ʿillah, xviii, 160, 163, 168
ṭalab, xviii, 8
taladhdhudh, xviii, 146
ṭalāq bāʾin, xviii, 197
ṭalāq rajʿī, xviii, 197
tark, xviii, 208
taṣarrufāt, xviii, 66
tashahhud, xviii, 200
tawātur, xviii, 14
tawbah, xviii, 253
tayammum, xviii, 86, 159, 264, 265
Thaubah b. Nimr, 125

U

ʿUbayd Allah bin Masʿūd, 23

'udūl, al-, xviii
'ulamā', xviii, xxxii, 14, 17, 18, 23, 27, 28, 41, 72, 76, 142, 170, 173, 174, 176, 179, 181, 185, 210, 212, 214, 215, 217, 283, 303
'ulū al-amr, xix, 19
'Umar ibn al-Abd al-'Azīz, 122
'Umar ibn Khattāb, 67, 118
Umayyad, dynasty, 88, 122, 123
ummah, xix, 28
umūm al-balwā, xix, 261, 264
'Uqbah bin 'Āmir, 86
'urf 'āmm, xix
'urf khāṣ, xix, 39
uṣūl al-fiqh, xix, xxxiii, xxxiv, 3, 5, 7, 14, 15, 18, 45, 298, 306
uṣūlī, xix, 5, 8, 23

W

Wael Hallaq, 74, 301
wahmī, xix, 35
waḥy, xix, 11, 75
wājīb, xix, 9, 10
waqf, xix, 241, 242, 249, 273, 274
wasā'il, xix, 41
waṣf, xix, 24, 32, 34, 189
wujūb, xix, 4, 8, 9, 299

Y

Yaḥyā b. Ādam, 193
Yaḥyā b. Saī'd al-Anṣārī, 84
Yā'lā bin 'Umayyah, 93
yanqadihu, xix, 151
Yusuf Ali, 142

Z

ẓāhir, xvii, xix, 11, 78, 133, 168
zakāh, xix, 15, 100
Zakiyyuddīn Sha'bān, 132
Zamakhsharī, 38
ẓann, xix, 21, 27, 41, 58, 68, 167,
ẓanni ghālib, xix, 45
Zarkashī, 147
Zayd b. 'Alī, 97
zinā, xix, 26, 203, 266

www.ingramcontent.com/pod-product-compliance
Lightning Source LLC
Chambersburg PA
CBHW031612160426
43196CB00006B/101